Qur'anic Matters

Bloomsbury Studies in Material Religion

Bloomsbury Studies in Material Religion is the first book series dedicated exclusively to studies in material religion. Within the field of lived religion, the series is concerned with the material things with which people do religion, and how these things—objects, buildings, landscapes—relate to people, their bodies, clothes, food, actions, thoughts and emotions. The series engages and advances theories in "sensuous" and "experiential" religion, as well as informing museum practices and influencing wider cultural understandings with relation to religious objects and performances. Books in the series are at the cutting edge of debates as well as developments in fields including religious studies, anthropology, museum studies, art history, and material culture studies.

Christianity and the Limits of Materiality, edited by Minna Opas and Anna Haapalainen
Figurations and Sensations of the Unseen in Judaism, Christianity and Islam, edited by Birgit Meyer and Terje Stordalen
Food, Festival and Religion, Francesca Ciancimino Howell
Material Devotion in a South Indian Poetic World, Leah Elizabeth Comeau
Museums of World Religions, Charles D. Orzech
The Religious Heritage Complex, edited by Cyril Isnart and Nathalie Cerezales

Qur'anic Matters

Material Mediations and Religious Practice in Egypt

Natalia K. Suit

BLOOMSBURY ACADEMIC
LONDON • NEW YORK • OXFORD • NEW DELHI • SYDNEY

BLOOMSBURY ACADEMIC
Bloomsbury Publishing Plc
50 Bedford Square, London, WC1B 3DP, UK
1385 Broadway, New York, NY 10018, USA
29 Earlsfort Terrace, Dublin 2, Ireland

BLOOMSBURY, BLOOMSBURY ACADEMIC and the Diana logo
are trademarks of Bloomsbury Publishing Plc

First published in Great Britain 2020
This paperback edition published in 2021

Copyright © Natalia K. Suit, 2020

Natalia K. Suit has asserted her right under the Copyright, Designs and
Patents Act, 1988, to be identified as Author of this work.

For legal purposes the Acknowledgments on p. xiii constitute an
extension of this copyright page.

Cover image © Fabrizio Troiani/Alamy Stock Photo

All rights reserved. No part of this publication may be reproduced or
transmitted in any form or by any means, electronic or mechanical,
including photocopying, recording, or any information storage or retrieval
system, without prior permission in writing from the publishers.

Bloomsbury Publishing Plc does not have any control over, or responsibility for,
any third-party websites referred to or in this book. All internet addresses given in this
book were correct at the time of going to press. The author and publisher regret any
inconvenience caused if addresses have changed or sites have ceased to exist, but can
accept no responsibility for any such changes.

A catalogue record for this book is available from the British Library.

A catalog record for this book is available from the Library of Congress.

ISBN:	HB:	978-1-3501-2138-6
	PB:	978-1-3502-6729-9
	ePDF:	978-1-3501-2139-3
	eBook:	978-1-3501-2140-9

Series: Bloomsbury Studies in Material Religion

Typeset by Integra Software Services Pvt. Ltd.

To find out more about our authors and books visit www.bloomsbury.com
and sign up for our newsletters.

To my children Aniela, Alicya, and Karsten, who grew up with this project; to my very patient husband Kenny; and to my supportive parents Maria and Zbigniew Kasprzak

Contents

List of Figures	viii
Preface	ix
Acknowledgments	xiii
Note on Arabic Text	xiv
Introduction	1

Part One   The Makers
1	The Beginning(s)	17
2	Pens, Letters, and Techniques of the Body	37
3	Mechanical Reproduction and Its Effects	57

Part Two   The Custodians
4	Politics of Correctness	81
5	The (Ortho)Graphic Blueprint	95
6	What Eyes Cannot See but Hands Can Touch: The *Mushaf* Braille	113

Part Three   The Users
7	How Printing Created Manuscripts: Aesthetic and Historical Approaches to *Mushafs*	127
8	Uses and Abuses	139
9	Body, Gender, and How to Enact "Electronic Qur'ans"	157

Conclusion	177
Notes	181
References	199
Index	208

Figures

All photographs have been taken by the author unless noted otherwise.

1	*Mushaf* printed at Bulaq in 1882. Photograph courtesy Tradigital	29
2	The word *al-khatt* (calligraphy) written in various calligraphic styles: *ruq'a, farsi, naskh, diwani,* and *thuluth*. Penned by *Ustaz* 'Adel ('Adel Kamal Muhammad Zaki)	45
3	For example, the letter *nun* in its isolated, frontal and, middle positions (the last two)	47
4	The letter *nun* in connection with other letters	47
5	*Basmala* penned by *Ustaz* 'Adel. Here the *kashida* is applied to the elongated letter *nun*	48
6	The same *basmala* without any *tashkil* and with various types of diacritics, progressively added until it reaches its "Qur'anic form"	50
7	"Cracks" in the typographically printed letters	66
8	The early *rasm* without the short vowels, dots that differentiate between consonants of the same shape (such as ت and ث), or any other diacritics present in contemporary *mushafs*. Wikipedia public domain, originally submitted by Mandel, Gabriele: *Das Arabische Alphabet–Geschichte, Stile und kalligraphische Meisterschulen*. Wiesbaden: Matrix, 2004	97
9	*Mushaf* in a Moroccan style printed at Subih in 1952. Its diacritics and calligraphic style are visibly different from *Mushaf* Fu'ad	110
10	*Mushaf* in Braille	114

Preface

Actors. There is a book on the table in front of me, bound with dark green matte plastic covers. Quite ordinary looking. It is about a quarter of the size of a regular book. It has 544 pages but it's not heavy, as the paper is rather thin and slightly transparent. A charcoal-color ribbon peeks out from between the pages. This book can be easily purchased in many places all over the world. I got mine from a friend in Egypt who had a few of them at home and gave me a spare copy. Before handing it to me, he kissed it and lifted it up to his forehead in a gesture of deference. On the cover, in the middle of a faded golden arabesque it read in Arabic "al-Qur'an al-Karim." The book 'Ali gave me was the Qur'an, traditionally described in English as "the Muslim holy book."

Counter to the prevailing modern inclination to read *through* the text[1] without paying attention to its material surface nor its social context of circulation and use, I have chosen to explore how the Qur'an's graphic design, paper, covers, embellishments, script, and other physical characteristics matter to those who, broadly speaking, interact with it. In other words, this narrative is an account of a physical object that carries the text of the Qur'an and circulates in millions of copies in the Muslim world and beyond; an object that people read, touch, put in their bags and pockets, and appropriate in many other ways in a concrete place: Cairo, Egypt. The perspectives of those who make, safeguard, and use the book highlight its materiality as a vehicle of meaning.

Historically, the Qur'anic book is now over one thousand years old. To narrow down the scope of my study, I have adopted printing as a point of departure to think about "the book as object," with writing and digitization as analytical counterpoints. Both of these technologies, when thought of in conjunction with printing, defamiliarize the relationship of the Qur'anic text to the tangible "thing" that mediates it, redefining the notion of a "holy book" as being more than just the message. Yet as this account is not simply a history of Qur'anic media, but rather an exercise in thinking about what the material form of a religious text may do for those who handle it, digitization and writing make only a partial appearance vis-à-vis printing, which, after recitation, is still the dominant technology for disseminating the Qur'anic message in Egypt.

I became interested in the ways my friends and random acquaintances approached and handled their ordinary, quotidian copies of the Qur'an, and in some ways this defined my further work in Cairo as "praxiography"[2]—an ethnographic narrative of religious practices through which the meaning and authority of the book in its entirety is established. The more I observed ordinary people and talked to them about what they did with their Qur'anic copies, the more I realized that my interlocutors discussed issues and performed activities that pertained to both theology and technology in ways that made it impossible for me to think about the Qur'an without simultaneously thinking about its material medium—how it is made, safeguarded, distributed, and handled by people. Egyptian Muslims print, sell, give, buy, and use Qur'anic books in large quantities. Undoubtedly, Qur'anic books that circulate in the Middle East and beyond participate in shaping the Islamic *umma* (the community of all Muslims) and mediating the divine message in ways that called for my attention.

Locales. As a site for thinking about the Qur'anic text as object, Cairo has been both representative and unique. Egypt was the first Arab country to begin mass-producing the Qur'an on typographic printing presses. Until recently, Egypt has been one of the largest manufacturers of Qur'anic books in the Middle East and is home to most of the religious publishing houses in that region. Apart from the historical and contemporary importance of Cairo as a center for the production of Qur'anic copies, it is also a place where relations between producers of Qur'anic books and religious authorities have a long and complicated history.

Cairo is also the location of al-Azhar, one of the oldest Islamic theological universities, whose scholars have been supervising the printing of the Qur'anic text in Egypt for the past century or so, having direct influence over the numerous publishing houses and print shops. Although at different points in time the fluctuating economic situation has caused some houses to lower publishing costs by outsourcing Qur'anic printing abroad, even those copies have had to be authorized by al-Azhar; as have the books manufactured by foreign publishers, such as those located in China and Indonesia, who have also tried to open up the Egyptian religious book market to their printed editions of the Qur'an. Al-Azhar's supervision over the printing of Qur'anic books, although necessary to ensure their quality and correctness, is nevertheless met with mixed feelings on the part of those who produce them. Some Egyptian publishers perceive it as necessary and unavoidable while others find it a nuisance, as the same regulations that are meant to protect the integrity of the Qur'anic message impose limitations and create obstacles for those interested in reproducing and distributing its text. Printing Qur'anic copies is not an easy business, engendering contentions about how to do it in a way that fulfills both economic objectives and religious obligations alike.

Once sold, Qur'anic books enter the realm of personal use and pietistic practice. The proliferation of circulating copies and their now permanent presence in places where they were not available before have created an environment in which users inevitably reinterpret the old forms of handling the book and come up with new ones. After all, there is a difference between having only one expensive copy of the Qur'anic book versus having multiple ones in different sizes, editions, and levels of quality and fatigue. Some of them may have been bought intentionally, and others may have been received as gifts, passed on, or acquired as souvenirs at a pilgrimage to Mecca. Regardless of their provenience, most of the Qur'anic books on the Egyptian market are inexpensive and easily replaceable and, in the age of mechanical reproduction, they spin their own forms of authority and power through their sheer numbers.

Digitization has speeded the process of dissemination even more as Muslim practitioners have begun dealing with electronic devices and digital bytes instead of paper and print. So in what ways is the religious practice that generates meaning affected by a change in medium itself? I looked for the answer to this question in multiple ways. First, in this unique milieu, where the physical presence of the Qur'anic text has long been established, I came to see how the Qur'an in its tangible form participates in the daily life of Muslim practitioners, lingering in their hands and pockets, lying on their desks and in their cars. I also spoke to those who produce and distribute Qur'anic texts and the *'ulama'* (scholars of al-Azhar) who have to address not only the content of the message but also the forms in which it becomes accessible to its consumers. In my efforts to map out the past relationships between the manufacturers of the Qur'anic books and the religious and governmental authorities, and to trace the scattered pieces of the history of printing in Egypt, I drew on secondary sources and archival documents from the National Library in Egypt. The Internet and newspapers helped me to fill in the gaps when face-to-face conversations were not possible.

Second, one cannot understand the questions and debates about the printing and use of Qur'anic copies without being familiar with religious knowledge. Preoccupation with the ways in which a Qur'anic book should be handled is not unique to Muslims in Egypt. It is part of an Islamic tradition that, as Talal Asad points out, "consists of discourses that seek to instruct practitioners regarding the correct form and purpose of a given practice."[3] Asad calls a given dialogue with a foundational text a "discursive tradition" and defines it as a relationship to a body of knowledge with which Muslims engage and through which they actively shape their present practice. Apart from the Qur'an itself, the texts on which religious reasoning is based include the *hadith* which are the compilations of the words and deeds of the Prophet Muhammad that were assembled by Muslim scholars in order to direct the comportment of all members of the *umma* (community). Collections of *hadiths*, such as *Sahih al-Bukhari* by the Persian Muhammad Ibn Ismail al-Bukhari (810–870); *Sahih Muslim*, also by the Persian Muslim Ibn al-Hajjaj (817–874); or more recently the work on Islamic law *Fiqh al-Sunnah*, compiled by the Egyptian scholar Sayyid Sabiq (1915–2000), are continually consulted, interpreted, and debated in the process of evaluation and validation of contemporary practices and ideas. People's conversations about the mundane affairs of daily life often evoke specific verses from the *hadiths* that, among others, comment on particular uses of the Qur'anic book. They create a frame of reference within which what is permissible and what is prohibited can be discussed. Therefore, my story about the materiality of the Qur'anic book would not be persuasive without references to classical sources in the sciences of the Qur'an that ultimately constitute a basis for many decisions surrounding the printing of Qur'anic books and inform many popular practices related to its use—even in digital form.

Third, apart from political turbulences, my research in Egypt coincided with a time of digital change. The last decade of the twentieth century and the first decade of the twenty-first century marked a significant shift toward the use of computers and the internet in Egypt. This new technology was quickly embraced by the public who appropriated it for social, political, and religious purposes. I was able to witness many of the early stages of this digital revolution, with its now nostalgically remembered floppy disks, bulky monitors, and primitive web pages that soon gave way to CDs, portable drives, and interactive sites. My initial interviews about the use of computerized machinery in the Qur'anic printing process reflected many of the early technical hang-ups as well as the excitement associated with the introduction of new and liberating technologies. Within a decade, however, the new had become a norm and during my last visit in 2018, I already saw a fully established digital market in Cairo, offering an array of digital devices in various shapes and sizes, including smartphones. It was a coincidence, then, that my interest in the physical form of the Qur'anic text concurred with a time when the Qur'anic message itself had expanded into a new medium, the digital one.

Times. The beginning of this research goes back to 1995 and my first trip to Egypt, its middle stage took place in 2012 after the fall of Hosni Mubarak's old regime and the beginning of Mohamed Morsi's brief tenure as president of Egypt, and its final stage occurred in 2018 after the consolidation of the new military government of 'Abdel Fattah el-Sisi. A considerable part of my fieldwork happened in the context of riots and strikes, water and electricity shortages, and growing anger. In uncertain times people are cautious and fatigued. Familiar channels of bureaucratic command and ways of going about daily institutional life cannot be assured from one day to another. After a while a statement such as "we had to close because of the protests" becomes as prosaic as the traffic congestion at Tahrir Square. I was sheltered from all these things although not unaffected by them. I felt sympathy for al-Azhar officials, library workers, and many other administrative assistants who tried to facilitate my research as best as they could in circumstances that were far from typical. I visited some places and institutions many times only to find out that the office was unexpectedly closed, or that the materials I was looking for were not there, or that the people I wanted to talk to were absent.

In many ways my research has been a testimony to Egyptian efforts to go on with life in spite of and against the prevailing hardships. Perhaps because so much about everyday existence in Cairo was unpredictable, I accepted chance as part and parcel of my fieldwork. Sometimes, an inadvertent conversation with a metro passenger or a casual stroll in the streets provided me with the most insightful knowledge and unusual artifacts. So I have carried an unpayable debt to all of the Egyptian friends, acquaintances, and strangers who were willing to share their time (and food) with me and without whom I would have nothing to write about. Time and again, I was humbled by their hospitality and kindness in spite of the tough political and economic times in which they had found themselves.

Acknowledgments

This book has been written with the support of many people and institutions. I will begin chronologically with those who set the foundations for this project: Margaret Wiener, Silvia Tomaskova, Carl Ernst, Gregory Starrett, Tod Ochoa, and James Peacock from the University of North Carolina, Chapel Hill. My research and writing have been possible thanks to the grants received from a Research Fellowship with the American Research Center in Egypt, the Fulbright Hays Doctoral Dissertation Research Abroad Scholarship, the Wenner-Gren Dissertation Fieldwork Grant, the Charlotte W. Newcombe Doctoral Dissertation Fellowship from the Woodrow Wilson National Fellowship Foundation, the National Endowment for Humanities Fellowship, and the American Research Center in Egypt Scholar in Residence Program. In particular I want to thank Ms. Djodi Deutsch from the American Research Center in Egypt and Ms. Eman Shaker from the Fulbright Office for facilitating my work in Cairo.

I was privileged to be supported in my research by Egyptian institutions, especially the National Library Dar al-Kutub, the University of al-Azhar, and the Library of Mashyekha. I want to thank all the staff and faculty—Dr. Ahmad 'Isi al-Ma'asarawi in particular—who so generously helped me find the threads of knowledge I wove together in this book.

It is hard to remember all of the individuals who contributed to this project, but I want to especially thank Radi Rahman, 'Ali Foda, Sa'ad Eddin 'Ali, Sahar Ramadan, Ahmad 'Ali Hasan, 'Adel Kamal Muhammad Zaki, and Dr. Yousri Ga'far for taking time to attend to my needs and countless questions. I am also thankful to Davidson MacLaren, Jake Benson, and Ana Beny for sharing their knowledge of Qur'anic manuscripts with me.

Intellectual incitement, so essential to the emergence of any ideas, has been liberally provided and nurtured by J. R. Osborn, Nadirah Mansour, Kathryn Schwartz, James Bielo, James Watts, Dorina Miller Parmenter, Brent Plate, Thomas Milo, and many other interlocutors with whom I have shared these ideas at a number of AAA and AAR conferences and workshops.

Finally, I am indebted to Mike and Marty Reimer for offering their home as a safe space for writing while I was in Cairo, and to Kenny, Aniela, Alicya, and Karsten for letting me take so much time from our family life to work on and complete this project. Thank you!

Note on Arabic Text

In order to make the main body of the text accessible to people who are not familiar with Arabic language and grammar, I simplified the transliteration of Arabic words by removing most of their diacritics and providing their English meaning. In some cases, I also retained the pronunciation characteristic for the Egyptian dialect rather than the classical, written language. Moreover, I do not tend to use the plural forms of Arabic words. Instead, I have often Anglicized them to reduce the amount of foreign words in the text.

However, for those who are interested in the Arabic sources used in this book, I have provided endnotes with the original titles, names, and citations in Arabic. I also retained transliteration in the sources that had already used it.

Introduction

The Qur'an and a *Mushaf*

In an act of defiant iconoclasm, Terry Jones, pastor of a small non-denominational church in Florida, announced in 2010 that he would "burn the Qur'an" on the anniversary of 9/11. Soon the press was full of reports about why and where he was planning to do it. Yet the press had it all wrong. Neither Jones nor anybody else for that matter could "burn the Qur'an." There were theological reasons for this. In Muslim theology, the word "Qur'an" does not describe a physical book but rather God's revelation itself. However, what made Reverend Jones's iconoclasm possible was a uniquely modern understanding of the nature of a printed text—of which I will speak later—and the fact that the immaterial Qur'anic message cannot be disseminated in an extrasensorial way. Instead, in order to reach its audience, the Qur'an requires a material medium: voice, stone, parchment, digital bytes, or paper that, conveniently for Jones, happens to burn easily.

If we consider all these forms of transmission, it is undeniable that the story of Qur'anic dissemination embodies a long and rich history of rendering it by voice more than by paper. Qur'anic recitation has always been central to Muslim religious practice. The word "Qur'an" itself comes from the root "q-r-a," which means "recitation" or "reading out loud." The emphasis on vocal mediation of the Qur'an is firmly grounded in the teachings of the Prophet Muhammad, who encouraged his companions to memorize and recite the message. "Chant it, for whoever does not chant it is not one of us," says the Prophet in a well-known *hadith* (account) narrated by a famous scholar named Ibn Kathir.[1] There are many narratives like this in addition to verses in the Qur'an itself that remind Muslims of the importance of recitation. As in the past, memorizing the Qur'an and reciting it aloud constitutes a large part of Muslim religious education in Egypt today. Children learn to recite the Qur'an in public schools, although in order to memorize the whole message they often have to take additional private lessons from licensed instructors. In recent decades the larger mosques and religious centers in Cairo have started offering courses in Qur'anic recitation. Radio and television channels broadcast international contests hosted in Egypt and in other parts of the Muslim world, featuring children and adult Qur'anic reciters. Apart from beautiful voices and musical virtuosity, participants in these competitions demonstrate their knowledge of the rules of *tajwid*—a particular form of recitation characterized by vocal embellishments.

The performance of recitation elicits strong emotional responses and it is common to see the audience weep during performances of their favorite *qari'* (reciter), although a less elaborate form of recitation called *tartil* (slow and ordinary chanting) may also bring a performer and his listeners to tears. Once a friend was reciting to me the Qur'anic story of the Virgin Mary. His voice suddenly trembled. "Give me your handkerchief," he asked his son, attempting to control his emotions.[2] The recited Qur'an accompanies Egyptian Muslims at birth, marriage, and death. Recitation of the Qur'an marks holidays, especially the Prophet's birthday (*mawlid*), the night of his journey from Mecca to Jerusalem (*mi'raj*) and—most of all—Ramadan, the month during which the Qur'an was sent down to people for the first time. Muslims recite the Qur'an as part of their daily prayers and devotion. The aural landscape of Egyptian cities is imbued with Qur'anic recitation, chanted by professional reciters or played on TVs, CDs, or phones during the day and long into the busy urban nights.

Yet the emphasis on vocal mediation of the message does not mean that other forms of mediation of the Qur'an are inconsequential. Muslims themselves have not neglected the Qur'anic codex, whether to beautify it through calligraphy, or to address it through acts of ritual purity, or to treat it with particular forms of deference. Given the persistent presence of the Qur'anic book within the Qur'anic soundscapes—and the occasional iconoclastic mistreatments of its material body—it has been increasingly hard for me to think of the Qur'an solely in terms of its abstract, ethereal message, and the voices that mediate it. But events like the one in Florida, or other reports of the extreme uses to which the Qur'anic book has been put, are not the only reasons why I have begun paying attention to the material presence of the Qur'an in its written or printed form.

Unlike it is customarily done with the Bible, where a proper noun denotes both the content and the object that carries it, scholars in Islam make a categorical distinction between the revelation—the Qur'an—and the physical object that mediates it—a *mushaf* (pronounced with a distinction between the letters *s* and *h*—"mus'haf"). The word *mushaf* comes from the root *suhuf* (bound pages) and is primarily understood to refer to the pages that carry the text of the Qur'an. It is not mentioned in the Qur'an itself but appears later in scholarly writings about the Qur'an. Grammatically, unlike the word "Qur'an," "*mushaf*" has a plural form: *masahif*,[3] indicating an essential difference between the ontological status of the two. One is singular (or unique) and divine; the other is not. In the Arabic language, the Qur'an is always preceded by the definite article "al" and often followed by the collocation "*al-Karim*," which means "bounteous" or "generous," although many English translations prefer to use the words "glorious" or "noble." Despite the fact that reporters covering Pastor Jones's memorable "Burn the Qur'an Day" often used the word "Qur'an" in plural form—"the Qur'ans"—in Arabic the word "Qur'an" does not have a plural form. There is only one Qur'an—al-Qur'an—*the* Qur'an—mediated by a tangible book, a *mushaf*. However, this distinction, although theoretically clear, has sometimes unexpected implications on a practical level when, for instance, the way in which the *mushaf* is made mixes technological concerns with theological pronouncements, or the *mushaf*'s material presence evokes actions that blur the crisp line of what is divinely-created and what is human-created. In other words, the distinction between the book and the message is theoretically easy to draw, but in practice this task is more complicated—as my story that follows the *mushaf* will show. But before I begin, let's correct the press reports: it was a *mushaf*, then, not the Qur'an, that Reverend Terry Jones wanted to burn.

Following the *Mushaf*

Thinking about a book as a material object entails two things: seeing texts as more than just conduits of meaning and meeting them in their mundane materiality. Although the forms in which texts circulate have never been inconsequential as far as their meaning and use have been concerned, readers do not often pause to think about a book beyond its content nor ponder how a book's material characteristics affect our responses to it (except, perhaps, when we buy a book tempted solely by its intriguing cover). Nonetheless, the precarious state of books as something other than text was already noted a century ago by Walter Benjamin in his essay *Unpacking My Library*, where he spoke of books not as a source of intellectual or spiritual enrichment but as collector's pleasures. For Benjamin, book editions, dates, publishers, bindings, and collector's memories all constituted an assemblage—a book—whose meaning went far beyond its immediate content.[4]

Since then, other scholars have become interested in the social lives of books, investigating the relationships between the texts, their material forms, the readers, and the social milieus in which they all operate. The bibliographer and book historian Donald F. McKenzie (1931–1999) was one of the first scholars to promote the idea that books—by means of their materiality and practices they engender—should be approached as more than mere textual representations. "In any study of a codex," McKenzie suggested, "it is impossible to divorce the substance of the text on the one hand from the physical form of its presentation on the other."[5] Criticizing the tendency to see texts as a category of things whose material form is irrelevant to their use and signification, he has also made it clear that the meaning a text evokes at a particular time cannot be separated from its historical place and technology of manufacture. McKenzie's "sociology of texts" was based on a conviction that "the book itself is an expressive means."

A similar approach to thinking about books has been taken by the book historian Roger Chartier who echoes McKenzie by saying, "Readers and hearers, in point of fact, are never confronted with abstract or ideal texts detached from all materiality."[6] Addressing directly the connection between how a book is made and what it means, he says, "One must state that forms produce meaning and that a text, stable in its letter, is invested with a new meaning and status when the mechanisms that make it available to interpretation change."[7] In this approach to studying books, Chartier pays attention to the ways readers engage the texts not only on an abstract, intellectual level but also as a physical object that gives cues to particular forms of reception and interpretation. The reader's body participates in this act of engagement, often following the cues and responding according to patterns prevalent in her or his community of readers. In short, for Chartier studying books also means studying practices that seize on these objects.

The writings of McKenzie and Chartier—and other scholars since then—have opened up new areas of exploration in research on printed texts. Their comprehensive and sociologically sensitive approach to written and printed forms encouraged others to look at the textual traditions in non-Western settings as well. Working with different scripts and diverse technologies, these studies—such as, for instance, a collection of essays on printing and materiality in China edited by Patrick Hanan,[8] or J. R. Osborn's work on Arabic printing and script design[9]—complicated not only the notion of printing as an essentially "Western" technology but also variegated even further the forms and meanings of practices surrounding books as objects. For instance, they made us aware of the multifariousness of reading techniques, which, as embodied practices, are always connected with particular forms of script and demand alternative ways of seeing. Through their materiality-oriented approaches, these scholars have once again shown that treating books as mere repositories of meaning neglects the corporeality that surreptitiously shapes human responses to them. For scholars working with texts, it has become obvious by now that books, apart from their "message," are tools of both social and material praxis.

Consequently, to become interested in the Qur'an requires one to also look at how *mushafs* mediate the message and ask questions about the potential effects of the Qur'anic books in their circulatory realm. To ask these kinds of questions does not mean, though, that I render the Qur'anic message itself insignificant or that the *mushaf*'s materiality is paramount to the text it mediates, delineating the possible field of practices focused on the book. Instead, I heed both the Qur'an and the *mushaf* in order to explore how matters of paper, design, script, digitization, Braille, etc., intermingle with and inform theological debates, economic choices, bodily habits, and political arguments that relate to the Qur'anic text.

Moreover, my approach to thinking about technology and Qur'anic production has been primarily ethnographic. I am not interested in creating a history of the *mushaf*. For that reason, I feel that my inquiry into the effects of the corporeality of the Qur'anic message does not need to exactly follow the normative historical narrative of its beginnings as a codex at the dawn of Islam; instead, as a point of departure I can evoke a much later event—the introduction of the printing press in nineteenth-century Egypt. I have intentionally chosen the moment at which the Qur'anic text transitions from its handwritten medium to a printed one not because I have focused on fleshing out the historical details of the Qur'anic printing, but because examining this transition helps reveal multiple layers of connections between the text, the message, and a religious practice that must be recollected and rethought by the public and scholars alike in relation to the new technology.

Objects as Actors

Texts and their socio-material aspects constituted one theoretical space in which I situated my project. A broader theoretical approach that ran parallel to developments in research on textual production informed my inquiry as well. This approach could be succinctly put this way: material things in general are more than hapless bearers of human projections.

For over two decades now, numerous scholars have challenged the view that the objects that surround us are mere repositories of meaning and instruments for human action. These scholars have done so not in order to promote a new kind of material determinism, but to draw attention to the things themselves: to challenge prevalent theoretical formulations of material culture in which material objects, although significant, always remain "a step behind" human actions and motivations. In other words, these works on materiality have attempted to problematize our relationship to and relationship with objects rather than analyze objects as merely a means to social ends.

These concerns were captured by Bjornar Olsen in his critical assessment of scholarship on material culture,[10] where he provocatively stated that objects that are loci of academic inquiry had been ignored by scholars for a large part of the twentieth century. To be sure, material culture always appeared in anthropological writing, but most of the time, he said, it was obscured by the common narrative about how the social world constitutes the world of objects and was shrouded by the academic tendency to exaggerate human agency over things.

What Olsen and other scholars have been weary of, then, is the propensity to think of things primarily in terms of their functions or symbolic efficacy. Both instances imply a problematic idea that things "serve" us to fulfill functions we assign to them and they "serve" us as vehicles of symbolic meanings we ascribe to them. But objects defined by their functions cannot tell us much about any activities they are able to perform when unconstrained by their ascribed utility and they cannot add much to a conversation when all they can do is reflect what humans think and feel. Any evidence of objects' capacities to act, perhaps even lurking in rough ethnographic field notes, is eventually trimmed away because it is mostly "auxiliary" to the objects' "true" function or "irrelevant" to the ideas people invest in them.

Yet, in the nitty-gritty of daily action, the material world anthropologists and other scholars study is rather "lumpy, recalcitrant, and inconsistent." In other words, things are "thick."[11] I appreciate this handy phrase coined by Ken Alder, as it evokes Clifford Geertz's notion of "thick description," a rich ethnographic narrative that is sensitive to multiple and often conflicting layers of meaning invested in action by its participants. Thick description can be juxtaposed with a narrative that "thins out" the richness of possible interpretations by collapsing the meanings of action into a set of particular functions. Similarly, things can be "thick," as Alder suggests, if we remember that by the virtue of their physical characteristics they can oppose our actions (things can break, be difficult to work with, or turn out differently than we intended them to be) and can escape attempts to be permanently stabilized (they can become something else over time).

Alder's propitious notion of the "thickness of things" dovetails with what Bruno Latour in particular has been telling us for quite some time now: that objects do not merely "'express' power relations, 'symbolize' social hierarchies, 'reinforce' social inequalities, 'transport' social power, 'objectify' inequality, and 'reify' gender relations."¹² Social theorists may think of them as docile but their action is more varied and their effect is much more ambiguous than such a narrow list of competencies would suggest. On the contrary, they may be found at the origin of social affairs by actively participating in the formation of assemblies of people and things. Tracing these assemblies allows us to see the kinds of agencies that make up the surrounding world. In other words, objects are as social as they are material, and they relentlessly (albeit without acknowledgment) contribute to building what we commonly call "the social world" even as they are commonly excluded from it by those who write about it. The exclusion of objects as actors hinges on the assumption that "the social" is constituted by intentional human actions for which objects form only a backdrop. If this is not the case—as Latour, Alder, Olsen, and others argue—it is reasonable to ask what objects can do and how.

Although objects cannot act intentionally, they do have agency that impacts our choices and limits our decisions; because of their materiality, objects have the ability to make people do things. In practice, human dealings with objects are much more intricate and symmetrical than many social theories would have it. "Try to bike without a bike"—suggests Olsen—"try to think of your day-to-day practices without things" and you will quickly notice "how the routines, movements, and social arrangements of our daily lives are increasingly prescribed, defined and disciplined, as well as helped or encouraged by networks of material agents."¹³ As a result, accepting objects as agentive elements of the social realm has far-reaching consequences for the way we understand, occupy, and act toward the world we live in. Removing the veil of transparency from objects changes the way we grasp facts and define objectivity, and it makes the subject-object divide less settled.

In this sense, then, my narrative aims at removing the transparency of the *mushaf*. It does so by looking at the moments when the book acts independently of or in addition to what the Qur'anic message produces. Again, I need to emphasize that I do not try to turn Muslim doctrine on its head by suggesting that a *mushaf* takes precedence over the Qur'an. I simply propose an inquiry into how objects, such as *mushafs*, help to construct the world in which Muslim practitioners live. By "construct" I mean make solid and durable. So instead of bracketing practices involving a *mushaf*, I foreground them to map out the material-social reality this produces. In this undertaking, I have been led by concerns, problems, discussions, projects, agreements, and disagreements generated by the material form of the book. I ask who is allied in these developments and what other actors are enlisted along the road, for as Latour says, "If you mention an agency, you have to provide the account of its action."¹⁴

Tracing the associations between humans and other objects that emerge thanks to the fact that the Qur'an is mediated not only through a sound but also via paper, ink, script, orthography, diacritics, and so on has allowed me to see what builds the world without deciding ahead of time what kind of reality is actually being produced: political, economic, religious, or something else? This way I did not limit my inquiry in advance: I did not constrain myself to fields that are commonly associated with the study of religious texts and media. As a result, I have extended my study to various technologies involved in disseminating the Qur'anic message—writing, printing, and digitization. As a "side effect," this approach added one more critical voice against the popular myth of religion as the "other" of modern media practice.[15] In fact, as the coming chapters will show, mediating the Qur'an has always had as much to do with technology as it has with theology.

Because I did not know ahead of time in what social spaces I would find the *mushafs*, searching for them became the catalyst of an inadvertently interdisciplinary project. James Clifford, in the opening to his now classic essay "Partial Truths," wrote, "To do something interdisciplinary, it's not enough to choose a 'subject' (a theme) and gather around it two or three sciences. Interdisciplinarity consists in creating a new object that belongs to no one."[16] In my project, to tell the story of what happens with the Qur'anic book, I searched for vernaculars and idioms to capture and assemble the seemingly idiosyncratic instances of the book's physical presence in places that didn't neatly fall under the category of the religious, the historical, the economic, or the aesthetic. In the process, the *mushaf* emerged as an autonomous actor belonging simultaneously to all of these places and yet stable enough to take its own stage.

Objects as Mediators

So far, I have spoken of the material medium of the Qur'anic message without specifying what I mean by that. I have used a neutral word, "medium," as it does not indicate what kind of a job a "medium" does and whether what it does has any consequences for what it mediates. But as the following chapters will show, it would be more pertinent to say that what we are dealing with here is a Qur'anic mediator, as opposed to an intermediary. There is a vast difference between the job performed by intermediaries and mediators, says Latour. Unlike intermediaries that can be ignored, mediators "transform, translate, distort, and modify the meaning or the elements they are supposed to carry."[17] An intermediary can be easily forgotten, transporting meaning or force without transformation; a mediator always exceeds its conditions and its output cannot be defined by its input. In this Latourian sense, we can say that at times a *mushaf* acts as a mediator. Moreover, it is a complex mediator, as one cannot always say for sure if it is the paper that mediates the message. Or is it the spelling? Or perhaps the script? Or all three at once? Or separately, at different times?

Marshall McLuhan already pointed out the complexity of the process of mediation by thinking of technology—including printed books—as multilayered environments in which multiple media, like a set of Russian matryoshka dolls, "nest" in each other. "The 'content' of any medium is always another medium,"[18] proposed McLuhan, seeing speech mediated by script used in printing and reproduced through books as an example of such a conglomeration of media, each of which had the ability to introduce change into human affairs through its process of mediation. However, as W. J. T. Mitchell has reminded us, we should not see this "nesting" phenomenon as a historical sequence.[19] For example, my study of the *mushaf* highlighted the overlapping nature of different forms of text mediation. As much as handwriting did not end with the introduction of printing so digitization did not entirely eclipse printing. Computers may have produced new forms of text consumption and thereby reshaped the meaning of printing as a dominant type of text reproduction, but historically, the appearance of one medium rarely eliminated the older ones. For instance, almost a century of coexistence between the two earliest ways in which the Qur'anic text was rendered spans the time from the first local print productions in Egypt to the decline of the manuscript economy. During that time both media had an effect on each other, transforming each other's forms and meanings.

Similarly, both printed and digital *mushafs* are nowadays available on the religious market and the growing numbers of both underlie the diversification of their users, including generational, economic, aesthetic, or educational differences. And, as in the past, the digitized text of the Qur'an is in many ways affected by its predecessor—the book. So thinking chronologically may prevent us from noticing that newer media can become incorporated into coexisting older media. The contemporary Qur'anic manuscripts produced for printing and digitization purposes, although very much grounded in the tradition of Qur'anic writing, clearly embrace elements of print and digital culture, such as the composition of the text on a page, the ornamentation of the page, or the calligraphic style of the script.

While McLuhan analyzed the effects of this mediation at the level of an individual's perception, Latour is more interested in tracking how the mediation of things "glues" humans and non-humans (things) together. They both emphasize that the costs of mediation can be found in the unpredictability of its results. Moreover, for Latour it is never certain ahead of time what thing will act and how it will act, but this uncertainty should not be seen by scholars as an obstacle. It only confirms that the reality constituted partially by objects is defined by constant movements, displacements, transformations, translations, and enrollments.[20] Tracing them makes *things* more interesting, and in the case of the Qur'anic text these movements, displacements, and translations have been at play for over a thousand years.

Mushaf in the Muslim Tradition

A written Qur'anic text has its place in well-known narratives about the birth of Islam. In addition to the accounts of the time when the Qur'an was written down for the first time by the Prophet's companions, a *mushaf* appears in the story of the third Caliph, 'Uthman Ibn 'Affan, who is said to have been assassinated while reading it. This dramatic event is described by a collector of *hadiths*, Abu Dawud al-Sijistani, who writes "the Caliph fell mortally wounded by a sword, with his blood dripping on the verse: '... God will suffice you for them; He is the All-hearing, the All-knowing' (Q. 2:137)." There are also narratives that disclose the presence of *mushafs* at crucial moments in the history of the early *umma* (Muslim community). Travis Zadeh, a historian of religion who traces early Muslim writings that mention material copies of the Qur'an, notes that "in the Battle of the Camel" (35 AH/656 CE)[21] and again at Siffin (37 AH/657 CE), *mushafs* appear prominently.

> In the course of these separate battles, the raising up of Qur'anic codices (*raf' al-masahif*) is used to signify a move for arbitration. In the case of caliph

Mu'awiya I (r. 41–60 AH/ 661–680 CE) at Siffin, several traditions detail how his forces lifted the *mushafs* on the tips of their spears to demonstrate their desire for a resolution to the conflict through arbitration based on the book of God (*kitab Allah*).[22]

These accounts date from the second and third centuries *hijri* (AH)—the Muslim calendar, counted from year 622 CE—and although Zadeh is not entirely sure of their provenance they indicate that at least in the times when they were written (two to three centuries after the events they describe) the material form of the Qur'an had started to attract the attention of Muslim authors and chroniclers.

Material copies of the Qur'anic text not only participate in historical accounts of events that affected the shape and development of the Muslim community but also—starting in the second century AH/eighth century CE—they become part of the broader discourse defining and codifying the practice of ritual purity (*tahara*). The *mushaf* as an object of particular concern appears in a number of legal writings starting with the works of the Medinan jurist Malik Ibn Anas (d. 179 AH/796 CE), who quotes a story of a letter the Prophet sent to Yemen's governor in which he urges people to teach the Qur'an to others but notes that the person who touches it must be in a state of purity. This story is used as the basis of a legal pronouncement that prohibits an impure Muslim from carrying a *mushaf*, including carrying it by a strap, in a cover, or on a cushion. Zadeh suggests that this example—as well as other pronouncements that prohibited the use of the *mushaf* in particular circumstances—coincides with the beginning of debates on the nature of the Qur'an that by the early third AH/ninth century CE produced a particular religious genre called "*fada'il al-Qur'an*," the "excellent qualities of the Qur'an."[23] The writings of well-known scholars 'Abd al-Razzaq and Ibn Abu Shayba and later of Abu 'Ubayd Ibn Sallam (d. 224 AH/838 CE), Ibn Durays (d. 294 AH/906 CE), al-Mustaghfiri (d. 432 AH/1040 CE), al-Razi (d. 454 AH/1062 CE), and al-Nawawi (d. 676 AH/1277 CE) all included—among narratives pertaining to the Qur'an—passages referring to the use of *mushafs* in different contexts. Dispersed in these writings are legal pronouncements concerning embellishments of the written text, the sale of *mushafs*, sprinkling a *mushaf* with perfume, the use of *mushafs* in the mosque and during the prayer, and, most notably, how to handle *mushafs* properly according to the rules of *tahara* (ritual purity required for prayer). A number of authors also addressed whether it is permissible for a non-Muslim to touch a *mushaf* and—by extension—whether a Muslim may travel with a *mushaf* to a non-Muslim land, where the book might be touched by unbelievers.

Legal discourses surrounding the corporeality of the Qur'anic text were by no means homogeneous, says Zadeh.[24] In fact, they included a variety of conflicting opinions concerning what one is permitted to do (or not do) with a *mushaf*. For instance, a few scholars—including al-Hasan al-Basri (d. 110 AH/728 CE) and Abu Razin (d. ca. 90 AH/708 CE)—argued that touching a *mushaf* in a state of minor impurity is permissible. Others debated whether the use of proxy objects (such as cloth or containers) would change the requirements of *tahara* (purity) and if a menstruating woman (who in the consensus of many scholars is automatically in a state of major impurity) might handle a *mushaf* hidden in a cover, coming to the conclusion that this was not permitted. On the other hand, according to Ibn 'Abbas, laying a *mushaf* on a bed where someone made love, sweated, or had nocturnal emissions did not violate the rules of *tahara*. The examples are many but the injunctions suggest two things: one, that a book that carries the text of the Qur'an is somehow special, and, two, that it needs to be handled with care. Obviously, as Travis Zadeh observes, such deliberation about the proper handling of Qur'anic copies would not make sense unless they took place in a society where a *mushaf* was already an important object of use.[25]

Questions about the proper handling of *mushafs* during the first few centuries of the development of Islamic tradition occurred among much more consequential debates about the ontological status of the Qur'an. As the Muslim doctrine of *tawhid*—the absolute unicity of Allah—was taking shape some scholars became increasingly uncomfortable with the idea that the Qur'an, as Allah's eternal speech, resembled the Christian concept of Logos. They were also disturbed that this suggested that Allah could speak, uttering sounds like a human, and thus that he shared some similarities with his creation. To avoid any likeness of this sort, a group of scholars known as the Muʿtazilites proclaimed the Qur'an to be the *created* word of Allah out of the need to communicate with His creation. This opinion was unacceptable to scholars who did not want to compromise the uniqueness and authority of the Qur'an by putting it on the same level as the creation itself. The debates, which lasted for over a century, had political as well as theological ramifications, with supporters of both camps being prosecuted at different times and in different places. The arguments ended by the third century AH/ninth century CE with the defeat of the Muʿtazilites's doctrine and the victory of those who thought the Qur'an eternal and who treated Allah's speech as one of his uncreated attributes. The crystallization of the doctrine of *tawhid* and of the ontological status of the Qur'an helped also to clarify the relationship between the message of the Qur'an and its human-made medium. A major fifth-/eleventh-century Ashʿarite scholar, Imam al-Haramayn al-Juwayni (419–478 AH/1028–1085 CE), articulated this affinity in the following manner:

> The words of the Exalted God are written in copies of the Qur'an, preserved in the breast, but they do not inhere in the copy nor subsist in the heart. The writing by which [the message] is expressed, either through the movements of the person who writes or through inscribed letters and imprinted lines, is altogether temporally contingent. What the lines signify is the eternal speech.[26]

Al-Juwayni's position on the nature of the relationship between the text of the Qur'an and the Qur'an itself was shared by other scholars and became a part of the *ʿaqida* (creed) that has defined Islam to the present. Al-Juwayni clearly distinguished the temporal text of the Qur'an, "that which is between two covers," and the eternal Qur'an, by stating that the *writing*, which is impermanent, points to what is *written* and everlasting. Attention to the *mushaf* as a temporal "safeguard" of the Qur'an has continued among practitioners even though the need to theorize about their relation ceased to be important to Muslim scholars once the doctrinal principles had been established (around the third century AH/tenth century CE). After this writing about *mushaf* became a part of normative literature (the *sunna*, or Prophetic tradition, and the *fikh*, or jurisprudence); questions about how to handle a *mushaf* became a matter of personal piety.

An "Invisible" Object

Perhaps because of the absence of discussions of *mushafs* in later Islamic literature and attention to recitation in general, non-Muslim academic writings are rather silent about the presence of *mushafs* in the fabric of Muslim social life. The book carrying the Qur'anic text has generated interest in only two fields—art history and codicology. Art historians have long paid attention to the *mushaf*, extensively documenting the history of Qur'anic manuscripts, discussing the technology of their production, addressing the relationship between the materials used and the visual characteristics of Qur'anic codices at different points in time, and occasionally discussing the social relations involved in inscribing and distributing manuscripts. Art historians, however, have ignored undecorated (from their perspective "ordinary" or "ephemeral") *mushafs* written by mediocre calligraphers and pious laymen that nevertheless circulated among Muslims and were extensively used in religious practice. Understanding how these *mushafs* were made and used did not belong to the purview of knowledge art historians produced. Is it, as Hala Auji ponders, "because art historians are better equipped to read image as text than to analyze text as image"?[27] Neither were codicologists inclined to analyze the materiality of the book in relation to its effects on the *mushaf*'s producers and users. Mechanically printed *mushaf* have received even less attention among academics, as they do not seem to have much of interest to offer anyone except a few historians of print.

A tendency to overlook the material medium of the Qur'an has been perpetuated in academia by a position that emphasizes the oral/aural features of Islamic practice, to the point of ignoring the book altogether.[28] For instance, in his work on writing and authority in Islamic scripture, Daniel Madigan says:

> Islam is [...] characterized by an almost entirely oral approach to its scripture. One finds no physical book at the center of Muslim worship; nothing at all reminiscent of the crowned Torah scroll or the embellished lectionary. On the contrary, the simple ritual and the recitation of the Qur'an that forms part of it are carried out from memory. Even the prodigious effort of memory required to have the entire sacred text by heart is not considered at all out of the ordinary for a Muslim. To have to consult a written copy to quote the Qur'an is thought a failure of piety.[29]

Such generalizations are in part shaped by an unstated comparison with images of the Bible held in the hands of Christian worshippers or, as in this example, by a more explicit contrast with the use of the Torah in Jewish ritual. But if Madigan's description accurately portrayed the role that memorization plays in contemporary Muslim practice there would be no need for 10 million *mushafs* to be published every year in Saudi Arabia alone,[30] not including a few million copies printed in the rest of the Muslim world.

Road Map

While tracking the connections, transformations, translations, and enrollments of actors in relation to the Qur'anic text, I follow three main groups of human-object networks. The first one consists of printing presses, fonts, moveable types, calligraphic styles, people who work in the Qur'anic printing business, and other networks. The second involves permits, orthography, religious pronouncements, governmental institutions, and the scholars who have much to say on the subject of the Qur'an and its material media. The third group of actors includes mobile phones, museums, radiocarbon dating, and multiple users of the Qur'anic text. Of course, those who produce *mushafs* also use them, and those who define their graphic format in a sense produce them, so this tripartite configuration of actors is only provisional, helping to create situations in which the *mushaf* matters. This configuration also allows me to map out patterns of authoritative claims, practical concerns, economic interests, and personal piety, all of which have the Qur'anic text at their center.

Chapter 1 is about "The Makers." My explorations in the materiality of the *mushaf* begin with the first attempts to print the Qur'anic text under the rule of Muhammad 'Ali Basha and the subsequent concerns and problems that arose as a result of this decision. Over the centuries, the Qur'anic message had developed very characteristic forms of graphic representation that were disrupted by the new technology. The relationship between the Qur'an and its graphic medium is a focus of Chapter 2. I discuss here why typographic printing was a particularly problematic technology when it came to dissemination of the Qur'an. Chapter 3 covers the more recent developments in the history of Qur'anic printing and reveals conflicting ideas about the role of *mushaf* as a commodity and a medium of the Qur'an. This conflict of interest is especially prominent when the Egyptian religious publishing market and its output are compared to the way the Qur'anic text is printed and distributed in Saudi Arabia.

As the beginning of the second section of this book, Chapter 4 discusses "The Custodians" and describes the complex relationship that exists between the makers of the Qur'anic copies and the religious authorities who act as guardians of the message. Since the beginning of the twentieth century, the production of *mushafs* in Egypt has been officially supervised by the University of al-Azhar. Chapter 5 discusses the reasons why the interests of those who produce *mushafs* and those who have authority over the text do not always converge. It also explores how Muslim theology and the practicalities of spreading the message amalgamate and how dissemination of the Qur'an is a matter of constant negotiation and decision-making. Muslim scholars have valid arguments for keeping the traditional Qur'anic orthography in place, yet at the same time they are willing to reinterpret tradition to make exceptions to that very tradition. Chapter 6 speaks to the question of what constitutes a *mushaf* and why the Qur'an in Braille is a rather remarkable although problematic undertaking for Muslim scholars.

The third section, entitled "The Users," takes us into the realm of those who deal with *mushafs* as practitioners. It starts with Chapter 7 that addresses the effects of printing on handwritten *mushafs* and the ways in which they turn into "manuscripts" in institutionalized settings. Although the *mushaf* as a mediator of the Qur'anic message is to be treated with particular care, every so often Egyptian journalists note instances of "Qur'anic abuse" in which a *mushaf* is used for purposes unacceptable by the religious authorities. In Chapter 8, I examine some of these unorthodox uses of *mushafs*, the contexts in which they take place, and the media narratives surrounding them. The closing Chapter 9, like the first one, is focused on a moment of Qur'anic transition between two technologies: in this case, print and digitization. Among Qur'anic theologians, this more recent transition has brought back some of the same concerns expressed during the evolution from handwriting to print but has also generated entirely new questions about the uses of the "electronic Holy Qur'ans," their value and meaning.

All of these chapters together are meant to highlight that although we tend to think of a religious experience, including the reading and interpretation of a holy text, as a predominantly human-generated, abstract (cognitive or affective) practice, this practice is often not only prompted but also shaped and limited by the material qualities of the object that mediates the holy text in unexpected and interesting ways.

Part One

The Makers

1

The Beginning(s)

The idea that printing is necessary for the growth of civilization is uniquely European, yet it has become a measuring stick of modernization in other parts of the world. Unsurprisingly, the assessment of Egyptian readiness to embrace modernity has been tied, first by European and later by Egyptian historians, to the presence of printed books. However, the discourse of advancement and the immediate association of print with the origins of modernity obscures the local conditions in which mechanical reproduction of text emerged in non-Western parts of the world.[1] For instance, until recently many academic works written on the subject of Ottoman printing took for granted the idea that the assessment of how printing spread in the Middle East should be done from the perspective of European and American development of printing.[2] Historical works produced before the mid-twentieth century were especially inclined to follow a chronological trajectory of print evolution and to underscore how important European printing establishments and printing traditions were for the development of printing in the Middle East.[3] By placing Arab printing within this teleological framework, such works often debated why this particular technology was "delayed"[4] in the region and how it contributed to the speed of Middle Eastern political and economic changes once it was embraced. Consequently, works written with this focus failed to notice the unique environment out of which printing emerged in the Middle East and overlooked the interface that already existed between manuscript and print cultures in the Ottoman literate world during most of the nineteenth century.[5] The scholarly assumption was that the printing press "naturally" addressed a growing need to increase the mass production and distribution of written content. But in fact, each Ottoman province had its own, idiosyncratic history of events that led to the introduction and eventual spread of printing.[6]

The discourse of necessary advancement is common in many cultural establishments in Egypt, including the Bibliotheca Alexandrina—a modern institution built to replicate the fame of its renowned ancient antecedent. Among other symbols of progress, the Alexandrian Library hosts a permanent exhibit about the dawn of printing in this region. But while the exhibit's visitors may see printing machines, letter casts, lithographic stones, and other objects in the Library's display hall as harbingers of a new era in the history of their country, I suggest instead that we should think of these objects in relation to what happened as they began printing *mushafs* within the culture of hand-written books and how this event was neither necessary nor certain.

Bodies and Artifacts

The library was cold. It was January and the concrete walls of al-Azhar Headquarters did not offer much protection from the creeping chill. A man sitting at the computer across the library table was warming himself up with a cup of strong tea. He would come every day and occasionally exchange a few niceties during the long hours we spent in front of our screens. He always wore white shirts, long and untucked, and had his arabesque rug ready for the noon prayer, prostrating himself right by our table. One day he asked what I was doing.

"Looking at old printed *mushafs*," I replied.

"Ah," he said briefly and seemingly disinterested returned to his reading.

After a moment of silence, he said again, "So why do you study these *mushafs*?" He must have been bothered by the books on my table for without waiting for my answer he said, "Look, my dear woman, I will tell you what you should do and where you should start from. Go to the College of Foundations of Islam, or go to …." He gave me a list of libraries in Cairo where I could find manuscripts and academic books on the Qur'an. "You don't need to bother yourself with these books," he said, pointing at my pile of printed *mushafs*. "It is not the right place to begin."

In a sense, he was right. In Muslim tradition, the narrative of how the spoken text of the Qur'an became secured in a physical object always originates at the moment in which the skilled and trusted scribe Zayd Ibn Thabit was given the task of collecting parts of the message revealed gradually to the Prophet Muhammad over many lunar years. These parts of the message had been recorded on pieces of parchment, leaves, and other materials but had not been collated into one object. Here the story hesitates: maybe only Zayd assisted Muhammad in writing down revealed portions of the Qur'an, or maybe others aided him. It is hard to tell, but a general knowledge of these early events is part of the ordinary religious education disseminated through various media, including TV, the internet, and mainstream newspapers. The Ramadan lesson, printed in *al-Ahram* during the fasting month of 2010, illustrates such teaching, unfolding the story further: the first compilation of scattered portions took place after the Prophet's death under the guidance of Abu Bakr, who was concerned about the mounting casualties of the Muslim wars and the diminishing numbers of those who could recite the text from memory. This particular lesson ends with a discussion of the editorial efforts exerted by the third Caliph, 'Uthman Ibn 'Affan, who was one of the Prophet Muhammad's companions and took over leadership of the Muslim *umma* (community) twelve years after the Prophet's death. Upon hearing rumors about the different ways in which the Qur'anic text was being recited in far corners of the caliphate, he enlisted Zayd Ibn Thabit's help in finalizing the compilation process to gather the Qur'anic text into one authorized codex. Then he ordered the burning of any text—presumably including those recorded by some of the Prophet's followers—that did not follow the version Zayd produced and was not confirmed by other companions. This is the canonical story of the beginnings of the *mushaf*.

But beginning at this point would lead me into the murky terrain of academic discussions of historical truth and veracity in which Western scholars have various stakes. Talking about the origins of anything that pertains to religion inevitably leads to debates of facts versus beliefs, because for many non-believers and believers alike the need to impose a test of credibility on certain events and narratives is crucial. Participation in such disputes, although expected from someone interested in the Qur'an, would divert me, however, from the tangible, present-day ubiquity of printed Qur'anic texts. As Travis Zadeh points out, investigations into when the event took place or how it proceeded—for instance, whether the first *mushaf* was assembled during the Prophet's lifetime or after—are "mired in the very epistemological positivism necessary for such endeavors."[7] These issues would also direct my attention away from examining what the *mushaf* as an object does to modern practitioners, manufacturers, and scholars (Muslim and non-Muslim), as well as what concerns, aesthetic pleasures, and deliberations it produces in the course of its use. I have to admit that my interest in the early history of *mushafs* goes only as far as its history is invoked in the present; my story of the Qur'anic book does not aim to be a full chronology of its earliest past.

I choose, instead, to link the history of the *mushaf* to a different constellation of events that highlights in a practical manner the untidy relationship between the text and the object. That constellation, it seems, has not left many traces in the collective memory of contemporary Egyptian Muslims, having been slowly buried under the weight of the affairs of the past century. The history of the printed *mushaf* has not been particularly significant for non-Muslim scholars interested in the Qur'an, either, for very different reasons. Yet, if we trust Marshall McLuhan's insights about the consequences of the medium for the message it mediates, this history may have had a great deal of consequence for Muslim practitioners because for over a hundred years now, it has been a different kind of book—a mechanically reproduced one.

"History begins with bodies and artifacts," wrote anthropologist Michel-Rolph Trouillot.[8] Taking this statement as my guide, I set off to understand how these concrete entities—bodies and artifacts—instigated changes that made printed *mushafs* ubiquitous elements in Egypt's contemporary religious landscape. I also wanted to let archives and historical records reveal the decisions that created the conditions of possibility for the following encounter to occur over a century later. This encounter took place some years ago, before the upheavals of 2011, when Egyptian peddlers were still hurling jokes at the neighborhood police officers down the street, rather than stones and homemade explosives. I was in an old mosque, one of those timeworn structures that tourists are allowed to visit "after hours," polluting it with the modern ambivalence of the spectator with a guidebook in hand. There was a tomb in the mosque behind ornate bars, covered in green fabric and artificial flowers, and ringed by a guarding circle of open, upright *mushafs*. I was curiously walking around the tomb, trying to peek through the latticework to see to which verses of the Qur'an the *mushafs* were open. In my circumambulation, I passed an older man in a long beige tunic and a gray shawl wrapped around his head, who seemed to be snoozing in the corner of the room with an open *mushaf* on his lap. During one of my circuits the man opened his eyes and gestured me to come closer. I remember a flash of surprise when he placed his *mushaf* over my head, smiling encouragingly, and murmured a little blessing. I wondered: would it have been possible for this somewhat shabby-looking man to bless visitors to the tomb with his own *mushaf* two centuries ago? Who exactly was responsible for the change that allowed my well-wisher to snooze in the corner of the mosque with his own copy of the Qur'anic text on his lap? To answer these questions, I chose to begin with an unlikely actor—the printing press—because, as Michel-Rolph Trouillot says, we should not "exclude in advance any of the actors who participate in the production of history."[9] Although Trouillot in his narratives did not include objects as historical agents, if we agree that inanimate things can act, then they cannot be omitted from accounts of the past. So here is the beginning of the story I offer.

Muhammad 'Ali's Printing Project

After the last French troops were forced to leave Egypt in 1801, the Ottoman Sultan in Istanbul, Selim III, tried to re-establish control over the unstable province. He thought it would be a good idea to send the energetic and ambitious Albanian-born commander Muhammad 'Ali Basha al-Mas'ud Ibn Agha to reoccupy Cairo after Napoleon's withdrawal. Muhammad 'Ali turned out to be so successful in his mission that he soon managed to become a *wali* (governor) and in 1805 forced the Sultan to acknowledge him as a viceroy only nominally subordinate to Istanbul. The new viceroy sought to turn Egypt into a military stronghold, matching the powers of the European states. The memory of Muhammad 'Ali as a well-organized but ruthless military general has morphed over time into that of an enlightened ruler and the founder of the modern Egyptian state; he is introduced as such to those who come to admire his headquarters in the Salah al-Din Citadel towering majestically over old Cairo. Even so, Muhammad 'Ali's interest in military power can be seen in the improvements he made to the interior of the citadel, which he also generously splashed with the blood of his Mamluk opponents in 1811.

Sometimes particles of the forgotten find their ways into present consciousness in the form of contingent knowledge expressed by unexpected interlocutors. In the course of a chance conversation about the first printing press in Egypt with a taxi driver on my way to the library, I heard an unanticipated assertion that questioned 'Ali's popular image. The driver had a master's degree in history from Cairo University and drove the taxi as a second job. He was convinced that the radical modernization of the country carried out by Muhammad 'Ali was not necessarily intended to improve his subjects' living conditions, but was merely a way to create an efficient army for his own, less altruistic, purposes.[10] My driver agreed, though, that 'Ali's robust military reforms were assisted by the organization of new military schools, which, in turn, needed textbooks. These were to be speedily provided through the industrialized printing that had just made its way more decisively into other regions of the Ottoman Empire, especially in Lebanon, Syria, and Turkey, where Sultan Selim III also promoted printing as a practical tool to facilitate administrative work.

Muhammad 'Ali had to look for assistance in establishing his new printing enterprise and he needed people and appliances that would enable him to accomplish this project. Italy was close, militarily non-threatening, and had a long history of printing in Arabic. By 1815, the Basha had sent to Milan a delegation of four men headed by Niqula al-Masabki (who already had had some experience with printing during the French occupation) to learn the principles of this art and to bring the necessary equipment, including the casts of the Arabic, Turkish, Latin, and Greek alphabets in different sizes.[11] Equipped in knowledge and machinery, the same delegation was able to establish a few years later an official Egyptian governmental printing house known as Matba'a bi-Bulaq (Printing House at Bulaq).[12] Historians disagree about the exact date of its establishment, in either 1821 or 1822, but since then its history has been closely woven into the wider story of printing in Egypt. In fact, Matba'a bi-Bulaq itself has often served as a symbol of modernity in later Egyptian historiography. Over the years, the printing house has changed not only its location but also its name, and the old walls of the establishment no longer remain where they were once built. It is now known as al-Amiriyya and its original printing machines are long gone. It is al-Amiriyya's equipment from later in the nineteenth century that is displayed at the Bibliotheca Alexandrina, exemplifying the Western discourse of successful modernization in the form of book printing in Egypt under the rule of Muhammad 'Ali.

In spite of Muhammad 'Ali's interest in books, publishing the Qur'anic text was not the Basha's priority. The first publications of his official print house at Bulaq (and a few other secondary print houses established by him for professional schools and governmental offices soon after the press at Bulaq) were directly related to his project of developing an efficient administration. They printed textbooks often translated from Italian and French, dictionaries, and legal manuals, which provided practical knowledge for doctors, engineers, and government and military professionals. In the next few decades, the press began including in its output various collections of poetry, popular literary works such as the popular Middle Eastern collection of animal fables *Kalila wa Dimna*, and classical texts in Islam like *Sahih al-Bukhari*, a well-known compilation of narratives about the Prophet Muhammad.[13] However, most of the publications of literary and religious genres were not commissioned by the Basha and his administration, but by customers who paid to have them published (mainly at Bulaq) in order to later sell them for profit.[14] Muhammad 'Ali's orders were much more pragmatic. His decision to print the Qur'anic text came only a decade after the establishment of the press at Bulaq and was most probably inspired by his need to teach the growing future cadre of soldiers and clerks to read and write. Throughout the Middle East, Qur'anic verses were commonly used in teaching literacy, so perhaps the Basha—who was illiterate himself—elected to print them with this didactic purpose in mind.

Muhammad 'Ali's edition of the Qur'anic text printed in Egypt was not, however, the first mechanically produced *mushaf*. Being interested in printing and its benefits, the Basha might have even heard of some of these controversial early attempts to produce a Qur'anic book undertaken in Europe. In 1537/8 in Venice, the father and son Paganino and Alessandro de Paganini printed a complete copy of the Qur'an for export in the Muslim world. It was a daring project to attempt to sell copies of the Qur'an printed in Europe to customers in the Ottoman Empire.[15] It was daring but risky for a number of reasons. Both the Qur'an and *sunna* (the canonical narratives about the Prophet Muhammad) explicitly forbid those without proper ablutions and non-Muslims to touch the book. For this reason Muslim scholars discouraged Muslim travelers to carry their *mushafs* to non-Muslim lands out of concern that the books might fall into the hands of those who did not follow the rules of *tahara* or ritual purity. So *mushafs* produced by a non-Muslim outside of the Muslim territories had a very problematic status to begin with. Moreover, exporting them to the Ottoman Empire must have violated some other regulations, as the archives indicate that Paganini's books were eventually confiscated by the Ottoman administrators.[16]

Apart from the religious and legal problems, there might have been aesthetic and scholarly factors at work. For one, the typeface of Paganini's *mushafs* looked very different from the handwritten Qur'anic copies. Across the board, the script exemplified "the difficulty typesetters had in reconciling the exigencies of setting type on a line with the piling up of letters in Arabic,"[17] which naturally overlap and flow on a page in a cascading pattern, instead of lying flat on the line. Another and equally difficult to accommodate feature of the Arabic script is that the connections between the letters are very important to the legibility of the written text.[18] Thus, the printed letters were hard to read and appeared much more static *in comparison with the dynamic lines of the written words*. (The change of fonts in this sentence only partially demonstrates this effect.)[19] Moreover, the books contained errors, including wrong vowels and missing diacritic marks, which changed the meaning of words.[20] It was bad timing for the Paganinis as well—their ungainly Qur'anic text appeared when Ottoman calligraphy was reaching its pinnacle.[21] All in all, the Paganinis' venture failed to produce a satisfying edition of the Qur'anic text, but this fiasco did not discourage others from trying to achieve better results. Still, subsequent publications made in Hamburg (1694), Padua (1698), and Saint Petersburg (1787) gained no popularity among Muslims either.[22]

These unsuccessful attempts in publishing the Qur'anic text undertaken by non-Muslim advocates of print are much better documented than the early efforts of those to whom the text belonged. I cannot claim that my record of events in Egypt is complete. There are gaps and contradictions, the result of conflicts, politics, and the limitations of human memory. Documents that would allow glimpses into that period are rare and scattered. The archival passion so well known to Europeans (and perhaps to the Chinese) has not feverishly consumed the Middle Eastern part of the world to lead people to produce equally large repositories of fragmented pasts. On the other hand, Egyptian political changes that shifted the country's position from that of a semi-independent Turkish province to a colonial protectorate, to a nominally independent kingdom and then a military regime, did not always secure a long-lasting interest in the preservation of materials documenting the deeds of predecessors. What is left, at least in connection to the printing of *mushafs*, can often be found in the margins of records of other, more pressing, affairs. Some dates and descriptions of events come from secondary sources, additionally mixing up the layers of historical accuracy, personal endorsements, and interpretations. And so my story continues, propelled by choices that in the end are somewhat arbitrary, dictated by chance encounters and a network of people and objects of which I happened to become a part.

Early *Mushafs*

Of course, it is just a speculation that Muhammad 'Ali might have heard of the printed European versions of the Qur'anic text, or perhaps he might have been informed about the first edition printed in Iran that took place somewhere between 1820 and 1830.[23] It is much more likely, however, that he followed the printing developments in Turkey. At the time when the Basha was busying himself with his project at Bulaq and getting the necessary printing equipment from Italy, the Turkish printing shops were already casting their own letters (matrices) and printing all sorts of books, except the Qur'an.[24] So in this sense, Muhammad 'Ali's decision to add the Qur'an to the list of printed publications coming out of Bulaq around the year 1832 was rather cutting edge. The first indication of this event comes from the newspaper *al-Waqa'i'a al-Masriyya* (*Egyptian Affairs*), praised today as the pearl of early journalism in the Middle East. It was a daily review established by Muhammad 'Ali in 1828 to inform the elites and administrators about various doings of the government. The issue from January 8, 1832, included a paragraph that stated:

> Mahmud Agha, the supervisor of the school gave a presentation to the Army Council [that supervised Bulaq], in which he was asked about the amount of what is necessary for the students of the aforementioned school when it comes to the parts of the Glorious Qur'an and other supplies. He replied that they need four complete readings of the Qur'an and sixty sheets. The members of the Council said that this proposal should be signed by his excellency the supervisor of the army, Bik Effendi, and directed to 'Amr Effendi, the supplies manager, to provide students with the previously mentioned items, as they are needed for their education.[25]

In and of itself, this memo is somewhat equivocal in its content. The word *lawh* used in the original text has many meanings and does not necessarily mean *printed* sheets. It can also mean wooden tablets on which students learn to write. The word *khatma* means a complete *reading* of the Qur'an and may refer to a handwritten *mushaf*. On the other hand, since the supervisors of Bulaq participated in this event, it is likely that the discussed supplies did refer to the printed sheets of *mushaf*, possibly parts of it, as it has been customary for teachers to divide the text for more convenient reading. This note as well as another governmental document issued a year later, in which the actual printing of the Qur'anic text is mentioned explicitly, indicate that certainly by April of 1833 Bulaq had released the first local, mechanically reproduced text of the Qur'an in Egypt.[26] This printed edition had a utilitarian value, as it was meant to be used in the governmental school and maybe also offered for sale to the general public.

Nevertheless, this first domestic printing in Cairo caused concerns among Muslim scholars at al-Azhar University, the intellectual hub of the learned Islamic community in the country. There is a long-standing opinion among Western and Egyptian historians—an opinion that has seeped into public imagery[27]—that the reluctance of the *'ulama'* (Muslim scholars) to endorse the Qur'anic text in print was a result of their visceral dislike of new technology and the fear of losing their monopoly over the consumption of religious knowledge.[28] Both of these reasons purportedly grew out of their reactionary attitude toward modernization in general. For instance, this opinion surfaces in a comment by Abu al-Futuh Radwan, who notes that the Egyptian religious authorities, in response to Muhammad 'Ali's decision, issued statements (*fatwas*) in which they were critical of the printing of the Qur'anic text, as opposed to writing it by hand. Radwan says:

> If al-Azhar scholars forbade printing religious books, they would make prohibition to print the Qur'an their priority. And indeed, printing of the Qur'an remained prohibited under *fatwas* of the scholars for a long time during the reign of Muhammad 'Ali. This [decision] was based on flimsy arguments, such as incompatibility of printing machines with the [requirements of] *tahara*, lack of permissibility to press the verses of Allah with the metal machinery, and a likelihood of error in the process of printing.[29]

It is clear that the Azhari scholars had primarily two objections: one related to the conditions of printing and the other concerning the outcomes of this undertaking that might result in mechanically multiplied errors. Although Radwan dismissed the arguments presented by the Egyptian *'ulama'* as "flimsy," these concerns were part of a wider discussion about the appropriateness of disseminating the Qur'anic text in print that had also taken place among Turkish scholars. It seems that Turkish religious intellectuals had not been comfortable with printing the Qur'anic text, nor with the *tafsir* (explanations of the Qur'anic text), *hadith* (narratives about the deeds and saying of the Prophet Muhammad), *fiqh* (jurisprudence), and *kalam* (a branch of Islamic theology)—all of which often contained considerable portions of the Qur'an. However, they did not object to any other forms of printing, which is clear from the exchange that had taken place already a century earlier between the printer Ibrahim Mütefferika (1674–1745) and the Grand Sheikh (Sheikh al-Islam) 'Abdallah Effendi regarding the permission to use a printing press to disseminate books in the country. Mütefferika did not request to be allowed to print religious texts, and the Grand Sheikh's response to his inquiry in 1726 was quite obliging:

> Being able to produce this great benefit, this person receives permission with the condition that several educated persons be appointed as proofreaders. Great benefit will come from the order based on that legal opinion, allowing for the exception of the religious subjects mentioned in the tract written with the pearl pen of wisdom.[30]

Clearly, the Grand Sheikh recognized that the new technology offered certain benefits, but he was also aware that it had to be used with caution. His concerns (supported by other religious leaders) were similar to those expressed later by the Egyptian *'ulama'* in response to Qur'anic printing undertaken at Bulaq under Muhammad 'Ali.

Furthermore, the legal objections to printing the *mushaf* lasted longer in Turkey than in Egypt. Although an 1871 edition of the Qur'an was produced in London by a Turkish national, Namik Kemal, and his British friend, Aristidis Fanton, they received permission for it to be sold in the Ottoman Empire only as a countermeasure to "illegal" *mushafs* coming from Iran and India.[31] The Ottoman government did not lift the local restriction on printing the Qur'anic text until 1874. When it became clear that the influx of *mushafs* with unclear provenance could not be stopped, the first official photolithographic edition of the Quar'an was printed in Istanbul, supported by the government and Muslim scholars alike, and featuring the handwriting of a well-known calligrapher Şekerzade Mehmed Effendi (d. 1752) who imitated the penmanship and Qur'anic design of one of the most famous Turkish calligraphers, Sheikh Hamdullah (1436–1520). In order to increase the legitimacy of this project, Ahmet Cevdet, its supervisor and a celebrated scholar, included in the *mushaf* a publisher's note that—says Brett Wilson—"in a one broad sweep evoked the authority and gravitas associated with first/seven-century Medina and four hundred years of Ottoman calligraphic tradition" by mentioning by whom and in what conditions the original manuscript was written.[32]

The project was done under the aegis of the Ministry of Education, which made sure to let everyone know that the conditions of printing were acceptable to the *'ulama'* (Muslim scholars), that there was no impure equipment used in the process of printing, that the workers performed necessary ablutions, and that any unused paper with the Qur'anic verses was properly disposed of. The project was also advertised as a nonprofit venture that meant to make *mushaf* affordable for an ordinary person and the book's exactitude was guaranteed by a committee of scholars who worked on its corrections. In 1880, another person took over the printing venture—a trained calligrapher and Chamberlain in the Sultan's Palace, Osman Zeki Bey, who received exclusive permission from Sultan Abdulhamid II to print the Qur'anic text, also imitating a Qur'anic copy of the seventeenth-century calligrapher Hafiz 'Uthman (d. 1698).[33]

His very profitable printing business was viewed with resentment by other entrepreneurs who did not want to be excluded from such a lucrative undertaking, so locally produced black-market copies began popping up in the country almost immediately. The initial amount of printed Qur'anic copies was quite impressive. Within the first decade, a number of officially produced *mushafs*—if the declared goals were actually met—might have reached 1 million books, not including the illegal editions.[34] Yussif Sarkis (1856–1932), a Lebanese scholar who moved to Cairo in 1912 and set up his own Maktabat Sarkis in the famous book street al-Fagala, notes in his bibliography of early printed Arabic books the lithographic *mushaf* ordered by the Turkish Ministry of Education. Interestingly, he also mentions an anonymous typographic *mushaf* printed in Turkey in 1871/1872.[35] If Sarkis was correct, this *mushaf* might have been an example of one of the black-market editions.

This unfolding of events in Istanbul has its own fascinating trajectory, but what matters for the story of *mushafs* in Egypt is that there was one major question which surfaced in both places, namely: what exactly happens when the Qur'anic text is manufactured mechanically in multiple copies made by a printing press? The religious scholars were obviously alarmed by the unfamiliar conditions of producing the Qur'anic text and anxious about the potential errors that might creep into this process of multiplication. It is clear that their objections were not directed toward the technology itself as much as toward the actual circumstances in which the text was reproduced as well as the potential consequences of reproducing the text with errors.

I suggest that we do not gloss over these expressions of concern as nothing more than the reactionary sentiments of conservative old-timers. In fact, I believe that unpacking the reasons the Egyptian and Turkish *'ulama'* were cautious about the idea of printing the Qur'anic text will not only help illuminate the relationship between the Qur'anic text and the book, but also challenge Western academic bias in thinking of religious practice mainly in terms of abstract ideas that underscore actions. Changes in religious practice do not simply happen when people change their minds. These alterations also come through changes in the forms of engagement with the material world in which these practices take place. Yet, as Ken Alder said, things are "thick and recalcitrant"[36] and, therefore, sometimes harder to act upon than one might wish them to be. The initial objections of the Muslim scholars to printing the Qur'anic text were, on the one hand, solidly grounded in the centuries-old debates and practices of Qur'anic orthography and script. On the other, these objections were also based on concrete examples of printing that in its earliest iterations clearly could not deliver copies of the same quality as those produced by hand. Therefore, the *'ulama'* in both parts of the Ottoman Empire viewed the Qur'anic printing project with circumspection and initially considered the printing press as *bid'a* (an innovation of an unreliable character)—a legal concept that denotes an event without a precedent that should be avoided in religious matters. They were—justifiably as we will see later—worried that the use of machines could distort a text that, above all, should be reproduced with the utmost care and attention.[37]

The issue of *tahara*, ritual purity, was not a minor obstacle, either. Traditionally, not only was the person copying the text by hand expected to be in a state of personal purity, but so too the place and objects used in the process of copying would have been surrounded by constraints. So, for instance, the 1833 document directly addressing the question of printed *mushafs* at Bulaq requested an investigation into the actual circumstances in which they were produced:

> In regard to the occasion of printing the noble mushaf, it is needed to recruit a head of the press and ask him whether some parts of the press are made out of canine skin or not, and send a report about it to Habib Effendi, by the end of Dhu al-Qa'ada 1248 [April 30, 1833].[38]

The authorities wanted to know the construction materials of the printing machine to exclude the possibility that the text might come into contact with items such as the skin of dogs—animals that, according to some *hadiths*, were impure.[39] About a decade later, the same concerns about the conditions of production voiced by the religious authorities resulted in the creation of a separate space at Bulaq for printing *mushafs* only. Radwan says, "Out of concern for printing the Qur'an it was decided to apportion a part of the printing house for special printing. It was known as 'Print House of the Noble *Mushaf*,' and there was an independent person, 'Abd al-Rahman Effendi, in charge of it."[40]

Considering the initial polemics about the appropriateness of using printing for Qur'anic production, it is not surprising that religious authorities at al-Azhar reluctantly gave Muhammad 'Ali permission to print. As chronicled by Andrew Archibald Paton, a British traveler to Egypt, it seems that arguments about the prudence of this action continued for a while, even though the newly appointed *Mufti* of Egypt (and Muhammad 'Ali's friend) Sheikh Ahmad al-Tamimi (1801–1851) put his seal on it at the Basha's request.[41] In this way, Muhammad 'Ali could ensure that the *mushaf* was officially approved and—if this was also his intent—would, in fact, sell.[42] But inspite of the seal, the *mushaf* printed under the rule of Muhammad 'Ali was nevertheless criticized for its less than satisfying quality. According to Abu al-Futuh Radwan, in 1853 the *'ulama'* were finally able to convince Muhammad 'Ali's grandson, Viceroy 'Abbas I, to withdraw these *mushafs* from circulation. Yet in spite of this prohibition, the authorities were not able to curtail the trade of printed *mushafs*; copies continued to circulate. A year later, another decree was issued by the governorate of Alexandria that stated:

> The printed *mushafs* that contained numerous mistakes and misspelling in multiple places have been forbidden to buy and sell. Therefore disposing of them in a religiously proper manner is legal. In regard to those who own such *mushafs* or possess them, they should be punished in proportion to their offense [determined after investigation].[43]

And so, printed *mushafs* were confiscated and collected at the Ministry of the Interior[44] but, as Abu al-Futuh Radwan records, there was a quandary about "disposing of them in a religiously proper manner." Perhaps nobody was sure what to do with them; for the next four years they lay stored in the ministry's warehouse. The problem continued through the reign of 'Abbas I's successor, Viceroy Sa'id Basha, who ruled Egypt and Sudan from 1854 to 1863. Upon inquiry from the Ministry of Interior in 1858 about what to do with the 296 confiscated *mushafs*, Sa'id Basha decided to appropriate some of them for students in the military school. He consulted the *'ulama'* who recommended corrections to the existing copies before their dissemination. So fifty-two *mushafs* were sent to the military school and revised there for the use of the pupils. Then, a qualified governmental employee who memorized the Qur'an and copied the work of Ibn Khaldun, calligrapher Sheikh 'Abd al-Baqi al-Jari, was charged with the task of correcting another 150 copies. The cost of these corrections was an incredible sum of 4,890 piasters.

Confiscation of these *mushafs* caused friction between their owners and the government. Radwan tells us a story about al-Hajj Amin who requested the return of 134 confiscated copies and al-Hajj 'Uthman who requested the return of twenty-six of them. Their representative, al-Hajj Hasan, argued at the Ministry that they should receive their *mushafs* back without having to pay 2,800 piasters it would cost to correct them. He claimed that his clients could take care of the mistakes themselves, presumably by asking someone else to correct them. The Ministry directed the case back to Muslim religious authorities who declared that the owners of the *mushafs* had not asked for the corrections to be done so they did not need to pay for them. Whatever *mushafs* remained, Viceroy Saʿid Basha ordered them to be corrected at his expense, and for the pleasure of Allah, before giving them back to their owners. Unclaimed ones were to be distributed in the appropriate (that is, unadulterated) places for recitation, reading, and studying.⁴⁵ It is hard to say whether the buyers of the corrected *mushafs* purchased them because of their relatively lower price compared to handmade copies, because they viewed the books as collector's items, because they saw printed *mushafs* as examples of Islamic modernity, or because they simply thought of these Qur'anic copies as useful tools in teaching literacy.

The records Radwan investigated are silent from that time on about disagreements concerning the printing of *mushafs* at Bulaq, but the production of Qur'anic copies continued. An 1887 inventory of books in the first national library al-Kutubkhana al-Khidiwiyya includes eighty-three complete *mushafs* and eighty-eight fragments (*rubʿat*) printed in Egypt, eighty-seven *mushafs* printed in Istanbul, eighty-eight printed in India, and eighty-eight printed in Persia.⁴⁶ In his *Dictionary of Arab and Moroccan Publications*, Yussif Sarkis lists editions of the Qur'anic text published at Bulaq in 1864/5, 1866/7, 1882, and 1886/7.⁴⁷ He also mentions other private enterprises that printed *mushafs* that were operating in Cairo between 1882 and 1904.⁴⁸ Some of them, like the establishment of Muhammad Abu Zayd, released a wide range of titles, including a *mushaf*. (Abu Zayd himself published the acclaimed *Mushaf* al-Makhallalaati.) Other printing presses were more ephemeral—or specialized—managing to print only one title that, in some cases, happened to be the Qur'an. For instance, ʿAbd al-Khalaq Haqqi appears on the Sarkis's list as one of those who successfully produced a number of Qur'anic editions during the last decade of the nineteenth century. But from the records of the historian ʿAyda Nossir, we can learn that he also belonged to those entrepreneurs who managed to publish only one title.⁴⁹ The number of circulating *mushafs* at the end of the nineteenth century was significant enough that many survived to pass into the general collection of printed *mushafs* in the Library of Mashyekhat al-Azhar where they are now available for general use (Figure 1).

Visual Practice

Let's go back a few decades to the first printed *mushafs* and look more closely at some of the reasons why the first attempts to copy the Qur'anic text in a mechanical manner were so vexing for the *'ulama'*. The decisions made first in Iran and then in Egypt to use machines to reproduce the Qur'anic text were soon followed in India, mainly in Lucknow (1850), Bombay (1852), and Delhi (1863).⁵⁰ Indonesia's first printed copy of the Qur'an appeared in 1848 and sold well.⁵¹ In Morocco, print was introduced in the mid-1800s and included religious books from the start, but the first Qur'anic text there didn't appear until 1879. Determining which one of these was the "first printed Qur'an" in each country is, of course, an elusive project and likely to be questioned; I prefer to leave the task of establishing priority to historians. What I find more interesting in this inventory of dates is that although for a long period of time printing did not constitute a popular technology for the dissemination of religious texts in general and *mushafs* in particular, once it *did* start, printed Qur'anic books quickly

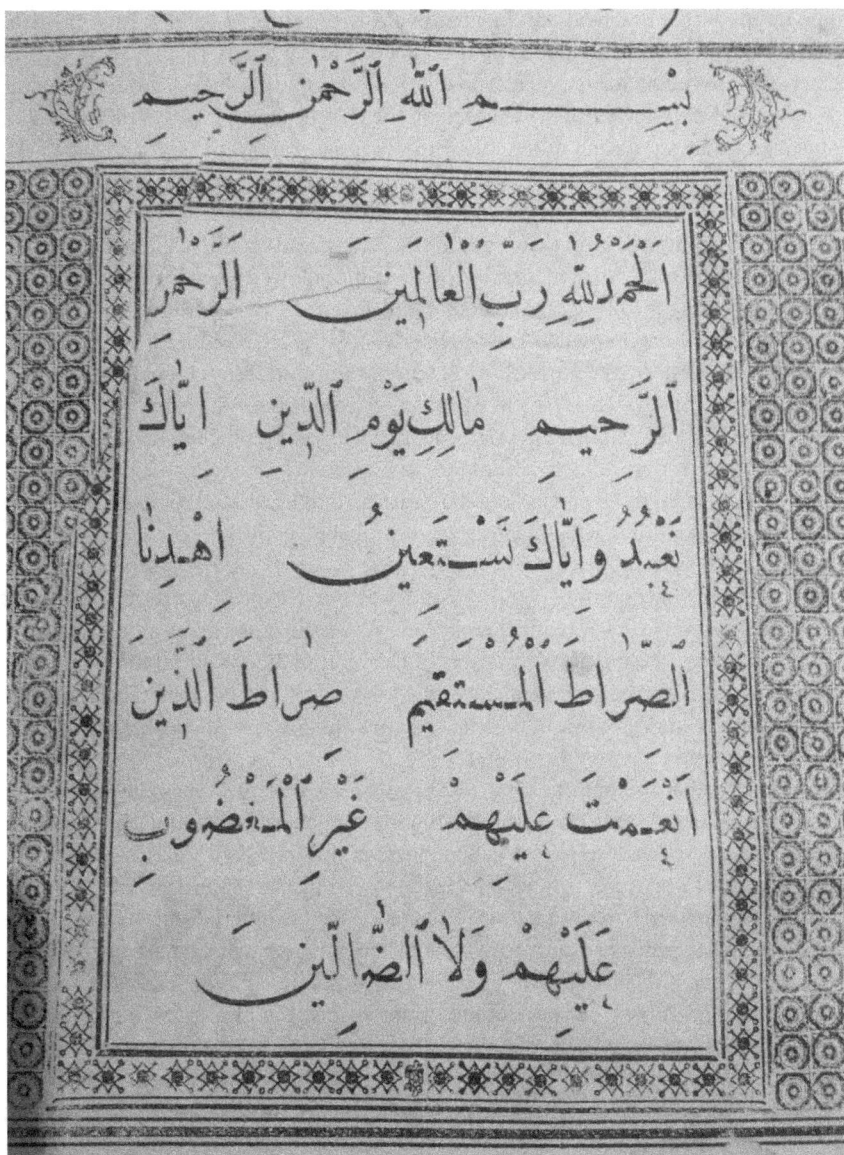

Figure 1 *Mushaf* printed at Bulaq in 1882. Photograph courtesy Tradigital.

spread throughout the Muslim world. What is also interesting is that print editions in different countries relied on two very different techniques.

In Euro-American societies, consumers of print are mainly familiar with letterpress (typographic) printing in which a movable type is arranged into the bed of a press, before being inked and stamped onto paper. For a long time typography was a practical and inexpensive way to multiply texts written in Latin script. However, it turned out to be less effective for Arabic script. In some places, especially Southeast Asia, experiments with lithographic printing produced better results. Lithographic printing was based on the chemical properties of oil and water, substances that repel each other. The image was not carved out but applied to the surface of a flat stone with the help of oil or wax, using specially prepared paper. Ink adhered to the greasy image and was repelled from blank areas by a thin film of water and a mixture of gum arabic and nitric acid spread on the surface of the stone. This kind of printing yielded smaller editions but allowed greater flexibility. Little print shops using the lithographic method mushroomed all over northern India and were primarily Muslim owned and operated.[52] "By the 1870s editions of the Qur'an and other religious books were selling in tens of thousands," says Francis Robinson,[53] obviously also making their way to Egypt, as we could see in the catalogue of the al-Kutubkhana Library. Unlike Egyptian and Turkish typographic books, lithographed publications in India and Persia from the beginning included religious literature and the Qur'an, although the *fatwas* issued by Turkish and Egyptian religious authorities dictating the conditions for printing were probably known in other parts of the Muslim world as well.

Some interesting questions could be asked here. For instance, once it was introduced in Southeast Asia, why was lithography not successful elsewhere? Why didn't the Levant embrace lithography as eagerly as India and Iran did? Why did the official and private presses in Turkey and Egypt continue to work with typography? The historians of print have addressed some of these questions. I will focus on those that are relevant for the production of *mushafs*.

It is likely that the objections of Muslim scholars toward industrialized printing were to some degree entangled with the mundane demands of making a living, since many of these scholars were also calligraphers and artisans. However, if we look at colophons of the privately printed *mushafs* in Egypt, by the 1880s many of the people who participated in the production of Qur'anic copies, especially the lithographed ones, were also graduates from al-Azhar and were religious scholars themselves. That said, the *'ulama'* (Muslim scholars) were mostly dependent on less-educated copyists who, at least in Turkey, put up a unified front against the idea of the governmental production of *mushafs*. Brett Wilson reminds us that in the Ottoman Empire, *if* a person owned a book it would most probably have been a *mushaf*, but the copies that we eagerly consume as spectators in Western museums are adorned masterpieces of calligraphic artistry.[54] Museums do not display *mushafs* written by average scribes who produced mediocre copies of the Qur'an. Many of these books stay hidden away in the storage rooms of archives and libraries. But even the inartistic scribes manufacturing not-so-sophisticated *mushafs* had to have a certain degree of religious education. With the introduction of print, theoretically even a person who did not have a licensed knowledge of the Qur'an could produce a printed *mushaf*. Thus, this new form of reproduction undoubtedly concerned those who had to master the text by heart to qualify as copyists. Still, qualms about the future of one's profession do not fully explain the reluctance with which printing of the Qur'an was initially met throughout the Ottoman world.

Although the concerns of religious authorities about the new typographic technology certainly stemmed from the practical problems related to its use and, perhaps, the threats it posed to those who copied the Qur'an by hand, I suspect that early controversies over printing the text of the Qur'an also were due to the relationship between printing and the past. The introduction of the printing press created an interruption in the chain of authority produced by generations of copiers who learned from their teachers. Before print, what authenticated the accuracy of the text, whether written or recited, was the *isnad*, a method of transmission by which the provenience of a text was traced through a person-to-person, student-to-teacher connection. Printing disrupted such connections. Francis Robinson explains this predicament succinctly, if somewhat dramatically: "Printing attacked the very heart of Islamic systems for the transmission of knowledge; it attacked what was understood to make knowledge trustworthy, what gave it value, what gave it authority."[55]

Isnad as an authoritative method for the transmission of knowledge was fundamental to the formation of Islamic law, theology, and science. It was, and still is, an indispensable part of certifying the professional qualification of reciters of the Qur'an. When asked about his credentials, a professor of recitation at al-Azhar proudly showed me his *ijaza*, a license to teach Qur'anic recitation and a proof of his *isnad*. It was a plain document, rather like a governmental booklet, a few pages long, that consisted of a long sequence of antecedent reciters, traced all the way back to the Prophet Muhammad. I found it interesting that this *written* document confirmed the credentials of a person who testified to the credibility of the text via its transmission through a chain of teachers emphasizing a pedagogy of vocal training and *memory*. (This is a method known as *talaqqi*, in which student has to memorize and recite the whole text of the Qur'an to his sheikh teacher, who can trace through the *isnad* his own teachers, and their teachers, and so on, all the way back to the Prophet Muhammad.)

The introduction of printing also interrupted the *isnad* of person-to-person instruction in calligraphy and writing. "Printing," writes Wilson, "unlike the calligraphy and writing, could not trace its origins back to the early Muslim community but rather to fifteenth-century Germany and to the non-Muslim printers who developed the technology. Therefore, printed books lacked a lineage that provided Islamic authenticity and guaranteed the quality of work."[56] Printing is a technology of multiplicity and assemblage. Each *mushaf* produced by a more or less accomplished copyist was nonetheless singular and unique, easily checked for accuracy and completeness, and easy to correct if any mistakes occurred in the process of writing. A printed *mushaf* could multiply the same shape of a letter or a space between words—or a misspelling— hundreds of times. A missed word in a handwritten *mushaf*—a rare event—was added in the margin of the text. The correction of an orthographic mistake was not difficult, either. But correcting hundreds of printed copies carrying the same mistake defeated the benefits of fast multiplication, as we saw in the case of the flawed *mushafs* printed at Bulaq under Muhammad 'Ali Basha. In this circumstance, the question of the text's correct spelling was crucial. Previously secured by *isnad* but now produced by printers without *isnad*, how could the accuracy of a written text be preserved? With printing as the primary technology of dissemination, the orthographic mediation of the Qur'anic message was at risk.

Moreover, the way the early typographically reproduced texts "looked" different from the handwritten one was a cause for concern. Evidently, the first set of letter casts brought to Bulaq from Italy did not produce print of the required quality: letter imprints were clunky and inconsistent in thickness. The set also lacked *harakat*—marks for vowelization indicating declension. But most of all, the letters did not follow the rules of "the eastern style" of calligraphy. The print just did not "look Arabic" and the letters from Europe were "stylistically strange for the Eastern taste."[57] Within a few years, these casts were replaced by locally made ones that were more aesthetically pleasing. A professional calligrapher designed the second set, made in the two writing styles known as *farsi* and *naskh*, and it was "accepted with great praise."[58] It was probably this type that the printing team at Bulaq used in printing the Qur'anic text, but—judging from the look of other texts printed at that time—even the improved lettertypes did not make the first impression of a typographically printed Arabic script less jarring.

The strangeness of printed *mushaf* was a problem, then, in areas where letterpress technology was the predominant form of printing. In the typography so prevalent in Europe, each letter was set separately. This method was not easily transplanted to places using non-Latin alphabets, especially Arabic. We get a glimpse of these problems in the history of printing in Malaysia. Walter Henry Medhurst, a nineteenth-century European missionary printmaker who worked primarily with letterpress typography, discovered that lithography was much more suitable for printing Malay, which was then written in Arabic script. This method allowed the printer to produce a whole page at one time using print that resembled handwriting. His readers found this much more acceptable. Medhurst noted,

> The Malays have few or no printed books; and when they are presented with one executed by letter press, they find it altogether so unlike their own, and so foreign in its appearance, that they are inclined to reject it on this ground alone.[59]

This rejection was not surprising. Even a person who did not grow up with a handwritten Qur'anic text could—by looking at early printed *mushafs*—understand the challenges of graphically representing the Qur'anic text in print: artificial-looking spacing between letters and words; awkward positioning of letters on the baseline; rigidity and disproportionate sizes of particular signs, diacritics above and below the line placed at the same unadjusted heights; and familiar ligatures and letter conjunctions oddly altered. These predicaments must have been even more disturbing for those who for years incorporated a particular image of the hand-lettered text into the practice of reading and grew up within the flourishing and prosperous scribal culture in the Ottoman Empire.

The documents about efforts undertaken to produce manuscript-like *mushafs* in Indonesia, where lithography was the dominant technique of printing, help demonstrate "the problem of the look." It seems that lithographed, handwritten-like printed editions of the Qur'an did not stir up the same controversies in that part of the Muslim world as letterpress printed editions did in Egypt or Turkey. Ian Proudfoot, a historian of Asian print, tells us that Muhammad Azhari, a native of Palembang in southern Sumatra, undertook printing the Qur'anic text in 1848.⁶⁰ He printed his *mushaf* on a press that he purchased in Singapore on his return from Mecca. He also brought to Palembang a trained lithographer to help in his venture. Azhari's *mushaf* imitated manuscript conventions very closely, including handmade verse markers. Proudfoot says that the degree to which he succeeded was indicated in the description of his second edition by a contemporary Dutch scholar who made a visit to Azhari's press,

> The script is quite clean and neat, in the so-called Lahore hand .... The text itself is written in frames, in the usual way. The pages are numbered continuously by numerals at the foot; at the head of each page is the name of the *Suraj* [book]. The thirty *Juz'* [sections] are indicated in the margin. The end of each verse is marked by a small golden circle above the line of script. The verses are not numbered, that practice occurring, if I am not mistaken, only in Qur'ans printed in Europe. On the second side of each leaf, outside the frame on the lower left hand corner, is the catchword (*rakiba*).⁶¹

Indeed, this description sounds very much like a handmade manuscript although page numbers were a new addition. Of course, the text of the colophon printed on the last two pages of the 1848 edition would have a different content as well. The reason for placing such editorial comments in this copy, says Proudfoot, was to make known Azhari's religious standing and where he printed his *mushaf* in order to give credibility to the text reproduced through this new technology. Perhaps such information aimed to reassure the reader that the printing was done by a Muslim and according to the rules of *tahara* (purity). This colophon read:

> To begin with, this holy Qur'an was printed by lithographic press, that is to say on a stone pressing the handwriting of the man of God Almighty, Haji Muhammad Azhari son of Kemas Haji Abdullah, resident of Pelambang, follower of the Shafi'i school, of the Ash'arite conviction [etc. ...] The person who executed this print is Ibrahim bin Husain, formerly of Sahab Nagur and now resident in Singapore, a pupil of Abdullah bin Abdul Kadir Munshi of Malacca. The printing was finished on Monday the twenty-first day of the month of Ramadan according to the sighting of the new moon at Palembang, in the year of the Prophet's *hijra*—may God's blessings and peace be upon him—twelve hundred and sixty-four, 1264. This coincides with the twenty first day of the month of August in the Christian year eighteen hundred and forty-eight, 1848, and the sixteenth day of the month of Misra in the Coptic year fifteen hundred and sixty-four, 1564 [etc. ...]. The number of Qur'ans printed was one hundred and five. The time taken to produce them was fifty days, or two Qur'ans and three sections per day. The place where the printing was done was the city of Palembang, in the neighborhood of the Third Upstream Village, on the left bank, going upstream from the settlement of Demang Jayalaksana Muhammad Najib, son of the deceased Demang Wiralaksana Abdul Khalik. May God the All-Holy and Almighty bestow forgiveness on those who have copied this, who have printed this, and who will read this, and upon their forebears and upon all Muslim men and women and their forebears.⁶²

Unlike *mushafs* printed in Cairo during the reign of Muhammad ʿAli, printing these editions became profitable, so by 1854 Azhari had printed "several hundred Qurʾans, for which he finds ready buyers at 25 guilders per item."[63] There have been no historical documents from this period found so far that record any religious scholars in Malaysia or Indonesia who objected to the printing of the Qurʾan in this manner.

Qurʾanic Printing after Muhammad ʿAli

Printing of *mushafs* outside of Bulaq began after the death of Muhammad ʿAli in 1849, most probably in the late 1850s or early 1860s. Geoffrey Roper suggests that these Qurʾanic texts were generally embedded in the texts of well-known commentaries.[64] However, it seems that al-ʿAbbasi al-Mahdi, *Mufti* of Egypt between 1848 and 1887, gave permission to print *juzʾ tabaruk* and *juzʾ ʿam* (various portions of the Qurʾanic text) as separate books.[65] The number of books preserved in archives does not always indicate how common these books were in the past, but I believe that by the 1880s the Qurʾanic copies without exegesis must have been very popular as well, as they represent the majority of the nineteenth-century *mushafs* in the collection at the library of Mashyekhat al-Azhar. Moreover, most of the preserved *mushafs* are lithographed,[66] in spite of the fact that the early private presses in Egypt relied predominantly on typographic equipment sold out of Bulaq in the early 1860s.[67] It is not quite clear from Sarkis's notes whether any of the Qurʾanic editions of which he took notice were actually typographic prints. He does specifically say that *Tafsir al-Baydawi* and *al-Jalalayn* were printed "on the stone" (lithographic) and that the *mushaf* printed in 1891 with the introduction written by Shaikh Muhammad Radwan al-Makhallalaati[68] (and printed by Muhammad Abu Zayd) was also lithographed, but he does not say anything concrete about other editions.[69] But we know that other *mushafs* printed by Abu Zayd were lithographic as well.[70] The anonymous Moroccan edition mentioned by Sarkis might have belonged to the Printing Press Subih whose Maghrebi *mushaf* was also a lithography;[71] so was the *mushaf* penned and published by Hasan Ahmad al-Tukhi in 1898.[72]

The lithographic method, then, had a number of advantages when it came to Qurʾanic production in particular. It provided a better control over the orthography of the text and its provenance (*isnad*), as the person making the template had to be a qualified calligrapher. Also, as I suggested earlier, lithography allowed a publisher to create a manuscript-like appearance of the text. For instance, al-Makhallalaati's edition printed by Muhammad Abu Zayd in 1891 still looked very much like a manuscript.[73] Its "editorial" notes were shaped in a typical triangular manner, the organization of the text on the page and its framing did not differ from a handwritten *mushaf*, and the binding was the same as the one used in manuscripts at that time. In fact, it is mainly the lack of any color, the "blurriness" of the letters, and smudges of ink that draw attention to this book as a lithographic production.

The influence of writing on printing technology in general and the comparatively long coexistence of handwriting and printing in Egypt are also reflected in changes made to letter casts in successive Qurʾanic editions printed in Cairo and Alexandria. Between 1866 and 1872, the equipment at Bulaq was thoroughly modernized, with new mechanized presses imported from Paris and with greatly improved typefaces.⁷⁴ These enhancements changed the visual effects of the printed text by giving it more clarity and flow, and by making the letters less clunky, overall. In particular, the new typefaces contained a variety of letter shapes that attempted to comply with the rules of calligraphy, diversifying the script in a handwritten-like manner.⁷⁵ Certainly, by the end of the nineteenth century the script on typographically printed pages of religious as well as secular texts resembled handwriting more than the mid-century ones did.

Improvements in typeface design continued into the twentieth century. Today, booksellers who trade old books at the al-Azhar book market have difficulty telling whether some of the *mushafs* printed in the first half of the twentieth century were lithographed or letter-pressed. They falter because the improvements undertaken at the presses using typeset were meant to blur the difference between typographically and lithographically reproduced texts. For many older booksellers in Egypt as well as younger bibliophiles, a *mushaf* is *helu* ("pretty" or "nice") if it looks like a manuscript— but a manuscript written a century ago at the most, rather than one penned two or three centuries earlier. Ultimately, a particular aesthetic makes some *mushafs* more acceptable than others. A 1905 copy I found sandwiched between other religious books in a flea market was "nice," I was told, because the text looked as if it were written by a calligrapher. An older antique copy, although neat and readable at first sight, was "not as nice" because, in the words of the onlookers, the type looked "mechanical" and the letters lacked "character."

The interplay between handwriting and its imitation works only for Arabic script that is recognizable and readable, which is the script that developed about two hundred years after the first codification of the Qur'anic text, containing diacritics that distinguish letters and full vowelization. An undertaking such as the 1905 facsimile of the early handwritten 'Uthmanic *mushaf* done in St. Petersburg is not common. This large text—reprinted in a small number of copies, of which some were sold and some given as gifts to the heads of various states—was a copy of a handwritten *mushaf* said to be one of the famous first *mushafs* made by the third Caliph 'Uthman about twenty years after the death of the Prophet Muhammad. What is odd about this particular project is that hardly anyone can read it, other than a person who has memorized the Qur'anic text or is a Qur'anic scholar. The *mushaf* of 'Uthman was written before Arabic consonants took their final shape; short vowels were not in their final form either. But the *mushafs* that were reproduced at the turn of the nineteenth and twentieth centuries using lithography or letterpress typography did not imitate this kind of early unmarked script but instead chose to imitate the then-contemporary style of writing, which was visually very different from early seventh- or eighth-century characters.

Whether handwritten or printed, the aesthetic appearance of the Qur'anic text is derived from two essential visual elements: calligraphy and diacritics, making it visually distinctive. Its "look"—the visual composition of the Qur'anic text and its script—is so characteristic that even from afar it is not difficult to distinguish it from other printed texts. My friend Khaled made me aware of this visual distinctiveness of the Qur'anic text when, walking on a busy Cairo street one day, he suddenly stopped and leaned over to inspect a piece of paper sticking out of a pile of trash on the side of the street. Halted halfway through our conversation, I watched him struggle to pull a printed page out of the mound of plastic bags, metal cans, empty containers, rotting food, and rubble. The paper turned out not to be what Khaled expected. He tossed it. "I thought it was a passage from the Qur'an," he said with relief as we resumed zigzagging between scurrying people and honking cars. "It is easy to recognize it, you know," he added. What I also learned from my walks with Khaled and his explanations was that print allowed the creation of calligraphic styles that do not have prototypes in handwritten *mushafs*. While calligraphies associated with *mushafs* can be used in non-Qur'anic publications—for example, in the title on the front cover of a book or even inside a book like the one Khaled found in the trash—the reverse does not happen. Modern Arabic fonts, whether manufactured for a letterpress publication or a digital design, cannot be used in producing a *mushaf*. I confirmed Khaled's casual remarks later in my conversations with scholars at al-Azhar who upheld the opinion that none of the contemporary Arabic font styles—no matter how clear or popular—could be used in Qur'anic production. This practice, again, emphasizes the importance of the visual, manuscript-like characteristics of the Qur'anic text and suggests that it is not the technology itself but rather what technology does to the text that matters most to Azhari scholars.

The concerns of the '*ulama*' over the use of new technology in the dissemination of the Qur'anic text that I discussed earlier in this chapter, the aesthetic preferences of common readers of the Qur'an reflected in their buying preferences, and efforts of Qur'anic publishers to satisfy both scholars and users all intersect at the point at which the Qur'anic message is rendered in a graphic form as a text. The message-content of the Qur'an takes precedence, but the materiality of the inscribed message undoubtedly affects reader's responses. The way the Qur'an is inscribed matters. The way it looks is important. Moreover, there is a connection between the message and its inscription that goes beyond customary efforts to make sure that the content is preserved correctly. This connection is best articulated by another group of "makers"—the calligraphers. So in my next chapter I will turn to their concerns about the ways in which the Qur'anic text is mediated via Arabic script.

2

Pens, Letters, and Techniques of the Body

Each written language has a visual "topography" that is reflected not only in the abstract notion of letters, words, and grammar, but also in the practice of producing a text. Script, apart from being a system of signs, includes the materials used to produce it, the practices that make the signs appear, and an overall understanding of the role of writing as a form of expression. "Writing," says Kathryn Piquette, "is fundamentally material. (…) From this vantage point, understandings of things that are written must therefore go beyond study of textual meanings and take account of the material worlds in which writing is inextricably embedded."[1] In the Islamic world, writing developed far beyond the needs of rudimentary communication. For almost ten centuries, it endured as an activity intimately connected to a spiritual worldview on one side and existing technologies on the other. The Qur'an was its primary object of beautification. The introduction of print drastically changed the visual characteristics of Arabic script and initially limited the role of the Qur'anic visual landscape to a utilitarian function of communicating the text's meaning. With the introduction of typographic print, the Qur'anic text was to be read but not necessarily admired with one's eyes. The story that unfolds in this chapter aims to map out some of the characteristics of Arabic writing in order to convey the scope of the changes that took place with the introduction of printing technology into the visual culture of the nineteenth-century *mushafs*.

Let's begin with handwriting, understood to be a technique of corporeal training in which both the hand and the eye are conditioned to follow certain movements and patterns. This conditioning, however, is not simply a matter of learning a particular kind of aesthetic, but it is always immersed in a wider sociopolitical context, which determines the ways in which the practice of calligraphy is articulated. Handwriting in early nineteenth-century Cairo certainly did not mean the same as handwriting in the late twentieth century—a transformation that unfolds in this chapter. Yet, as a "technique of the body"[2] and a form of a physical engagement with the Qur'anic text, handwriting is able to offer us glimpses of understanding why those familiar with work within the constraints of one medium—calligraphy—were reluctant to suddenly shift to another. Moreover, thinking of calligraphy as bodily training formed over a long period of time—in the life of an individual as well as the communities of practice—in response to and as a result of working with particular materials and characteristics of Arabic script will bring forth another layer of connection between the Qur'anic text and its material medium.

Calligraphy—Art or Artisanship?

In front of the Egyptian National Library, in the middle of a green lawn, there is a small, one-room glass pavilion full of hardbound, heavy books stacked on shelves and tables. *Ustaz* (Mr.)³ 'Adel sits at the big desk at the back of the room always surrounded by other workers, helpers, and tea makers. I met him for the first time while looking for a particular book about Arabic calligraphy. The book was not in stock but *Ustaz* 'Adel promised to find it. Drinking hot, dark, and strong sweet tea with speckles of mint, we chatted about his unfinished degree in calligraphy. For in addition to his occupation as a manager of the pavilion belonging to the General Egyptian Book Organization,⁴ *Ustaz* 'Adel was also a *khattat*—a maker of *khatt*.

The multivolume *Lisan al-'Arab* (the Arabic equivalent of the unabridged Webster's Dictionary) defines *khatt* as lines written with a pen. But in contemporary Egypt, penmanship indexes the rapidly changing social position of professional calligraphers and the limited opportunities to train in this field. "Becoming a *khattat* requires time and patience," reflected *Ustaz* 'Adel, sipping his hot tea and signing documents scattered on the desk, "now people are too busy." His words revealed more than just regret over the modern affliction of time shortage. Over the last hundred years, new technologies have slowly relegated this previously widespread and indispensable artisanship into the peripheries of art. Employment opportunities for calligraphers have gradually shrunk in all areas of their activity: manuscript writing, street sign design, illumination, document writing, architectural design, home decor, or journalism. The convergence of growing literacy and technology might also explain the disappearance of "writing offices." In my neighborhood, I came across only one, located in the most timeworn and impoverished part of Ma'adi. The office was a single alcove slightly below the ground floor level, completely open to the street, and screened from it by a big desk that filled the whole room leaving just a bit of space for the person sitting behind it. The sign read: "Muhammad 'Ali, calligrapher, writing documents and making signs." Ironically, when I tried to call the number listed on the sign to make an appointment, a pleasant female voice told me that the number was out of service. I would have liked to ask Muhammad 'Ali which calligraphy school he had attended and whether he, like *Ustaz* 'Adel and some others, thought his craft was in peril.

Sometime later, I visited Dr. Mustafa Muhammad 'Imari, a calligrapher recommended to me by Munir, a friend who came to Egypt to study penmanship. Munir was interested in developing a computer font that would imitate some of the calligraphic features, an idea that Dr. 'Imari abhorred, Munir warned me. I had with me a piece of calligraphy written by *Ustaz* 'Adel from the Dar al-Kutub bookstore. It turned out that Dr. 'Imari and *Ustaz* 'Adel had been good friends at the calligraphy school. To make sure we were talking about the same person, Dr. 'Imari said, "He smokes a lot, doesn't he?" I laughed and said, "He smokes, all right." Dr. 'Imari welcomed me with most solicitous greetings. He wore round glasses, a small moustache, and a trimmed goatee. His hair was peppered with gray, making him look to be in his early fifties. A gracious host, he offered me tea and snacks, slightly upset that I had already eaten.

To discuss his work, we set at a large desk where jugs full of bamboo and reed pens surrounded a computer screen. He made sure I knew that he used his computer to study examples of calligraphy done by other artists, but he did not use any software to create his own designs. He perceived his activity as "pure art" rather than artisanship and subscribed to a modern notion of calligraphy as a form of intellectual, spiritual, and aesthetic expression that drew its power from the past and, therefore, should be preserved "as it has always been."

Dr. 'Imari shared his passion for penmanship with students in one of the well-known schools of calligraphy, Tahsin al-Khutut al-'Arabiyya in Gizah. He had studied under some of the famous Egyptian calligraphers, Muhammad 'Abd al-Qadir 'Abdallah, Husayn Amin 'Ajaj, and 'Abd al-Rahman Sha'ib, and had participated in a number of exhibitions, competitions, and seminars promoting calligraphy in the country. His office room testified to his achievements, displaying numerous diplomas hanging on the walls between shelves tightly stacked with academic books. Yet it was not the awards or media interviews that he considered his biggest accomplishment, but four copies of the Qur'anic text that he penned over a number of years for different publishing houses, one of which was printed in Algeria. In spite of his successful career, Dr. 'Imari also lamented over the general state of affairs, "Calligraphy goes through a crisis," he told me, "because there is no close relationship between people and the language that naturally sustains calligraphy. There are no people who would defend it through an artistic engagement with it."

I found that his conviction about an organic relationship between the language and its visual representation was shared by many traditionally trained calligraphers. However, the visual form of the written language meant much more for them than simply giving form to signs in an expressive and artistic manner. They saw practicing calligraphy not only as a skill, but also as a moral force shaping individual values and the condition of the society in general—an argument absent from works produced about calligraphy before the appearance of print. A good example of this modern understanding of calligraphy comes from the conference of calligraphers organized in 2014 at the Bibliotheca Alexandrina. In his opening, and rather poetically dramatic words, calligrapher said al-Sayed al-Qaftanji stated:

> We need to accept this painful truth that we have become part of a charming past and parcel of a deteriorating present. We have become the middlemen between the handsome gone-bys and the hideous today, as if suffering from schizophrenia. This, imposing itself upon us, contrast between where we were and what we have become—the contrast between the lines of beautiful writing that pleases the soul and delights the heart, and the lines that slap us in our face, hurt our eyes, and pollute our taste—this contrast breaks in on us and thrusts itself upon us with the utmost force.
>
> Truly, I feel incapacitated when I read many of the contemporary signs [or banners] that are distorted and warped, and whose writers think that they are capable of inventing something new. Then, they hang them or fix them in front of their shops and companies like corpses and spotlight them, although they should be hiding them instead.

And there is no law that would avert this crime of art and language, as if our language has lost its owner who would protect it and keep it safe with jealousy. And it has become true everywhere that one messes with it as one pleases.[5]

Street Banners and Techniques of the Body

Let's follow the link al-Qaftanji made between language, calligraphy, and banners in the streets of Cairo that would also come up in conversations with other calligraphers. The frequency with which this connection was mentioned in discussions about writing suggested that street signs and banners in early twenty-first-century Cairo did more than communicate promotions, advertisements, political endorsements, or religious invocations. They also served as spaces where various understandings of Arabic *khatt*, its role, and power were contentiously negotiated. A plethora of handmade signs, especially white spreads of canvas, has characterized the city landscape for decades. Even with the use of computerized printing, it is still cheaper to pay men with good handwriting to make signs than to print them out. The number of white sheets floating in the air on ropes strung between two buildings increases significantly around times of elections or other important events, such as the first anniversary of the Egyptian revolution. Banners commemorating the martyrs who died in clashes with the police, and in prisons the previous year, sprouted all around the city, visible and inconspicuous at the same time because of their ubiquity.

I first learned about the banner-making business from Sa'ad 'Ali, a high school teacher directly affected by the Ministry of Education's decision to close his calligraphy school before he managed to complete his degree. "To be fair, though," he said, "these schools could have been a waste of money because few people applied for admissions." Strangely, an *al-Ahram*'s editorial about the state of calligraphy in Egypt, published about the time of my conversation with Sa'ad, claimed the opposite; it was hard to get accepted to calligraphy schools in Cairo, students had to reapply, and only two hundred were admitted annually after a very difficult entry examination. Sa'ad lived in the remote suburbs of Cairo. Perhaps his school had not placed high in the ranking of places to study good handwriting? Was there not enough demand for banner making in Tukh? While talking about his passion for calligraphy, and defending its importance in the face of the Ministry's decision, Sa'ad informed me that it is common for wealthy or well-sponsored political candidates to employ professional calligraphers to create eye-catching banners for their campaigns because "people's eyes are drawn to beautiful handwriting." A similar sentiment was expressed by al-Shami, one of the students from the school featured in *al-Ahram*'s article, who spoke about benefits of learning calligraphy also using the street banners as an example. In his opinion, signs and banners in Cairo had lost their artistic quality, particularly those designed by computer programs, because they could not reproduce script with the visual appeal of the traditional calligraphic styles.[6]

Such conversations about calligraphy and street signs speak not only to the history of the public display of text and contemporary politics, but also about the materiality of objects on which Arabic script could appear, how particular materials have been capable of enabling certain practices, or how other materials make them impossible to perform. This interplay was already at work in the first two centuries of Islam when parchment was one of the materials available for inscribing the Qur'anic text. It was much more durable in comparison with papyrus, and because at that point the durability of the text was more important than its portability, most of the early *mushafs* were inscribed on parchment. But in order to manufacture one *mushaf*, it took on average a few hundred sheep skins requiring weeks of treatment to be ready for binding them into a codex. The weight of such a book was quite considerable, and picking it up for the purpose of reading it the way we would today would have been impossible. Paper, which began appearing in the Middle East around the eighth century,[7] enabled Muslims to produce *mushafs* that were fairly durable but also more manageable than those made of parchment. Although initially expensive, in time the cost of paper went down and the speed of codex production increased. Paper books were less heavy, easier to carry, and took less space. But when a new paper-making technique developed in Iran in the thirteenth century, it became possible to produce large sheets of paper, creating an extra space around the text that could be lavishly decorated. Calligraphers made good use of this space, of course, but the larger sheets of paper also increased the size of *mushafs*. Some of the most monumental Qur'anic copies come from that period.

The connection between the material characteristics of an object and their relationship to the displayed text was not always noticed in the past. In his famous essay on typography, Eric Gill wrote, "The mind is the arbiter in letter forms, not the tool or the material."[8] Although no innovation can be viewed solely as a result of the material characteristics of objects used in the process of production, the ease with which some materials render themselves to particular uses will obviously encourage experimentation. "Every material has inherent properties that can be either expressed or suppressed in use," says Tim Ingold.[9] The ways in which various calligraphers spoke about the palpable characteristics of various kinds of surfaces on which they write—softness, absorption, roughness, spaciousness, smoothness, thickness, gloss, flatness, porosity, moisture, and so on—show a level of intimacy with the materials they use that can only emerge from long-term corporeal engagement with them. These techniques of the body, including ways of seeing things, once habituated, are hard to change. Perhaps for that reason, Egyptian streets signs, although on one level instrumental in discussions about calligraphy and politics, illustrate the idea that habituated bodies become extensions of particular technologies.

Street signs and banners began appearing in Egypt—and probably in other parts of the Middle East—in the nineteenth century and, apart from a culture that relied upon and buttressed the public display of texts, they were dependent on the availability of spaces and materials conducive to their production, including inexpensive fabric. At the same time, the characteristics of Arabic letters, their movement and flair, rendered them easy to write on long stretches of spacious material stretched between buildings. Human creativity, combined with the materiality of sheets and the movement of air, produced a unique form of expression. In banners, the mechanics of writing became entangled with the physical qualities of the objects that bear the letters. It seems to me that this synergy was palpable enough to explain why Sa'ad, al-Shami, al-Qaftanji, like many others, thought that freehand banner calligraphy followed tacit aesthetic rules too complex to be imitated by mechanical typesetting, emphasizing once more the intricate relationship between what is inscribed, how it is inscribed, and where it is inscribed.

A similar understanding of writing as more than a technology of communication was expressed by 'Ali Mahmud, the student featured in *al-Ahram*'s article about the downfall of Egyptian calligraphy. 'Ali admitted that he treated the process of acquiring skills in calligraphy as a form of self-discipline and an activity that gave him personal satisfaction. "I'm learning something that I like," he told the reporter. "I feel the beauty and energy inside me, and I am also learning to draw by co-existing with the letters."[10] Unless the English translation distorted the meaning of his words (the article was published in English), 'Ali was clearly suggesting a bodily disposition beyond his rational experience, but this also reminded me of another occasion when I saw a calligrapher writing the *basmala* (a common phrase *bismillahi ar-rahmani ar-rahim*—"in the name of God, the Most Merciful and Compassionate") on a classroom blackboard. I was attending a calligraphy workshop. Muhammad took the time to painstakingly finish every letter and every diacritic mark. I watched his body and hands move in slow motion as if the letters flowed from within him, through his arm and hand down to the board. His body seemed to remember not only each letter but also the motion that produced it. He was so concentrated on the cadence of writing that he did not hear the growing fidgetiness of his American students. The volume of conversations slowly rose behind his back but he did not stop until he finished the whole sentence.

While watching Muhammad, I pondered the idea of Islamic authenticity offered by a calligraphic tradition rooted in bodily training and artisanship that is missing from new techniques of textual reproduction. Handwriting the Qur'anic text was a technique of the body combined with spiritual training. Religious education intersected here with bodily exercises that included hand-eye coordination and a breathing rhythm that corresponded with the movement of the pen. Writing the text of the Qur'an was not only a profession but also a pious act that brought the writer personal blessings. Over the centuries, calligraphers have liked to quote the Prophet's words—"Whoever writes the *basmala* beautifully will enter the Paradise"[11]—and point to Qur'anic verses that mention writing, such as "Recite, and your Lord is the most Generous—Who taught by the pen—Taught man that which he knew not" (Q. 96:3–5) or "And if whatever trees upon the earth were pens and the sea [was ink], replenished thereafter by seven [more] seas, the words of Allah would not be exhausted. Indeed, Allah is Exalted in Might and Wise" (Q. 31:27).[12] Printing technology certainly thwarted this form of piety, as interest shifted toward the benefits of the text's fast multiplication. Before the introduction of print, laymen who had an interest in calligraphy could write the Qur'anic text for their own benefit and donate what they wrote to the mosque.[13] I have not heard of such copies being donated to mosques these days. Although it is unlikely that over the centuries every Muslim calligrapher and copyist treated his or her[14] profession with equal piety and wonder,[15] nevertheless, up to the present calligraphy has continued to represent for its practitioners a creative act that requires special manual skills and a particular predilection of mind. Reminiscing about his days in calligraphy school, *Ustaz* 'Adel evoked the visceral habits acquired through comprehensive training. He said,

"Writing is connected with the state of mind. If I am angry I don't write things in the same way." After a pause, slouching in a squeaky chair and exhaling smoke from the cigarette nonchalantly stuck between the tips of his fingers, he added: "There is a secret in each style of calligraphy. There is an atmosphere in each of them.[16] One should not write before he learns about the secret of each style and immerses himself in its atmosphere."

Calligraphic Styles

Noticeably, each calligraphic style has its own peculiar characteristics that often have been considered suited to particular genres of text. For instance, *naskh* and *ruq'a* are quite plain and easy to read or write quickly. Students learn these styles in elementary school. *Naskh* is also the style imitated by print fonts and the most common form to find in books. In the past it was the script of general knowledge and science. Its everyday character and legibility made it, then, an appropriate model for print, unlike *diwani* (which was used in the past specifically for protected royal decrees) or *thuluth* (which had more religious connotations). *Thuluth* in particular was not a suitable choice for everyday use. Its extremely elongated vertical lines and narrow, upright letters give it a monumental character. Stately in its features, it requires more space and is often chosen for headings and more spectacular inscriptions. For instance, the confession of faith ("There is no god but Allah and Muhammad is Allah's Messenger") on the flag of the Kingdom of Saudi Arabia is written in *thuluth*. Arabesque-like and curvilinear, *diwani* is famous for its intricacy, its intertwined letters, and its use at Ottoman courts for governmental messages and official documents. It is the most agile and vivacious of the main styles. With the expansion of Islam, the Arabic alphabet was adapted to the Persian language and in the process yielded the *nasta'liq* style. Persian poets liked its thick and thin, diagonally running, "hanging" or "swooping" lines that save space horizontally and give the writing a rhythmic look. In Arabic, *nasta'liq* is used to embellish book titles or, more recently, to fashion elegant postcards and posters with Qur'anic inscriptions.

The main calligraphic styles are products of different exigencies and conventions. They were designed for particular purposes yet disposed to evolve under the fickleness of calligraphic fashions and through the artistic sensibilities of individual masters. Each style developed variations, and each calligrapher could add unique features deriving from his or her own technique, while still preserving the rules of proportion and spacing. These rules were dictated not only by the artists' inspirations but also by the tools and materials they used. The size and shape of letters could be measured by the number and relative positions of hypothetical dots made by the nib of a pen. For instance, *alef* (long a), the first letter of the Arabic alphabet, looks like a single, long, vertical line. In the *naskh* style the length of the *alef* should be no longer or shorter than five measures of the pen's nib (in *thuluth*, on the other hand, this length is equal to seven measures).

Another important element of each style was defined by the angle at which the lines were written. Whenever the letters followed more angular lines and were based on a square or rectangular grid, as in *kufi* style, the angle of the parts of each letter was carefully calculated. In *kufi*, the complexity of measurements of the length and height of the letters, the angles at which they are drawn, and their thickness and thinness of different sections is remarkable. In Bookstore al-Husseyn, another bookstore belonging to the General Egyptian Book Organization and located in an out-of-the-way building behind al-Husseyn Mosque, I came across a textbook on *kufi* style and its variations prepared and drawn by Muhammad 'Abd al-Qadir 'Abd Allah (1917–1995), a professor of calligraphy in the College of Applied Arts—and Dr. 'Imari's teacher—who received his calligraphy diploma with honors at the age of eighteen. This very technical book contained over two hundred pages of calculations and patterns for letters written in *kufi* style and their Qur'anic variations. It also contained examples of ornamentation and particularly well-composed pieces in other calligraphic styles. The descriptions of letters and examples were preceded by a short history of the most influential calligraphers in Egypt who were listed in a familiar fashion: a long sequence of teachers and their students who then became teachers as well. I have already spoken about this form of authentication of knowledge within Islam. The introduction to the book written by Awas al-Ansari, professor of calligraphy and teacher of Arabic language at Cairo University, suggested that despite being the oldest calligraphic style, *kufi* went through a period of renaissance in mid-twentieth century in Egypt through the teachings of Muhammad 'Abd al-Qadir 'Abd Allah. *Kufi* was the only style that *Ustaz* 'Adel did not master and could not use to design cover titles for some of the books printed at *Dar al-Kutub*. He had left his calligraphic program before the end of the fourth year, during which students wrestled with *kufi*. Years later, *Ustaz* 'Adel considered *kufi* to be the least "atmospheric" style of calligraphy on account of its angular features. But some calligraphers, such as Sa'ad, thought it was most challenging because the precision of measurement and complicated calculation of angles required the use of additional measuring tools. In addition to studying *kufi*, during the last year of calligraphy school students practiced the rules of text ornamentation. Their final exam required them to create a small piece of calligraphy surrounded by a lacy frame of decorations. Elements of writing such as contour and flow of line, proportions, elongations, tension, and correct alignment were carefully scrutinized by the examination committee.

Examples of *Ustaz* 'Adel's writing lay collected in a small pile of papers on his large metal desk. Pushing away books and files, he pulled a set of bamboo pens from the drawer, carefully opened a little bottle of black ink, dipped the nib, and on a scrap of paper began to set down strokes of curvy, unwavering lines, running from right to left. With few exceptions, the line was unbroken like a ribbon of narrow black satin meandering on a white surface. He held his breath whenever his hand was in motion. *Ustaz* 'Adel first wrote in different styles to accentuate the differences, stopping now and then and cautiously putting dots and strokes over and above the baseline of writing. He was visibly proud of what he was doing. Distinctive, smooth lines crept from under his pen: tall and narrow, thick and stubby, or slanted with each word running down at an angle like oblique traces of raindrops on an automobile's window glass. The movement of these lines depended on the established characteristics of a style, *Ustaz* 'Adel's skills, and the width of the nib of the pen he held in his cigarette-stained fingers. On his desk were also a few projects in the *diwani* style that visually epitomized scholarship and aesthetics. They allowed the reader not only to enter a world of knowledge and erudition but also fastened the content of the book to the aesthetic experience of reading an artfully and studiously designed title. The level of one's refinement was already tested at the moment a potential reader looked at the book cover and could understand the words hidden in the arabesque of intertwined strokes pressed in gold on its crimson, indigo, dark green, or charcoal leather binding (Figure 2).

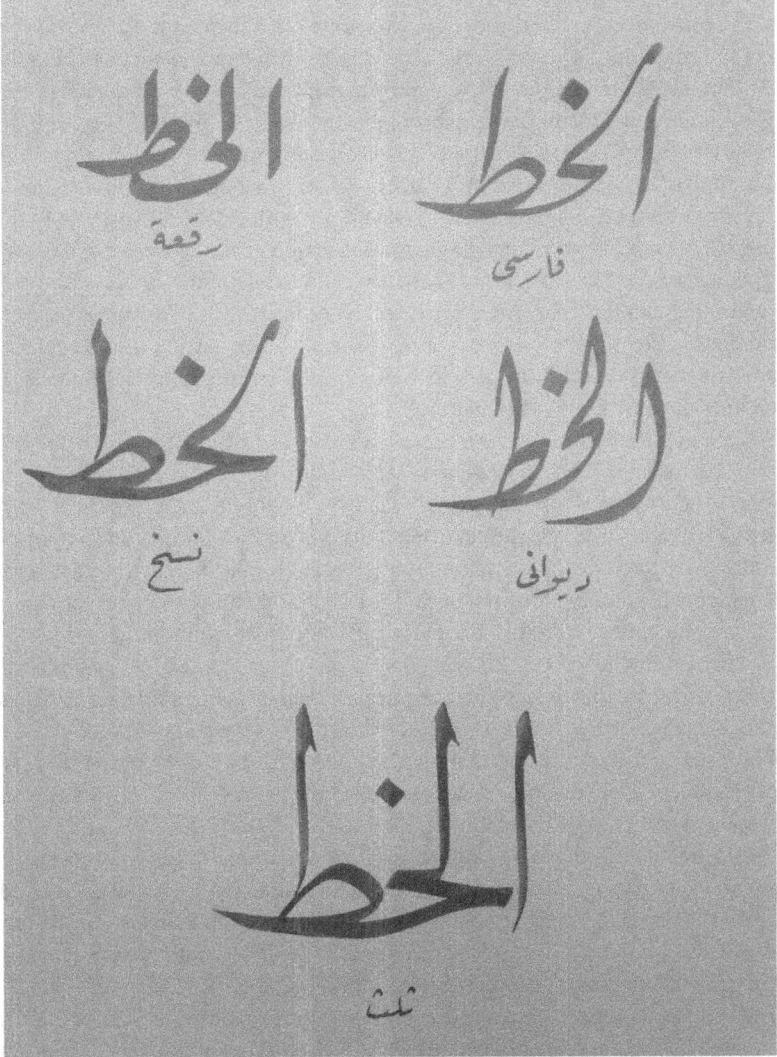

Figure 2 The word *al-khatt* (calligraphy) written in various calligraphic styles: *ruq'a, farsi, naskh, diwani,* and *thuluth*. Penned by *Ustaz* 'Adel ('Adel Kamal Muhammad Zaki).

Arabic Script

The connectedness of Arabic letters gives the writing its decorative quality and richness of form—a feature that had caused headaches to entrepreneurs of mechanical, typeset printing in Arabic. These dramatic effects are hard to achieve in Latin handwriting, where letters forming words only have two forms, upper- and lower case, and can only stand alone as individual graphemes,[17] breaking up the optical flow of the line. In Arabic, most letters are not separated within a word, which means that they are always written in cursive. There is no block writing in Arabic, but to create desired aesthetic effects a calligrapher can alter spaces between the sentences, words, and a few letters that do not connect in some circumstances. Or he can keep all the spaces the same, unlike the contemporary Latin script where spaces between sentences and words are larger than those between letters. As I already mentioned, *alef*, a single, long, vertical stroke and the first letter of the alphabet that denotes a long vowel "a," is the only letter that always stands alone. In the past, this exception intrigued Muslim linguists and scholars of Islam, who devoted monographs to this phenomenon and assigned to it spiritual significance. Also, the letters ز (zayn), ر (rayn), و (waw), د (dal), and ذ (dhal) connect only with the preceding grapheme and leave a space between themselves and the following sign. But the rest of the twenty-eight letters of the alphabet always join the preceding and the following grapheme. Over the centuries, Muslim artisans have intentionally used this property of connectedness, creating artifacts that contributed to a religious-artistic tradition in which ornamental writing has been the main and sometimes the only form of decoration.

A calligrapher writing in Arabic is not constricted by the interruptions of punctuation used in Western languages—an addition that was introduced into Arabic writing systems only in the nineteenth century. In Arabic, there are other ways of directing a reader through the text: the ends and the beginnings of sentences are identified with the help of particular phrases. Also, in Arabic there are no capital letters that mark the beginning of the sentence. These letters in Latin can be very ornamental but it is not an option in Arabic. Instead, an artist can play with multiple shapes of the same letter within the words. This is possible because, depending on its position within the word, each letter has at least three slightly different forms: an initial form that starts a word, a medial form within a word, and a final form at the end of a word.

For instance, beginning from the right to the left, these are the forms of the letter *nun* in its independent position (this form is not used very often), in its medial position between two other letters, in its initial position when it starts the word, and in its final position when it ends the word (Figure 3). However, Arabic letters are very malleable so the same *nun* in the middle of the word can be written in different ways depending on the style, the calligraphers preferences, and the letters immediately preceding and following it. In other words, a letter "responds" to the letter that precedes and follows it. But, in whatever form, it is still the letter *nun* (Figure 4).

Apart from changing their forms, letters within words can be "kerned." Kerning requires adjusting the spaces between the letters to achieve a visually pleasing result. A calligrapher can stretch, shorten, or modify a letter and then use kerning to overlap the spaces of the letters around it so that the end of one letter is above or below the

Figure 3 For example, the letter *nun* in its isolated, frontal and, middle positions (the last two).

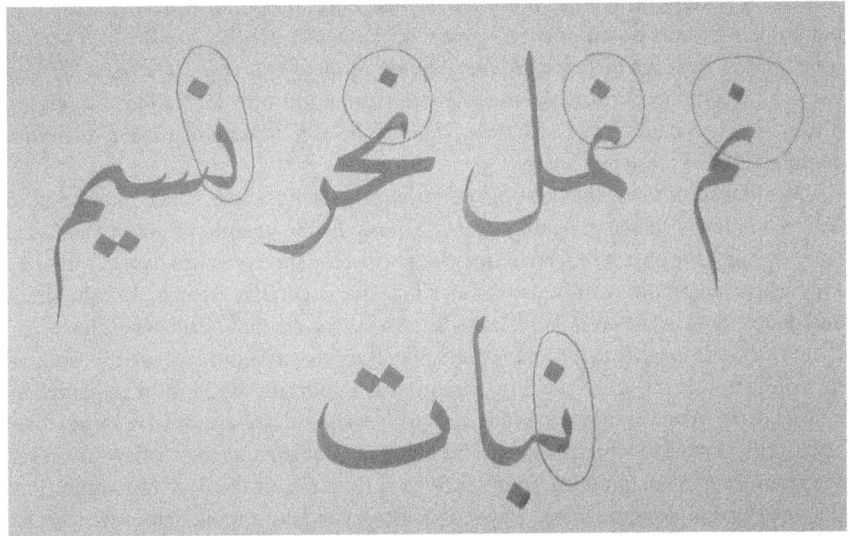

Figure 4 The letter *nun* in connection with other letters.

next. Some letters, like *sin*, are more often adjusted in this manner than others. The calligrapher will use these modifications so as to achieve an aesthetically pleasing effect of harmony and proportion or one of drama and agitation. *Kashida* ("lengthened" from Persian) is one of the most common ways of altering the shape of a letter. Instead of stretching or constricting the white space between words or individual letters, *kashida* involves stretching or constricting the letters. Some letters are prone to stretch horizontally and some, like *alef* or lam, stretch vertically. And so the *basmala* I watched being written at a calligraphy workshop (visually composed of the four words بسم الله الرحمن الرحيم) became an inscription in which the tail of the letter *sin* is so elongated that it doubles the length of the whole phrase (Figure 5).

Figure 5 *Basmala* penned by *Ustaz* 'Adel. Here the *kashida* is applied to the elongated letter *nun*.

Another characteristic of Arabic letters that is commonly manipulated by calligraphers is the similarity between some graphemes. For instance, the letters *ba*, *ta*, *tha*, *nun*, and *ya* have the same initial and middle forms in the shape of a small vertical stroke and are differentiated only by the number of dots placed below or over the stroke called *i'ajam* (dots that mark the phonetic distinctions between consonant letters). There are other letters that have an identical base or "footing" but a different number of dots. The shape of the letters predisposes them to certain transformations—for instance an intertwining of *alef* ا and *lam* ل ("a" and "l") into لا—and calligraphers will make use of these shapes and transformations to develop distinctive characteristics of each style. *Thuluth* and *kufi* in particular like to play with combinations of these two letters.

Dots that accompany the "footing" of the letter and whose basic role is to distinguish between letters also serve a calligraphic purpose. In the ligature *basmala*, the initial letter *ba* starts the phrase and has a single dot below the short, vertical base of the letter. Precisely arranged dots can be used as an additional decorative element, like the single and double dots in the *basmala*, thus adding an overall rhythm to the whole line.

In Arabic, as in other Semitic languages, short vowels can be, and usually are, omitted in writing and print. This "docility" of vowels is important for Muslim calligraphers and scholars. When written or printed, short vowels and declensions are represented by diacritical marks (*harakat*) above and below the consonants they follow. However, in certain cases their presence or absence has practical and theological ramifications that may lead to debates. To see why, it is necessary to take a small detour into Arabic linguistics.

In Arabic, the short sound "u" is represented by the comma-like mark called *damma* (و) and placed above the letter (as in this example: سُ, where it is placed above the letter *sin*; together they represent the sound "su"). The short sound "i" is represented by a single oblique stroke called *kesra* below the letter *sin* سِ (here *kesra* and *sin* denote the sound "si"). *Fatha*, which looks like *kesra* but is placed above instead of below the letter (سَ) gives the short sound "a" (here, *sin* and *fatha* represent sound "sa"). The grammatical structure of Arabic, which relies on a system of three (or sometimes four) consonant word roots from which all other parts of speech (nouns, adjectives, adverbs) are derived, allows a writer to omit short vowels (*damma*, *kesra*, and *fatha*). All parts of speech, stemming from a root word (which is a verb in the third person of the past tense: he said, he slept, he came, etc.), follow regular patterns of consonants and long and short vowels, and native speakers easily recognize them in the context of a sentence. Therefore, printed Arabic texts skip the short vowels that are, nevertheless, vocalized in speech or reading aloud. For instance, the verbal noun *salaam* سَلام (well-being) derives from the root verb *salima* سَلِمَ which literally means "he was safe, intact," according to a grammatical pattern: first consonant "s"/short vowel "a" written over the first consonant/second consonant "l"/long vowel "a"/third consonant "m". Three consonants in this pattern are the same as consonants of the root verb: *sin* س "s", *lam* ل "l," and *mim* م "m." Another root verb, *kallama* كَلَّم (he spoke), gives us a verbal noun *kalaam* كَلام (speaking) that follows the same pattern: first consonant "k"/short vowel "a" over the first consonant/second consonant "l"/long vowel "a"/ third consonant "m." The root consonants here are *kaf* ك, *lam* ل, and *mim* م. In theory, Arabic has endless possibilities for the formation of words that follow the established patterns of vowels and consonants, although in practice not all patterns are utilized for each of the root words. However, because they follow recognizable patterns, the existing words may have their short vowels omitted in writing. *salaam* and *kalaam* would skip the first *fatha* (short vowel "a") and would be written without diacritics as *slaam* سلام and *klaam* كلام, although every Arabic reader knows from the context of the sentence and practical knowledge of the language that these words should be pronounced as *salaam* and *kalaam*.

This detailed discussion of Arabic diacritics may seem to be only of interest to linguists and calligraphers. But diacritics are extremely important in the production of graphic representations of the Qur'anic text. The *harakat* (marking vowels and declensions) that are conveniently ignored in contemporary printed texts cannot be omitted or modified in a printed *mushaf*. For that reason, it is easy for an Arabic reader to spot text from the Qur'an. It is fully vowelized and therefore visually characteristic, unlike most other contemporary texts in print.[18] The uniqueness of the graphic representation of the Qur'anic text becomes accentuated, then, through comparison of printed *mushafs* with other, non-vowelized texts (Figure 6). This is the reason why, in his opening speech at the conference in Alexandria, al-Sayed al-Qaftanji also mentioned the value of studying Qur'anic script as a form of ocular training. He said:

> Indeed, there is a problem that has caught my attention in the course of my work [as an administrator in the field of education]—that among millions of *mushafs* we find in our hands today most of them are written in the *naskh* style, the most lucid of all Arabic styles. But, I noticed that the students don't read their *mushafs* and they grope their way around in navigating the strangeness of this style—as it appears to them that way at first—because they don't know it, they don't study it, as they are used to reading only poor contemporary fonts.[19]

The ability to artistically modify the shape of Arabic letters, to change their proportions or use diacritics like the strokes that represent short vowels, or to enhance their ornamentation, all these are aesthetic qualities not simply related to the characteristics of the graphemic system itself. These aesthetic qualities also depended upon the materials on which inscriptions could be made. The introduction of paper from China in the eighth century created more possibilities for changes in calligraphic styles. The smooth surface of paper offered more freedom to experiment with the

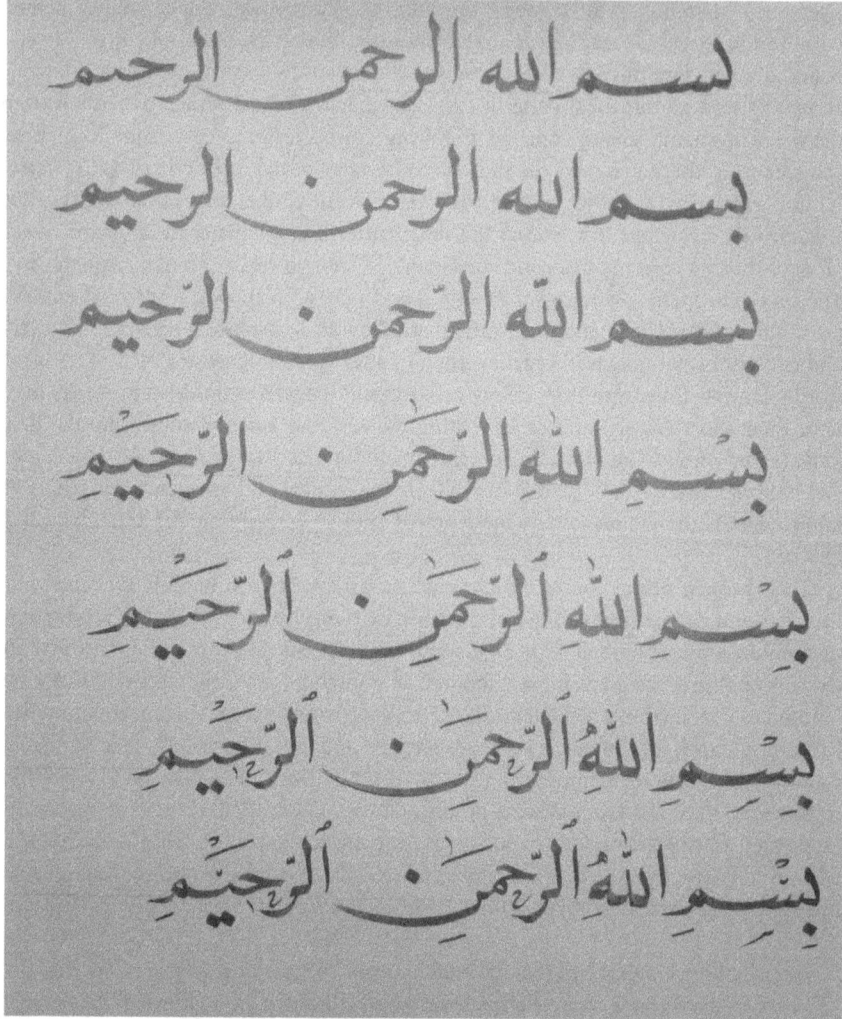

Figure 6 The same *basmala* without any *tashkil* and with various types of diacritics, progressively added until it reaches its "Qur'anic form."

contours of letters and allowed greater litheness of lines. The early "squarish" inscription in *kufi* was executed on rough surfaces, most commonly stone and parchment, but sometimes wood, papyrus, or textile, which may have initially contributed to the characteristic features of this style.

Today the use of particular calligraphic styles in typeset and lithographic printing is dictated by a combination of factors that include tradition, materials, the calligrapher's skills, and the cost of production. Countless shops and stands clustered around the al-Husseyn Mosque constitute a major *bazaar* in Cairo. Their clientele is diverse, as shopkeepers cater to Egyptians as well as tourists. Among thousands of cheaply made products, many of which come from China, numerous objects display calligraphy: postcards, jewelry, framed ornamental textiles, clocks, posters, and stickers. Radi, a master's student in the department of history at al-Azhar, had a stand across the al-Azhar street that divides the al-Husseyn area from the booksellers' quarter. Radi sold textbooks but made money on the side using the penmanship he learned at the university. We had known each other for a few years, during which Radi was struggling to finish his master's thesis on the slave trade in Zanzibar. In return for help in finding English language sources, he assisted me in procuring copies of *mushafs*. One hot and sticky day, I was photographing *mushafs* he had borrowed from another seller a few bookstands down the road. At the same time, I watched Radi writing something in Arabic in his elegant handwriting. A boy of about ten had brought him a list of five or six names, which Radi was now carefully drawing on a piece of paper. I kept photographing books, drawing curious, furtive looks from passing customers. The same boy came back twenty minutes later.

"Abu-l-Hasan, can you write these names too!" He held out the same list with a few more names. Radi, laughing, shooed him away.

"Go, don't bother me again. I am busy."

"Please, Abu-l-Hasan, just this last time."

"No! I told you. Go away!"

"But it will take you only a minute." The boy was throwing meaningful looks in my direction. I joined him.

"Come on, Radi. Write them for my sake," I said, jokingly using a popular pleading phrase. With a theatrical sigh, Radi wrote two more names on the wrinkled page. Giving the paper back to the grinning boy, he started saying,

"Next time when I say go, you go!" He finished the sentence yelling after the running boy who swiftly vanished into the crowd, skipping and waving the page with Radi's handsome calligraphy. I saw the boy later, selling copper pendants with the names cut out using templates copied from the skillful penmanship of Radi.

A lot of what Radi learned about calligraphy came from books that had passed through his stand. He did not have extra income to purchase the latest books and periodicals on calligraphy published in Turkey, Saudi Arabia, or the Emirates, but he carefully studied examples illustrated in older publications and on book covers. The newer, imported guides were too expensive. It was *Ustaz* 'Adel who lent me an example of a foreign publication: the beautifully edited *Journal of Arabic Letters*,[20] published quarterly in the United Arab Emirates and printed on a thick, glossy paper. In recent decades, efforts to revitalize the art of Arabic calligraphy in that country (especially by the Ministry of Culture, Youth and Development[21]) have involved organizing workshops and competitions for calligraphers from all over the world. *Ustaz* 'Adel had a few issues carefully wrapped in a plastic bag waiting for me on his desk. "There is a saying that the Qur'an was revealed in Mecca,"—said *Ustaz* 'Adel in his gravelly voice while handing me the journals—"written in Istanbul, and recited in Cairo. This means that the best calligraphers come from Turkey but here in Egypt we have always had the best reciters." I nodded agreeably, having already heard of the fame of Egyptian reciters and their popularity in Saudi Arabia and other Gulf countries. I had also heard of the fame of the Turkish calligraphers among Egyptian lovers of penmanship. In fact, beginning in the sixteenth century, the Ottoman Empire became a major center for the development and production of artistically acclaimed calligraphy, competing with and often superseding older centers in other parts of the Islamic world. It would be wrong, though, to think of the history of Islamic calligraphy as an uninterrupted, linear process. Rather, it is the product of many overlapping artistic endeavors, intersections between the mundane work of ordinary copyists and the creativity of individual artists, all dispersed over time and space and influenced by the economic and political situation in the Middle East and the individual interests of particular rulers.

According to *Ustaz* 'Adel and a few other professional calligraphers—based on knowledge gathered at schools they had attended—throughout the nineteenth century Egyptian pen artists were as accomplished as their Turkish colleagues. But the most famous artists would often be claimed by different regions as they learned and worked in multiple locations, like the acclaimed penman 'Abdallah Bik al-Zuhdi who was born in 1836, probably in Damascus, studied calligraphy in Turkey and later practiced in the school of Khedive Isma'il Basha in Egypt. His skills were so highly regarded that he designed inscriptions on *kiswat al-ka'aba*, the fabric covering the shrine in Mecca that was periodically produced in Egypt. After 1927, Saudi Arabia took over the right to manufacture the cloth for this shrine.

On several occasions, some of my Egyptian friends expressed a nuanced deprecation of their Saudi neighbors. A note of jealousy also surfaced in *Ustaz* 'Adel's remark that the growing wealth of Saudi princes allowed them, especially in recent decades, to sponsor calligraphic events, competing with Turkish and other established centers of calligraphic production. What still makes Turkey special, however, is the promotion of calligraphy done by women. For instance, in 2010 Turkey hosted the International Female Calligraphers Exhibition. The prominence of female calligraphers in Turkey, such as Hilal Kazan or Soraya Syed, was echoed in *Ustaz* 'Adel's mini-lecture on the day I borrowed *The Journal of Arabic Letters*: "There is a family of calligraphers in Turkey," he noted, although he could not remember their name, "and the girl from that family is very famous for her calligraphy and ornamentations." Without warning, he passed me a sheet of white paper and asked me to write the title of a text on calligraphy, obviously testing my writing skills. I laughed and grabbed a pen.

Writing the Qur'an

In my efforts to understand the principles of Arabic calligraphy, I had learned the *naskh* style although I have never studied it enough to become really skilled, a task that would require a year or two of regular practice. In the process, I realized that producing Arabic calligraphy is not only an exercise in aesthetics but also a lesson in religious ethics. All five of my penmanship teachers had a religious education and, with only one exception, had graduated from al-Azhar University. Moreover, they all insisted that no one could practice calligraphy properly without being immersed in "the study of Qur'anic writing" or literally "the study of 'Uthmanic writing,"[22] a specialization in the broader field of Qur'anic studies taught at al-Azhar. While learning about the proportions and shapes of letters or the placement of short vowels and other diacritics, I could not ignore Islamic precepts and the theology of the Qur'an. Over time, I started sensing an intricate connection between the text's graphic representation, the act of writing, and understanding and knowing by heart the Qur'anic message. I also realized that this tenacious relationship between message, act, and representation has particular effects. One, already mentioned earlier, is that no *mushafs* have been executed in any of the calligraphic styles invented after the introduction of print. As I mentioned in the previous chapter, the *Mushaf* Committee, a branch of the Islamic Research Academy at al-Azhar[23] that oversees production of all media that carry Qur'anic text, does not accept them.

The connection between memorizing and understanding the Qur'anic message, the act of writing it, and graphic representation is not mystical but rather historical and practical. To a certain degree, this connection has always been negotiable and negotiated, mainly through evolving practices of writing Qur'anic copies but also through other, more mundane, aspects of life, such as the production of jewelry, coins, architecture, home decor, textiles, and more recently advertising, souvenirs, newspaper headlines, and banners. A "secular calligraphy" that does not reference the Qur'an, or boldly alters its stabilized calligraphic styles, is another such negotiation that tests the limits of al-Azhar's authority and public sensitivity by developing new fonts for print and by experimenting with letters as aesthetic objects. However, in Egypt such efforts have always been cautious and partial, so as not to disengage the final product completely from its "heritage." For since at least the twentieth century, calligraphy has been presented as an essential part of the Arab and/or Muslim heritage, with greater emphasis on one or the other depending on the circumstances. No one wants to be completely separated from such a powerful network. Otherwise, instead of benefiting from the aura of participation in "centuries of tradition" an artist risks entering the dangerous grounds of blasphemy.

Attempts to unravel the relationship between the Qur'anic message, its carrier, and calligraphy may create trouble. Those unaware of this tradition, such as Karl Lagerfeld and the Chanel fashion house, learned a hard lesson in 1994, when during a fashion show in Paris, they featured an evening gown that displayed a fragment of Qur'anic text. Although the verse ran across Claudia Schiffer's bosom, I would argue that what aggravated Muslim authorities most was the complete removal of that verse from its stabilized context, including the medium authorized to carry it. Therefore, I disagree with Kenneth George's statement that "What Lagerfeld would learn is that a custodial ethics for displaying Qur'anic script subtends an interest in Arabic orthography from an 'aesthetic point of view.'"[24] To be sure, Muslims often use Qur'anic verses for decorative purposes. Quotations from the Qur'an are displayed on "secular" walls, ornamental textiles, posters, dishes, or furniture, but what allows them to be "visually pleasing" are the ethics of their production, the "tasteful" manner of their display, and the fact that their display is immersed in the network of theological and calligraphic knowledge and practice. Sheila Blair concludes that the point of calligraphy is to "impress the receiver visually"[25] but also to reflect the audible beauty of the Qur'anic message. Verses on display have an *aesthetic* value in part because they are a part of the *aesthetic* Qur'anic message. The historical association of particular calligraphic styles, executed by hand, with the Qur'anic message has become stabilized and intertwined to the point that styles initially developed and refined for the purpose of writing the Qur'an are considered by many Muslims to be the most aesthetically pleasing. Printed copies of the *mushaf* resemble handmade manuscripts, as I was told, because of their beauty. "The old calligraphic styles are meant to preserve the beauty of the writing and bring pleasure to the eye," said one of the workers in the print shop that I visited. In other words, the connection between certain styles of writing and text has become so close that what originally was meant to beautify a *mushaf* is now considered beautiful by virtue of being a part of the *mushaf*. That is why during my visit to Dr. 'Imari, in speaking about lengthening of certain letters to space them harmoniously over the page, he said in a matter-of-fact voice, "You can get illustrations of this technique from different places in the *mushaf*. And take pictures of them and you can use them as examples." For a calligrapher, like 'Imari, it is a deeply ingrained habit to look for illustrations of perfect writing in a *mushaf*. It reflects an education in which aesthetic and religious knowledge is complementary rather than oppositional.

Yet, in Dr. 'Imari's opinion, religious institutions in Egypt such as the Islamic Research Academy have not been promoting calligraphy. I asked him why he thought this. He shook his head and said:

> The governmental administrators are not likely to promote calligraphy, because they specialize in academic reviews of the mushafs. Scholars like Dr. Ahmad 'Isi al-Ma'asarawi are preoccupied with memorizations and reading of the Qur'an, they are not interested in teaching how to write the Qur'an. They are interested in the Qur'an from the perspective of special legal affairs and listening, not things pleasing for the eye. I studied Arabic language and I have experience in writing the Qur'an so, naturally, I am interested in it. However, there should be more interest on the side of the scholars to specialize in everything that pertains to the Qur'an, including calligraphy.

Dr. 'Imari was correct in his perception of the rather lukewarm interest of the Azhari scholars in promoting calligraphy (at least in comparison to other religious institutions in the Gulf countries), but he was amiss in saying that the sheikhs of al-Azhar concentrate mainly on Qur'anic recitation or legal interpretations of the text. Qur'anic orthography is one of the important branches of knowledge in the College of Islamic Sciences and an essential subject for scholars in the *Mushaf* Committee. How the message is inscribed *does* matter for the sheikhs of al-Azhar and I will discuss their concerns in Chapter 4 devoted to the "custodians of the text."

For now, let me just conclude by saying that in Egypt, calligraphy, whether understood as art, communication, artisanship, or an obsolete technique, is still grounded in the Qur'an as an inscribed text. Calligraphy itself developed historically in relation to the production of material inscriptions of the message. Therefore, regardless of circumstances, *to graphically represent the Qur'an in print means to wrestle—even today—with its long tradition of writing.* In the previous chapter, I sketched the circumstances of early attempts to print the Qur'anic text in Egypt and highlighted some of the initial arrangements that made this undertaking possible. Having made a detour in this chapter into the techniques of writing as a bodily practice and some of the idiosyncrasies of the Arabic script essential to the practice of its inscription, I will return in the next chapter to the discussion of how the interplay of writing and printing played out in further attempts to create acceptable editions of the Qur'anic book that would satisfy both scholars and the public alike.

3

Mechanical Reproduction and Its Effects

Printing in Egypt, especially printing of the Qur'anic text, was from the beginning marked by the efforts of many people to define the role and capacities of this new technology in relation to writing. As we will see in this chapter, the discussions over printed editions of the Qur'an continued into the twentieth century and were soon followed by new concerns.

In the second half of the nineteenth century, with the number of printing establishments growing exponentially,[1] the following question became quite relevant for Egyptian religious authorities: how should they regulate the printing process of the Qur'an now taking place in multiple locations and in numerous private publishing houses, with editions reaching into the thousands of copies? Such supervision had not been needed in the past, as the calligrapher's *isnad* provided a "quality control" mechanism and any mistakes—if made—were easily correctable. This state of affairs changed within half a century. Some of the early, small, family businesses that began printing *mushafs* in the second half of the nineteenth century continued to flourish and expand their production, building up a market in which Qur'anic texts circulated as a particular kind of commodity. In this milieu, the religious task of disseminating the message of the Qur'an intersected with the profit-making interests of individual publishers. The earlier equilibrium between religious duty and ordinary life was sustained as long as everybody agreed that although the Qur'anic book should not be sold like any other object, those who produced *mushafs* still needed to make a living.[2] (Until recently, the idea that a *mushaf* cannot fully be a commodity has affected the rhetoric of purchasing it: buyers often avoided words such as "purchase" or "sell" when acquiring a copy of the Qur'an.)

Yet, at the turn of the twentieth century—accompanied by steadily rising numbers of mechanically reproduced copies—this *status quo* was impossible to maintain any longer. A number of interesting phenomena took place as a result of alignments between the benefits of broad dissemination offered by printing and an adherence to the legacy of Muslim discursive tradition. The most important outcome of these alignments was a momentous institutionalization of the Qur'anic text via its iconic editions, especially *Mushaf* Fu'ad in the early twentieth century and *Mushaf* al-Madina sixty years later. For that reason, in this chapter I will focus on the process of institutionalization of the Qur'anic text and its effects on the material form of the Qur'an as a book.

Private Businesses

As we saw in Chapter 1, the printing shop at Bulaq and its branches operated regularly during the reign of its founder, Muhammad 'Ali Basha. In 1848 'Ali's son, Ibrahim Basha, took over the throne but died the same year. 'Ali's grandson, 'Abbas I, reigned from 1849 until 1854. He did not have much interest in his grandfather's printing establishment and let it deteriorate to a point when Bulaq became a financial drain and, eventually, was sold to a private owner in 1862 by 'Abbass's uncle, Sa'id Pasha, who took over the throne in 1854.

Let's pick up the story of Qur'anic printing again around the time when the press at Bulaq began losing its importance so that we can meet a new protagonist—Muhammad Effendi Mustafa, a progenitor of the 'Abd al-Rahman family. Muhammad Effendi Mustafa was one of the workers at the Bulaq press. But perhaps because of the deteriorating situation at the press, or maybe encouraged by growing public interest in print and a new opportunity to make money, he left his governmental job in 1851 to establish his own business known as Matba'at Muhammad Mustafa.[3] Maybe he learned from those who had previously specialized in providing cheaply copied manuscripts and now foresaw a profitable alternative for himself in producing inexpensively printed books. Working at Bulaq certainly gave him firsthand experience and knowledge of the burgeoning book market. Mustafa began by printing popular religious books, but with time he also ventured into publishing *mushafs*. Muhammad 'Ali's Qur'anic text published at Bulaq had paved the way for entrepreneurs like Mustafa to take advantage of this new and promising niche in religious publishing. When making a decision to add the Qur'an to the list of his titles, he might have heard about print developments outside of the Ottoman lands and how successful printing the *mushaf* had turned out to be in other parts of the Muslim world. For example, Indonesian entrepreneur Muhammad Azhari, whom I mentioned earlier, did not hesitate to advertise in his first edition of the Qur'anic text that the new method of reproduction allowed him to produce "two Qur'ans and three sections per day," while generating a handwritten copy could take weeks at best (and, if done that quickly, it would have certainly been a rather poor copy). For this special undertaking, Muhammad Effendi Mustafa, like Muhammad Azhari, had scholarly support—he was assisted in his work by a certain Sheikh al-Dardir.

Within a decade, Mustafa's printing business became quite successful and he even exported his books to the Levant, thanks to the mercantile connections of his friend, Sheikh Ahmad al-Babi al-Halabi, another founder of a family-run printing business, whose descendants continue to work in the publishing sector in Egypt today. In 1866, Muhammad Mustafa opened a second printing establishment out of which he also produced copies of the Qur'an.[4] His presses quite significantly contributed to the growing number of printed books available on the Egyptian market, reaching at least 256 titles by the end of the nineteenth century.[5] Matba'at Muhammad Mustafa also added to the supply of mechanically reproduced *mushafs* whose numbers were slowly increasing in the shops surrounding al-Azhar University.

During the lifetime of Muhammad Effendi Mustafa (he died in the early 1900s), a significant change had taken place. At first, if anything in print was controversial, it was the *mushaf*. But by the end of his life, if anything was printed, it would include the *mushaf*, especially if the price was affordable for less wealthy customers. The conviction that a *mushaf* was the most important of all Muslim books to possess probably encouraged private and governmental publishers to take more interest in this unique enterprise. Thus, during the fifty years Muhammad Effendi Mustafa operated his press, printed *mushaf* became common and normalized as an object of pietistic practice.

I have already mentioned a *fin de siècle* publisher, Muhammad Abu Zayd, who at the same time was perpetuating and capitalizing on this state of affairs. His *Mushaf* al-Makhallalaati was a big hit—at least with the Azhari scholars—and its multiple editions appeared between 1882 and 1907.[6] As I discussed earlier, this was a noteworthy *mushaf*. Because of its visually classic format, it nicely ushered the calligraphic tradition of writing the Qur'an into the lithographic medium. It was a fairly well-done scholarly work as well, effectively connecting the traditional Qur'anic sciences of orthography and recitation to a new form of mass reproduction. Also, it was acclaimed because the heads of al-Azhar had accepted it, which was not true of most editions available around that time. Typographic *mushafs* in particular tended to have more problems, as it was easier to make a mistake while setting manually separate casts of letters, diacritics, and all other additional reading signs.[7] Moreover, some of the *mushafs* did not follow what was understood to be the traditional 'Uthmanic *rasm*—the consonant base of the text according to caliph 'Uthman Ibn 'Affan—instead adjusting it to contemporary norms of spelling. Even al-Amiriyya was guilty of this innovation, releasing in 1905 a section of the Qur'anic text (*juz*') printed according to the conventional, not 'Uthmanic, orthography.[8] This state of affairs was making the scholars of al-Azhar exceedingly concerned.

However, what also made *Mushaf* al-Makhallalaati interesting is that it participated in introducing new forms of authorization of the Qur'anic text that were developing to supplement the traditional teacher-to-student chain of transmission (*isnad*). In addition to the common supplications and praises characteristic of handwritten copies of the Qur'an, *Mushaf* al-Makhallalaati included a scholarly introduction that discussed classical sources used in reviewing the *mushaf*'s orthography (including the markings for recitation). At the end of the book, al-Makhallalaati also placed a note that, as in the introduction, drew a direct line connecting the science of Qur'anic spelling, calligraphic tradition, scholarly authority, and the printed text. This is worth quoting in its entirety to illustrate its purpose, style, and rhetorical devices:

> These are the words of Radwan Ibn Muhammad known as al-Makhallalaati,
> the servant who put writing of this gracious mushaf in a correct way,
> the proofreader of its script and orthography according to the Qur'an,
> the captive of his own sins,
> the one who is in need of God's mercy,
> the one who hopes for the forgiveness of his transgressions in the past and in the future, and the one who says that the words of God are the most noble words being uttered by a human tongue and the most amazing knowledge by which people of science adorn themselves.

"No falsehood can approach it from before or behind it: It is sent down by the One Full of Wisdom, Worthy of all Praise" [Q. 41:42]. "[This is] a Book, with verses basic or fundamental [of established meaning], further explained in detail—from the One Who is Wise and Well-acquainted [with all things]" [Q. 11:1]. The book from which the light shone and the blessings flowed to include everything, young and old.

God beautified writing of his own words by guiding the scribe to know the best ways of putting them down. And, He also brought respect to the one who can evoke in his recitation the marvels of the Qur'anic orthography. And, He adorned those who memorized it with respect and dignity and praise. And, it is proved by the verse: "Then We have given the Book for inheritance to such of Our Servants as We have chosen." [Q. 35:32].

And peace and prayer be upon our master Prophet Muhammad who spreads the mercy and who says: "the noblest of these nations are the ones who carry the Qur'an by heart."

And peace and prayer be upon his kin who abide by the decrees and teachings of the Qur'an. And when the verses of the Qur'an are recited before these people their hearts naturally long for them. And peace and prayer be upon the companions who inscribed the Qur'an and upon the followers and those who perfectly followed after, and upon every one who follows this path, serving the Book that clarifies everything. For those people "the reward is forgiveness from their Lord, and Gardens with rivers flowing underneath—an eternal dwelling: How excellent a recompense for those who work [and strive]" [Q. 3:136].

And then, when printed, this noble *mushaf* became like a full moon and a sweet smell that spread everywhere with the fragrance of completion—a book that is grammatically and linguistically perfect and written according to the 'Uthmanic script. I mentioned this subject in the book "A Guide for the Reciters and Scribes in the Knowledge of the Script of the Clear Book"[9] discussing the issue of numbering the verses and the rules of pausing and resuming the recitation, which I retrieved from the book "Pause and Recommencement"[10] by Sheikh al-Islam and used the [letter] *kaf* for *kafi* [a pause at the beginning or in the middle of the verse where the meaning is completed], and the [letter] *ha* for *hasan* [if the reciter stops here he/she needs to be careful from which word to resume recitation because this may change the meaning], and the [letter] *jim* for *ja'iz* [permissible stop—indicates that it is a good place to pause], and the [letter] *sad* for *saleh* [the reciter can take a break if needed for breath, but it is preferable to continue], and the [letter] *mim* for *mafhum* [the reciter has to stop, otherwise the meaning will be changed], and the [letter] *ta* for *tam* [a pause for the beginning and end of the verse].

They were placed in the beginning of my introduction, complementing the system of script, diacritics and numbering in easy and beautiful words. And so came this mushaf by the grace of God—drawing the eyes of those who look at it and elucidating the hearts of those who read this Clear Book. And its noble printing and beautiful execution took place at the lithographic printing press al-Bahiya located in the street al-Mughrablin in the area of Darb al-Unsiya, under the management of the press's owner—responsible in front of his Lord the Creator—Professor and Sheikh Muhammad Abu Zayd.

This event happened at the end of the month of fasting [Ramadan], the ninth month of 1308 [1891] *hijri* of the Chosen One [the Prophet], peace and prayer be upon him.

Al-Makhallalaati's note is important for a number of reasons. He presented himself not simply as a calligrapher of the text prepared for this lithographic edition, but also as a scholar who had the authority (backed up by the authority of the sources he cites) to implement changes to the orthography of the text. These amendments were meant to facilitate its recitation in a correct way as well as to make this *mushaf* resemble the very first edition of Caliph 'Uthman, of which I will speak more in the next chapter. By quoting the verses *from* the Qur'an *about* the Qur'an, he reassured the readers that it was indeed the same Qur'an with which they were familiar in its recited form. He also cited a work of another scholar of Qur'anic diacritics and his own book on the same subject. Finally he indicated that the person who was in charge of the printing house (Abu Zayd) was a Muslim scholar himself.

For over two decades, the lithographic edition of al-Makhallalaati remained distinctive, causing a well-known member of the Institute for Recitations,[11] Sheikh 'Abd al-Fattah al-Qadi (1907–1982), praise Radwan Ibn Muhammad for his outstanding job. Years later, in a little felicitation he wrote, "[al-Makhallalaati] produced a *mushaf* of sublime quality and great significance."[12] He also mentioned that al-Makhallalaati paid particular attention to the rules of 'Uthmanic orthography and made a few important improvements. First of all, he indicated the count of verses in each chapter. He also marked the *fawasil*—the last word of each verse—on which the scholars disagreed and which affected the count of verses in each chapter. Finally, he applied six different *'alamat al-wuqf*, signs for obligatory, optional, and forbidden pauses while reading or reciting the Qur'an, and placed them above the line of *tashkil*. In an appendix to the Qur'anic text, he gave credit to the scholarly sources on which he had drawn in making these improvements and offered a short account of the *mushaf* in the time of the Prophet and his followers. Finally, he briefly summarized existing research on *rasm* (the base consonants) and *dabt* (diacritics), cited several famous scholars in this field, field, defined the words *sura* and *aya*, and "he did all of that in simple words and an eloquent manner."[13]

This was not an ordinary *mushaf*, with the editorial notes clearly exceeding those found in other printed *mushafs* on the market,[14] including the average manuscript copies. Unfortunately, says Sheikh 'Abd al-Fattah al-Qadi, "[*Mushaf* al-Makhallalaati] did not distinguish itself in a positive way among its beholders and disquieted the readers by the poor quality of the paper and badly done printing lithographic job."[15] It is difficult to say whether the complaints about the poor material condition of this particular *mushaf* reflected the general poverty of lithographic technique among Cairo's printers or the readers' heightened aesthetic expectations of printed *mushafs* in general. One reason this might have caused al-Qadi to make such judgment was that *mushafs* produced in Turkey available on the Egyptian market were of better quality on average—the paper was thinner, the print more crisp and delicate, and the binding lasted longer—so the *mushafs* printed by Muhammad Abu Zayd, although comparable in printing quality to other lithographic Qur'anic copies made in Egypt, could not successfully compete with "foreign" ones.

These late nineteenth- and early twentieth-century *mushafs* can still be found on occasion in used book stands and fleas markets in Cairo. I was in search of such a copy in Darb al-Atrak, an old, narrow, and curvy street tucked behind the al-Azhar Mosque when I came across *Ustaz* Yussif who was selling books in the entryway to the old *wikala* (warehouse) at the side of the eighteenth-century Mosque Abu Dhahab. The warehouse is a monumental stone building, raised with beige blocks of rock, cool, dark, and dusty inside but hot and bright outside. The doorway stands perpendicular to the entry of al-Azhar and opens to a small courtyard, where another well-known press, Maktabat Muhammad 'Ali Subih, opened up in 1900 (some family members think it was 1890). Muhammad 'Ali Subih, like Muhammad Effendi Mustafa, also started a prosperous family business whose members did well for a long time, printing and selling religious books. But after a century of operation, the business has been closed and sold to a stranger outside of the family. *Ustaz* Yussif did not mind sharing the few facts he knew about the place, reminiscing that the original machines used at Maktabat Subih were bought from Germany, they were automatic, and they needed four people to operate them. The enterprise was very successful, but the family grew so big, with so many descendants, that running the business smoothly became impossible, and they collectively decided to sell it in 2001.

When I spoke to *Ustaz* Yussif, he was still unpacking and dusting off the books stored over the decades in the printing house's back rooms. He remarked begrudgingly that dealers would buy these books to resell them for a much higher price to collectors, usually from abroad. The locals, on the other hand, would often buy his books to reprint them. I stepped into the entryway of his bookstore, enticed by the books with covers faded and tattered, laying on tables in front of a big stone gate and along the breezy hallway leading to the courtyard. Tables obstructed the other end of the passage, barring the shoppers from entering the courtyard where cool, dark, and sand-smelling rooms were hidden along the stonewalls. A forlorn printing machine stood in one corner of the open space, its greasy gears and handles reflecting the brightness of the afternoon light. *Ustaz* Yussif let me browse the books that his assistant was bringing out of the darkness of the rooms, every now and then vigorously blowing at a stack, raising clouds of dust in the air. I fished for *mushafs*, putting them aside to look at them when I had more time.

A week later, I returned to Maktabat Subih, or what was left of it, the stacks of worm-eaten books and forsaken equipment. The morning air was still brisk, but I could feel the heat slowly rising in the open spaces between the buildings. I hoped Radi could help me—he was an al-Azhar student who also traded books by the mosque—but he was not in his century-old nook yet. I called him and asked if he could meet me at *Ustaz* Yussif's shop. I needed Radi's expertise in calligraphy. When he finally came, *Ustaz* Yussif waved him into the cellar-like room full of books. "You know, we normally don't let any Egyptians in there," he whispered again what he had already told me before, stressing the word "Egyptians." Radi did not hear his whisper or chose not to, stepping into the stone chamber. It was placed somewhat above the level of the hallway and we squatted to get some light by the opening in the wall right over *Ustaz* Yussif's table. My *mushafs* were stacked up on the floor on a piece of cardboard, set aside from the pile of books in the middle of the room. Ismail, the assistant, was still sorting them out and we would occasionally pass some of them to *Ustaz* Mustafa. According to the lunar calendar, some of the books were printed in the thirteen hundreds of *hijri*—almost a century ago—and we would pause to discuss the value of the volumes passing through the void in the wall.

Muhammad 'Ali Subih printed religious books in tandem with the *'ulama'* of al-Azhar, including textbooks for the courses offered at the university.[16] He hoped to revive interest in religious classics by publicizing them to students and the broader public. His cooperation with the religious authorities was very fruitful, to the point that Maktabat Subih gained a reputation as an important printing house specializing in Islamic and classical books, including the Qur'an. The *mushafs* from Subih were both lithographed and typographic. At least one of the lithographed editions was penned by an acclaimed Turkish calligrapher, Mustafa Nazif (1846–1913)—known as Qadroghli.[17] Subih also published *mushafs* for the North African market in a Maghrebi script that differed slightly from the script and calligraphic styles used in Egypt and the Levant.[18] On the other hand, his typographically printed Qur'anic texts resembled *mushafs* published in al-Amiriyya, displaying much improved typeset and font design. Muhammad 'Ali Subih's brother, Sheikh Mahmud 'Ali Subih, also participated in this business, branching off with time to his own establishment called al-Maktaba al-Mahmudiyya al-Tigariyya, located not far from Maktabat Subih. Like his brother and nephews, he printed *mushafs* among religious texts "under the approval of al-Azhar."[19]

Radi and I were squatting on the stone floor, sorting *mushaf* by *mushaf*, stacking them in two piles on a piece of cardboard. Twenty volumes of different sizes and styles. Only a few were printed by Muhammad 'Ali Subih, but these were undated. All the rest, except one, were printed in the twentieth century and had poor binding and cheap print—they certainly did not resemble the elaborate and richly decorated handwritten *mushafs* on display in the museums. They were small, thin, with soft covers. They looked like any other ordinary book. I was making notes and comparing fonts. Radi squatted before me, every now and then pointing to interesting particularities in the print. Some of these *mushafs* were obviously lithographed, preserving the tighter, overlapping, and wavy lines. The lithographic print undeniably expressed the writer's individuality: *waw* و curved more here or there; *nun* ن now round and pudgy, now a little flat; *kesra* adjusting its length to the width of its neighbors. These letters existed in a mutual dependency, making space for each other, stretching and squeezing to accommodate each other's shape and curve.

Each of the lithographed *mushafs* looked slightly different from the others, with *harakat* wrapping around the letters rather than running above and below them in their own separate trajectories, a feature characteristic of many typographed Qur'anic texts. All of these *mushafs* lay in piles not as museum objects but as used books that nobody knew what to do with. Not new, but not too old either, like the misprinted *mushafs* in the time of 'Abbas I they needed "disposal in a religiously proper manner." But, as before, such disposal was not going to happen, not yet. The very moment I lifted them from the dusty pile, their worn-out covers and yellowish pages were already changing them into something else: they were becoming antiques, potential collectibles. My preoccupation with the dates and places printed on their binding, instead of the message itself, was adding to their transformation. After all, *Ustaz* Yussif requested that I pay for the privilege of photographing his *mushafs*. My salvaging conflicted with the purpose for which these books were made. They were to be read and recited, not photographed for money. Yet such early printed Qur'anic texts can be found in the antiques stores; not old or fine enough to make their way to the exhibit halls or museums, but old enough to draw the attention of a book collector or a tourist, they bridge the gap between a museum object and a commodity. If collected, they do not necessarily speak to the artistic skills of individual makers, but rather to processes of technological change in the twentieth-century Egypt.

Institutionalization of the Qur'anic Text

In one of the decaying piles of books I found a *mushaf* that was bound like a textbook: a black taped spine between soft, brown covers, with the following words running in various calligraphic styles across the front:

ministry of education[20]
juz' twenty nine

juz' tabarak

second edition
al-matba'a al-amiriyya in cairo
1329 hijri

In the corner of the cover someone had written in red and blue pencil: Ahmad Hilmi Nufal, and repeated the name in a little rectangle on the title page, and again on the last empty page of the *mushaf*, adding the words: "eighth of the month of October 1926 from al-Qur'an." I paused for a moment. Was this the date by which Ahmad Hilmi Nufal was to memorize this particular part of the Qur'an? Or the day on which he received it from his teachers in one of al-Azhar's preparatory schools? He must have been a young student who did his best at ornamenting his words with two color frames. If he was already a student at al-Azhar he was probably just starting his education: *juz'* (part) twenty-nine would have been only the second out of thirty portions to memorize. The length of the Qur'anic chapters decreases toward the end of the book, so it is not uncommon for students to start memorization from the end. Perhaps it was one of the *mushafs* the Ministry of Education ordered for courses in Qur'an at al-Azhar, as they did from Subih. After all, al-Amiriyya—the new name of the press at Bulaq—was a governmental printing house that supplied limited orders of *mushafs* free of charge to students. How did it get mixed up with the books in storage at Subih? Was Ahmad Hilmi Nufal a member of the family? Or did he give away the copy that he had already memorized to a *ruba bikya* man—a collector of unwanted objects, who then resold it to someone else? Did the printers at Subih use it as a proof copy with which to compare their own Qur'anic textbooks?

On the back cover I could see a note in small print: corrections to this *mushaf* were made thanks to the knowledge of *Ustaz* Hussayn Zaghlul, a teacher at the Muhammadiyya School. It had always been necessary to solicit the assistance of a person with a solid knowledge of the Qur'anic text, whether to write down the text for printing on a lithographic stone or to make sure that none of the individual letters, diacritics, or other recitation signs were missing or changed in the final version, lithographic or typographic. Hussayn Zaghlul was probably not directly involved with the printing activities at al-Amiriyya, but rather served as a corrector of this particular edition. Still, the involvement of a variety of Qur'anic scholars of different levels of education as editors and proofreaders of the *mushafs* from private and governmental publishing houses most likely produced varying results.

In spite of its cheap look, this inconspicuous *mushaf* was a much-improved "descendant" of the text ordered by Muhammad 'Ali in the 1830s. It was printed in 1911—fifteen years before Ahmad Hilmi Nufal signed his name on it in red and blue pencils. Like other books from al-Amiriyya, it was another letterpress edition. By then, the *mushaf*'s typographic design had gained a grace and artistry of its own, independent of the proper rules of the *naskh* style in which it was supposed to be printed. In spite of their dissent from traditional calligraphy, I could not deny that these typographic letters had their own elegance and clarity—the result of efforts in improving the font design by the designers at al-Amiriyya. The print was easy to read, with loosely arranged words and an extra line of space between the twelve lines of text. The diacritics unobtrusively floated below and above the consonants. The changing thickness of letters imitated the effects of a writing pen. There was an overall sense of order and rhythm without exuberance. It was obviously a *mushaf* meant to be read, easily and conveniently. But still, there was something that must have vexed the professional calligraphers working with fonts at al-Amiriyya—the minuscule cracks between letters, almost invisible to those who did not know about them, but hardly hidden from the professional eye of a *khattat*. The cracks were irksome, unbecoming, and they interfered with the ideals of Arabic calligraphy, which focuses on the perfection of a continuous line (Figure 7).

In spite of its modest appearance, this and other *mushafs* coming out of al-Amiriyya at the beginning of the twentieth century participated in establishing a new visual standard for Egyptian readers of the Qur'an. They created a new model of beauty, elegance, and clarity of script that was different from its traditional calligraphic counterpart—the handwritten *naskh* style. With time, the "'al-Amiriyya font" has become an embodiment of "beautiful writing" and an iconic part of governmental *mushafs* produced in Egypt.

Mushaf Fu'ad

However, it was the 1924 edition known at the *Mushaf* Fu'ad that has become famous for its fusion of the visual attraction of earlier improved fonts with academic effort

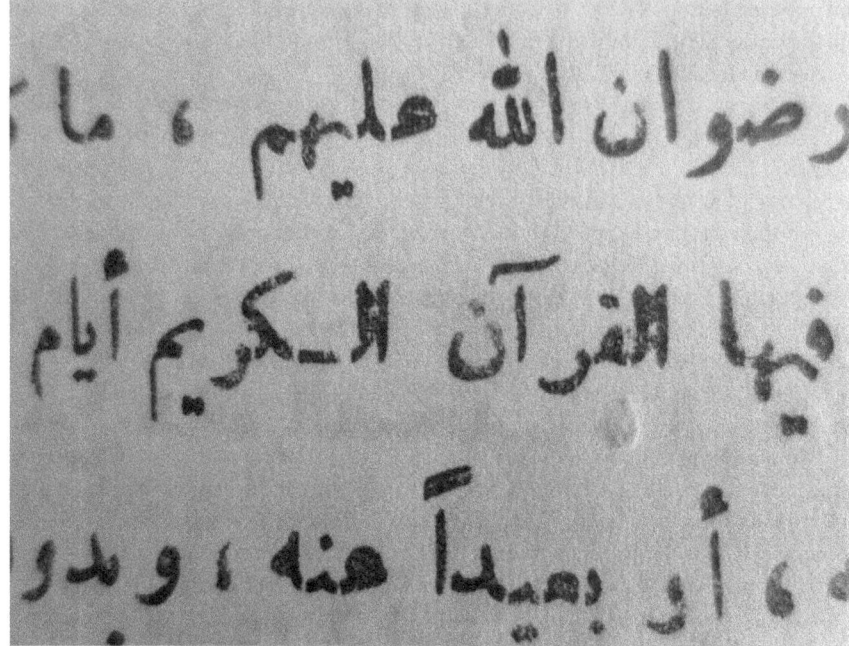

Figure 7 "Cracks" in the typographically printed letters.

and traditional Islamic scholarship. The pressure to standardize the Quranic text was growing with every decade of the twentieth century. Some of the Turkish *mushafs* being sold in the Egyptian market did not adhere to the 'Uthmanic spelling.[21] Neither did some of the local *mushafs*, including even the *mushafs* coming out of al-Amiriyya, like the already mentioned 1905 edition. Auspiciously, King Fu'ad I, a descendant of Muhammad 'Ali and the ninth ruler of Egypt and Sudan who came to the Egyptian throne in 1917, was responsive to the concerns of Azhari scholars. He is said to have been benevolent toward religious establishments and is known for his support of the al-Azhar professors, expressed in part by his monetary donations to the university and his provisions for mosques both in Egypt and outside of the country. King Fu'ad I in his benevolence expressed a desire to fund the printing of a well-prepared Qur'anic edition at his own expense. Preparations began in 1918 and the Sheikdom assembled a committee, including the most competent *'ulama'* experts in Qur'anic science and literature. The committee was led, in what Sheikh 'Abd al-Fattah al-Qadi called "this serious and arduous assignment," by Sheikh Muhammad 'Ali Khalaf al-Hussayni al-Haddad (1865–1939), Head of the Egyptian Reciters,[22] who was joined by a professor of linguistics, Hefni Nasif, and two other members, Mustafa 'Anani and Ahmad al-Iskandari. This committee was given the task of adjusting the diacritics (*dabt*) and the spelling of the baseline consonants (*rasm*), according to the rules of *al-rasm al-'Uthmani* (the baseline used in the *mushaf* produced under the rule of the third caliph 'Uthman). It took them five years to complete the task, according to 'Abd al-Fattah al-Qadi.

And they thoroughly revised the orthography of the Qur'an according to opinions of the experts among the *'ulama*'. In the heading preceding each *sura*, they indicated the number of its *ayas* and whether the *sura* was revealed in Mecca or Madina, and after which *sura* it was revealed. They also inserted into the text a verse number corresponding with each *aya* and set the signs of pause, and text dividers that split the text of the Qur'an into thirty parts and their subparts. Finally they marked *al-sajadat*, the signs of prostration. They divided the marks of pause into five signs: "necessary to pause and not to continue with the next word after" and gave it a letter *mim*, "preferred to pause but permitted to continue" and gave it a "*qilla*" ligature (قلى), "permitted to pause but preferred to continue" and gave it a "*silla*" ligature (صلى), "permitted to pause or to continue" and gave it a letter "*jim*", and finally, "necessary to continue" and gave it the ligature "*la*"(لا).[23]

As a result, the committee produced a text that according to the classical sources they used allowed them to recreate, in their opinion, the appearance of the original seventh-century consonantal text. At the same time, it included all the vocalization and other markings required for a better understanding of the meaning and for correct recitation by contemporary readers. Muhammad 'Ali Khalaf al-Hussayni al-Haddad himself prepared a handwritten draft of the Qur'anic text that was used as a model. The printing took place in 1923. The letters the printers used had been designed a decade earlier by a famous calligrapher, Muhammad Ja'afar Bik (d. 1916), and were cast by the Print House al-Amiriyya. King Fu'ad was lauded for his benevolence and the *mushaf*, printed in different sizes and in considerable numbers, "was accessible to the wider Muslim population in the world. The printing was precise and mastery in what was produced was a picture of the king's sincere interest in it."[24]

This *mushaf*, later known as either the *Mushaf* Fu'ad,[25] the *Mushaf* Bulaq, the *Mushaf* Amiri, the Egyptian *Mushaf*, the *Mushaf* Dar al-Kutub, or the Cairene *Mushaf*, soon became an iconic edition not only in Egypt but in other Islamic countries.[26] A note at the back of this edition read:

> This *mushaf* is based on the *Mushaf* of al-Matba'a al-Amiriyya and was printed in the division of Messaha in Giza in 1924. It was written by his Eminence Professor Sheikh Muhammad 'Ali Khalaf al-Hussayni [al-Haddad], the sheikh of recitation and the Head of the Egyptian Reciters at present. It was endorsed by the committee appointed for this task under the supervision of the Sheikhdom.

The note is followed by an "Introduction to this *mushaf*," which asserts that it complies with the spelling approved by the scholars of *rasm* following the orthography of the *mushafs* edited by the third caliph 'Uthman Ibn 'Affan. Yet in spite of the efforts to use the correct spelling, a few words, in the opinion of the next generation of *rasm* scholars, were still incorrect. For instance, the letter *ta* normally written at the end of the word *kilmatu* (كلمة) as *ta marbuta*, according to the rules of *rasm al-mushaf al-'Uthmani*, should be changed to *ta maftuha* (كلمت). This is an example of spelling that was initially "corrected" according to the rules of modern orthography but later changed back to the irregular version present in the early *mushafs*.

Therefore, during the reign of King Faruq I, the son of King Fu'ad who ascended to the Egyptian and Sudanese throne in 1936, the *Mushaf* Malik Fu'ad went through another series of editing revisions. A new committee was formed at al-Azhar to prepare the second edition, which al-Amiriyya was ready to print. This committee was presided over by Muhammad 'Ali al-Diba'a, Head of the Egyptian Reciters at that time. He was joined by 'Abd al-Fatah al-Qadi (Supervisor of the Institute for Recitations), Muhammad 'Ali al-Najar (professor in the College of Arabic Language), and 'Abd al-Halim Basyuni (a supervisor from al-Azhar). This committee reviewed the *mushaf* according to the classic sources in recitation/reading, *rasm*, diacritics, *tafsir* (exegesis), and Qur'anic sciences, correcting the first edition. This is how committee member Sheikh 'Abd al-Fattah al-Qadi summarized the committee's efforts: "We worked to the best of our knowledge to avoid these defects and to improve these flaws, and we ask God to make this work count among our good deeds, purely for His sake. He is the best patron and the best supporter."[27]

The committee finished its work in 1951. This second and revised edition of *Mushaf* Fu'ad was printed in 1952, the year of the Egyptian Revolution when King Faruq I was forced to abdicate in favor of his infant son Ahmad Fu'ad II. The abdication did not appease the revolutionaries so a year later the monarchy was abolished and Egypt became a republic with Muhammad Najib as first president. The dynasty that sponsored *Mushaf* Fu'ad ended, but subsequent editions of *Mushaf* Fu'ad have continued to appear.

New Authority, New Authenticity

In contrast to a handwritten copy, a printed *mushaf* follows a pattern of writing and page design sanctioned by the *Mushaf* Committee and is sold to the general public, not created for a particular person. Yet in spite of an aesthetic, religious, academic, and cultural bias against mass-produced objects, printed *mushafs* resist this opprobrium. In his classic essay, "The Work of Art in the Age of Its Technological Reproducibility," Walter Benjamin says that "for the decline of the aura, one thing within the realm of production is of overriding importance: the massive reproduction of the image."[28] While lamenting the disappearance of auratic properties in mass-produced objects, Benjamin suggests that a new kind of aura arises through the reproduction of images. In the context of printed *mushafs* what emerges is, in the words of Brinkley Messick, "a new authority, a new truth value, enhanced by the definitiveness of the technology."[29] It is a different kind of authority produced and reproduced by a particular font, vocalization, and spelling sanctioned by the scholars of al-Azhar. But paradoxically—and contrary to what Walter Benjamin suggests—a printed *mushaf* is not detached from the "original." It may be emancipated from its dependence upon particular rituals of manufacture but a mechanically multiplied and non-individualized Qur'anic text becomes even more universal and closer to "original" than ever before. This happens because the font and the editing introduced by the *Mushaf* Committee have made the *mushaf* graphically "traditional," and for that reason, it is easy to spot the text of the Qur'an among other printed texts. The difference between the Qur'an and other written texts was not as obvious in the past. The tenth-century scholar Ibn al-Nadim, an early author on the subject of calligraphy, lists about sixteen scripts used to transcribe the Qur'an. This number stands in sharp contrast to the limitations on calligraphic style and format of the text that al-Azhar has imposed on Egyptian publishers. Thus, a printed *Mushaf* Fu'ad epitomizes a reified tradition by its adherence to a particular script, calligraphic style, orthography, and recitation signs, all of which are being further authorized through the book's multiplication as print copies roll off the press. The aura of this *mushaf* expands and is not diminished.

The temptation to see the typographic *mushaf*, such as *Mushaf* Fu'ad, as less valuable than a handwritten one is clear. For collectors, scholars, and institutions that deal with manuscripts, the handwritten Qur'anic copies possess the power of authenticity—an authenticity that printed codices lack. Printed *mushafs* cannot be examined to verify anything else beyond their own historical "lateness" on a continuum of technological progress. They are not one-of-a-kind in terms of either their content or material form (although I am sure that partisans of the mid-century al-Shimarli edition would disagree).

So from an aesthetic perspective, as a result of the acceptance of print, Egyptian Muslim practitioners began using a less individualized and less artistically refined object. But aesthetics aside, they obtained a text that was understood to be more fixed and thus seen as unalterable, like the word of God. A handmade *mushaf* may have been the product of artistic skills and sensibilities, individual knowledge shaped by a line of transmission (*isnad*) and devotion. However, in line with Benjamin's suggestion that mass production generates its own form of preeminence, the King Fu'ad's *mushaf* firmly anchored the text in the sphere of tradition by giving it a standardized form and by making an explicit connection with the *mushafs* of 'Uthman Ibn 'Affan. The use of print to reproduce the Qur'anic text led cumulatively to a reassessment of earlier works on *rasm* and *qira'at* (recitations/readings) and, as a result, a standardization of the rules for writing *mushaf* was accomplished.[30] Paradoxically, then, new technology solidified tradition. If treated as art objects, mass-produced *mushafs* lost the aura of an authenticity rooted in scholarship, calligraphy, and individualized manufacture. But at the same time, mass production enhanced the Qur'an's authority with individual readers through the mechanical multiplication of a particular version considered closer to the original and therefore more correct or accurate.

Moreover, the 1923 Fu'ad edition finally transformed eighteenth-century calligraphy and page design into the standard "look" of the Qur'anic text. This *mushaf*, endorsed by al-Azhar and used by its students, became for a while the most popular edition in Egypt and was well known and appreciated elsewhere in the Muslim world. What was the source of its popularity? It had authority: it was the product of the cumulative effort of religious and political leaders to disseminate an edition of the Qur'anic text prepared by a committee of scholars and published by a governmental publishing house. It also appealed to Middle Eastern aesthetic sensibilities with its evocation of the rules of Arabic calligraphy. The Publishing House al-Amiriyya (old Bulaq) printed thousands of copies of this edition and many other publishing houses copied and reprinted it later as offset technology allowed.

Interestingly, the very font used to print *mushafs* at al-Amiriyya, now so praised for its classic beauty and so closely identified with *Mushaf* Fu'ad, initially was a source of contention. A report written in 1948 by Muhammad Nadim, the Director of the National Library, reveals dissention and conflicting points of view on the relations between printing and calligraphy. Muhammad Nadim writes that in 1902, the Ministry of Finance requested general improvements to the letters used in printing to make them more legible. A committee led by Ibrahim Najib Basha, a representative of the Ministry of Interior, and made up of four others (Amin Sami Basha, Ahmad Zaki Basha, and Sheikh Hamza Fatah Allah, and Shilu Basha) undertook the task of improving the letter casts. In the process, the committee decreased the existing set of casts from 900 to 464 graphemes. They also decided to establish new rules for printing in *naskh* and chose for this job Muhammad Ja'afar Bik, a calligrapher known for his elegant inscriptions on street signs and Egyptian banknotes.

The committee wanted to simplify the writing and move away from adherence to the strict rules of *naskh* style, especially when it came to certain ways of connecting or overlapping letters. They also wanted to standardize forms of single letters that until then came in a variety of shapes. Here they encountered a problem. Muhammad Ja'afar abhorred the idea of moving away from the rules of the calligraphed *naskh* and insisted on preserving the connecting and overlapping letters as they were. He argued that this decision was necessary to preserve the calligraphy of *naskh* as one of the fine arts. "I was informed by Sami Basha, a member of the committee," wrote Muhammad Nadim,

> that the late Muhammad Ja'afar Bik threatened the committee to withdraw from the project if it insisted on their plan. Under the pressure, the committee accepted his objection to simplify connections and overlappings between the letters, even though Ja'afar increased their number. These letters, finished in 1906, have been until now used at Matba'a al-Amiriyya and other governmental printing houses.[31]

The committee did not succeed in simplifying the diacritic system either. The markings indicating short vowels and some other signs facilitating pronunciation were left as before: in two separate rows below and above the main line of writing. This division of script into three lines continued until a few changes were made by Mustafa Nadim, an expert in calligraphy who joined the committee later, who also happened to be the father of Muhammad Nadim. Mustafa Nadim managed to move the positioning of the lower vowels but was not able to change the upper ones. When it was all said and done, the set of letters designed by Muhammad Ja'afar Bik was promoted in official printing beyond the religious domain. For a while, it was used in governmental newspapers and books, even though now it is mainly remembered as *the* font of *Mushaf* Fu'ad.

Mushaf Fu'ad dominated the religious book market until 1985.

"Cultural Colonialism"

In the city of Madina in Saudi Arabia there is a statue. It does not represent a human being but a gigantic open book—a *mushaf*. The statue marks the location of the

"King Fahd Complex for the Printing of the Holy Qur'an."[32] Since its establishment in 1984, the company employs as many as 1,700 workers and has been producing about 10 million *mushafs* a year.[33] The *mushafs* printed by the King Fahd Complex are distributed for free and has one primary calligrapher, 'Uthman Taha.

Taha was born in Syria in 1934 and was educated in Damascus where he studied religious law, Arabic language, and Islamic arts. He received a certificate in calligraphy and in 1970 he prepared a *mushaf* for the Syrian Ministry of Religious Endowments.[34] In 1988, he traveled to Saudi Arabia where the religious authorities appointed him head calligrapher at the King Fahd Complex. "It took Taha three years to prepare a copy of the Qur'an for the royal printing house,"[35] and after another year of revisions, the first edition of *Mushaf* al-Madina al-Munawwara based on Taha's handwritten copy was ready for publishing. Since then, 'Uthman Taha has prepared a template for reproduction three more times, making more corrections and improving the book visually. More than two hundred million copies of the *mushaf* written in his hand have been distributed around the world.

Like many other accomplished calligraphers, Taha learned his art from other calligraphers, in his case calligraphers located in Syria and Turkey. As part of his training he also remembers copying other handwritten and printed *mushafs* available at the time. He says that printed ones that were good were scarce, except a couple of *mushafs* from Turkey and *Mushaf* Fu'ad from Egypt. Taha learned clarity and simplicity of style by imitating these books. Indeed, contemporary Egyptian readers praise *Mushaf* al-Madina al-Munawwara for its clear and easy-to-read calligraphy. But Taha's *mushaf* does not simply continue the calligraphic tradition of his teachers. It does more than that. *Mushaf* al-Madina has introduced Muslim readers of the Qur'an to a style of calligraphy that has been influenced by the simplified mechanical typography of printed *mushafs* that by Taha's time already dominated the book market. The calligraphers in Egypt recognize that the Syrian artist employed the calligraphy of the *Mushaf* Fu'ad as a model for his writing. Perhaps this is why calligraphers in Egypt are fond of saying that "*Mushaf* al-Madina is easy to read but it lacks individual character."

Nevertheless, *Mushaf* al-Madina, known in Egypt also as the Saudi *Mushaf*, is now the most common edition of the Qur'anic text in the country. The ubiquitous presence of *Mushaf* al-Madina in Egypt has had a seminal impact on the Egyptian religious publishing market as well as on users of the Qur'anic text. What are the consequences of the introduction of this Saudi *Mushaf* in Egypt?

Let's begin with a vignette that illustrates some of the interesting entanglements between *Mushaf* al-Madina and other *mushafs* produced in Egypt, especially *Mushaf* Fu'ad.

I spotted Muhammad, my old teacher of classical Arabic, in the common room of a language center. It was two years since I had seen him last. He wanted to know how my project was going. I told him about my visits to the publishing houses that print *mushafs*, including a recent trip to the Publishing House al-Shimarli. Two other teachers were engrossed in a conversation, sitting on a couch next to us. After a moment, they went silent and began listening to our chat.

Suddenly one of them interrupted.

What's *Mushaf* al-Shimarli, Muhammad?

"It's a *mushaf* used at al-Azhar in the past but they don't use it anymore," Muhammad replied. "I memorized the Qur'an from it and when I started reading from *Mushaf* al-Madina I was confused."

"Aaah," said the teacher with evident curiosity on her face. "I have never heard of it. I use *Mushaf* al-Madina al-Munawwara. Now they distribute it for free to people who go on the pilgrimage. When I went to Mecca maybe ten years ago I found a *mushaf* that had mistakes, so I gave it to the police there. I think it must have been left by a pilgrim from another country. Because, you know"—she looked at me—"people come with their *mushafs* and then donate them to the mosque. That's why the Saudi king decided to print one *mushaf* and give it to everyone to make sure that there are no bad copies."

This little dialogue brings to light two interesting issues: one, the easy availability of *Mushaf* al-Madina in the market of contemporary religious publications; and two, its growing dominance over Egyptian editions of the Qur'anic text. In order to understand the significance and the effects of the latter, it is necessary to go back in time again and wrap up the story of Muhammad Effendi Mustafa and his successful printing press. I left the narrative about this publishing house at the turn of the twentieth century, in the times when a printed *mushaf* was already a common book, and when the sons of our entrepreneur 'Abd al-Rahman Muhammad and Mustafa Muhammad, continued printing Qur'anic text. 'Abd al-Rahman Muhammad worked at the family printshop while studying at the Royal School of Calligraphy.[36] In addition to his involvement in the family business, after graduation he became a teacher at the Royal School and was known for inscribing the Qur'an by hand a few times. Given his education and experience, he was most probably an advisor on the text of printed editions. His brother, Mustafa Muhammad, opened his own print shop where he published other religious books in addition to the *mushaf*. Qur'anic copies from their company were available when the *Mushaf* Fu'ad entered the market during the first half of the twentieth century.

Muhammad Effendi Mustafa's grandson, Muhammad 'Abd al-Rahman, studied printing in England and received his engineering diploma there in 1933. He worked in his grandfather's printing business and later in England, where—when an opportunity came—he designed a one-page *mushaf* with print so minuscule that it needed to be read with a magnifying glass. He must have been fond of miniatures for later he also printed a whole *mushaf* as a book in the size of a postage stamp. It was a complicated undertaking considering the then-accessible technology and, therefore, was "considered a miracle in 1952"—at least, this is how al-Sa'id Dawud lauded this print curiosity.[37] Al-Azhar authorities inspected these miniaturized *mushafs* to check if they were correct and permissible to be released on the market. After Muhammad 'Abd al-Rahman's return to Egypt, he continued printing and distributing regular *mushafs* through his father's Cairo establishment, the "Bookstore and Print Shop 'Abd al-Rahman Muhammad." In 1963, Muhammad 'Abd al-Rahman published an edition of the Qur'anic text for the "foreign" market. He printed this edition in the Maghrebi calligraphy—a style derived from *kufi* and used predominantly in northwest Africa—in order to make the text easily readable for Algerian, Moroccan, or Nigerian practitioners. According to Dawud, this initiative met with great success and was particularly well received in West Africa. Muhammad 'Abd al-Rahman's commitment to printing *mushafs* was reflected in the change he made to the name of his father's shop in 1971: "Dar al-*Mushaf*: Company of Bookstore and Print Shop 'Abd al-Rahman Muhammad." A year later, he embarked on a new project: a *mushaf* with an appendix discussing the basic religious obligations: prayer (*sala*), alms (*zaka*), fasting (*siyam*), and pilgrimage (*hajj*) with a tabulation of the *ayas* (verses) that pertain to these obligations arranged in a topical index. Published under the name *al-Mushaf al-Muʿallim* (*mushaf* that instructs), this edition garnered "fame throughout the Arab and Muslim world."[38]

The 'Abd al-Rahman family publishing establishment, as we could see earlier, was not the only family business dealing with printing of the Qur'anic text. The large Subih and al-Halabi printing houses count among them, as well as al-Shimarli—the publisher of the *mushaf* my friend Muhammad had used when studying at al-Azhar. The story of this publishing house begins in 1944 with a man named Hajj Ahmad Hossayn al-Shimarli al-Kabir, grandfather of the company's present director, who employed a calligrapher named Muhammad Saʿad Ibrahim Haddad (1929–) to write the copy of the Qur'anic text to be used for publication. Haddad was famous for his calligraphy not only in Egypt but also in other Muslim countries, including Kuwait and Saudi Arabia where he had prepared copies of the Qur'anic text for printing houses there.[39] It took Haddad five years to prepare a copy of the Qur'an for al-Shimarli, and since the 1950s this version has been printed as *Mushaf* al-Shimarli, a text well known among Egyptian calligraphers and admired for its beauty and elegance. Haddad's distinctive calligraphy, coupled with decades of corrections and reviews,[40] has made this *mushaf* highly reputable. As a result, the company has been extremely protective of its rights to publish it—rights that al-Azhar guarantees and confirms every five years.

Unlike many other publishing houses, al-Shimarli employs its own specialists in calligraphy whose primary task is to attend to the *mushaf* and its correctness. Because of its exactitude and refinement, the copy of the Qur'anic text that al-Shimarli produced competed for decades with *Mushaf* Fu'ad; al-Azhar even recommended *Mushaf* al-Shimarli to its students. Moreover, each year al-Shimarli exported considerable numbers of this *mushaf* to Saudi Arabia and other Gulf countries. But the introduction of *Mushaf* al-Madina in the mid-1980s was a game changer. Within a decade, *Mushaf* al-Shimarli, *Mushaf* Fu'ad, and other local and foreign editions were outnumbered on the market by the Saudi *Mushaf* that is now the most commonly used *mushaf* in Egypt.

Several factors have made *mushaf* al-Madina so ubiquitous. As one of the language teachers at Muhammad's school noted, it is commonly brought into the country by Egyptian pilgrims returning from Mecca, where it is distributed for free. Thousands of Egyptian workers who find temporary jobs in Saudi Arabia bring it home as well, often as gifts, because the quality of paper and print is better than the *mushafs* made in Egypt.

Different Saudi institutions, including the Saudi embassy, distribute *Mushaf* al-Madina for free to people who want it. But the most significant factor in the increase of its popularity in Egypt is the strange fact that it is also printed in Egypt. The King Fahd Complex for the Printing of the Holy Qur'an does not claim the copyright over the Qur'anic text written by 'Uthman Taha.[41] Thus, many small and sometimes flyby-night printing houses in Egypt copy or download the text and reprint it in cheap editions that flood the market. On the other hand, the long and thorough revisions made by a committee of religious scholars in Saudi Arabia have prompted al-Azhar's *'ulama'* to recommend *Mushaf* al-Madina to its students, which also encourages its local reproduction.

The emergence and dominance of *Mushaf* al-Madina has corresponded with a decline in the production of other *mushafs* in Egypt. The story of 'Abd al-Rahman's family illustrates the causes behind the decline. After the death of Muhammad 'Abd al-Rahman (the printer fond of miniature versions of the Qur'an), his sons Ahmad, Mahmud, and Muhammad Wafiq continued to print *mushafs* until 1988. After that, they decided to significantly scale back their production of the Qur'anic text. The eldest brother Ahmad explained some of the reasons behind this decision. He said,

> First, techniques of printing developed in other countries allowed them to establish their own printing houses specializing in printing *mushafs*. Second, the newly established Qur'an Printing Complex of Malik Fahd in Saudi Arabia produced high quality *mushafs* and distributed them for free among Muslims in all Islamic countries. Third, the costs of production, taxes, and customs fees became too high to continue the printing of *mushafs* only.

In its stead, the brothers began to print books for the Ministry of Schooling and Education in a new printing house they called al-Dar al-Taysir, printing religious books and *mushafs* at Dar al-*Mushaf* as a supplement to their main business.

The decreased presence of other Qur'anic editions on the Egyptian market is evident in two ways. First, one may peruse the *mushafs* for sale in Egyptian bookstores and street stands. In the little religious shops mushrooming around al-Azhar Mosque or in the French-owned Carrefour, a multinational retailer built on the outskirts of the city, the *Mushaf* al-Madina al-Munawwara is by far the most common *mushaf* available. The measure of its popularity is also visible in the places of its disposal. It is common to donate an aged *mushaf* to one's local mosque where such books fill spaces on the shelves if they are not kept in closets. I browsed these surplus collections occasionally, looking for editions other than the Saudi one. They were hard to find among the rows and rows of colorful covers protecting the characteristic green and black text written in the hand of 'Uthman Taha.

For Egyptian producers of *mushafs*, then, the *Mushaf* al-Madina is a problematic book. On the one hand, its ubiquity is good, because it is the Qur'an. As the Azhari scholar Sheikh Tareq 'Abd al-Hakimi points out, the Qur'an is "the most precious possession of all Muslims, their constitution, a secret of their strength, a source of their rejuvenation, a cause of their success, a unifier of their judgment, and an object of pride to which they adhere."[42] But on the other hand, the Saudi *mushaf* has caused an economic crisis for Egyptian publishers whose livelihood depended on printing and selling the Qur'anic text. Al-Shimarli is perhaps the only publishing house that claims to continue its production in the same numbers since the appearance of *Mushaf* al-Madina but even they have had to look for new markets outside of Egypt to distribute what they print. For instance, they have turned to Palestine as a new market. *Mushaf* al-Shimarli's firmly established position among Qur'anic readers and the company's careful protection of its copyright have over time turned this particular *mushaf* into a sort of connoisseur's book. In Egypt at least, it is used primarily by those who learned from it in their youth or by those who specifically appreciate its unique and graceful calligraphy, which is very different from the one exercised by 'Uthman Taha in the *Mushaf* al-Madina.

There is one major difference between the ways these two Qur'anic texts are written, a difference not easily visible to the untrained eye but obvious to those who know calligraphy. *Mushaf* al-Madina is the product of a practical sensibility: it is clear, simple, and easy to read. In order to facilitate its reading or recitation aloud it is designed according to the rule demanding that no verse of the text should continue on the following page. In order not to interrupt the reading by turning the page, the verses always end at the end of the page. This method of text adjustment, easy to achieve in digitized typography by automatically adjusting the width of the letter or word, is much harder to implement when a text is handwritten. Therefore, Taha's calligraphy, instead of solely following its inner harmony and composition, is forced into an external framework of page design. The writing in *Mushaf* al-Madina does not flow naturally, crossing the page as necessary, but rather is expanded and contracted on the page to ensure that it ends with the end of each verse in the left bottom corner of every page. Thus, the differences in the density of the writing go against the rules of proportion and evenness so cherished by Egyptian calligraphic artisans.

On a practical level, the differences between *Mushaf* al-Madina and *Mushaf* al-Shimarli create a problem for their readers. Those who memorized the Qur'an following the text of *Mushaf* al-Shimarli, like my teacher Muhammad, find it confusing to use *Mushaf* al-Madina and vice versa. It is because the mnemonic techniques of memorizing the Qur'an include remembering the position of the words on a page. A different location will confuse the reader who has memorized the text and who looks for passages in particular places within the rectangular space of the white sheet of paper that constitutes a printed page. Of course, it is not impossible to read from another *mushaf* but an individual's preference for a particular copy is usually shaped by the early experience of memorizing a text that has a particular "look," placement, and distribution of words on each page. Younger generations of Muslims in Cairo have grown up with *Mushaf* al-Madina however, so when they purchase a new copy of the text they are likely to buy the same, familiar, and easy-to-follow edition.

The inconvenience of adjusting to another edition is exemplified by a question posted on a Qatari *fatwa* website that provides, like other websites of its kind, a direct way of obtaining authoritatively sanctioned pronouncements on a variety of religious issues. The most common are questions pertaining to permissibility of a particular action. One of the requests submitted for scholarly opinion had to do with the *Mushaf* al-Shimarli. An anonymous person accustomed to *Mushaf* al-Shimarli was finding it increasingly difficult to find copies in the mosques where he or she taught recitation. To correct this problem this person came up with a plan to look for copies of *Mushaf* al-Shimarli in other mosques, remove them, and place them where he or she needed them to be. To compensate these mosques for their loss, this person offered to replace the removed copies of al-Shimarli with newly purchased copies of *Mushaf* al-Madina.

The question was whether such an exchange was permissible. The replying *mufti* was not sympathetic, pointing out that it does not befit a teacher of Qur'anic recitation to be limited to a single type of *mushaf*. The *mufti* was also concerned by the issue of donation. If someone intentionally had donated a particular *mushaf* to a particular mosque, he stated that it should not be removed from there.[43]

The dominance of the *Mushaf* al-Madina concerns some Egyptian publishers for yet another reason. They ask: should the Qur'anic text have a copyright (like *Mushaf* al-Shimarli) or not (like *Mushaf* al-Madina)? By claiming intellectual property rights to a particular edition of *mushaf*, a publisher could watch over his own economic interests and, in some cases, ensure the survival of his business. But at the same time, since it is the word of God, the Qur'an should be distributed widely and in the best condition possible. The King Fahd Complex in Saudi Arabia not only produces Qur'anic copies of good quality but can also afford to check each individual copy for correctness. After such inspection books are stamped as a proof of control and only then are made available to the public. Unfortunately, no publishing houses in Egypt can afford such quality control. At present that's not a problem; the *Mushaf* al-Madina can be legally reproduced by other publishers. But what if the law changes? Who will be able to afford to pay royalties? Will retroactive payments be demanded for copies already sold? These and similar questions worry some who work in Cairo's printing houses.

As the owner of a private Egyptian publishing company that used to print *mushafs*, Ustaz Ahmad has an office in an old condominium in downtown Cairo. From the street, dark wooden stairs lead to a three-room apartment full of books stacked along the tall walls up to the ceiling. The stairwell has the characteristic musty smell of an old building. I greet the doorkeeper who is sitting on a small chair by the building's entry. His dry, wrinkled face shows no emotion but he acknowledges my greeting with a slight nod of his head, which is wrapped in a beige shawl. He sometimes dozes on the cardboard boxes stretched on the floor behind the door. Later in the day he drinks tea, squatting in the sun before the entrance, but most of the time just sits in his chair, staring at the ceaseless flow of cars and people in the street.

Ustaz Ahmad's office is on the first floor. The men who work there are always busy, sorting out the stacks and filling out forms, but they do not mind my visits. I pop in there quite often to ask about the latest news from the Egyptian publishing world, and I'm always welcomed with a cup of tea. Ustaz Ahmad is one of those who worry about copyright issues. His company does not produce *mushafs* anymore, although it used to print some before *Mushaf* al-Madina. "It is all a matter of politics," says Ustaz Ahmad one muggy day over a glass of refreshing lemon juice. "Like America, Saudi Arabia wants to be the leader. It dominates other countries through money. They give *mushafs* away by the boxload for free while in Egypt production is more expensive." The honking of cars bursts through the open window. A small breeze lazily undulates the dusty sheer curtains. He shifts to the subject of illegal printing but eventually comes around to his original subject, remarking that "the relationship between Saudi Arabia and other neighboring countries is that of control, including culture. Yes, it is cultural control. They want to have everything best, including the *mushaf*."

As I discovered in many conversations, people outside, on the streets of Cairo, take the *Mushaf* al-Madina for granted. Most people do not even know that this *mushaf*'s original template used for printing was not written in Egypt but in Saudi Arabia. Many Cairo shop owners do not know its history either. Egyptian publishers who reproduce the Saudi text often do not include their company's name but simply reprint information about the King Fahd Center. Yet like al-Shimarli and other publishing houses that print their own editions, to be sold in Egypt these *mushafs* of Saudi origin have to have a printing permit issued by Cairo's al-Azhar University.

In this chapter, I have outlined some of the ways in which printing and writing—two technologies that disseminated the Qur'an as text—were shaping the Qur'anic book *and* each other during the decades following the introduction of mechanical reproduction in Egypt. By the turn of the twentieth century, Qur'anic printing was visually reminiscent of writing even more than before, and the improvements in the shape and design of the letter casts were partially a result of the efforts to make printing more like handwritten calligraphy. The editorial commentaries about the process of production that began appearing in both the typographic and lithographic copies of the Qur'an were meant to ground them more solidly in the textual tradition of the written copies and, thus, to assert their legitimacy among their readers and religious scholars alike. Printed Qur'anic copies began creating their own forms of authority through the process of multiplication and editorial innovations that were directly attempting to connect this new medium of the Qur'an with the 'Uthmanic blueprint. Yet the potential to multiply the blueprint in great quantities also created a need to assert that a given *mushaf* was, in fact, a correct version of the original text. Therefore, the research on Qur'anic orthography became important once more. Moreover, because of the number of Qur'anic copies that did not meet the standards of the Azhari scholars in terms of their content as well as quality, the *'ulama'* recognized the need for greater institutionalized control over Qur'anic production, which began with the iconic edition of *Mushaf* Fu'ad. All early attempts to print the Qur'anic text were undertaken by people with some religious education or with the help of religious scholars. However, with the making of *Mushaf* Fu'ad in the 1920s, control over the content and editorial commentaries included in the printed copies shifted to al-Azhar. The way in which contemporary production of Qur'anic texts from Egypt, Saudi Arabia, and elsewhere is institutionally guarded and the political and material implications of this custody will be the subject of the next chapter.

Part Two

The Custodians

4

Politics of Correctness

In this chapter, I will turn to affairs that reveal a broader political context in which the Qur'anic text is manufactured and distributed. In her discussion of mass-produced religious images, Birgit Mayer says, "The successful public presence of religion today depends on the ability of its proponents to locate it in the marketplace of culture and to embrace audiovisual mass-media so as to assert their public presence."[1] The presence of Qur'anic books in Egypt is undeniably ubiquitous; however, asserting it comes at a cost. The constant increase in the number of circulating copies may easily spin things out of control, as the capacities of the institutions responsible for their condition are not able to match the printed output. Fast and cheap production not only lowers the costs but also decreases quality. It is not an easy task to balance the need for dissemination of religious content, quality production, and profit-making. The dilemma of how to maintain this balance is at the center of this chapter.

The production of *mushafs* takes place under the supervision of religious authorities—the Grand Sheikh of al-Azhar and his subordinates—who have the power to define what, how, and where the *mushafs* may be printed. At the same time, however, they have no direct means of enforcing their decisions. In order to effectively regulate the production of *mushafs* they need to deploy other institutions that, through their legislative measures, provide practical ways of reinforcing the decisions of al-Azhar. This means that what would seem to be solely a matter of religious jurisprudence instead becomes a case of multilayered negotiations and agreements between religious authorities, governmental officials, and representatives of the publishing industry. During these debates all parties define their stakes: for al-Azhar officials it is the theological integrity of the text and their own authoritative position, for politicians and lawyers it is their aptitude in creating passable and enforceable laws, and for the Qur'anic publishers it is their ability to reconcile economic profits with religious requirements and spiritual edification. In this complicated process, scholars and producers have to address issues that speak as much to the content of the text as to its material form. It is necessary for them to confront a question that has a very peculiar nature, which is: what does it mean to "distort" the Qur'anic text? Here I offer a narrative of efforts to overcome technological pitfalls in order to properly attend to the text—efforts that bring together politics, religion, and the materiality of the book, producing a reality that is at odds with the secular/religious divide of modern (i.e., Enlightenment-influenced) political practice.

Defining Distortions

On Monday, May 28, 2012, the daily newspaper *al-Akhbar* published a short editorial by Raja' al-Nimr entitled *Elections and Printing of the Noble Mushaf*.[2] The first round of presidential elections had just ended with two candidates, Muhammad Morsi and Ahmad Shafiq, selected as finalists running for the presidential office. The press was brimming with opinions and speculations about the voting process and what one might expect when the final election was held. Madam Raja' commented on rumors about voting fraud but did not end there. She went on to speak about another event that had been overshadowed by the frenzy of the first free presidential elections since the 2011 revolution. While the general public discussed the strengths and weaknesses of the two presidential candidates, a group of parliamentary members at Majlis al-Sha'ab (the Egyptian lower house) gathered to resolve a very different set of issues. They debated how to avoid flaws in the printing of the Qur'anic text. The discussion focused on the requirements and penalties to be imposed on publishers whose print copies of the Qur'an contained "errors or distortions."[3] The discussion of a new law that would severely punish those who release *mushafs* with defects met with strong opposition from the body representing the Chamber of Printing Industries,[4] who—according to the editorial—threatened to stop printing *mushafs* altogether if the law in its proposed form were to pass. Apart from the severity of the monetary penalties and the excessive length of prison time suggested for those convicted, the Chamber contested the very definition of text "distortion." They argued that some defects, such as wrinkled paper, missing pages, or ink blobs, simply happened during the printing process and were a natural and unavoidable by-product of the process of mechanical reproduction. They were by no means intentional or insidious "distortions" of the Qur'anic text.

A couple of weeks before *al-Akhbar* published the editorial on the legislative debates regarding the printing of *mushafs*, Ustaz Ahmad, the owner of a Cairo publishing house, spoke to me of his concerns. As someone familiar with the legal propositions being discussed in parliament, he simply said—while clicking his tongue in a characteristic sign of disapproval—"This bill is a bad idea." I asked why. "It will create a climate of fear in which the publishers might not want to print the *mushaf* at all." After a moment of thought he added rather angrily, "If one gets fewer years in prison for dealing drugs than for misprints, people will prefer to make a living by selling drugs rather than printing the *mushaf*. A fine of two or three thousand pounds is a reasonable amount to pay for a mistake but not tens or hundreds of thousands, as the proposal suggests." He reiterated his opinion, making sure I understood him correctly, "The proposed penalties in this case are disproportionate to this sort of crime." In principle, Ustaz Ahmad was not against punishing the wrongdoers, but he felt that by proposing such penalties the parliament disclosed a complete lack of understanding of the realities of the printing profession, its technological constraints, and profit margins. In short, it did not take into account the "thickness of things" that those who work with machines and objects know so well. Machines sometimes break and objects sometimes don't turn out exactly the same in spite of the efforts to make them identical.[5]

Madam Raja' thought otherwise. "Is it reasonable to print a *mushaf* with a number of defects and then argue that they were not intentional or that they were misprints?" she asked in her editorial. "The Chamber of Printing Industries should first solve this problem, instead of threatening to stop publishing the *mushaf*. And anyway," she concluded, switching her line of attack, "Egyptians do not need *mushafs* printed by big publishing companies. Every household already has at least ten copies. What is important is to read them and to memorize them. And, if publishing companies fear for their export they should also discuss it with the Parliament, as it is a matter of commerce." She ended her piece rather facetiously, "Not every industry threatens to stop the production when they don't like the law that is there to regulate it."

Her editorial was subsequently picked up by Jabar al-Qarmuti, a host of a news program *Munshet* ("Headlines") on ONTV, a private Egyptian television station that presents news and politics. Al-Qarmuti was also taken aback by the protests of the Chamber of Printing. "So a school book is inspected three times before it goes on the market and it's not possible to do the same with a *mushaf*?!" exclaimed the host over the *al-Akhbar* newspaper spread out on his desk, opened to the page with the editorial by Madam Raja'. "Our Lord preserved the heavenly books, the Qur'an," after a momentary pause he added,

> and the *Enjil* [Gospels] and *Tawra* [Torah], and now we distort them?! Do you want to print this book as you like?! No! It's one of those laws that we have to respect. Not every law comes from Freedom and Justice Party [the Party of the Muslim Brotherhood]. How can a Muslim or a Christian buy the book, bring it home and find that it has mistakes? It may lead to more distortions and soon you will find that the whole *sura* is wrong. And, anyway, there are houses full of *mushafs* and people don't read them. There are cars with a *mushaf* in front of you and behind you, and people don't know anything of it.

He closed the newspaper with a flourish. "I think it is good that there is a law that regulates printing of *mushaf*. Something positive will come out of it."

In his journalistic monologue, Jabar al-Qarmuti not only managed to sneak in a jab at the then leading Muslim Brotherhood party that was receiving a flurry of popular criticism for its inability to deliver laws that would invigorate the spiraling economy, but he also got himself in trouble for his politically correct but theologically faulty inclusion of the Gospel and Torah in the list of books preserved by Allah. "And where does this idea come from?" commented a viewer under the YouTube recording of the program. "Allah pledged to save the Qur'an only, not other books."

Al-Qarmuti's very pragmatic approach to printing the Qur'anic text was at odds with the equally pragmatic attitude of the Chamber of Printing Industries. From the Chamber's perspective, there was a significant difference between a printing error that changed the meaning of the text and a flaw that merely made the text look less attractive. Similarly, there was an even bigger difference between a purposefully made corruption of the text (accusations of such efforts by "Israeli spies" have periodically circulated on the internet) and an accidental flaw, created by the printing machine or human neglect. All of these gradations of errors, the Chamber argued, should be taken into consideration when discussing penalties that could possibly bring a publishing house to financial ruin.⁶

During the course of these arguments, the fact that "mistake or error" (*khata'*) has multiple meanings was never addressed. In an interview with an official from a sister organization, the Union of Book Distributors, the word *khata'* came up so often that I asked for specific examples of the defects in question. The official looked around his small office, furnished with a desk, a coffee table, a few armchairs, and a bookcase standing along the wall. He reached for one of the *mushafs* on the shelf, opened it randomly, and after a few seconds of quick skimming he pointed to a letter *kaf* that was missing its top part. A few pages further, there was an ink smudge in the middle of the text—also a defect, he said, flipping through the pages. Suddenly, he came across a blank page; strangely, only the red numbers that should mark the end of the verses were suspended in the empty space of bare paper. "Look at that!" he exclaimed obviously surprised. "This is impossible! It's sixteen pages like that! One sheet of printing contains sixteen pages, so any mistake of this sort affects all sixteen pages!" He looked at the first page to see who printed the *mushaf*. A nervous smile covered his discomfort, "Don't tell anybody at al-Azhar. The publisher is my friend and he might end up in prison."

The issue of printing defects in the Qur'anic text that spurred the editorial and its discussion on television was addressed by the president of the Chamber of Printing Industries, Khaled 'Abduh, at a council that took place on 22 May 2012 when members of the organization gathered to discuss their official response to the proposed law. Representatives of the publishing houses that printed *mushafs* attended the council as well as some officials from al-Azhar who were asked to deliver their opinions on this matter. Short news reports appeared in the media thereafter, informing the public that the representatives of the Chamber criticized the Grand Imam and Sheikh of al-Azhar, Dr. Ahmad al-Tayyeb, as well as the Ministry of Justice,⁷ for stipulating a fine of an inconceivable 50,000 Egyptian pounds (LE) and fifteen years of imprisonment for the owner of any publishing house that prints the Qur'anic text without a license and a 200,000 LE fine for misprints in the text (one news agency quoted a range between 100,000 and 1,300,000 LE. To compare, an average salary at that time was a couple of thousand pounds).⁸

News agencies stated that the Chamber's president, Khaled 'Abduh, intended to form a delegation that would include three members of the Chamber, three members of the Union of Book Distributors, and three representatives of the houses that publish *mushafs*. This delegation would subsequently meet with the Sheikh of al-Azhar and the President of the Parliamentary Council for Religious Affairs,⁹ Sheikh Sayed 'Askar, to discuss the proposed law and the alleviation of the problems it would create for the publishing sector. The news reports emphasized that according to the Chamber's representatives the printing of *mushaf* has always been given a priority but mechanical mistakes such as pages in the wrong sequence, blank pages, or missing pages sometimes occur, although—of course—they are not desired. To help in finding a resolution Sheikh al-Tayyeb should offer a clear definition of what it means "to distort" the text of the Qur'an. If the proposed law were implemented, Ahmad Hossam (a member of the Chamber's Board) warned, "the publishers who print *mushafs* in Egypt will face a threat to stop production. This will open the door to other countries, such as China or countries of Southeast Asia, for printing the Qur'anic text and will result in the loss of prestige on the part of al-Azhar."[10] Hossam's reference to the *mushafs* printed in Asia was not only a concern of a commercial nature—obviously, for financial reasons it is always better to export rather than import copies of the Qur'anic text. But he also hinted at an ethnic and cultural hierarchy of Qur'anic production, with Chinese *mushafs* having a reputation for being notoriously erroneous and, therefore, not as good as locally produced Middle Eastern ones.

A week later, internet news websites and newspapers announced that yet another round of negotiations had taken place. This time it was the Union of Book Distributors that met with the members of the Parliamentary Council for Culture and Information[11] headed by Muhammad al-Sawi. The issue of penalties for misprints in *mushafs* was not the only one discussed by the Union's delegation, but it was contentious enough to remain unresolved and, eventually, any decisions were postponed to yet another council. At the meeting, the Union delegation expressed, among other grievances, its discontent with the slow speed with which al-Azhar issued licenses to print the Qur'an (often a year or more) and the lack of standardization in printing procedures. The author of one of the longer articles reporting on this meeting juxtaposed these complaints with the rather unyielding opinion of Muhasin Radi, a parliamentary member, representative of the Council for Culture and Information, and Secretary of the Freedom and Justice Party, who called for the imprisonment of any person involved with printing a *mushaf* with distortion, appealing to al-Azhar to exercise "its rightful authority in that matter."

Muhammad Rashad, the Union's president, had his own agenda to defend. According to Law Number 25 of the year 1965, only publishers belonging to the Union had the right to print the Qur'anic text. In his opinion, al-Azhar should indicate the publishing houses that are capable of printing the *mushaf*, and each printing house should employ a reviewer in addition to the review done by al-Azhar to make sure that the text is printed correctly. The report ended with the words of Muhammad Hossam, a member of the Union's delegation, stating, "We [Egyptians] are no lesser than the Kingdom of Saudi Arabia where *mushafs* are printed as well and where it is done according to standards and specifications, and penalties are enforced on those who violate them."[12] He meant, of course, the King Fahd Glorious Qur'an Printing Complex in Madina, a place that produces, apart from millions of copies of the Qur'anic text, mixed feelings of pride and jealousy on the part of some publishers in Egypt.

The next meeting took place in June. Khaled 'Abduh, representing the Chamber of Printing Industries, and 'Asim Shalabi, representing the Union of Book Distributors, met with 'Ali 'Abd al-Baqi, Secretary General of the Islamic Research Academy.[13] Negotiations continued, with each side defending its position. The meeting reported by the newspapers *al-Wadi*, *al-Ahram*, *al-Yum 7*, and a few others[14] became an opportunity for 'Ali 'Abd al-Baqi to denounce most of the printing defects as, what he called, "professional errors,"[15] blaming them on negligent workers. Therefore, in his opinion, a publishing house that applied for a license to produce the Qur'anic text should be responsible for the quality of its printing. If it published a *mushaf* with misprints, a house should be penalized even if it claimed that the mistakes were accidental and they did not represent a case of willful distortion. Publishing houses should monitor the standards of their printing, concluded 'Ali 'Abd al-Baqi, acknowledging that the *'ulama'* and administrators at the Islamic Research Academy had been working on a revision of Law Number 102 of the year 1985 to better address the problem of printing errors and to deflect public criticism of al-Azhar for neglecting its supervisory role. 'Asim Shalabi, on the other hand, made more general comments about the development of Qur'anic printing over the last fifteen years. In spite of improvements, he admitted, misprints in *mushafs* have occurred, including those printed in Beirut for Egyptian distributors. Even the Saudi *Mushaf* al-Madina printed in Egypt was not free from printing errors, claimed Shalabi. So there was an evident need, he said, to put new rules into place and to create regulations that would efficiently manage the printing of *mushafs*.[16]

These news reports gave an impression that, however united in their opposition to the proposed law, the Chamber of Printing Industries and the Union of Book Distributors had their own internal disagreements to overcome. Perhaps this is why Khaled 'Abduh spoke at length about the growing ties between the two institutions and their willingness to cooperate in solving the printing problem. After all, there was a question of at what stage—printing or distribution—responsibility for the quality of the text should be assigned. He also responded to al-Baqi's denunciation of negligent workers by emphasizing that the workers in this industry clearly desired to be rewarded by Allah for their efforts. Yet printing is a human activity, prone to problems and in need of correction. In any case, he reassured everyone that the Chamber had no desire to be profiteering from printing Allah's words.

The meeting ended by declaring that its proceedings would be presented to the Sheikh of al-Azhar, Ahmad al-Tayyeb, with whom the representatives of the Chamber and the Union would meet again. Meanwhile, 'Abduh and Shalabi would draft a statement about the importance of recognizing the difference between accidental errors that happen in any printing process and willful distortion of the text. This statement was to be discussed with the Sheikh during the upcoming meeting.

A few days later, Khaled 'Abduh, 'Asim Shalabi, and Ahmad al-Shimarli met with the Grand Sheikh of al-Azhar, Ahmad al-Tayyeb. The Egyptian media reported that the men agreed to create a committee to once more review the proposed fees for license to print the Qur'anic text, define clearly what it means to "distort" the *mushaf*, and decrease the proposed penalties for misprints to more reasonable amounts.[17]

Although the series of official meetings I describe above occurred within a single month, the parliamentary project to impose penalties for misprints of *mushafs* in Egypt had already been under discussion for a year prior to these events.[18] A proposal to penalize those who misprint the Qur'anic text or print it without a license came from the Islamic Research Academy in al-Azhar after a growing number of incidents in which *mushafs* with misprints, missing pages, or pages out of order were discovered for sale. In 2008, *al-Yum 7* reported that 371 *mushafs* containing errors had been confiscated from a bookstore located in the al-Husseyn area and belonging to a certain 'Abd al-Tuwab.[19] Two years later, journalists reported another incident. A parliamentary member belonging to the Muslim Brotherhood, Yasir Hamud, requested an inquiry from the Parliamentary Religious Council regarding *mushafs* printed by the Publishing House al-Ghad from Mansura. In copies he had found, page 419 was followed by pages 196–227 and then jumped to page 452. The *mushaf* seemed to be missing some pages as well. The briefing was evidently not well attended by the governmental representatives, who were criticized by another Muslim Brotherhood MP, Sheikh Sayed 'Askar, for their lack of concern.[20] Interestingly, he blamed the Islamic Research Academy for the publication of faulty *mushafs* even though he was intimately familiar with the difficulties the Academy faced in controlling the final product, having been its member a decade earlier. The head of the Council for Religious Affairs, at that time Ahmad 'Amr Hashim, asked Grand Sheikh al-Tayyeb to withdraw the flawed *mushafs* from the market and to cancel the license the Islamic Research Academy had given to the Publishing House al-Ghad.[21]

In 2012, *al-Masri al-Yum* ran a short piece on a Qur'anic reciter from Sharqiyya who found errors in a *mushaf* licensed by al-Azhar and printed in al-'Abur City. The book did not contain a standardized picture of the printing permit the *Mushaf* Committee insisted must be present in every legally produced copy of the Qur'anic text. Some of the verses in this *mushaf* were merged together, the titles of chapters were mixed up, and some chapters appeared twice.[22] The reciter who bought the *mushaf*, Muhammad 'Abd al-Hakim al-Muhammad, said in an interview with the reporter:

> I bought this *mushaf* because I was impressed with its cover and printing but when I started reading it I realized that there were changes in the meaning of the verses and that there were repetitions. Had I not memorized the Qur'an I would not have noticed these mistakes. [...] I took the *mushaf* and went immediately to its publisher who told me that the *mushaf* with which I had problems had been distributed in ten thousand copies, out of which three thousand went to the mosques and nobody has complained so far. So I took the *mushaf* and went with it to al-Azhar but nobody listened to me.[23]

The story ended without revealing what eventually happened to the erroneous copies of the Qur'anic text that Muhammad 'Abd al-Hakim al-Muhammad discovered.

This anecdotal sketch of events and debates surrounding the process of printing the Qur'anic text in Egypt could be interpreted as an example of the mixing of religion and politics. Moreover, it would be easy to think of these negotiations merely as a form of confrontation between religiously motivated concerns for the integrity of the holy text and the mercenary imperative of money-making enterprises. That said, it might be better to think of this as a conflict between realms of ideas: one set of ideas about what is *right* encountering another set of ideas about what is *necessary*. When ideas float unanchored in any material reality, we can readily see them as belonging to unrelated spheres of human activity. After all, religious matters in modern imagination mostly involve the realm of spirit and belief while economic matters are focused on much more mundane and grounded knowledge of how to run a business. The historical roots of such a vision of the world in which ideas tend to be grouped by categories such as politics, religion, economy, kinship, or education are only about three or maybe four hundred years old and coincide with a particular approach to the exclusion of the material realm from what we understand to be the social realm. The social, then, designates what people think, say, and do, sometimes using objects in the process.

It is the human ideas that drive the world while the objects they use assist them in accomplishing their purpose.

In my opinion, however, this is not what these confrontations over the distortions of the Qur'anic text reveal. To the contrary, the ink smudges, missing pages, or incomplete letters point to what Bruno Latour calls *Dingpolitik*[24]—a more realistic explanation of the way material things contribute to the establishment of human affairs and how effectively they mix what modern people try to keep separate, in this case religion and economy. *Dingpolitik* assumes that things may stand in the center of human affairs and affect decisions that at a first glance seem to be of a discursive nature only. But a more commensurable picture of how the social realm is constructed would include a depiction of how things—such as millions of Qur'anic books—not only reflect people's ideas about the ethics and aesthetics of life but also force them to make decisions that would not need to be made if these books did not exist. For that reason, the discussions about the correct printing of the Qur'anic text cannot be left ungrounded but have to be related to the creation of a concrete institution that had been established in order to address the very presence of Qur'anic books within the Egyptian book market. This institution is known as the Committee for the Review of the Noble *Mushaf.*

Committee for the Review of the Noble *Mushaf*

The tepid reaction of al-Azhar officials to the existence of 10,000 erroneous copies of the Qur'an discovered by the intrepid reciter from Sharqiyya, Muhammad 'Abd al-Hakim al-Muhammad, could have been exaggerated by the reporters of the story discussed above, or it could have been factual. After all, this was not the first time this sort of problem had been brought to the Islamic Research Academy's attention. But to be realistic, how could anyone expect al-Azhar to retrieve each and every one of those copies of the Qur'an from their owners? Nevertheless, Muhammad 'Abd al-Hakim al-Muhammad was correct to turn to this institution with his complaint. Law Number 102 of the year 1985, evoked in the negotiations between the Parliament and the organizations representing printers and distributors of the Qur'an, stated that only the Islamic Research Academy at al-Azhar was authorized to oversee the printing, dissemination, and trading of *mushafs* and of any books containing *sunna*. The same body was in charge of granting the licenses and keeping records of companies and individuals who apply for permits to print and distribute the Qur'anic copies, and the general secretary of the Islamic Research Academy is designated as the proper authority to issue the document itself. The law also stipulated that the Grand Sheikh of al-Azhar is the person to establish the conditions and regulations for manufacturing *mushafs*. Only *mushafs* produced by the Ministry of Religious Endowments[25] were exempted from the obligation to obtain a license.

Law Number 102 imposed monetary penalties and imprisonment on those who printed and distributed *mushafs* or audio recordings of the Qur'anic text without a permit. Similarly, it listed penalties imposed on those who would violate the rules decreed by the Sheikh of al-Azhar and the Islamic Research Academy. According to

Article Two of the Law, printing and distribution without a license would result in a fine of 3,000–10,000 LE and five years in prison, while any deliberate distortions to the text would result in a sentence of hard labor and a fine of 10,000–20,000 LE. The law did not stipulate penalties for "accidental distortion" resulting from mechanical printing; nor did it define the meaning of "deliberate distortions."[26]

In theory, al-Azhar's control over the distribution of the Qur'anic text in Egypt is unquestionable. Its branch, the Islamic Research Academy, is a parent institution to the *Mushaf* Committee (the full name of which is the "Committee for the Review of the Noble *Mushaf*").[27] The Committee includes a chair, two deputies, and a number of members selected from among the scholars of Qur'anic orthography and reading by the Grand Sheikh and his advisors. The Committee oversees all Qur'anic production and distribution in Egypt by reviewing the texts submitted for printing and assigning permits to print and sell. It also supervises the audio recordings distributed on CDs and digital texts for portable electronics. Any complaints about the poor quality of the Qur'anic text or any defects such as missing words or letters, wrong *i'ajam* (dots that make differences between the letters), or incorrect *tashkil* (short vowels) should be directed to this body as well. After reviewing the case, if the distributor or producer of the *mushaf* is found guilty, it has the power to direct the case to court.

Several stages of examination are required in order to obtain a license. A publishing house must first submit a copy of the Qur'anic text to be reproduced for inspection. The text is returned to the publisher with comments and corrections to be made. Then, ten test copies of printed text, with pages folded and bound, are requested. Once proofed again and found correct, the Committee grants the house a permit to print. Several random copies of the Qur'anic text are selected from the run and forwarded for further inspection. Once the house passes this inspection the Committee issues a license to sell the Qur'anic book. There is a fee for each of the stages, and each of the reviews takes at least a month. On average, about four hundred publishers apply each year for a permit to print the Qur'anic text.

Procedures for obtaining a license to print and distribute the *mushaf* are the same for every individual and institution, and, in theory, every printing house that distributes *mushafs* includes a copy of a valid license in every copy they print. However, a temptation to make a profit without following these complicated procedures—or, in some cases, a lack of familiarity with the law—brings about a situation in which unregistered printing houses copy *mushafs* prepared by companies such as al-Shimarli, including the page that contains the license, and sell them without putting the original publisher's name on the cover. If any mistakes are discovered, it might be the Printing House al-Shimarli that would be made responsible for them. In a similar way, some print shops reproduce the Saudi *Mushaf* without a license from al-Azhar. Their *mushafs* are usually inexpensive, but of poor quality (very thin paper, poorly glued pages, flimsy covers) and likely to contain errors, such as the ones mentioned by Muhammad 'Abd al-Hakim al-Muhammad.

Al-Azhar's ability to firmly control text production has been undermined by the sheer number of Qur'anic books annually produced in Egypt. Unsurprisingly, the main problem the *Mushaf* Committee has faced is that there are too many unlicensed printing businesses and too few al-Azhar employees to police the book market in search of illegal or misprinted copies. Moreover, the *Mushaf* Committee is not capable of supervising the printing process after the license has been issued and cannot inspect every single Qur'anic copy that enters the market, even from officially licensed publishers.

Sheikh Ahmad al-Ma'asarawi, the President of the *Mushaf* Committee during the time of my fieldwork, was not pleased with this situation because, as he pointed out, no substantial errors showed up in the *mushafs* brought for a review. The distortions that the press highlighted (missing pages, verses, words, or letters; merged lines; smudges; etc.)—and for which al-Azhar was criticized—would not be found in the copies inspected by the Committee. They were, in al-Ma'asarawi's opinion, the result of slapdash negligence of the workers in the publishing houses and of their purely mercenary attitudes. "A worker may leave the room for a moment or press the wrong button that will result in blank pages," said al-Ma'asarawi in an interview given in 2009,[28] implying that such copies were nevertheless sold on the market and that al-Azhar could not be held responsible for these kinds of production errors. However, he suggested there was a solution to this problem. Those who print *mushafs* should employ their own reviewers to inspect the books after they have been printed and bound. He repeated this view three years later when I spoke to him about the recurring issues surrounding the printing of the Qur'an.

We met at the Islamic Research Academy, which was located in one of the modern, 1960s, socialist-style office buildings in one of Cairo's newer neighborhoods. A rabble of security police in navy blue and shabby looking doormen lounged in front of the building. A Fulbright liaison had arranged my visit ahead of time. When I showed up at the entry to the building one of the doormen who looked very much like a security officer asked, "al-Ma'asarawi?"

"*Na'am* (yes)," I replied.

He threw away his cigarette. "Come with me."

We got into an elevator. The space was bedecked with dainty white and orange curtains with frills. I found out later that regular visitors took a less fancy elevator on the other side of the hallway. We got off on the fifth floor. The rest of the building was quite sterile. Long, straight corridors were lined with offices on both sides. Concrete floors echoed the steps of the "offise bouy" (office boy) delivering tea and interdepartmental mail.

One of the department's workers said that doctor al-Ma'asarawi had not come yet, so I was invited to wait with his secretary Ronda, an amiable girl who had graduated from Cairo University with a degree in classical Arabic. Her room was small with two desks, a few chairs, and some metal shelves full of boxes and videotapes loosely stuck on top of each other. Ronda did not know much about the review procedures, but when I asked about the videotapes behind her chair she said that TV programs were brought here for theological inspections as well. "It is necessary because you would not believe what kind of mistakes they may have," she said with a merry twinkle in her eye. "For example, one of the animated films for children presented the circumambulation around the Ka'aba in the wrong direction!" "But," she added, "the division of audiotapes does not have a lot of work anymore because of CDs."

We snacked on dried dates, chatted about work, and drank tea to keep us warm while waiting. Ronda's office had a pretty view of Cairo but, like many other governmental buildings, had neither central heating nor insulation. She laughed, watching me pour more hot tea to warm up my hands, and said, "When I get too cold I go to my friends on the other side of the building. Their windows face the south. But in the summer it is much cooler on this side and they come here. I like it that way."

Sheikh al-Ma'asarawi arrived two hours later. He was tall and redoubtable, with a white and red *'amama* (cap) on his head and a well-tailored robe of fine gray wool. He joked with Ronda, who offered him a cup of tea. A man walked into the office and kissed al-Ma'asarawi's hand, thanking him for something. There was a hustle and bustle around the sheikh that marked him as someone important. He finally sat down, looked at me, smiled, and said, "I have visited North Carolina." Ahmad al-Ma'asarawi is the embodiment of a modern Muslim scholar, traditionally educated (he memorized the Qur'an by the age of eleven), yet aware of the dramatically changing needs and precarious political situation of the institution for which he workes. Representing the elite of Azhari textual experts, he specializes in the history of Qur'anic recitations with a particular emphasis on variant schools of reading. He is well respected in the Muslim academic world for his *magnum opus*, the *Mushaf of Fourteen Schools of Reading*, in which he explained the idiosyncrasies of each school by coding in different colors the Qur'anic text printed therein—a very innovative approach, as I was told by many sellers of *mushafs*.

Since Ahmad al-Ma'asarawi was the head of the *Mushaf* Committee, I was very interested in his opinion about the project entertained for a while in Azhari circles tied to the production of *mushafs*: that Qur'anic printing be unified. It meant that there would be only one institution in Egypt responsible for printing of the Qur'an. I found out about this proposal for the first time in 2010 when I came across an article titled "Unification of Printing Necessary for Preservation of *Mushaf* from Errors." The article was in the religious section of the popular Egyptian newspaper *al-Ahram* and featured an interview with Sheikh Tareq 'Abd al-Hakim, a member of the *Mushaf* Committee who did not find the current system of supervision of printing very efficient. 'Abd al-Hakim said:

> The proliferation of entities that print is one of the reasons that leads to the creation of defects in *mushaf*.[29] Everybody who wants to print obtains a permit, and this is a big mistake. So the number of institutions that print *mushafs* grows, causing problems, and the quality of printing differs from one house to another. This happens because the same machine can produce one page correct and the other with a letter missing its part or omitted altogether. Errors can also happen during the process of binding. Most of all, the attitude of some of the printing houses to printing *mushafs* as a commercial undertaking causes a lot of harm. These print the whole edition before obtaining the final permit for selling the *mushaf*. So instead of printing only ten copies requested for inspection they go ahead and print the whole amount and in the case of presence of mistakes they correct only a few copies, distributing the rest on the market. Therefore in Egypt there should only be one printing house that prints *mushafs*.[30]

It was not only Sheikh Tareq 'Abd al-Hakim who argued that Egypt should have a printing house resembling the King Fahd Complex in Saudi Arabia. Such a proposal came from the Grand Sheikh himself. Not all members of the *Mushaf* Committee, however, supported it. In fact some, including Ahmad al-Ma'asarawi, found the idea preposterous. "This was Sheikh al-Tayyeb's idea," he told me, "but it was a short-sighted vision that did not account for the situation of the Egyptian publishing market and the fact that there are at least two hundred publishing houses that print *mushafs*." He shook his head. "If we shifted the responsibility for printing *mushafs* onto al-Azhar alone, it does not have the potential to print millions of copies. Such an undertaking could have hurt the Egyptian economy and the publishing houses, and it did not have support from the public, so it went into the dustbin of history."

There were other reasons for which Sheikh al-Ma'asarawi spoke about the project as unrealistic. In 2009 the Ministry of Finance agreed to spend 200 million Egyptian pounds to create a printing house that would produce *mushafs* in a manner similar to the King Fahd Complex in Saudi Arabia but the Egyptian government took no steps to implement the project in spite of efforts to gain President Hosni Mubarak's patronage. The printing center was to be under the presidential supervision and bear the name "Publishing House Mubarak for Printing of the Noble *Mushaf*," as reported by Sheikh Tareq 'Abd al-Hakim and a few other officials familiar with the campaign.

In January 2011, weeks before the collapse of President Mubarak and his government, the project was still on the table. In an interview for the Saudi newspaper *al-Ray*, Sheikh al-Ma'asarawi mentioned that a proposal to build a centralized publishing house for printing *mushafs* was under consideration at al-Azhar. The center would print millions of copies for distribution to local and international markets. However, such an effort would require a considerable amount of start-up money and a special operating budget that al-Tayyeb as the Sheikh of al-Azhar was still seeking to secure. The project would also need large grounds to build three or four individual buildings equipped with advanced technology.[31] Three weeks after the interview, the unthinkable happened and after thirty years Mubarak and his government fell from power. Thus, the promises of the Ministry of Finance to subsidize the project were left unrealized.

It is unclear whether the idea of building a single, large printing complex would have come to fruition had Mubarak's regime continued. The deteriorating economic situation in Egypt cast doubts on either the government or al-Azhar's capacity to finance an undertaking that would require at least 30 million US dollars. The change in Egypt's political configuration and increasing friction between different factions at the University of al-Azhar led to a hounding of Azhari figures associated with the deposed president. Mubarak had appointed al-Tayyeb the Grand Sheikh of al-Azhar in 2010 and in the opinion of Sheikh al-Ma'asarawi this caused unfounded rumors. He said, "Ahmad al-Tayyeb tried to approach the ex-president Hosni Mubarak with the idea of Complex Mubarak—like Complex King Fahd. But Mubarak's reaction was cynical. He said he was not able to do that. But whoever wrote about it made a futile effort to ridicule al-Tayyeb and overplay his connections to the old regime."

In any event, the Grand Sheikh of al-Azhar certainly did not originate the idea that al-Azhar should centralize printing of the Qur'anic text. A note saying that "the Islamic Research Academy is studying the ways and means of avoiding typographical mistakes in printing copies of the Holy Qur'an, after a number of copies that were being sold on the local market were found to contain such mistakes" appeared in English in 2003. The IPR Strategic Business Information Database that tracks the major newspapers, magazines, government reports, and websites in the countries of the Middle East and North Africa contained a short article that stated:

> A senior official of the Academy [Islamic Research Academy] said that the Azhar Printing Press prints 30,000 [*mushafs*] annually, while the market needs around 450,000 each year. But the Azhar lacks the material and financial wherewithal for expanding its printing activities, and therefore an appeal has been made to the well-to-do to contribute to a project for printing the Holy Qur'an, under the supervision of the Azhar. An official of the Academy said that such a project would require financing in the region of a billion Egyptian Pounds.[32]

A desire to centralize printing of the Qur'anic text, or at least increase al-Azhar's control over printing, may seem solely to be an imitation of the Saudi King Fahd Center. This was, at least, *Ustaz* Ahmad's interpretation of these events as well as that of others in the printing business who disapproved of the initiative. "King Fahd's Center is an institution financed by the royal family who can invest a lot of money in printing *mushafs* of high quality," argued *Ustaz* Ahmad in defense of private Egyptian publishing companies. "They are later distributed for free, while al-Azhar is not able to carry out a similar undertaking. It's not financially capable and does not have enough qualified workers to supervise such a big project. Centralized printing would hurt family businesses like Shimarli that have their own traditions of publishing the *mushaf*." *Ustaz* Ahmad is not alone in his opinion. Certainly at least some officials at the Islamic Research Academy have been aware of the fragile symbiosis between Egyptian *mushafs* and the publishing companies that manufacture them. Obviously, those who participated in negotiations surrounding the proposed laws delineating penalties for printing errors have had many chances to listen to an array of grievances and points of view. But would their concerns have been mollified if sufficient funding had been available to carry out the centralization project?

A Matter of Concern

Printing defects are a very delicate and sensitive issue in the eyes of Azhari scholars, as they directly relate to a number of issues. Apart from genuine concern for the integrity of the Qur'anic text, printing errors undermine the authority of al-Azhar as a leading religious institution and could be effectively used by those who, ironically, saw al-Azhar as the puppet of a secular Egyptian regime and a defender of the old political status quo. More importantly, printing errors in the Qur'anic text tacitly undercut the credibility of religious education at al-Azhar, already challenged on many levels by the more radical and independent Egyptian sheiks who did not receive Azhari diplomas and who often have Salafi affiliations—a Saudi theological orientation not welcomed at al-Azhar in 2012. Flawed Egyptian Qur'anic copies could thus lead to lost national prestige, especially when compared to the Qur'anic copies coming out of the King Fahd Complex. Further, they could produce fear that Coptic and international Christians might use such mistakes in debates about the veracity of the Qur'an and by extension Islam, and, if that news is presented in a sensational way outside of Egypt, it might lead to broader anti-Muslim internet campaigns. Printing defects could even trigger rumors about the "foreign efforts" and "hidden hands" that purposefully aim to discredit the Qur'an and, by extension, institutions like al-Azhar that are meant to guard it. Such insinuations did appear in a few news articles reporting on negotiations between al-Azhar, parliament, and publishers, and some Azhari scholars treated these issues very seriously. But most importantly, printing defects besmirched efforts to recreate the ultimate authoritative graphic representation of the Qur'anic text, an issue that preoccupied the scholarly attention of those who specialized in the *rasm* and *dabt* of the Qur'an—in other words, those who specialized in Qur'anic orthography. The next chapter will expound on why the immaculately printed and orthographically perfect representations of the Qur'anic message matter so much for al-Azhar scholars and academics versed in the Qur'anic sciences. To borrow a word from Latour, I will continue exploring the *Dingpolitik* of the Muslim sheikhs who have been attuned to the materiality of the Qur'anic book.

5

The (Ortho)Graphic Blueprint

In *Things: Religion and the Question of Materiality* Birgit Meyer and Dick Houtman write:

> Materializing the study of religion means asking how religion happens materially, which is not to be confused with asking the much less helpful question of how religion is expressed in material form. A materialized study of religion begins with the assumption that things, their use, their valuation, and their appeal are not something added to a religion, but rather inextricable from it.[1]

This is the case because religion is never just a set of beliefs; it also includes and is sustained by practices, and these practices are never completely immaterial. People practice their religions *with* things. Even rituals without objects cannot happen without our bodies, which ultimately become objects of our actions. Even more ephemeral things, like air, dust, or sound, can still be acted upon. And, even the most iconoclastic religions in their radical rejection of tangible objects still destroy *material* things. Following this argument on a smaller scale, the material qualities of a holy book are not something added to the spoken message and irrelevant for the way the message is interpreted, debated, understood, and read, but rather the materiality of the book and its message materially captured by text participates in and instigates discussions related to the content of the message. Let's look, for instance, at ink—a medium that allows one to visualize the message. Ink can be applied to a surface with a variety of tools and technologies that will either limit or expand the possibilities of how well the text is inscribed. In other words, a particular technology that applies ink will either create a satisfactory image of spoken words or represent them in a way considered inferior to their acoustic equivalent.

In this chapter, I discuss some of the debates surrounding (ortho)graphic representations of the Qur'anic message. Those debates, although existing in the past, became in many ways more relevant and pressing in contemporary times when instead of applying ink by hand, the producers of *mushafs* applied the ink using machines of particular capabilities and limitations. In other words, discussions of how to properly inscribe the Qur'anic text were rekindled by two factors: the difficulties of recreating the Qur'an's exact letters and diacritics in print, and general social pressures to update the orthography of the Arabic language in relation to the technology used to disseminate it.

Deliberations over the Arabic language and its spelling were carried out over multiple sites: the institutions that directly dealt with the production of *mushafs*, the associations of linguists with ideas about the graphic form of the Arabic language, and the Muslim leaders responsible for delivering legal pronouncements on how to properly visualize the Qur'an. An interesting question emerged from such discussions: what precisely is the written representation of a text supposed to *reflect*? The sound of the Qur'anic words? Their meaning? Was there something in the letters themselves that required the graphic representation of the message to look in a particular way? In other words, if a letter in a word was not pronounced and its absence would not change the word's meaning, was there still a need for it to be there? The Egyptian *'ulama'* (scholars) who ultimately declared that the orthography of the Qur'anic message should not be changed under any circumstances—thus giving Qur'anic printers a considerable headache—had very substantial arguments in favor of their position. In order to understand them, we need to return to Arabic grammar and script.

Rasm

The Qur'anic message in its handwritten form, reproduced in individual copies with the use of calligraphic pens, nicely accommodated some of the practical questions of visual representation that appeared almost as soon as the Qur'anic message was committed to writing. The reasons for putting the message into a form other than sound were quite pragmatic. In case of disagreements between reciters, a material copy of the text could assist in adjudicating the argument. But, visualizing the message in a material medium led to a new question: what was the most correct way to write down words not inscribed by the messenger himself?

Twenty years after the Prophet Muhammad's death, when according to classical sources the third Caliph, 'Uthman Ibn 'Affan (d. 35 AH/656 CE), was asked to supervise a compilation of the first official codex containing the full text of the Qur'anic message in one book, his scribes recorded the text according to a writing system that represented only the consonant baseline of the words, known in Arabic as *rasm* (from *rasama*, to draw). Nevertheless, this script was easy to read for native speakers of Arabic who were familiar with the morphological patterns of the language and had already memorized the message. This *rasm* is referred to as *al-rasm al-'Uthmani*—the consonant base (without any diacritics that make distinction between the letters) authorized by the third Caliph 'Uthman Ibn 'Affan (Figure 8).

Yet the Muslim *umma* (community) rapidly grew and soon the Qur'an was recited far away from the center of its origin and by those who did not speak Arabic at home. This necessitated modifications to the existing system of graphemes, which introduced a more complicated orthographic inscription of the message. The first person credited by many Muslim historians with improving the written Qur'anic message was Abu al-Aswad al-Du'ali[2] (d. 69 AH/688 CE), a companion of the Prophet's son-in-law, who added a system of dots to indicate three short vowels—*u*, *a*, and *i* (*harakat*)—and to signal the grammatical cases (declension) of the Arabic language (*i'rab*)—nominative, accusative, and genitive. Later, Abu al-Aswad al-Du'ali or one of his successors added

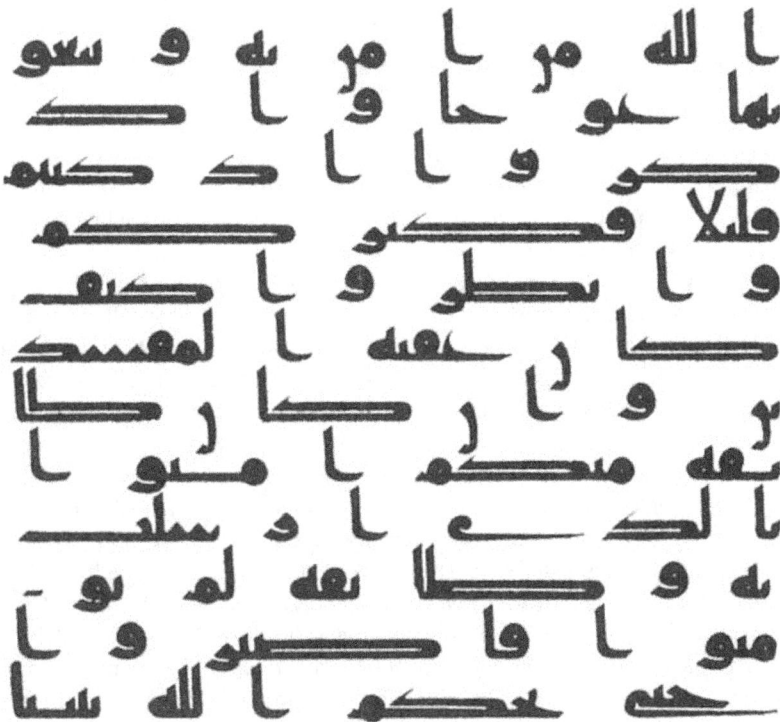

Figure 8 The early *rasm* without the short vowels, dots that differentiate between consonants of the same shape (such as ب and ت), or any other diacritics present in contemporary *mushafs*. Wikipedia public domain, originally submitted by Mandel, Gabriele: *Das Arabische Alphabet–Geschichte, Stile und kalligraphische Meisterschulen*. Wiesbaden: Matrix, 2004.

more dots to mark differences between consonants of similar shape (*i'jam*). The dots distinguishing letters of the same shape and short vowels were of different sizes and colors, as opposed to black *rasm*, and were intended to enable the nonnative speakers to read the Qur'an without errors.

Some Muslim scholars opposed any additions to the original *rasm*, but most agreed that they were permissible, if not necessary, as long as they facilitated correct recitation.[3] Still, the initial dot system must have been seen as imprecise (perhaps in small codices the limited space made the dots accompanying the *rasm* hard to tell apart?), so for the next couple of centuries Qur'anic scribes continued expanding and improving the system of diacritical signs. The science of their correct use (*'ilm al-naqt*) that prompted Muslim scholars to study Arabic syntax became a part of Qur'anic studies and its grammar. By the beginning of the third century AH/ninth century CE, the system of Qur'anic diacritics facilitating reading was fairly well established, although small changes continued to be introduced until about the fifth century/

eleventh century. These developments went hand in hand with efforts to explicate the rules of writing the consonant baseline of the Qur'anic text. Thus, *'ilm al-rasm* (the science of *rasm*) dealt with the orthographic form of the text's consonant baseline and long vowels.

At first, the 'Uthmanic *rasm* was one of the most important sources of Arabic orthography in vernacular use, but with time the common spelling of certain words began to differ from the spelling used in Qur'anic copies. The question of whether Qur'anic *rasm* should be updated to reflect the changing rules of spelling was raised as early as the third century AH. When asked whether such changes in Qur'anic orthography should be executed, Malik Ibn Anas (*c.* 93–179 AH/711–795 CE), founder of one of the major Islamic schools of religious law, emphatically replied, "No, [it should be written] according to what was first."[4] Malik was not the only scholar who felt that the *rasm* of the Qur'anic text should be left unmodified. Among those who explicitly opposed any alterations to Qur'anic orthography were Abu 'Amr al-Dani (371–444 AH/981–1053 CE), who wrote a famous treatise on the Qur'anic *rasm* entitled *A Persuasive Book of Knowledge of What Has Been Decreed in Relation to Masahif of People of the Region*;[5] Abu Dawud Suliman Ibn Najah (d. 496 AH/1103 CE), who wrote on the same subject in his *Revelation*;[6] Imam al-Shatibi (d. 590 AH/1193 CE), who discussed schools of reading in relation to orthography in *The Best of the Lowliest of Poems Regarding Loftiest of Goals Concerning the Science of Qur'anic Orthography*;[7] Abu al-'Abbas al-Marakashi (Ibn al-Bina') (d. 721 AH/1321 CE), who prepared a *Manual for the Orthography of the Revelation*;[8] Muhammad Ibn Bahadur Zarkashi (744–794 AH/1344–1392 CE), who wrote multiple treatises on this subject; and al-Suyuti (849–911 AH/1445–1505 CE), who produced a classic work entitled *The Perfect Guide to the Sciences of the Qur'an*.[9]

These studies of *rasm* were well known among Muslim academics many hundreds of years ago, but they have become even more relevant in the last two centuries (al-Makhallalaati used some of these sources to produce his introduction as well) and have been cited as authoritative in contemporary writings that discuss the 'Uthmanic orthography. Al-Suyuti in particular is an important source, as he wrote extensively on the matters of orthography, compiling earlier works on rules and patterns characteristic of Qur'anic spelling. His work on Qur'anic grammar has served as a foundation for general grammar courses and its elements are still taught in Egyptian public schools.

At al-Azhar, study of the Qur'anic *rasm* represents a narrow but complex branch of Qur'anic knowledge that takes years of rigorous scholarship for those who want to specialize in it. Yet, it is an essential study for the contemporary *'ulama'* who supervise the production of Qur'anic copies, as they are the ones who ensure that the rules of classical orthography have been preserved, that no diacritics missing or altered, and that no form of contemporary spelling has fraudulently wormed its way into the written or printed text.

It is very hard to understand what is at stake in such a rigorous control of the text without a thorough knowledge of the Qur'anic grammar. A brief example below only partially reflects the complexity of this issue and indicates how the rules of *al-rasm al-'Uthmani* compare to contemporary spelling. The Qur'an's orthographic patterns are grouped into six categories:[10]

1. The pattern of deletion. Qur'anic orthography: the letters *alef, ya, waw, lam,* and *nun* are omitted in writing some words although they are pronounced (example: *al-il* instead of *al-lil*[11]). Contemporary orthography: some of these letters are now written in contemporary modern standard Arabic.
2. The pattern of addition. Qur'anic orthography: the letters *alef, waw,* and *ya* can be added even though they are not pronounced (example: *qalu* with an extra *alef* after *waw*[12]). Contemporary orthography: this *alef* is not written in vernaculars but is retained in contemporary standard Arabic.
3. The pattern of writing the *hamza* (ء), which is a glottal stop that can be pronounced in different ways depending on the surrounding letters. Its writing in the Qur'an differs from non-Qur'anic orthography.[13]
4. The pattern of changing. Qur'anic orthography: the letter *alef* changes into the letters *waw* or *ya, nun* into *alef*, and the final feminine *ha* (*ta' marbuta*) into an ordinary open *ta'* (example: *zaku'a* instead of *zakaa*[14]). Contemporary orthography does not preserve this form of spelling.
5. The pattern of joining and separating where pronouns and prepositions are combined with other words (example: *yawmuhum* instead of *yawmu hum* or *fima* instead of *fi ma*[15]). This spelling is present in contemporary writing.
6. The existence of variant canonical readings— *'ilm al-qira'at* ("schools" or methods of recitation).

Although complex, these are not differences that would make contemporary reading of the ancient Qur'anic text impossible. Most of these discrepancies could be compared to the way the King James Version of the Bible is archaic but still able to be read and understood by contemporary English speakers. Why, then, do scholars at al-Azhar (and other places as well) still adhere to the unrevised spelling? I will come back to this question shortly but for the moment I want to turn to the last category on the list of orthographic patterns: variant canonical readings.

Schools of Reading

Historically, variant canonical readings of the Qur'an have been discussed from many points of view, and the tradition of these debates among Muslim scholars as well as scholars of religion is long, rich, and sometimes contentious. However, from an anthropological perspective, discussions of variant canonical readings instantiate an example of how religion appears and becomes tangible in the world through the negotiation of practices.[16] The science of variant schools of recitation of the Qur'an (*'ilm al-qira'at*) is very technical, practical, and intimately connected to the knowledge of *rasm*. It represents a separate branch of specialization in Qur'anic studies that is essential for people like Sheikh al-Ma'asarawi, who used to be the

Head of the *Mushaf* Committee and the Head of the Egyptian Reciters at the same time.[17] Such a position entails an immense comprehension of both: how to recite the message according to the science of *al-qira'at* and how to inscribe it so that there are no discrepancies between the sound of a particular recitation and its visual representation.

It is commonly understood among Egyptian Muslims that reading the Qur'anic text out loud (*tilawa*) is better than reading it silently. It is even more beneficial if one is familiar with the rules of *tajwid*, which is a desired way of reciting the Qur'an that is attentive to particularities such as the modulation of the voice, the length of syllables, accents, the assimilation of consonants to the following ones, or the places where one should pause and end the verse. Differences between variant readings include these particularities as well as simple pronunciation variants, different case endings or verbal forms, and synonyms or near synonyms. However, the question of how much difference the variants of reading actually produce when it comes to the text's meaning has been a matter of debate between Muslim scholars and some orientalists and does not belong here; neither does the history of the variants' development—also investigated by Muslims and non-Muslims alike. What I find relevant, and what is important for the printing houses that produce *mushafs*, is the fact that peculiarities of each school/variant of reading are reflected in the *rasm* of the *mushaf*, its diacritics, and the signs that guide the recitation (*'alamat al-wuqf*).

To illustrate the practical consequences of variant readings for the printed Qur'anic text, let's recall my conversation with Muhammad and two other instructors in the language center. The conversation concerned *mushafs* in the Grand Mosque in Mecca, in particular the one that was found to have "errors" and was turned in to the religious police. The teacher who discovered it could not recall what kind of "errors" the book contained, and it may well be that what she had come across were simply mechanical misprints. However, it is also possible that, instead of defects, the *mushaf* actually contained one of the less common recitation variants (*qira'at*), specifically one that the teacher did not know, as this kind of knowledge is mastered mainly by Muslim religious scholars and those who graduate from al-Azhar. Occasionally, a person without Azhari education may know one or two other variants which he or she learned through self-study or courses at various religious centers, but most Egyptian Muslims are unfamiliar with differences between the *qira'at* and know primarily one, their own reading.

The Grand Mosque in Mecca is a cosmopolitan place where a pious sojourner may easily come across a *mushaf* printed in another *qira'a*. Over 6 million pilgrims a year visit this impressive architectural complex and Muslims from all over the world gather there, many of whom bring their own *mushafs*, sometimes leaving copies worn out by prayer behind (especially when they receive in return a brand-new *Mushaf* al-Madina). An amalgamation of people and books in one building creates a space of juncture where objects can easily find themselves changing hands. Crowds of pilgrims pour in and out of this famous place daily, some clenching a *mushaf* in their hands, others looking for a copy left behind or belonging to the Mosque. The religious custodians of the Holy City strive to satisfy the needs of the pilgrims in this matter. In 2012, the Director of the Administration of Affairs Pertaining to *Mushafs*[18] at the Grand Mosque in Mecca, 'Abd al-Rahman Ibn 'Ali al-'Aqla, announced that the King Fahd Complex had provided *mushafs* of different sizes to be distributed around the Mosque so they would be available to visitors. This in and of itself might not be as surprising if not for the number of distributed codices—an astonishing 1 million copies of the Qur'an that year.[19] The Director did not mention whether they included *mushafs* with different *qira'at*, but from what I heard on different occasions from pilgrims coming back home it is reasonable to assume that most, if not all, contained the reading predominant in Saudi Arabia. One Azhari sheikh summarized the state of affairs in Egypt in a rather caustic way by saying, "If you want a different *qira'a*, get online and listen, or buy a CD with an old sheikh who was famous for a certain school of reading."

Auspiciously, for Egyptian pilgrims and visitors to Mecca arriving from Lebanon or Syria, that particular choice is not a problem. In Egypt, as in Saudi Arabia and the Levant, the common school of recitation is attributed to the reciter 'Asim according to the version narrated by Hafs, generally called "Hafs 'an 'Asim." It is one of seven officially accepted schools of *qira'at* (an additional seven more are considered less authoritative), each one deriving its name from a famous reciter (*qari'*) and his transmitter (*rawi*) through a chain of other well-known reciters, beginning with the Prophet himself. For instance, the reading variant "Hafs 'an 'Asim" is traced back to the reciter 'Asim Ibn Abi al-Najud (d. in 127 or 128 AH), who learned from Abu 'Abd al-Rahman al-Solammi and Zirr Ibn Hubaysh. Abu 'Abd al-Rahman was reported to have learned from 'Uthman, 'Ali Ibn Abi Talib, 'Ubayy Ibn Ka'ab, and Zayd Ibn Thabit, who were all companions of the Prophet. And Zirr Ibn Hubaysh was said to have learned from 'Abdallah Ibn Mas'ud, also one of the Prophet's close associates.

So a pilgrim from Egypt who receives a *Mushaf* al-Madina is not troubled by its orthography. A sojourner from Morocco, however, will spot a few differences. For instance, in chapter *al-Shura* (Q. 42:30) according to the school of Hafs she would read فَبِمَ (*fabima* "then it is what") and according to the school of Warsh popular in Morocco she would read بِمَا (*bima* "it is what"). Variant readings also affect the text's diacritics. Thus, in *al-Fath* (Q. 48:17), the school of Hafs has it: يُدْخِلْهُ (*yudkhilhu* "he makes him enter"), while Warsh contains the same *rasm* (the basic shape of the consonants) with altered *i'jam* (dots or diacritics): نُدْخِلْهُ (*nudkhilhu* "we make him enter"). The letters *qaf* and *fa* would also look differently, as their *i'jam* would be shifted: in the Maghrebi script the letter *qaf* has only one dot above instead of two and looks like a regular *fa* ف, while *fa* itself ڢ has a dot beneath instead of above (Figure 9). Variants of reading also include different ways of prolonging syllables, connecting words, and making stops to take a breath. These rules are marked in the texts of the contemporary *mushafs* and the reciters call them '*alamat al-wuqf*, "signs of punctuation," better translated as "guide to when to stop, pause, or continue recitation." They were added last to the Qur'anic text and differ, depending not only on the school of recitation but also on the expertise of the scholars who decided it would be beneficial to readers to use them.

After the introduction of print, the editorial notes in the form of an appendix that explained orthographic modifications, additions to facilitate recitation, and any other decisions made about the *rasm* of the text became standard only with the edition of *Mushaf* Fu'ad. This appendix ensured readers of the edition's accuracy and fidelity to the Qur'anic text considered to be original—the 'Uthmanic text. It also cited the scholarly treatises on which the opinion about the text's accuracy was formed. For instance, in the appendix to the *Mushaf* Fu'ad, the editors emphasized their efforts to follow strictly the rules of *al-rasm al-'Uthmani*:

> When it comes to the few letters that differed from *mushaf* to another, [the editors] followed the most common orthography according to the school of reading of the reciter who wrote the *mushaf*. They [also] complied with the rules formulated by the scholars of that *rasm*, based on what was said by Sheikhs Abu 'Amru al-Dani and Abu Dawud Suliman Ibn Najah with the preference [for the opinion] of the latter in the case of disagreement.[20]

Needless to say, this edition, like most of the *mushafs* printed in Egypt, followed the *qira'at* (school of reading) "Hafs 'an 'Asim." What is also interesting is this coda's emphasis on adherence to the rules of *al-rasm al-'Uthmani*, although at this point in time *al-rasm al-'Uthmani* already had come to mean not only the consonant base of the text but also all later additions: *i'arab* (markings of declension), *i'jam* (diacritic dots making distinction between the letters), and *tashkil* (all other diacritics functioning as phonetic guides including *harakat*, diacritics of short vowels).

Visualizing a particular *qira'a* always has consequences. As we learned earlier from the sheikh who gave a *fatwa* on the question of replacing *Mushaf* al-Shimarli in the neighboring mosques, a professional reciter should not have difficulty reading from any number of *mushafs*. But a person unfamiliar with the orthography of other variants will likely find them strange if not altogether "wrong," as my teacher Dalia did. Her story testifies to the unsettled reality in which different textual variants of the Qur'an coexist in the religious book market in Egypt. While some *qira'at* are printed in larger quantities than others, they all can circulate freely along contemporary channels of migration, such as international student exchange. Dalia's job was to teach the basics of the Qur'an to foreigners at the American University in Cairo. Performing this task, however, did not mean that Dalia had a good command of various *qira'at* other than "Hafs 'an 'Asim."

"I once found a *mushaf* with misprints," she told me.

"Oh really?!" I said, letting my voice trail off, hoping for more details.

"It was on the old campus." She spoke to me in English, "I once found one in the mosque. We had a mosque usually for the students. When I was a student …

"I remember." I interrupted, stirred by the memory. "The mosque was on the top of the building, the administrative …"

She interrupted in return.

"*Ayyywa*, it was on the top of the building. I once found a *mushaf* there. I think it was printed somewhere in Africa, in Sudan?" She hesitated trying to recall an event that had happened more than ten years ago. "No, I don't remember. But, I remember that I took it from the shelf. Usually, the stuff there is donated by students. And I think I gave it to security or something like that."

I was curious.

"So you just started reading and you noticed that it had a mistake?"

"Not only that I started reading. I first noticed that the version was different. *Bussi* (see). You know when you read *Wuthering Heights*, you have the Wuthering Heights published by Longman, and you have the *Wuthering Heights* published by... *ismaha eh* (whatchamacallit)... the Ladybird. So you know the version that you have, *keda* (just like that). I noticed a version that I never knew, so I started looking at it. Because, usually, we Muslims, especially Muslims who are practicing, you know by looks, you know them. You know?"

I didn't know. But I was intrigued by this comparison.

"So, what do you mean by versions when you talk about...?"

She got slightly impatient.

"*Ya'ani* (well). It's not the content!"

"Right, right. I know that."

"The cover, *habibti* (darling)." She stressed the word "cover" as an obvious answer. "The cover looked different. I never met this cover before."

"Oh, OK, so visually... it looked different from the ones you normally see around?"

Dalia made a typical throaty "ah" to confirm.

"I started looking and I noticed. What's this? And then I started looking at the print house and I never heard about this print house..."

At this point she digressed to the subject of printing houses in Egypt and penalties for misprints, but I kept thinking about what she said. So I called her again a few days later.

"Listen, Dalia." I said. "Do you think you could have found a *mushaf* in a different *qira'a* and you just didn't know it?"

She thought for a moment and then said, "Now that you said it, yeah... it could have been a different *qira'a*, you know."

Dalia did not seem bothered by the fact the *mushaf* she delivered to the security office could have been, in fact, errorless. As a devout Muslim, she felt a moral responsibility to make sure that the copy she came across and perceived as faulty would be removed from a place where other young Muslims could find it. But her lack of more specialized knowledge of the Qur'an prevented her from discovering a possible mistake caused by the fact that the two largest producers of the *mushafs* in the Muslim world—Egypt and Saudi Arabia—share the same *qira'a* (although there are other possible schools of reading) and Muslims in Egypt are mainly familiar now with copies of *Mushaf* al-Madina that dominates the religious market.

But what happens if an institution, such as the King Fahd Complex that produces millions of *mushafs* a year, uses predominantly one school of reading in all of its editions and distributes them for free? At what point will a historically developed adherence to a particular *qira'a* in places such as Yemen or Morocco give way to the sheer numbers of *mushafs* produced elsewhere? After all, it is not possible for any local religious authority to forbid the import of *mushafs* of this or that variant, as technically they all contain the same Qur'anic message. But precisely for this reason, some of the Egyptian scholars who specialize in science of recitation—*'ilm al-qira'at*—are concerned by the proliferation of the Saudi *Mushaf* al-Madina, printed in "Hafs 'an 'Asim," and its effects on the continuity of a tradition that supports a number of different schools of reading. Of course, religious authorities in Madina are aware that pilgrims from Libya or Tunisia may prefer "Qalun 'an Nafi',' that sojourners from Algeria and Morocco may be more interested in procuring "Warsh 'an Nafi',' or that travellers from West Africa and Sudan would rather have "Abu 'Amr Ibn al-'Ala' 'an Hafs al-Duri" and may cater to them in their Qur'anic production to a certain degree, but most publications that come out of the King Fahd Complex in practice promote only one *qira'a*.

So Qur'anic printing has had an impact on the spread of a particular reading school that constitutes part of a religious regional identity. Historically, this was already the case when Osman Zeki Bey printed his *Mushaf* Hafiz 'Uthman, which also followed "Hafs 'an 'Asim," while many readers in Turkey at that time followed the Maghrebi school of recitation. Bey's nicely executed edition quickly became popular and decreased the presence of the Nafi' school in the country and increased the popularity of "Hafs 'an 'Asim." Similarly, nowadays the spread of *Mushaf* al-Madina is problematic in northwestern Africa, where Warsh has historically been the established *qira'a*, resulting in governmental efforts to control the circulation of the *Mushaf* al-Madina in order to promote their locally produced *mushafs* containing the regional school of reading. A similar situation has taken place in Sudan, where *qira'at* al-Duri used to be widespread but now competes with "Hafs 'an 'Asim."

For average Egyptian Muslim practitioners (middle-class literates), such nuances are beside the point. After all, variant schools of reading are not essential in any way to the ideal of unity of the Muslim community often expressed in casual conversations. They are at stake, though, for scholars, and reciters in particular, who in 1971 at the Sixth Symposium of Islamic Research Academy were still affirming the importance of a diversity of Qur'anic readings, stating:

> In regard to schools of Qur'anic reading the [members] of the Symposium have decided that the variants are not [a matter of individual] discretion but of revelation, and they depend on the unbroken [chains] of narrations [*al-ruwayat al-mutawatira*]. (…)
>
> The [members] of the Symposium encourage the reciters of the Glorious Qur'an not to limit themselves to the reading of Hafs only but to safeguard from oblivion and extinction all the established schools of reading.[21]

These nuances are also at stake for those who choose to create *mushafs* for Moroccan or Sudanese markets. Yet, the changes in the preferences for this or that particular school of recitation would not occur as swiftly in certain regions without the help of printed books and their materially mediated orthographies.

Orthographic Reforms

Let us now return to the question of why Muslim *'ulama'* at the Islamic Research Academy time and again advocated strict adherence to the unaltered orthography of the Qur'anic text and why they have been so particular about the accuracy of printed *mushafs*. In the opinion of these scholars, only the 'Uthmanic *rasm* should constitute an orthographic template for contemporary *mushafs*. It is true that this position conforms to the opinion of most, though not all, classical scholars. Yet to say that merely the weight of tradition affects the scholars' opinions would be simplistic. What complicates matters is that the text's original orthography is mainly known through works and commentaries written by later scholars, and there is no consensus about whether a few manuscripts known as true 'Uthmanic copies were, in fact, written in the Caliph's time. Concerns about how to inscribe the words of the message in the most accurate way preoccupied the Muslim *'ulama'* during Islam's first few centuries, but interest somewhat abated later as other, more pressing problems needed attention from scholars and theologians. Yet this problem came back with new urgency alongside the growing use of print technology in the nineteenth century and with the language reforms contemplated by members of the Arabic Language Academy in Cairo[22] at the beginning of the twentieth century.

In Chapter 3, I spoke about attempts to modernize Arabic font at al-Amiriya and the frictions that arose between the calligrapher designing the letter casts and other more pragmatically oriented officials involved in the project. This dispute had as a backdrop other debates surrounding the Arabic language in general. One of the most crucial issues at that time was (and still is) related to the footing of Egyptian spoken dialect (*'amiyya*) vis-à-vis its literary register—modern standard Arabic (*fusha*). The former was commonly spoken in the country while the latter was taught at schools and used by the intelligentsia and the media. This meant that a large percentage of the population in Egypt did not have a working knowledge of the literary language that, although initially bound to the Qur'an, also had evolved and changed, as did its use (for instance, some inflections were dropped even from spoken *fusha*). Different ideas of how to ameliorate these language problems started emerging at the turn of the twentieth century.

Perhaps the debates about reforms to the Arabic alphabet that had already surfaced in the second half of the nineteenth century in the Ottoman Empire, and intensified significantly at the beginning of the twentieth century, were fueling similar discussions in Egypt. Of course, in Turkey the language matters looked quite different. Unlike Arabic, the Turkish language belonged to a non-Semitic linguistic group. So, in order to write Turkish words in Arabic script, some of the letters of the Arabic alphabet had to be modified to accommodate Turkish sounds that are nonexistent in Arabic. But Turks did not have the same ethnic or cultural affection for Arabic script that Arabs do. Arabic as a language was intimately connected to the story of the rise of the *umma*, the Muslim community that was only later joined by the Turks. "Adopting" the Arabic script (by the Turks) does not create the same passion as "emerging" with the Arabic script (by Arabs), even if that script later became an important element in the construction of Turkish culture and religion. Additionally, Kemal Atatürk's aggressive politics of modernization was ready to appropriate any arguments—such as the incompatibility of the Arabic alphabet with the use of the telegraph[23]—that would promote a swift transition to the Latin script, which he saw as a tool of development and a symbol of a new allegiance with Europe.

In Egypt, similar debates about ushering modernity in via script reform took place in the first half of the twentieth century.[24] As a result, a bold motion to relinquish the Arabic alphabet and to replace it with the Latin script was proposed by a prominent lawyer, diplomat, and poet, 'Abd al-'Aziz Fahmi (1870–1951), at the conference of the Arabic Language Academy in Cairo in 1941.[25] But after a serious discussion of the motion, the Academy rejected the proposal. Fahmi's plan was extremely radical, especially considering that only two decades earlier—in 1917—the Sheikhdom of al-Azhar had issued a decision that forbade, under penalty of confiscation, the printing and distribution of *mushafs* that did not follow the 'Uthmanic *rasm*.[26] Indeed, if the proposal to adopt the Latin alphabet in other areas of life had been accepted, such a shift would have put the Qur'anic text in the peculiar situation of being a calligraphically obsolete writ. More moderate proposals, submitted to a contest organized by the Academy in 1940s, opted for a preservation of the Arabic alphabet but suggested that orthography be modified to reflect the dialect spoken in Egypt.[27] Their authors were of the opinion that traditional spelling was becoming increasingly unrepresentative of people's speech, and so they urged its reform. Updated orthography would make reading easier, they argued—especially reading the Qur'an. Some promoters of language reform compared their efforts to modernize the Arabic language to a "religious revolution—like the Protestant Reformation" that would free the Qur'anic text from the constraints of traditional orthography.[28] In support of their cause, they emphasized that nothing in the Qur'an explicitly and irrevocably indicated that it had to be written according to any particular *rasm*. As long as the printed signs pointed a reader to the correct pronunciation, their format should not matter and could be changed as needed.[29]

None of these reforms, although carefully discussed at al-Azhar, were ultimately accepted. But if the need to modernize orthography was so pressing, what were the reasons behind the reluctance to revise the Qur'an's spelling? First of all, *'ulama'* who defended the 'Uthmanic way of writing relied on the opinions of earlier scholars who had faced similar questions and had to resolve a similar quandary about whether or not the 'Uthmanic *rasm* could be updated. In order to accept or reject changes, experts first had to define the nature of Qur'anic spelling itself: was it merely a human-made tool to record the divine words (*al-rasm al-istilahi*—a matter of convention) or was it a part of the revelation itself (*al-rasm al-tawqifi*—a matter of revelation) and, as such, unchangeable in any circumstances? With a few exceptions (the most famous of them being Abu Bakr al-Baqillani and Ibn Khaldun), most classical scholars were inclined to see *al-rasm al-'Uthmani* as revealed.[30] This meant that the text's written representation was part of Allah's plan to preserve the message intact; therefore, it was something that people should not tinker with. But even among those who did not believe in the divinity of Qur'anic orthography, some scholars preferred to preserve the 'Uthmanic spelling because of its value as a historical artifact or because the consensus of the *umma* (Muslim community) had always counted a great deal in any decision-making process. The Prophet's companions wrote the message under his guidance, many argued, and Muhammad's followers agreed with its form, so it would be unwise to change it. Besides, the scholars who seriously considered the issue asked: with what *rasm* should we replace the previous spelling? Language evolves and once updated the Qur'an would require constant revisions, revisions that might open the door to other, undesirable changes. A small group of scholars—'Az al-Din Ibn

'Abd al-Salam and Badr al-Din al-Zarkashi were among them—took the middle ground, suggesting that an updated spelling was permissible in *mushafs* written for the benefit of the public but the original orthography should be preserved in the texts used by the *'ulama'* and specialists as a "psychological heritage" that had been preserved by the previous generations.[31]

Clearly, any decision to keep or to change the 'Uthmanic *rasm* would consequently entail more adjustments and demand even more answers in other areas of Qur'anic knowledge. Most prominently, if the spelling were modified, what was to be done with the "mysterious letters" that open some chapters of the Qur'anic text? These combinations of single letters stand at the beginning of twenty-nine out of a hundred and fourteen *suras* (chapters) and have puzzled Muslim scholars for centuries. For example, the twentieth *sura* starts with two letters *ta* and *ha* (طه) that by themselves constitute the chapter's first verse. The *sura* itself is titled after them and is called Surat Ta Ha. Surat al-Shu'ara' (chapter twenty-eight) begins with *ta*, *sa*, and *mim* (طسم) and Surat Ghafir (chapter forty) has as its first verse *ha mim* (حم). These letters are recited along with the rest of the text. All Muslims consider them a part of the revelation, although there have been many different explanations as to what meaning they have or what their role might be. Some scholars suggested that they stood for abbreviations of the names of Allah or the Prophet, others that the letters signified abbreviated titles for the chapters or the ways to mark the separation of one chapter from another. Those who have participated in more esoteric trends in Islam saw the isolated letters as mystical signs with symbolic meaning based on the numerical values assigned to the letters. What everybody has agreed upon is that nobody could confidently explain why they were there. As it was difficult to decide the relation between the mysterious letters and the message, scholars concluded that it was better to leave them where the first scribes had placed them.

However, such a conclusion also led to another conundrum: if these letters had a potential symbolic meaning, perhaps the same was true of other letters in words that did not follow the rules of conventional orthography. More precisely, what should be done with instances of words in the Qur'anic text that had alternative ways of being spelled and, depending on the *sura*, were written according to two different orthographic rules? Any changes to the *rasm*, then, were not simply a matter of discarding traditional spelling and embracing an easier, modern one. Updating Qur'anic orthography required a rejection of a considerable body of theological thought and speculation developed over the centuries in this particular field of study. No wonder, then, that the decision whether to adhere to or update orthodox spelling was from the beginning fraught with difficulties and uncertainty.

There is also the matter of less canonical but traditional exercises Qur'anic readers have been performing in math and the Qur'anic text. Although Muslim scholars have not considered the knowledge of numerical equations based on the length of particular words in the Qur'an or formulas of how often they appeared in the text as part of official Qur'anic training, mathematical exercises of this sort, popular in the past, have nonetheless become even more in vogue with the increased use of computers. They have to do with not only the number of letters in words but also the overall organization of the Qur'anic text. In size, the Qur'an is roughly equal to the

New Testament. It is arranged in 114 chapters—*suras*—of unequal length. The longest *sura* (*al-Baqara*—*The Cow*) consists of 286 verses while the shortest one—*al-Kawthar* (*Abundance*)—consists of a mere ten words divided into three brief verses. The word *sura* derives from the root *s-w-r* that means a wall or enclosure that marks off a space. Except for *suras* eight (*al-Anfal*) and nine (*al-Tawba*), all other chapters of the Qur'an are separated from one another by the *basmala* invocation: "In the name of God, the Most Merciful and Compassionate."

Suras are divided into *ayas*. The word *aya* means divine revelation or a divine sign, but it also denotes a Qur'anic verse. The order of verses, or *ayas*, in each *sura* is believed to have been fixed by the Prophet himself. But the non-chronological order of the *suras* themselves was made by the original compilers of the 'Uthmanic *mushaf*, copyist Zayd and his collaborators. Generally speaking, they arranged the *suras* by length, so that although the book begins with *Surat al-Fatiha* (*Opening*), consisting of seven short verses, it is followed by the lengthy *The Cow* chapter and other long *suras*. Chronologically, the earliest revealed *suras* were placed mostly at the end of the *mushaf*. What is important for our discussion is to note that any changes done to the spelling of the words might throw off the computations between words, *ayas* and *suras*. In these calculations, the number nineteen has a particular importance. For instance, the invocation "In the name of God, the Most Merciful and Compassionate" contains words repeated in other parts of the Qur'an:

The word "name" *ism* is repeated 1 time
The word "God" *Allah* is repeated 2698 times = 19 × 142
The word "All-merciful" *al-rahman* is repeated 57 times = 19 × 3
The word "Compassionate" *al-rahim* is repeated 114 times = 19 × 6

If we add 1+142+3+6 we get a total of 152 which can also be divided by nineteen.[32] The same number nineteen is repeated in other combinations. For instance, the last revealed *sura* has nineteen words and the first *aya* has nineteen letters, etc.

Although these mathematical minutiae were not essential to the decision to preserve Qur'anic orthography, twentieth-century Egyptian scholars of *rasm* were familiar with them as well as other arguments against any changes of spelling. They examined different opinions expressed by classical *'ulama'*, carefully evaluating the effects of each potential decision. Moreover, they added a new, uniquely modern argument to the discussion: a broader concern for the preservation of Arab and Muslim culture, of which the Qur'an has been the source and the epitome. Within this argument, Qur'anic orthography represents the linguistic heritage of pre-Muslim Arabs that has contributed to the development of the Muslim faith and sciences. As such, the preservation of Qur'anic orthography not only spoke to theological concerns but also became an object of historical continuity immersed in the discourse of Arab unity and nationalism.

That said, the Language Academy's 1941 rejection of the proposals to modernize the Arabic language and the following decision by the *'ulama'* regarding modernizing the script used for the Qur'an did not close the subject altogether. Every so often, the matter would resuscitate to produce more debates and pronouncements. So when members of the Islamic Research Academy convened for their Sixth Symposium in March of 1971, one point of discussion was a research paper submitted by Muhammad Abu Shahabah, Dean of the College of Fundamentals of Islam[33] at al-Azhar University (Asyut branch), entitled "The *Rasm* of 'Uthmanic *Masahif*." Abu Shahabah presented the members of the symposium with a summary of his research on the history of the 'Uthmanic *rasm* and its rules, in which he once more reviewed earlier scholars' opinions about the revealed nature of this *rasm*, the benefits of its preservation, and the outcome of research by some Orientalist scholars on the subject. After a fresh consideration of the issue, the Academy delivered this memorandum: "The (members) of the Symposium recommend that Muslims abide by [the rules of] *al-rasm al-'Uthmani* in the Noble *Mushaf*, protecting it from distortion."[34] On the whole, the *'ulama'* at the Symposium affirmed the revealed character of the Qur'anic orthography. The memorandum they issued once again blocked any attempts to do away with the 'Uthmanic *rasm*. This decision carried extra weight, as the sheikhs gathered at the conference were to represent the consensus of the Muslim scholarly community, or at least its majority, in religious matters for the rest of the Muslim world.

Another round of conversations on this topic were published in 2002 in *Majallat al-Azhar*, a prominent journal and outlet for Azhari scholars. In three separate articles, three specialists of Qur'anic *rasm* expressed their views on three issues: why 'Uthmanic *rasm* should be preserved, why common spelling should not be implemented, and why writing Qur'anic text in Latin letters is not merited.[35] Again, after reviewing the pros and cons of each alternative, the importance of following the 'Uthmanic *rasm* was confirmed.

And yet there is one caveat that keeps the conversation going. The conventional, as opposed to traditional, way of writing a difficult text—and the Qur'anic text is grammatically complex—simply allows students to learn faster. Also, for education and convenience the text of the Qur'an is broken down into portions (*ajza'*) to facilitate memorizing and studying. Such *ajza'* have been commonly published since the nineteenth century and notices of their existence are mentioned in various compilations of early published book titles in Egypt. Perhaps such utilitarian copies of the Qur'anic text were also the reason why the need to print a thoroughly researched and academically endorsed edition of the Qur'an arose at the beginning of the twentieth century.

The idea that certain accommodations with the Qur'anic text can be made for the purpose of teaching has its roots in the *hadith*. The most common source is one discussed by al-Din al-Sakhawi (831 AH/1428 CE–902 AH/1497 CE) in his explanation of the work of Abu Ishaq al-Shatibi (720 AH/1320 CE–790 AH/1388 CE), who maintained that Malik Ibn Anas (93 AH/711 CE–179 AH/795 CE) was once asked whether a *mushaf* should be written in the then contemporary *rasm*. Malik replied that he didn't think so and that the calligrapher should follow the 'Uthmanic *rasm*. However, Malik also recognized the wisdom behind adding diacritics to the original text. Out of these conversations about the need to preserve the Qur'anic text as close to what was understood to be the original inscription and the need to teach the Qur'an correctly came a conclusion that for certain purposes—like educating children or taking notes—not all of the orthographic rules need to be followed and certain conventional rules can be applied. For that reason, the *Mufti*, Sheikh 'Ali Goma'a, stated in one of his opinions that it was permissible to write a Qur'anic verse according to conventional orthography for personal purposes. His reasoning was that the original *mushaf* did not contain many of the markings that were added to it over time for the purpose of correct learning and understanding, so the same logic should apply in reverse to any contemporary situation in which a person is studying the Qur'an for personal edification.

Azhari scholars were not the only ones who have debated the problem of Qur'anic spelling. The Organization of Senior Scholars of the Kingdom of Saudi Arabia[36] also held a conference on the same subject in the 1990s. Their Committee for Scientific Research and *Fatwa* carried out preliminary research that was presented at the symposium.[37] After consideration of the materials prepared by the Committee, the Organization confirmed the view that Caliph 'Uthman had ordered a codification of the Qur'anic text and had ensured that it be written in a particular way, and generations of Muslims that had followed him had consented to this decision. A move to a modern orthography, the Organization opined, would entail constant amendments to the text as vernacular language evolved. Over time, these changes would lead to growing discrepancies between *mushafs* from different parts of the Muslim world, and to possible friction, which would "turn the book of Allah into a toy in human hands." Because of such apprehensions, the Senior Scholars found it preferable to preserve the 'Uthmanic *rasm* and not to modify it according to the rules of contemporary

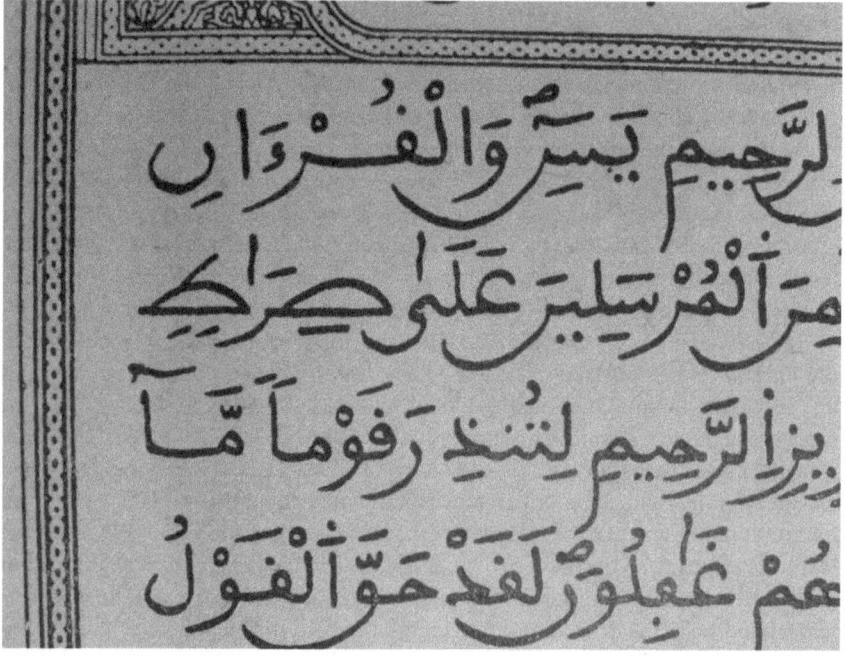

Figure 9 *Mushaf* in a Moroccan style printed at Subih in 1952. Its diacritics and calligraphic style are visibly different from *Mushaf* Fu'ad.

orthography, thus protecting the Qur'anic text from any "distortion." This decision, known as Decision No. 71, was consequently confirmed by other scholars of religious jurisprudence in the Kingdom, published in a scholarly journal,[38] and announced in the newspapers.

Rasm and Technology

The proclamations made by both the Egyptian *'ulama'* and the Saudi Council had a direct impact on the production of *mushafs* in these two countries and—by extension—the rest of the Muslim world. For publishers, to adhere to the 'Uthmanic *rasm* meant that, unlike all other books, templates for *mushafs* still had to be handmade by calligraphers schooled in Qur'anic orthography. This was so because of the technical difficulties in replicating the 'Uthmanic *rasm* via the letterpress technology available in the second half of the twentieth century. The texts of regular books were assembled using already simplified typeset fonts. This task did not require any specialized knowledge beyond that of the profession of printing. But when it came to the Qur'anic text, the use of *tashkil* not applied in common print made production much more demanding.

These difficulties were not alleviated by the introduction of computerized printing. For a long time after the establishment of digital printing systems, publishing houses in Egypt, and in other countries as well, continued to photocopy written Qur'anic texts. There were two reasons for this time-consuming practice. First, until the end of the twentieth century, the complexity of Arabic script made it impossible to create computerized graphic design programs that could successfully imitate the 'Uthmanic orthography with all of its diacritics and other signs added to the text to facilitate reading. (I will return to this problem of digital design in coming chapters.) Second, photocopying a written or already-printed text allowed publishers to be sure that their *mushafs* did not contain any typeset errors. Of course, the book still had to go through all the steps required by the *Mushaf* Committee to secure permits for printing and distribution. But scanning a handwritten text meant that the publishing house could start their production with a template less likely to contain mistakes and one that included all of the proper signs in the right places. So this was still preferable to the new (but primitive) computerized printing that was available at that time.

The continuing decision of the Azhari *'ulama'* to preserve the old orthographic system must not be an easy one to maintain. Despite the views of classical writers, there were (and are) scholars who support changes in the spelling. However, the official decision to adhere to the 'Uthmanic *rasm* has created additional pressure on members of organizations supervising the production of *mushafs* to make sure that the text's compliance with the 'Uthmanic *rasm* is upheld in all circumstances. Therefore, it has become a common practice to include in the *mushaf*'s appendix a paragraph stating that this particular *mushaf* follows the 'Uthmanic *rasm*—although I have never come across a contemporary *mushaf* that would be printed in any other style of orthography. So this particular note may not mean much to practitioners without an Azhari education. In fact, when I asked lay Muslims about *al-rasm al-'Uthmani* they often thought that it referred to an Ottoman style of calligraphy (in Arabic called *al-khatt al-'Uthmani*), or they referred me to a sheikh or a student from al-Azhar as being someone more likely to know something definitive about this subject.

This limited familiarity with the rules of 'Uthmanic *rasm* leads to various issues. Scholars must oversee not only *how* the Qur'anic message is written (or printed) but also *who* writes it or prints it. Obviously, a person without proper Qur'anic training is more likely to make a mistake. In this context, the critical reactions of the *'ulama'* to the Qur'anic quote on Claudia Schiffer's dress mentioned in Chapter 2 become even more understandable. To all the previous arguments against such use and display of the Qur'anic text already mentioned in Chapter 2, one might add one more: a Qur'anic text applied for its aesthetic quality by a non-practitioner as a decorative motif may be in danger of following an unauthorized simplified orthography. A text displayed in these circumstances not only does not evoke either its proper sound or its meaning for those who look at the dress (a dress is not a fabric to be read—at least not in the conventional sense of this word) but is also likely to have its graphic form altered. As I have already noted, although not all *'ulama'* would find contemporary spelling offensive, such changes should only take place within their proper context of scholarship and/or devotion.

In this chapter, I sketched out some of the discussions surrounding the ways in which the Qur'anic message is mediated through its orthography. As we could see, these concerns did not suddenly appear with the introduction of printing but had already belonged to a long tradition of scholarship focused on the visual form of the Qur'an. In Qur'anic orthography, the aesthetic interests of the calligraphers intersected with theological questions about the nature of script as a medium pondered by the Muslim (especially Arab) scholars. In fact, their attention to the problem of spelling indicates, in my opinion, a considerable dose of pragmatism mixed with an understanding that the Qur'anic message cannot be easily separated from its written (or printed) text. In other words, the meaning of the message was *and* is also grounded in its textual form, as opposed to the modern approaches to text that, while looking for meaning, tend to disregard the form. In fact, the importance of the way in which the Qur'anic text is mediated by physical objects like orthography will become even more obvious when I discuss another decision made by Azhari scholars in the mid-twentieth century—a decision to print the Qur'anic text in Braille. Here, instead of ink, the makers and the custodians of the Qur'anic text had to deal with a very different orthographic medium—perforated cardboard.

6

What Eyes Cannot See but Hands Can Touch: The *Mushaf* Braille

The decision to render the Qur'anic message in Braille is a watershed in thinking about the Qur'an as a uniquely aural phenomenon. Before the Braille *mushaf*, a sight-impaired or blind person could know the Qur'an only through its acoustic mediators, and for centuries, the primary acoustic mediator was a reciter. In the twentieth century, though, the live human voice was reproduced and multiplied by electronic audio devices. Visually impaired Muslims could use all of these, but with the choice to make the Qur'anic message available in Braille, vision-impaired practitioners were given a chance to become familiar with the Qur'an through a different medium in the form of perforated paper. In other words, they were offered a way to *read* the Qur'an. I am not suggesting that from that point on the Qur'an ceased to be a message highly reliant on the mediation of sound. To the contrary, the chanted words of the Qur'an, produced by a reciter or disseminated by various electronic audio media, still constitute a ubiquitous element of Cairo's religious landscape.[1] An image I associate with this phenomenon is that of a man (sometimes a woman) riding the metro and listening to a cell phone held next to his ear, his eyes closed, the chanting itself audible for other passengers as well. Over the last decades the practice of Qur'anic recitation has become even more popular, thanks to the growth of religious programming, internet sites promoting recitation, and recitation competitions broadcast internationally. But the decision to make the message available for blind and sight-impaired Muslims via perforated paper suggests that, apart from listening, *reading* the Qur'anic text has become an integral way of knowing it in modern times. According to some classical Muslim scholars, to read the Qur'an out loud was always the ideal, but few could attain this in the past. Now, with growing levels of literacy in Egypt and the easy availability of *mushafs* on the market, it has become the norm.

However, Braille is a tactile writing system that relies on combinations of raised dots grouped in rectangular blocks (or cells) to represent various sounds, the way the graphic design of a written letter represents a sound. But in Braille, these arrangements of tiny, palpable bumps, though acting like letters, do not resemble the graphemes of the Arabic alphabet and none of the rules of Arabic calligraphy can be applied to them. For example, all blocks (or cells) filled with indentations representing different letters are of the same size. They are also separate, and—in contrast to the letters of the Arabic alphabet—each cell/letter has only one form instead of three. Most of all,

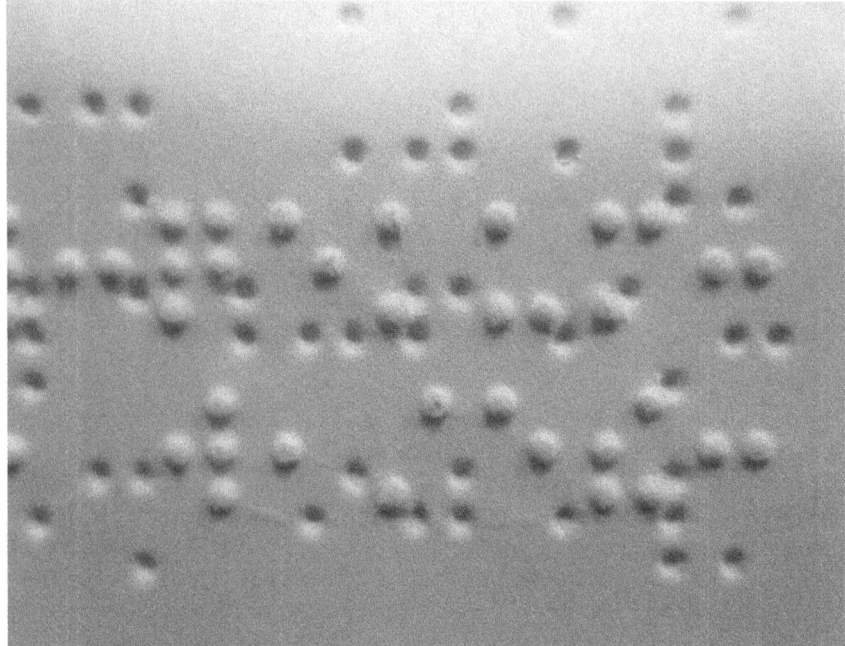

Figure 10 *Mushaf* in Braille.

they cannot be arranged into a main script line with smaller markings placed around it. In other words, Braille is not a *rasm*. For that reason, the decision to use Braille to disseminate the Qur'anic message can be contrasted to the polemics surrounding the issue of 'Uthmanic writing. After all, the same arguments against changing the graphic format of the Qur'anic text can be mustered against a *mushaf* in Braille. And yet the *Mushaf* Braille exists with the approval of Muslim scholars. So if the orthography of a printed *mushaf* cannot be altered, what arguments prompted the *'ulama'* to allow the use of a completely different writing system in *mushafs* for the visually impaired? Is a *mushaf* in Braille a *mushaf* at all? (Figure 10).

Another Point of View

I had passed by the al-Azhar University gate next to al-Husseyn Mosque many times on my way to other places, never crossing under its arches to the other side. In fact, I was not allowed to enter the campus without permission from the Azhari authorities. This time, though, I had permission to enter from the Dean of the College so that I could use the library there. Approaching the gate, I expected a routine set of questions from the security officers standing by the decorated iron bars. But the guard silently wrote down my name in a big book laying on the shaky table next to the wall that surrounded the university and the mosque, and let me in without further inquiry. The fringes of my head scarf were getting tangled in the bag strap on my shoulder so I kept shifting the veil, nervously holding onto the fabric with one hand and my bag with the other. This place made me uneasy, perhaps because I could palpably sense the unabashed interest of men's gazes from every corner of the courtyard. I certainly felt out of place on this predominantly male campus.

I found the library of the College of Islamic Fundamentals in a big, new building opposite the Department of Arabic Language. It was comprised of two rooms. The first had rows of stands along the walls, each holding books, and big, wooden tables crouching heavily in the center of the room. A few students were sitting in a group, talking to each other and laughing merrily. The librarian, who was reading a newspaper at the desk in front of the room, listened to my explanation about the purpose of my visit—to look for sources related to Qur'anic printing—and then asked one of the young men to assist me. The somber-looking student gave me a hesitant look, took a deep breath, and quickly recited what was evidently a memorized lesson on why 'Uthmanic *rasm* was *tawqifi* (divinely inspired). He ended his speech with the sudden and non sequitur assertion that Islam in its inception spread without violence, and immediately left the room, as if worried that I might ask him some questions.

The librarian observed us from a distance. He smiled with encouragement. "Now, go to the other room," he said, "and ask for help there." I crossed the hallway into a place that looked very similar to the first one. There was only one sheikh sitting at the table, making some notes in a simple, lined binder. The librarian working in that room asked him to spare me some time. "Doctor" Tareq was a matter-of-fact person and without much small talk led me to see his thesis supervisor, Sheikh Muhammad. We walked up to the first floor but Sheikh Muhammad was at a meeting. So I returned to the basement. Meanwhile, the second librarian accosted another person and cheerfully waved at me to come closer and meet the professor of *qira'at* (schools of reading), Dr. Yousri Ga'far, who immediately burst out with questions and advice. "You need to know about the *mushaf* in Braille," he said as his eyes wandered around the room. "We have to meet again. Not today. The library is closing soon. Tomorrow." It was Dr. Yousri's personal investment in this particular *mushaf* that opened up to me an entirely new dimension of the material mediation of the Qur'anic text.

Early the next day, I came to the library of the Kolleyat Usul al-Din. The librarian, *Ustaz* Shirif, and his coworker were just having breakfast and, having made sure that I was not hungry, let me browse the stacks. The newer part of the room looked neat and clean and was evidently used by students on daily basis. The back part contained uncatalogued books stacked in piles and on the shelves, some of them quite old, judging by the way the metal font casts perforated the pages, a feature characteristic to many books printed before the twentieth century. I enjoyed running my fingers over their yellowing pages, trying to decipher the ornamental titles that spoke to the concerns of people more than a century ago. A few students were sitting at the desk, working on an assignment and throwing furtive looks in my direction.

When Dr. Yousri came, he was greeted with joyous *salaams* by everyone in the room. He sat at the table in front of me. Sipping hot tea from a thick glass brought by *Ustaz* Shirif, he began with an unanticipated revelation. "I do not believe that *al-rasm al-'Uthmani* is *tawqifi*," he said bluntly. His words took me by surprise. "I think that whatever helps you read the Qur'an correctly is right. If it's a contemporary spelling, so be it." I did not expect to hear such an open contradiction of the prevailing opinion about the nature of the Qur'anic *rasm* from a member of the faculty. But Dr. Yousri was not a sheikh and he did not favor the "traditionalistic," as he described it, position of many Azhari sheikhs on the issue of *rasm*. "The traditionalists are used to only one way of thinking," he shook his head, sighing, "and it has affected decisions made about the *mushaf* in Braille. The discussions about printing this *mushaf* started in the fifties or sixties," he felt with his right hand for the glass on the table and sipped from it again as he talked,

> but not all sheikhs supported it. They thought that if such a *mushaf* were written according to *al-rasm al-'Uthmani* it would make Muslims incorrectly read the words that were spelled one way but read another.[2] They also could not decide what to do with the *tashkil* (diacritics) and chose to print the *rasm* in one line and the rest of the diacritics in the other. Reading from that *mushaf* was to be taught by memorization. It meant that students were to repeat the words after the teacher. But the opportunities to learn that way came to nothing, as there were fewer and fewer Qur'anic schools. People began listening to audiotapes and mobile phones, and Braille lost its relevance. Anyway, the blind always prefer to learn from hearing. But at the same time people initiated discussions about whether to adhere to the *rasm* of the *mushaf* or to replace it with a spelling that reflected the pronunciation. There was a lot of talking surrounding this subject.

He pulled out a cell phone from the pocket of his gray suit and called the department of audio recordings. "Let's go and see a copy of the *mushaf* in Braille printed here in Cairo," he said. We walked to another building, but a female librarian sitting at the desk informed us that they had none. Dr. Yousri winced. Obviously trying to make up for the bad news, he said, "Why don't you come and see my *mushafs* then?" We left the department and caught a taxi to Nasser City. Dr. Yousri's wife greeted us at the door of their apartment and, somewhat surprised, collected his *mushafs* from the bookshelves filling out the sitting room. Their white Persian cat, Mishmish, eyed me and the stack of books arranged by her on the coffee table.

"They printed a *Mushaf* Braille in Jordan." Dr. Yousri continued, sitting himself comfortably on a red, velvety sofa by the pile of *mushafs*.

> Scholars there also disagreed on this subject. This edition, like the one we printed in Cairo had a problem too. It came in six volumes and was too large to handle. This did not facilitate its reading, but they kept it as a "specimen."[3] It was printed according to the modern spelling; it was not constrained by the limitations of the 'Uthmanic *rasm*. Still, you needed a teacher to learn how to recite it.

Dr. Yousri's *mushafs* were new, printed mostly in the last couple of decades. He felt for them on the table. A few were made abroad. I noticed that some of them had twelve lines of text per page, others fifteen or seventeen. These were standard numbers. Even in that matter readers had different preferences, said my host, holding one of them very close to his face to count the lines.

> It helps to always recite from the same *mushaf*. Here in Egypt, we uphold the tradition of good recitation. Also in Indonesia. I have tapes by an Indonesian sheikh who beautifully recites with *al-muqamat* [particular voice intonations depending on the content of the sentence]. This is an Egyptian art, nonexistent in Saudi Arabia. In Egypt, there is a quality of scholarship on the Qur'an. You know of the museum at Sayeda Zaynab Mosque. They have a very old *mushaf* made in the times of the Prophet's Companions. It is said to be the *mushaf* of 'Uthman Ibn 'Affan, but I am not confident about it because one should not speak with certainty without documented proof. The scholarly research needs to be authenticated.

This kind of attention to details and accuracy has caused Dr. Yousri to grumble about the common confusion of *rasm al-mushaf* with *al-rasm al-'Uthmani*.[4] "It is not correct to call the contemporary *rasm* of the Qur'anic book *al-rasm al-'Uthmani*," he explained,

> because all of the diacritics used in contemporary *mushafs* [*tashkil*, *i'rab*, *i'jam*, and other signs] were not written in the *mushafs* produced at the time of the third Caliph 'Uthman; they were added only later by scholars with a purpose of improving the recitation. Also, those who inscribed the message did it according to the rules of orthography prevalent at that time, which does not mean that these rules cannot be changed.

In the light of these arguments, Dr. Yousri's endorsement for the so-called "*Mushaf Braille*" was not surprising. "You have to see it," he insisted, making arrangements to visit the library at Mosque al-Nur the next day in the morning.

Mosque al-Nur in al-'Abbasiyya square cannot be missed even from afar. Its two slender minarets tower well over the roofs of the surrounding buildings and highway overpasses. They resemble sharp pencils reaching to the sky as if ready to draw the outlines of the white, domed mosque. It is simultaneously a place of prayer and a bustling center of academic and political life. Here many specialists in services for Muslims with disabilities work, and the mosque's library holds a copy of the Egyptian edition of *mushaf* in Braille.

Next day, I waited for Dr. Yousri on the old campus of al-Azhar outside his departmental building, trying to warm up in the pale November sun while transcribing some documents on my laptop. A security man came up to me and asked what I was doing there. I said I was waiting for Dr. Yousri and he left me, apologizing for the interruption. Not wanting to draw more attention, I went back to his department and sat on the floor in an empty hall in front of the main office. A sheikh came out of a classroom nearby and, seeing me sitting on the floor, ordered a worker to bring a chair. Instead, the men inside the office invited me to come in. Some men wore *abayas* and some wore Western clothes, but all left their shoes at the edge of the ornamental carpet by the door to the office. A Saudi sheikh, conspicuous in the group because of his white *thawb* (robe), was also waiting for Dr. Yousri. He had once been Dr. Yousri's student but now was a professor at the university in Mecca. After finding out that I am not a *Muslima*, another man, sitting next to me on the opposite side, began a casual conversation about Jesus, unexpectedly asking, "So, how can you believe that Allah may have children?" and unapologetically demanding a response. A few minutes later, Dr. Yousri walked into the office. He must have heard us talk. Teasing the man humorously, he said, "It would have been better if you discussed her research." We left to a chorus of *ma'assalamas* (good-byes).

The Saudi professor walked out with us. Hearing that my research had to do with the Qur'an, he gallantly invited me to come to Mecca. Before I managed to think of an equally courteous reply, Dr. Yousri interjected, quickly changing the subject to the advantages and disadvantages of using the Egyptian dialect. His Saudi visitor had a taxi waiting for him, but Dr. Yousri and I took the metro to Abbasiyya to the Mosque al-Nur. Unfortunately, Sheikh 'Abd al-Rahim, who was responsible for *Mushaf* Braille, was not feeling good and had gone home before our arrival. The library was closed. Dr. Yousri was agitated, having expected the sheikh to call him about cancelling our meeting. After a few minutes of deliberation, he came up with another plan: "Let's go to the Center for the Blind in Nasser City."

The Center was located on the ground floor of a tall, administrative building. A few customers quietly went about their business, creating a monotonous buzz of voices and audio recordings. We approached a woman sitting at the computer and helping one of the visitors. She finished her search for the other petitioner and brought us four *mushafs*: Egyptian, Saudi, Kuwaiti, and Tunisian. The Egyptian edition was the oldest. It did not have a date but looked as if it had been produced in the 1950s or 1960s. It followed the system described earlier by Dr. Yousri in which the perforations for *tashkil* were placed above the line of consonants. I turned its thick, perforated pages that looked like strips of an old-fashioned computer printout. An Azhari student from the College of Fundamentals of Islam joined us at the table and offered to help us decipher the differences between the *mushafs*. I watched him run his fingers over the little bumps covering the pages. He was moving his palms from left to right. I had a fleeting thought, "He is reading in the wrong direction …," but then I realized that the Braille letters were arranged in the direction opposite to Arabic script. They were, as in the Western system of writing, oriented from left to right. The *Mushaf* Braille was very large in size, making it difficult for the librarian to bring all six volumes at once. Unlike Arabic books, it opened on the right side, like Western books. The front page was printed in regular Arabic script. I noticed that the print itself must have been typeset. The letters had minute cracks and lacked precision; occasional blobs of ink made them thick and blurred. Once again, it was obvious why calligraphers were not enamored when the Qur'anic message originally appeared in typeset format.

The Saudi *Mushaf* Braille was much smaller in size, although still larger than a regular book. It was almost new, printed in 2006 at the request of the Ministry of Education by the Press of the Custodian of Two Noble Mosques.[5] I recognized its green covers from pictures in the news posted on Saudi websites.[6] This particular edition had already reached its fourth reprint.[7] Both the Saudi and Kuwaiti *Mushafs* Braille followed a different system of text arrangement than the Egyptian one. Here *tashkil*, instead of being placed in a separate line, were interspersed between the consonants.⁸ Drawn by our voices, a few other visitors to the Center gathered around the table. Someone said, "This system is harder to read than the Egyptian arrangement." Others agreed. It surprised me, as in my mind reading one line of perforation seemed to be easier than reading two simultaneously. I asked the Azhari student how he learned to read the Qur'an in Braille and he replied that he knew some from al-Azhar. But after a moment of hesitation he grumbled under his breath, "It is hard to find someone there who can teach it to the students..." The Center's Tunisian *Mushaf* Braille was in *qira'at Qalun* but followed the *tashkil/rasm* arrangement of the Saudi *mushaf*.

The 1950s edition of the Egyptian *Mushaf* Braille, in spite of the disagreements that surrounded its publication, was not an isolated attempt to distribute the Qur'an in Braille. There was another reprint (or maybe reprints) that, according to Dr. Yousri, was also rather imperfect—a problem about which he wanted me to remind Sheikh al-Ma'asarawi during my visit to the *Mushaf* Committee. "Tell him that the mistakes are still there because they print each page from one whole tablet, which makes it difficult to make the necessary corrections." Dr. Yousri knew that the *Mushaf* Committee was working on a new *Mushaf* Braille. I had found out about it from the newspapers. In May of 2012 an Egyptian news agency reported that al-Azhar had inaugurated a project to create special *mushafs* for people with disabilities. The project was launched under the aegis of the Islamic Research Academy and carried out by a committee led by the Grand *Mufti* 'Ali Goma'a and a group of scholars from al-Azhar. The work of the committee was supported by the Braille specialists from the Mosque al-Nur, as well as organizations caring for the deaf and mute who sought to create a video recording of the Qur'an in sign language and a new printed edition of the Qur'an in Braille.⁹

Mushaf Braille and Its Producers

Perhaps what contributed to the launching of this project was the growing number of requests expressed by blind and vision-impaired members of the Muslim community. In February 2012 a group of Egyptians started a Facebook page entitled "Towards the Egyptian *Mushaf* Braille without errors."¹⁰ It aimed to gather Muslims interested in creating a support network "for those brothers and sisters who suffer from the presence of multiple printing mistakes in *Mushaf* Braille in Egypt and to exchange ideas on how to solve this problem." A few people responded, mainly with comments about which editions had the fewest errors and which were the most problematic. The Egyptian and the Saudi *mushafs* in Braille were criticized the most, although two respondents claimed to be able to read from them without any difficulty. One member of the group had worked for a committee preparing a *Mushaf* Braille in Libya. The committee used the Saudi and Jordanian *mushafs* in Braille as their models and—as he admitted—they tried to retain the 'Uthmanic *rasm* as much as possible but in order to make it easier for users to read they had to modify it in some instances. Another member disapproved of the Egyptian system that—as in early regular printing—separated the lines of *rasm* from the diacritics. He claimed that it was much easier to read when the *tashkil* were integrated with the writing and for that reason he preferred the Saudi and Palestinian *mushafs* in Braille. Someone suggested that they appeal directly to al-Azhar—as the institution responsible for printing of *mushafs* in Egypt—and demand a review of the existing edition. The postings practically ended in April 2012 except for a reply made two years later to my inquiry about whether there was any further news on this subject. The founder of the page wrote, "Unfortunately not."

The messages posted on Facebook suggest a few things. First of all, various editions have attempted to accommodate the 'Uthmanic *rasm*, but in the end its full preservation turned out to be impossible if the correct pronunciation of the words were to be preserved in Braille. Thus, makers of *mushafs* in Braille faced a dilemma: either follow the tradition that adhered to the 'Uthmanic *rasm* as the correct form of inscription—but this led to problems involving incorrect recitation and the need to have additional instructions from a teacher— or, follow a modified orthography that would render the correct recitation but use an "incorrect" spelling. Second, no single edition was unanimously voted best, indicating that *mushafs* in Braille are still undergoing experimentation and adjustments to the new technology of writing in Braille and its very different inscription system. The lack of agreement among contributors to the website on whether to place *tashkil* within or above the main line of the text demonstrates the varied preferences of Braille users, which at this point may only be satisfied by a variety of editions produced in different countries. Those who preferred the Saudi system of arranging the text probably followed the news coming from Saudi Arabia closely.

A short note released in 2013 on the Saudi website *al-Muwatin* announced that a six-volume *mushaf* in Braille had just been finished and would be distributed for free among the centers and institutions that serve the blind and vision-impaired both within and beyond the Kingdom. The Press of the Custodian of Two Noble Mosques, known for its services for Muslims with sight problems, had produced this particular *mushaf*. The Press's General Director, Sheikh Nasir Ibn 'Ali al-Musa, wrote that the project had been necessitated by the needs "of millions of Muslims who have been looking forward to acquire the Glorious Book of Allah according to Braille, especially imams and preachers, teachers and students of science, and so [the Press] will continue to fulfill its responsibilities to print the Glorious Qur'an in Braille."[11] Al-Musa also explained that the services of the Mekkan press would be complemented by another edition in preparation by the Malik Fahd Complex that would take over responsibilities for publishing *mushafs* in Braille.

It seems that in Saudi Arabia, as in Egypt, the decision to boost the production of *mushaf* in Braille might have come in response to the requests of Braille users and the organizations that represented them. A year earlier, the Saudi newspaper *al-Iqtisadiyya* ran a short article on an organization called *"Ibsar"* (Vision), purportedly one of the first to address the needs of people with sight disabilities in the Arab world, that was struggling to meet the needs of blind and vision-impaired Muslims in America, France, and Spain in addition to Muslims in Sudan, Iraq, Jordan, Palestine, and, of course, Saudi Arabia. In veiled terms, the Secretary General of the organization expressed his disappointment in the lack of response to the organization's needs on the part of "concerned authorities." He found it particularly discouraging that the organization itself owned only three copies of *mushaf* in Braille, while three-quarters of the people who turned to the organization for help needed assistance in reading it. Therefore, he called on the authorities and the *'ulama'* responsible for printing *mushaf* to implement more efficient support for the blind and vision impaired. For the latter, he also suggested other improvements. It would be beneficial, he said, to fully simplify the letters of the traditional calligraphic style *naskh* currently used in *mushafs* and to increase the contrast between fonts and their background to enable people with poor eyesight to read from regularly printed *mushafs*. Yet he concluded that all these efforts and ideas would be pointless if difficulties in contacting the King Fahd Complex, the Ministry of Education, and other institutions dealing with the production of *mushafs* in Braille persisted.[12]

I do not know how to account for the communication problems between *Ibsar* and other establishments responsible for the production and distribution of *mushafs* in Braille (purportedly, at the end of 2013 *Ibsar* distributed 200 such *mushafs* in the Kingdom and beyond). However, what I find significant is that both pieces of news convey a certain sense of urgency and an undeniable need to increase the number of *mushafs* available for the visually disabled, in spite of the easy accessibility of the recorded Qur'an on compact discs, mobile phones, computers, the Internet, televisions and cable, radio, and other electronic devices, which reraises the question of whether the Qur'an is preserved as an oral artifact or a visual-linguistic one. The conviction that there is a demand for *mushafs* in Braille may have been the result of a wider campaign in the Arab world to increase the awareness of the needs of the disabled and of efforts to produce more books in Braille, in general. But the campaigns of activists cannot fully explain the growing numbers of *mushafs* in Braille. I would argue that what has led to increased production of these Qur'ans is precisely the intensified and unresolved discussion about Braille by religious authorities in Egypt, Saudi Arabia, and other Muslim countries.

In a 2008 interview, the director of a printing house in Cairo that employs mainly blind and vision-impaired workers admitted that they had toyed with the idea of printing a *mushaf* in Braille for a very long time but the impossibility of adapting the 'Uthmanic *rasm* to Braille deterred them.[13] To solve this problem, they turned to al-Azhar, which created an advisory group consisting of a few blind members and a few experts in *qira'at* (schools of reading). After intensive discussions, the group agreed to replace *al-rasm al-'Uthmani* with *al-rasm al-imla'i* (the conventional orthography). But they agreed to do it only in cases where it was absolutely necessary to avoid any confusion about the way the word was to be pronounced. The advisers based their decision on *fatwas* that had justified writing the words of the Qur'an according to *al-rasm al-imla'i* in situations where such a surrogate was crucial for correct learning and recitation, as in Qur'anic verses printed for children. The rest of the signs and letters that could be represented in Braille without confusing readers were to remain unchanged. This statement suggests that it was a rather arbitrary decision by members of the advisory group that defined which words were confusing and had to be modified and which could stay unchanged. Unfortunately, the article did not mention when these decisions were made. They may have concerned the edition of the *mushaf* in Braille kept in the Center for the Blind, as the *mushaf* described in the article also consisted of six large volumes (each of them 35 x 25 cm large) and was characterized by a very thick paper (150–160 grams)—twice the weight of regular printing paper.

What attracted my attention, apart from mention of the advisory group, was a description of the process in which workers of the printing house inscribed the Qur'anic message in Braille:

> The director of the printing house said that the steps to print *mushaf* in Braille start from a translation of the Qur'anic writing into the perforated writing on the tin plates. It happens via recitation to the blind expert who specializes in Braille and who transposes what he hears into the letters written in Braille.[14]

It is interesting that in the context of this practice the author of the article, or perhaps the interviewee, chose to use the word "*tarjama*," which means "translation." This word is typically used in reference to translation from one language to another.[15] But technically speaking, the Qur'an in Braille is a script translation. Reading in Braille may produce the same sound as those produced when a person reads from a regular *mushaf*, but the writing system used is only a "translation" of the 'Uthmanic *rasm*. Yet when I asked Dr. Yousri what the Qur'anic text written in Braille is, he said: "It is the *mushaf*."[16]

Is It a *Mushaf*?

The Egyptian *'ulama'* must have discussed the relationship between the *mushaf* in Braille and *mushafs* printed in Arabic script as this issue was brought up by the Saudi sheikhs as well. I could not find transcripts of these discussions, but I did come across an insightful research paper by a Saudi scholar, Dr. 'Abd Allah al-Khamis, a professor at the Department of Jurisprudence and Graduate Studies at the College of Muslim Law at the Islamic University of Muhammad Ibn Saud in Riyadh.[17] His paper referenced the standard classical sources to summarize opinions of the *'ulama'* belonging to different schools of law in regard to the idea of replacing *al-rasm al-'Uthmani* with the *al-rasm al-imla'i*. This review allowed al-Khamis to address the permissibility of such a substitution in the case of *mushaf* in Braille. Clearly, al-Khamis thought that defining the degree of similarity between the writing system in *Mushaf* Braille and the script of the regularly printed *mushafs* was crucial for a correct pronouncement on the use of Braille. In an introduction to the part of his research that directly addressed the *mushaf* in Braille he wrote,

> It appears from what has been said that the prevailing opinion is that of adherence to *al-rasm al-'Uthmani* in a *mushaf*. In regard to writing Qur'anic verses in places other than *mushafs*, such as books for children, newspapers and academic journals, it is permitted to write them in a rasm different than the 'Uthmanic one. This concerns writing for the sighted. When it comes to the Braille system, or what is called *khatt al-bariz* (embossed style), do the same rules apply to it as well? Or, is it a specific code that has no relation to *al-rasm al-'Uthmani* or *imla'i*, and

requires a specific exigency? Does what has been said about the replacement of the 'Uthmanic *rasm* with the phonetic spelling apply to the replacement of *al-rasm al-'Uthmani* with the Braille system?[18]

Al-Khamis's way of dealing with these questions was very systematic. He first inquired into the structure of the Braille system and obtained specific examples of Qur'anic words that cannot be reproduced in Braille. Next, he searched for religious literature on the subject of Braille but admitted that he was not successful in finding any. This encouraged him to express his own views and to make suggestions about how to resolve the problem. He began by advocating complete adherence to the 'Uthmanic *rasm*. Strict endorsement of the traditional orthography, he concluded, would mean that a rendition of *mushaf* in Braille is not permissible. Of course, such a ruling would not prevent the vision-impaired person from learning the Qur'an through listening. However—changing the direction of his thought, al-Khamis admitted—this argument could be countered by the claim that among the visually impaired there are people with different capabilities and talents, and not everyone is able to memorize the Qur'an just by listening to it, as "such skill is bestowed by Allah according to his will." Moreover, not everybody has access to an audio device that helps to teach the Qur'an, so it is advisable not to leave such a person without assistance while waiting for the opportunity to take lessons in recitation. Besides, it would be a regrettable decision to deprive millions of visually impaired people of the opportunity to read the Qur'an on their own. In any case, concluded al-Khamis, a prohibition on printing *mushaf* in Braille in the Kingdom would not prevent others from producing such a book anyway.[19] Therefore, it would be better to make sure that such a job is done properly by the scholars in Saudi Arabia. As for those who opt for the use of fully phonetic spelling in *mushaf* printed in Braille, he pointed out that their arguments are based on the fact that in Jordan, Tunisia, Saudi Arabia, and Egypt the *mushafs* with phonetic spelling have already been printed and many people have benefited from these editions, so it is hard to find evidence against them. There is also a third path, suggested al-Khamis, to keep what can be preserved from *al-rasm al-'Uthmani* and to use the *imla'i rasm* only when it is impossible to write a word according to the Braille system. He personally preferred this approach, "as the benefits of printing *mushaf* in Braille outweigh the evils of its prohibition."

Al-Khamis's research paper was published in 2006 on a website that disseminates *fatwas* and other religious writings for Muslims. In 2010 a journalist who covered developments in the printing of *mushaf* in Braille at the Press of the Custodian of Two Noble Mosques quoted al-Khamis, juxtaposing the researcher's conclusions with the opinion of a member of the Organization of Senior Scholars of the Kingdom of Saudi Arabia, Sheikh 'Abd Allah Ibn Muni'a, who had said, "We have been familiarized with the case of *mushaf* in Braille, but we restrained ourselves from issuing any decision in that matter."[20] Differences of opinion existed among members of the Organization about the application of the rules of the "Qur'anic *mushaf*" to the *Mushaf* Braille.[21] They arose from the fact that the Board of the Organization had refused to recognize *mushaf* in Braille as a *mushaf*, perhaps seeing it only as a "translation."

The negative decision of the Board, as well as numerous articles announcing the printing of the *Mushaf* Braille in Saudi Arabia and Egypt, have been circulating on the internet in the last seven years. In addition, some internet activists have publicized al-Khamis's paper, including the owner of an Egyptian religious blog who plagiarized the research, extensively using uncited excerpts on his website "Light of the East."[22] Yet, all of this news, along with opinions and pronouncements increasingly accessible to the public in different Arabic-speaking countries, did not clarify what, from a theological perspective, a *mushaf* in Braille actually was.

On a practical level a *mushaf* in Braille constitutes a unique combination of the Qur'an and its "translation," placing itself in a curious position between the "original" and a significantly transformed rendition. The lack of consensus among the *'ulama'* about this *mushaf*'s status as a medium of the Qur'an reflects the competing priorities and objectives of scholars at al-Azhar. For some, it is spreading the message, albeit at a cost, that counts the most. Others are more concerned with attending to the medium through which the message is disseminated. And these priorities matter to different degrees. It is certain, though, that disagreements about the permissibility of using the conventional *rasm imla'i* in *mushafs* for blind and vision-impaired Muslims have once more separated scholars into those more inclined to see the orthography and, by extension, the *mushaf* as an integral part of the message and those who, in particular instances, step in the direction of divorcing the Qur'an from its graphic and tangible mediators.

None of the Azhari scholars, however, will claim that the same can be done in regard to sound. In the case of the acoustically mediated Qur'an, the meaning and the sound do not operate separately, invalidating any attempts to apply synonyms for the vocabulary used in the Qur'anic message. For that reason, in the eyes of all Muslim scholars, the Qur'an is essentially untranslatable. Editions of the Qur'an in languages other than Arabic are thought of as mere "commentaries" or "glosses" of the Qur'an in Arabic. The angel Jibril *recited* the Qur'an to the Prophet, emphasized the *'ulama'*, and this made him a depository and disseminator of the words, not a narrator. So it seems that the relationship between the message and its acoustic form is more stable than the one between the Qur'an and its visual medium. Yet, from what has been said above it is clear that the latter is also stable enough to produce anxiety and uncertainty about how to think of the Qur'an in a script and orthography entirely different from the ones instituted by the Prophet's Companions and endorsed by the Muslim community over its centuries of use. In spite of the religious context in which the *mushaf* in Braille has been produced, its radically different materiality puts it in a precarious position of being a medium whose mediation is seen as somehow flawed, at least from a scholarly point of view. Yet, the practitioners are not fully satisfied either because they generally find the *mushaf* in Braille to be not user-friendly enough. What they are able to assert, however, is that their voices are increasingly heard through the social media they use to publicize their needs and to put pressure on the religious institutions responsible for the Qur'anic production, thus transforming the public space of religious debates and the negotiation of authority. In the next three chapters, I will turn to other issues generated by the uses of the Qur'anic books as material objects and the ways in which their users enact the Qur'an through the use of *mushafs*.

Part Three

The Users

7

How Printing Created Manuscripts: Aesthetic and Historical Approaches to *Mushafs*

The previous chapters pointed to script, orthography, and perforated paper as elements that mediate the Qur'anic message. In this chapter, I turn to another source that generates change—the technology of making *mushafs*—and its reframing capabilities. In other words, I want to specifically consider how handwriting and its visual alternative—printing—define the uses to which the Qur'anic text is put. In order to do this, I first discuss manually written *mushafs* in relation to printed ones. The relationship between printed and handwritten Qur'anic texts is not simply a matter of the replacement of an older technology with a newer one (as we could especially notice in Chapters 1 and 3) or of a mechanically reproduced book displacing a handwritten one. To highlight the nature of the connection between a printed and a handmade Qur'anic text, I turn matters around. Instead of treating this relationship in a chronological or evolutionary fashion—when printing replaces writing—I reverse that perspective by asking: how did the appearance of printed *mushafs* affect those written by hand? What happened to handmade Qur'anic copies when printed *mushafs* became widespread commodities? And how does the way of making the book mediate the Qur'anic message when printing and writing are juxtaposed as two, mutually redefining technologies?

In this chapter, I consider situations when printing turns handwritten *mushafs* into something unprecedented. I specifically address Qur'anic *manuscripts*—texts written by hand that, by virtue of the way in which they were made, have become objects whose primary value is no longer the message itself but rather the fact that they are *not printed*. Thus, these *mushafs* are being moved into the realm of "tradition," to what *was before* rather than what *is still now*. As a long-term result of this transformation, handwritten Qur'anic copies that are now kept in the Cairo Museum of Bab al-Khalq or Dar al-Kutub serve mainly as proofs of Egyptian competence in protecting their Muslim and national heritage. Dar al-Kutub is particularly well known for its publications on handwritten *mushafs*. In 2011, its employees participated in the Frankfurt Book Fair, the biggest book and media fair in the world, displaying as one of their achievements a monumental survey of *mushafs* preserved at the National Library. The Museum of Bab al-Khalq shows—in the manner of the best Western museums—a collection of *makhtuts* (manuscripts), with gorgeously illuminated and calligraphed *mushafs* as part of the attraction. At Bab al-Khalq, these *mushafs* are not Qur'anic texts as much as they are *makhtuts*—museum pieces and handwritten books that testify to the greatness of the past.

What gives these *mushafs* their value most of the time is *not* what is written in them but the length of time that has passed since their production and the artistic sensibilities skillfully poured into them by a calligrapher. This is because, in Qur'anic manuscripts, writing itself can be treated as an object rather than as knowledge, and so handwritten *mushafs* always test the boundaries of the notion of a "book" as a text to be read. The capacity of Qur'anic manuscripts to act as "books" is limited by their physical properties: calligraphy, ornamentation, parchment or paper, binding, etc. In the aftermath of print, handwritten *mushafs* have become items in private and public collections, acquired for their historical importance, artistic qualities, and—in the case of museums—for their academic significance for both Muslim and non-Muslim (especially Euro-American) scholars. This transformation of Qur'anic *mushafs* into *makhtuts*, or manuscripts, could fully take place only when mechanical printing became not only possible but also ubiquitous. From this perspective, then, printed *mushafs* did not only follow handwritten ones, they also, in an important sense, recreated them by transforming them into the all-encompassing category of *makhtuts*.

Handwritten Qur'anic texts were not the only kind of textual production that underwent a dramatic change with the introduction of print technology. Brinkley Messick, who examined the changing relations between writing and authority in nineteenth-century Yemen, noted that with the spread of print culture

> the old diversity of handwritten texts, including the drafts and autographs of famous scholars, calligraphic exercises, copies made as pious pastimes, artifacts of formal study, products of professional copyists, and so forth, would eventually be reduced from the point of view of a print-oriented society, to a single basic and increasingly archaic type, the "manuscript," to be collected and curated, kept in library sections that would begin to resemble museums.[1]

However, unlike many of these genres of writing that disappeared after the introduction of printing, the Qur'anic text continued to be disseminated, acquiring new forms of authority vis-à-vis the handwritten *mushafs* but at the same time clearly relegating the latter into a category of objects rather than texts. How has this happened? Let's have a closer look at the conditions under which a Qur'anic text may be referred to as *makhtut* rather than a *mushaf*: conditions created through practices of preservation, collection, and academic investigation.

Practices of Preservation

How exactly does a *mushaf* become a *makhtut*, or, anthropologically speaking, what kind of practices reconstitutes *mushafs* into *makhtuts*? A conversation with the specialist in charge of the manuscript collection when I visited the Cairo National Library offered a glimpse of activities through which the Qur'anic message is minimized and the material characteristics of the book are accentuated. The *mushafs* that fill the storage rooms, the specialist explained, go through basic preservation, like other *makhtuts* (manuscripts). Basic preservation involves physical protection from the environment, or more specifically, from dust, mold, and moisture. That means the *mushafs* are kept in air-conditioned rooms, in boxes, at an optimal temperature and humidity to prevent the decomposition of parchment and paper. Some are selected by the staff to be digitized, a process that allows conservators to preserve a text without having to make costly little repairs to the object itself. The 3-D technology used for this purpose displays the *mushaf* in multiple ways, showing not only the text but also elements of its binding, the thickness of its paper, and other physical characteristics. Anybody interested in them (mostly academic experts) may view them on a computer screen, usually not at the *mushaf*'s original size but significantly enlarged and in fragments. "It all comes down to this," the specialist summarized his mini-lecture, "What does the manuscript need to be used for?"

Preservation, then, is a matter of use. It is a set of practices (chemical treatments, manual repairs, digital reproduction, etc.) that determine even further in what capacity the text will be used after it has been physically stabilized. Thus, handwritten *mushafs* are not merely texts but are objects entangled with potential practices through which they may be reconstituted into generic manuscripts. In other words, the material properties of the *mushaf*—the fact that it is handwritten and adorned—render it suitable to become an object of conservation and potential display: two acts of translation (in a Latourian sense) during which the Qur'anic text becomes a *makhtut*. In these circumstances, the need to attend to the Qur'an—the actual message—is not necessary. "If you want to look at a *mushaf*, the text is already known," declared the curator,

> so what are the other things that we are looking for? There are different kinds of priorities: things viewed as treasures get preference in conservation, which includes illumination and the name of the calligrapher. Copies of the Qur'anic text with titles of chapters, markings indicating where to take a break in reading, signs facilitating recitation and so on are always more valuable than the ones that lack these additions.

After a pause he added, "Some manuscripts are preserved because of their pseudo-historical value. In this case ... " here the man hesitated slightly, " ... it is the sentiments that matter." I realized that he is alluding to a Qur'anic copy that played a special role in the religious landscape of Muslims in Cairo, one of the famous *mushafs* prepared on the order of the third Caliph 'Uthman Ibn 'Affan. "There is a list on the internet that mentions a whole number of them in different places in the world. Of course, it is hard to say whether they really are the authentic ones."[2] His skepticism, however, does not reflect the wider Egyptian public opinion about this *mushaf*, which serves in the popular imagination as one of Egypt's more treasured possessions embodying for Muslims in a material way centuries of Qur'anic endurance and integrity.

My questions about the choices of what gets to be preserved and how it gets preserved intrude into the tender realm of the politics of preservation. It is a delicate matter to discuss the conservation of the Qur'anic copies with an outsider, for a lack of discretion may have serious ramifications internationally, and people working in the field are very much aware of this. The most recent example of frictions born of publicized information concerning the discovery and study of old Qur'anic manuscripts comes from Yemen. The candid comments of one of the researchers involved in that study were picked up and broadcast by the American and, later, Arab presses, stirring up tensions between the Yemeni government, foreign scholars, and local researchers in charge of the collection.[3] The turf wars that followed help one understand why specialists involved in the Qur'anic conservation project in Cairo may prefer to be cautious about publicizing their endeavors. In Egypt, the *makhtuts*, including the Qur'anic ones, also lie at the center of a complex network of exchange and dependency, entangling Egyptian cultural authorities responsible for preservation of the Islamic heritage, the financially needy National Library, foreign book preservation experts, tourist markets, and international publishing companies that, for a variety of reasons, are willing to invest in book conservation in Egypt.

One such company is Tradigital, a German publishing house that, through its support of conservation activities at the Egyptian National Library, has access to books rarely seen by the public. As a result of their arrangement with the National Library, the company has been able to carry out a number of important restoration and reprinting projects. The one most relevant here is the creation of a Qur'anic copy that imitates the calligraphy used in a beautifully executed personal *mushaf* that belonged to King Fu'ad I and was written by the renowned calligrapher Sheikh Muhammad 'Abd al-'Aziz al-Rifa'i. Tradigital's success in using a computer program that accurately recreates the calligraphic Qur'anic letters in a digital format without photocopying them is a recent technological breakthrough in the production of the Qur'anic texts to which I will return in the next chapter. It is also an undertaking that has allowed the company to produce a "New *Mushaf* Fu'ad." Incidentally, this name tends to create some confusion among those Egyptian practitioners who refer to the "*Mushaf* Fu'ad" as the 1924 typeset and printed edition of al-Amiriyya and have never heard about the personal, handwritten copy made about the same time for the king and kept now in the museum collection. The "New *Mushaf* Fu'ad" purveyed by the calligraphic experts from the Tradigital company—thanks to its artfully reproduced handwriting—offers simultaneously the individuality of a masterpiece and a personalized relationship with the text, allowed by the multiplicity of a printed edition. Yet this is not a typical Qur'anic edition. Tradigital's edition is printed in gold, blue, red, brown, and black on thick, glossy paper with a gold-embossed Balacron leather cover. One may read it at home but it is not a *mushaf* that would be—like many ordinary *mushafs*—carried in one's pocket or purse on the streets of Cairo. It is not designed to be affordable for most Egyptians either: its cost (40 USD) and workmanship make it a display book, hardly one that would be read in public. Furthermore, it is not a complete *mushaf*, as it contains only a thirtieth of the whole Qur'anic text. *Mushafs* divided into thirty smaller sections for easy use outside of the home are common in Egyptian bookstores, but in the case of this particular *mushaf* it is the only part available on the market so far and is sold exclusively via the internet. It is, essentially, an aesthetic object produced mainly for elites and bibliophiles among Western and Gulf Muslim consumers.

The company advertises its products—the "New *Mushaf* Fu'ad" and other religious publications—as an attempt to "reinvent the Arabic book."[4] What the company aims at is to produce highly artistic books that are illuminated according to the models and designs developed by Arab book artisans in the times when book production was a well-developed and highly appreciated craft in the Middle East and before those traits were considered characteristic of "*makhtuts.*" The official website of the company explains their venture as a project that "successfully cultivates the traditional art of bookmaking" by appropriating old designs and adjusting them to the modern artistic sensibilities of contemporary Muslims: "The designs of the current books produced by the company follow the designs of typical, old Arabic manuscripts and when necessary, develop their ideas further. For this, traditional documents are studied and examined intensively, in order to pick out the typical patterns and the specifications used in combination with their contents." This project is sustained by the company's access to manuscripts in the Egyptian National Library and carried out by experts who study the holdings in order to recreate the most "typically Arabic" patterns of book illumination. These designs incorporate discrete combinations of spandrels, mandorlas, stars, polygons, and arabesques that correspond with particular book genres, including ones for the Qur'an that are different from those for *hadiths* or *sunna*. Tradigital's design experts recreate the geometrical arrangements and use them in the books published by the company, giving their productions a distinctive "manuscript-like" character.

The arabesque illuminations used in the "New *Mushaf* Fu'ad," along with its font, paper, and decorative binding, turn this book into an object that one should *have* but not necessarily *use*. In this context, Tradigital's manuscript-like copy of the Qur'anic text potentially becomes an index of the owner's religiosity—the presence of the Qur'an at home—as well as an index of his or her artistic sensibilities and connoisseurship, as *mushafs* are often displayed in the house in a prominent manner.[5] A *mushaf* that looks like a museum object connects its owner with imagined past generations of Qur'anic users, members of the family, and the historical Muslim community who owned similar-looking although differently made objects. On the other side of the spectrum, a manuscript-like reproduction of this sort participates in building the prestige of contemporary institutions that own "valuable objects," particularly the one that owns the original manuscript from which the reproduction was made. At the same time a manuscript-like book, such as the "New *Mushaf* Fu'ad," has the potentiality to create an interest in the original manuscript by popularizing particular physical features—such as ornamentation and calligraphy—among those who are not museumgoers. An artistically adorned, manuscript-like *mushaf* on display in one's house creates, then, an atmosphere of sophisticated religiosity that communicates the personal piety and worldly refinement of the owner to visitors. Likewise, when presented as a gift to another Muslim, such a Qur'anic copy is a safe yet stylish purchase that is not likely to be criticized or refused—again reflecting the taste of the giver. All of these effects and uses may be produced without the owner or gift recipient ever reading the "New *Mushaf* Fu'ad."

Aestheticizing the Written

Muslim readers collected *mushafs* on the basis of their aesthetic qualities and as objects of aesthetic pleasure before printing existed. Historical sources speak of connoisseurs of penmanship who gathered calligraphic specimens, including *mushafs* produced by famous calligraphers, as early as the ninth century.[6] Demand created supply, and even forgeries. The story of the accomplished calligrapher and illustrator Ibn al-Bawwab is worth telling because it sheds light on the artistic markets in the eleventh-century Middle East. According to the twelfth-century chronicler Yaqut, the acclaimed tenth-century Ibn al-Bawwab himself stated that he had successfully imitated the hand of ninth-century master Ibn Muqla. Ibn al-Bawwab was in charge of the library of the Buwayhid prince Baha' al-Dawla in Shiraz. During his appointment, he found in the library a copy of the Qur'anic text written by another famous calligrapher, Ibn Muqla. The text was divided into thirty parts and those parts were scattered among other manuscripts in the library. One of the valuable volumes was missing and Ibn al-Bawwab could not find it despite a thorough search. The calligrapher reported the loss to the prince who asked Ibn al-Bawwab to make a new copy of the missing part, imitating Ibn Muqla's hand. They agreed that if the prince could not tell which volume was forged he would give Ibn al-Bawwab the handsome sum of one hundred dinars and a robe of honor. Ibn al-Bawwab prepared the missing portion and showed the whole *mushaf* to the prince. Baha' al-Dawla examined the volumes but could not tell which of them was written by Ibn al-Bawwab. The story says that the prince did not give Ibn al-Bawwab the promised reward but instead offered him sheets of Chinese paper from the library for his own use, which were also quite valuable.[7] After Ibn al-Bawwab's death his own work became widely renowned and, in turn, "forged" by others (closely copying the work of one's teacher or another master was a large part of traditional "calligraphic" scribal training).

Apart from calligraphic collections, wealthy Muslim elites kept richly decorated *mushafs* and also presented them as donations to particular mosques, where such gifts occupied shelves of honor, sometimes for centuries. Connoisseurs of calligraphy did not collect just any *mushafs* but only those written by particular artists. Caliphs and sultans did not commission plain copies of the Qur'anic text but rather versions that were abundantly decorated. That said, there is a difference between these older practices that led to accumulations of Qur'anic copies in royal libraries or private households and the institutionalized collections that began emerging in the nineteenth century in Europe, the United States, and the Middle East. Within an institutional framework, highly decorated *mushafs* were gradually seen less as beautiful repositories of the Qur'an and increasingly more as objects carrying other kinds of meaning. The shift in emphasis that took place during this period resulted in the transformation of *mushafs* from being primarily Qur'anic texts to being above all objects of art, creating a precedence in which a *mushaf*'s formal qualities might trump its semantic content. Museum collections in which Qur'anic texts have been displayed as objects praised for the artistry of their production are epitomized today by permanent displays of Islamic art at the Smithsonian, the Louvre, and the Victoria and Albert, as well as their counterparts in Muslim countries: the Islamic Art Museum in Doha, the Beyt al-Qur'an in Bahrain, the National Museum in Riyadh, and the Museum of Islamic Art in Egypt. In all of these institutions, *mushafs* serve primarily as didactic tools for lessons in the history of art.

Institutionalized Collections

Egypt has a long history of the institutionalized display of artifacts. In Cairo today, there are two major collections of Qur'anic texts: one exhibited in the Museum of Islamic Arts, the main museum devoted to Muslim art in Egypt, established in 1881 and considered as having one of the largest collections of manuscripts in the world; the other at the recently opened Museum at Bab al-Khalq that displays famous manuscripts from the holdings of the National Library. Both institutions are well known among art historians and Islamic Studies scholars for their acquisitions of Qur'anic copies produced in various historic periods and geographical regions. The *mushafs* exhibited in these institutions no longer serve the original purpose of a Qur'anic text. They cannot be read, pondered, recited, nor otherwise engaged in daily worship. As parts of *collections*, they are permanently thwarted in the task for which they were made: namely, giving guidance to individual practitioners of Islam. Instead, they are on public display and are meant to be looked at, like other museum artifacts. They are showcased to serve particular purposes of the institution that owns and displays them.

In the Museum of Islamic Arts, collections of *mushafs* are emphasized as being *Muslim* artifacts. It is only the rarest and most aesthetically pleasing specimens that constitute this collection, paradoxically creating an impression of the ubiquity of such objects through the uniqueness of the ones on display. Thus, even though the average *mushafs* used in the past were quite ordinary, museum viewers—mainly local school groups and foreign tourists—leave the institution with the impression of beautifully crafted Qur'anic texts as being quintessential "Qur'ans." These *mushafs* are cumulatively displayed as great achievements of Islamic art for the purpose of educating the public about the "Golden Age of Muslim civilization" (which in fact does not coincide with the period of the Golden Age as understood by many conservative Muslims today who consider the times of the first four caliphs the true Golden Age of Islam). At these museums, the attention of viewers is drawn to the mastery of production, perfection of design, and development of ideas, all discussed within the framework of what constitutes Islamic art.

Beyond their role as vehicles of aesthetic pleasure, cultural refinement, and historical knowledge made available to the public, these *mushafs* contribute to the making of Egypt's national heritage. From this vantage point, these manuscripts are a part of the legacy of the Egyptian nation. The catalogue issued on the occasion of opening Bab al-Khalq calls the whole exhibit the "memory of a nation" and claims that the history of the manuscripts from the museum's collection—including *mushafs*—"represents earnest efforts in preservation of the historical and intellectual legacy left by the past generations of this great country." The phrase "memory of a nation" clearly implies national consciousness, rather than a shared religious or Islamic consciousness/history. At the same time, in the Museum of Islamic Arts the collections of *mushafs* "belong to Muslim history," and in the Museum at Bab al-Khalq, these manuscripts are labeled "national treasures." Thus, national and religious agendas dovetail in the display of *mushafs*, connecting what it means to be Muslim *and* Egyptian.

But what most differentiates today's collections of *mushafs* from earlier ones is that these manuscripts are viewed as products of an outmoded technology that can be contrasted with newer, contemporary forms of dissemination. In this regard, they literally become *makhtuts*—objects written by hand, manuscripts, rather than printed books. Any handwritten book may be a *makhtut* but only the carrier of the Qur'anic text bears the name of *mushaf*. Yet at Bab al-Khalq and the Museum of Islamic Arts, Egyptian archivists in charge of old *mushafs* commonly call them *makhtuts*, not *mushafs*. The archivists know the manuscripts contain the text of the Qur'an and occasionally refer to one as "*mushaf*" or "the Qur'an" but it is clear that what makes these books valuable from an archival point of view is not the text that they carry but the fact that they are "handwritten and old." As such, they become objects of academic interest and investigation.

Private Collectors

Of course, the spread of institutionalized public displays of the Qur'anic manuscripts in the nineteenth century did not eliminate the practice of collecting *mushafs* by private connoisseurs around the world, although it limited the availability of the manuscripts on the market and circumscribed their circulation from a legal perspective. Private collectors now had to compete with state-sponsored "collectors" (that is, museums and other institutions), and with time private connoisseurs also became limited in their purchasing abilities by laws proscribing the circulation and trade of art objects. Nevertheless, the aesthetic qualities of Qur'anic manuscripts have been appreciated by all sorts of collectors, foreign as well as Egyptian. The foreigners especially constitute a diverse and somewhat amorphous group, including non-Muslim collectors (who may have no religious investment in their purchases) and Muslim buyers from the West, Asia, and the Persian Gulf countries who are familiar with the content of the Qur'an. These purchases are often a private affair with only some manuscripts advertised in places such as the Arab equivalent of Amazon, Suq al-Kutubiin. This fact helps to establish, even as it already responds to, the audience interested in purchasing such objects. Non-Muslim foreign collectors visiting Egypt, in spite of the national laws that prevent export without license of any objects over fifty years old, are certainly interested in making such purchases, judging from the number of offers I received from sellers around al-Husseyn Mosque who were ready to supply me with an antique Qur'anic manuscript if I wanted to buy one.

The reasons for which such objects are sought after vary, but in most cases it is their rarity that propels the desire to obtain them, thus turning these purchased *mushafs* into pecuniary investments. And where art and economy intersect, political concerns are likely to arise. A few years ago, the Egyptian Supreme Council of Antiquities launched a campaign aimed at combating trade in illicit antiquities and aiding in the recovery of stolen artifacts. As part of an effort to retrieve objects considered part of Egypt's heritage, the council has started monitoring Egyptian items offered for sale at auction houses in France, England, and America. In 2013, the Paris Fontainebleau Osenat Auction house had scheduled for sale on June 9 a Qur'anic manuscript that bore a handwritten note of the French owner, Jean Joseph Marcel, "This script was part of the books of the mosque at El-Azhar Kaire. It was saved from pillage and fire the days when this mosque was taken by the French on the revolts of the city."[8] News of the auction reached the Grand Sheikh of al-Azhar, Ahmad al-Tayyeb, who implored the Egyptian Minister of Foreign Affairs, Muhammad Kamal 'Ali 'Amr; United Nations Educational Scientific and Cultural Organization (UNESCO) chairman, Irina Bokova; and Islamic Educational Scientific and Cultural Organisation (ISESCO) director general, 'Abdel 'Aziz al-Tuwaijri, to take action against the sale of the manuscript. Initially, the auction house refused to accommodate his request by stopping the sale on the grounds that the manuscript had been removed from Egypt before 1970, the date the UNESCO convention on the protection of cultural property established as a cutoff for the legal excavation or export of artifacts from a source nation without government permission. The national newspaper *al-Ahram* reported,

> Ossama El-Nahas, reporter at the ISESCO and director of the department of the repatriation of antiquities, called for the immediate return of such a rare manuscript because it was taken from Egypt during the French expedition, which is against the UNESCO convention that stipulates the prevention and prohibition of illicit import, export and transfer of ownership of cultural property in a combat, conflict, and colonised country. "The French expedition led by Napoleon Bonaparte was a colonisation," said El-Nahas.

Yet when the Egyptian Embassy in Paris became involved in the dispute, the director of the house, Jean-Pierre Osenat, decided to pull the manuscript from the auction. He said, "We are aware of the feelings that the proposed sale has provoked in Egypt and after friendly exchanges with the embassy, we decided to withdraw the manuscript from this weekend's sale."[9] The Egyptian ambassador, Muhammad Mustafa Kamal, followed this decision with a letter to Osenat, in which he wrote, "The withdrawal of the said manuscript from the auction scheduled for June 9 reflects a great understanding of the very high moral and cultural value of this manuscript." Yet in spite of the al-Azhar request "to bring back the manuscript and other relics from Azhar's great human heritage,"[10] Osenat declared that he would have to think about what to do with the book as it belongs to a private collector.[11]

The story of this particular manuscript is a part of a longer history of the violent appropriation of objects by Europeans and takes us back to the French occupation of Egypt at the end of the eighteenth century. Only three months after Napoleon's arrival, the Cairene population, tired of the French presence, excessive taxes, and the hygienic regulations they imposed, rose up against the occupiers. French troops brutally suppressed the uprising. In a memoir written by one of Napoleon's savants, Jean-Joseph Marcel, a note for October 1798 described the desecration of the Grand Mosque in Cairo as punishment for Egyptian insubordination.[12] This act of revenge cost many Egyptian lives and provided French scholars with a chance to rummage through the collection of manuscripts stored in the mosque. Jean-Joseph Marcel, who had linguistic skills and an interest in printing, kept one of the nicely adorned copies (as did other scholars who had gone to the mosque) and, in spite of the tragic finale of the Napoleonic expedition, was able to bring it home. What prompted this French traveler to keep this object stained with violence as it was and carry it a long way to another place? Was it a souvenir? A piece to add to his collection of items in a cabinet of curiosity, so popular at that time? Did he read it or display it to tell the story of his adventure? I do not know but what I find significant is that the French savant singled out this *mushaf* for collection on the grounds of its material properties and, two hundred years later when the Grand Sheikh of al-Azhar sought to claim it, it was also treated as a *makhtut*, a "manuscript of cultural value."

The temptation to treat religious texts as artifacts may take different forms but for non-Muslim collectors who cannot and do not have the need to read such texts, it is only the text's format that affects its future use and future value. Another example of this aestheticizing and objectifying practice in relation to the Qur'anic text comes from Ebay. With accessibility of the internet, the location of an object no longer limits its global circulation. Purchases, sales, and general information about such antiquities are theoretically available in any place and to anybody. In early 2013 an American seller auctioned three handwritten pages of Qur'anic text. He had purchased them years ago, appreciating beauty and artistry of the miniature writing (the pages were very small) and obviously seeing in them something other than the Qur'anic message—even though in the eBay advertisement he did refer to the text's "spiritual energy." The pages were—like *mushaf* from the Cairo Grand Mosque—objects of violence, this time executed on the book itself by the original seller untold years ago. The book had been cut into pieces before being sold to the present owner, who was not distressed by this fact, posting his listing without trying to excuse or explain his sale of separate pages:

> These three miniature pages of handwritten calligraphy in Arabic from the Holy Koran are magnificent works of art with strong spiritual energy. The writing is on the front and back side, but the back sides seem to have smeared ink and a blurred image, as shown in the photos. I believe I purchased these in Algeria or Tunis many years ago.[13]

This destruction of the book in order to sell its fragments is, of course, an extreme example of the violation of the relationship between the text and the object that carries it. In the eyes of the *'ulama'*, such an act goes beyond an acceptable, although always somewhat risky, appreciation of the beauty of the written Qur'anic text. However, as I mentioned earlier, the *mushaf* can be divided into smaller parts, as it is often done to facilitate carrying and reading it. Yet a fragment of the text always forms part of the whole that should be read. A portion of the text that stands on its own without being preceded or followed by another act of reading has the potential to surpass the whole message. It may divert the onlooker from *what it is* to *how it looks*. It may become an object in itself.

Manuscripts as Objects of Academic Investigation

The practices of preservation, display, reproduction, and collecting of which I have spoken so far primarily emphasize the aesthetic value of manuscripts. Conservators, spectators, connoisseurs, and collectors who look at the manuscripts as expressions of artistic skills are mainly interested in their embellishment, in calligraphic craftsmanship, and in the kinds of materials used to produce them. These elements matter for both private collectors and for those in charge of museum collections, who treat adorned Qur'anic manuscripts in the category of potentially displayable and tradeable objects.

But another set of practices partly overlaps the ones just described, practices through which the Qur'anic manuscript becomes a subject of academic attention as a historical artifact. This approach is not very common in Egypt's academic centers where theological interest in the Qur'an's content prevails. Incidentally, the phrase "Qur'anic studies" has always had a different meaning in Muslim and non-Muslim scholarly communities. While Muslim scholars focus on exegesis of the text, non-Muslim scholars are just as interested (if not more) in the object that carries it as in the text itself. Moreover, Qur'anic studies in Europe grew out of a desire to investigate the origins of religious texts under an Enlightenment assumption that their history involved no evidence of divine intervention. So these manuscripts have been used as tools to construct theories about the Qur'an's human foundation. Such methods of inquiry have been irrelevant to scholars at al-Azhar, although some Egyptian researchers have undergone a Western "Qur'anic studies" training and specialize in the history of Qur'anic manuscripts. Thus, the approach of which I am speaking is mainly a characteristic of Euro-American academic institutions and could in theory be disregarded by Muslims. At the same time, however, neither the approach nor the conclusions that foreign scholars have reached have gone unnoticed by Egyptian *'ulama'* familiar with Western studies of Qur'anic manuscripts and they occasionally respond to such theories in academic journals in Arabic, English, German, or French. Both Muslim scholars and educated Egyptians know—through academic networks, media, and religious apologetic publications—that the Qur'anic text is also the object of secular investigation. So when Egyptian *'ulama'* discuss orientalist research they confront a very different kind of science and must engage with the materiality of the *mushaf* in a way that does not have a precedence in their own field. What does this kind of "Qur'anic studies" entail?

In this tradition, *mushafs* become historical artifacts that do not simply "carry" the text but apparently communicate information additional to the truths of the message they transmit—information independent of the circumstances for which the books were made and used. For centuries, inscriptions of the message aimed to ensure its preservation. Nobody expected the objects that contained the Qur'an to reveal more than the Qur'an itself. Yet in archival labs in the West, *mushafs* as *makhtuts* became tools to question the history and veracity of Muslim revelation itself. Scholars deploy radiocarbon dating, chemical analysis, and paleographic examinations as scientific warrants that may call in doubt the text's uniformity across time and space and contest Muslim certainties about the Qur'an's divine origins. In museums and academic halls, a Qur'anic *makhtut* holds answers to scholarly questions about the origins of the Qur'an—and by extension—Islam. The efforts to answer these questions concentrate on the manuscripts as unique material proofs of scientific theories. The things themselves serve to sift truth from mere belief or falsehood.

In this chapter, I specifically looked at the interplay of two technologies, printing and handwriting, and their power to affect the purpose to which books manufactured through these technologies can be put. Undeniably, Qur'anic manuscripts play a very different role than printed books, in spite of the same content. The material characteristics of the handwritten codex, then, determine its value and appropriation. In the next chapter, I will continue exploring the material characteristics of the Qur'anic book in relation to its daily uses and—occasionally—its daily abuses.

8

Uses and Abuses

Early on in this story, I mentioned Terry Jones and his followers who in 2010 took to burning *mushafs* on the anniversary of 9/11. Two years later, another incident of *mushaf* incineration occurred at an American base in Afghanistan and made the international news. Both times, the internet was full of pictures showing Qur'anic books consumed in flames. The images of scorched pages crumpling under the heat of fire provoked a chain of violent reactions, including injuries and death. Many Muslims expressed their shock and anger via the internet, public protests, newspaper articles, and vehement conversations with friends and neighbors. The situation was dangerous, so the heads of states and politically influential organizations got involved. The mass media were asked to stop reproducing the images—to self-censor—so as not to increase violence. The reaction to the burning of these *mushafs* was worldwide, creating a situation in which the books' burning matter became a burning matter of global politics.

These events could be interpreted in a variety of ways. The most immediate one would be to explain them in the context of Muslim beliefs about the uniqueness of the Qur'an. After all, Muslims do *believe* the Qur'an to be the very words of Allah and they place His message at the center of their religion. One could conclude, then, that it is their *beliefs* that prompted them to react that way. But was it? Why does explaining these events as a result of Muslim beliefs not seem to be fully satisfactory? It is so, David Morgan reminds us, because defining religion in terms of what people believe reduces it to a body of assertions demanding assent. He says,

> In fact, religions are rarely describable as this. Even the most prescriptive or Fundamentalist versions of Protestantism, Islam, or Judaism are much more than that. Their embodied forms of practice such as prayer, liturgy, and pilgrimage, their sensations of sound in corporate worship, their visual articulations of sacred writ, their creation of spaces that sculpt sound and shape living architectures of human bodies—all these vastly exceed the narrow idea of a religion as the profession of creeds or catechetical formulae singularly understood to represent an inner state of volition.[1]

How should we, then, approach these events? Apart from examining an abstract set of religious tenets, one could look at them through the political-historical lens of entangled "Muslim-Western" relations, which, without a doubt, played a role here as well. But to what extent? In and of themselves, both of these explanations, although germane, do not fully account for the magnitude and vehemence of the backlashes, as the reactions were too visceral and impetuous to be brushed off as merely the result of people's ideas about the divine nature of their holy text. And, I argue, such explanations have not been able to present a more complete picture of events because they do not reckon in any way with a less immediate sphere of Qur'anic presence—the plethora of transactions that typically surround the physical copies of Qur'anic text, the activities that, from an ethnographic perspective, make the sacred happen on the level of practice.

For that reason, I want to bring these transactions more fully into view. I also want to relate the ways in which Muslims in Egypt reacted to incineration of the Qur'anic books to the ways Egyptian users of *mushafs* handle their quotidian copies of the Qur'an in their daily life. From this angle, the various responses to Terry Jones's iconoclastic acts and to the careless treatment of Muslim books by soldiers on the American military base are meaningful because they indicate various levels to which Muslims in Egypt have been committed not only to the Qur'anic message but also to its material form. In other words, these reactions can be read as indicators of different semiotic ideologies that are always implicitly at work in any community but become explicit in moments of crisis. Taking a cue from Webb Keane, when I say "semiotic ideologies" I mean people's underlying assumptions about signs (in this case the material substance of the book), how much those signs matter, and how seriously they should be taken into consideration in religious practice.[2] One of the contributions of the material turn in anthropology and its reevaluation of approaches to material culture is by now the obvious conclusion that people's commitments to the materiality of things—their understanding of how material or immaterial they are—are not universal. Nor are their understandings of how effective those things are. Moreover, as I illustrate in this chapter, these commitments should not be assumed to be always the same within a cohesive community of practice. Rather, I argue, the relationship between the divine and the material that mediates it is always dynamic and debatable, as the following ethnographic account of the uses and abuses of Qur'anic books suggests.

Paper Burns

Let's begin with a useful observation that objects are prone to "bundling." "Bundling" is the term used by Webb Keane to describe the "contingent coexistence of an indefinite number of qualities in any object,"[3] whose combination permits the object to exceed the intended purpose of its maker. Books are generally made out of paper because it is an inexpensive and functional material to write on. It makes books light enough to carry them around. It can be easily cut to adjust the book's size, depending on the needs of its user. And various types of paper—for instance, coated, laid, recycled, or gilded—allow one to communicate diverse messages to different audiences. (Let's just imagine how much confusion a wedding invitation sent on a piece of toilet paper or Kleenex would create.) Yet paper is also flammable, which turns books into objects susceptible to other uses as well, or misuses, as in the case of the events at the military base in Afghanistan or at the church in Florida.

When the first reports of Pastor Jones's campaign in 2010 reached the press, I was in the United States. An Egyptian friend of mine walked into the room, shaking her head in disbelief. "Look," she said, handing me her laptop with a display of the news. "This is awful! How can he do that?" She was visibly angry. "But, anyway," she added after a pause, composing herself, "he can't burn the Qur'an." Doriya's faith in Jones's inability to destroy the Qur'anic book did not necessarily come from a conviction that the police or some other governmental body would step in and prevent the event from happening (although many people in Egypt thought so, used to their own government intervening at will in public expressions of opinions it deemed undesirable). I understood that Doriya was referring to the doctrinal distinction Muslims make between the eternal message of the Qur'an "preserved in the hearts of Muslims"—as the Qur'an emphasizes on multiple occasions—and the material and tangible book, the *mushaf*. However, she also might have been hinting at another part of the Muslim discursive tradition, the one that is recorded in some *hadiths* and scholarly works and even today effectively undermines a permanent distinction between the book and the revelation.

One of the earliest reports narrating the words of the Prophet, "If the Qur'an were on an untanned hide and then thrown into a fire, it would not burn," appeared in Abu 'Ubayd's *The Excellences of the Qur'an*[4] (d. 224 AH/838 CE). It was later repeated in other sources, including some important and influential books, such as Ahmad Ibn Hanbal's (d. 241 AH/855 AD) *Musnad* or al-Suyuti's (d. 911 AH/1505 CE) *The Perfect Guide to the Sciences of the Qur'an*.[5] The report was accompanied by a gamut of interpretations. After citing this *hadith*, Abu 'Ubayd explained it metaphorically, suggesting that it should be understood in the following way: the hide is the heart of the believer, which represents the vessel in which the Qur'an is preserved via memorization. Those who memorize the Qur'an and "have it in their hearts" will not perish in hellfire. However, on the other side of the spectrum were scholars like Ibn Qutayba (d. 276 AH/889 CE) who in his *Interpretation of Conflicting Narrations*[6] left space for a more literal reading. He suggested that it was conceivable that in the times of the Prophet the actual book could indeed be immune to harm by fire.[7] The debates about how much the physical inscription of the Qur'anic text partook in the immaterial message continued for a while (I mentioned some of them already in the Introduction to this book). Of course, scholarly treaties of this kind—many of which comprised multiple volumes—are not commonly perused these days. They were composed at times when the body of foundational theological knowledge was still emerging and the nature of the Qur'anic message (including its position vis-à-vis its material medium) was likewise debated. The scholars who engaged the subject created a margin of hesitation as far as the corporeality of the Qur'anic message was concerned, as if recognizing the necessity of material mediation in dealings with the divine. However, after the formative period ended, the question of how much the Qur'an participated in its tangible instantiations ceased to occupy most scholarly minds, which turned to more pressing jurisprudential concerns. An early exchange of complex arguments and sophisticated examples had concluded with a general consensus in the form of a cautious acknowledgment that although the revelation was immaterial and eternal, the material book somehow participated in its heavenly source and, therefore, should be treated with care.[8]

Yet although scholars may have considered this issue somewhat resolved, it did not prevent the question of how much the materiality of the *mushaf* should underscore the immateriality of the message from surfacing in other ways and other times, but in less formal contexts. I suggest that the *hadith* recorded by Abu 'Ubayd centuries ago and other reports of this kind have a contemporary "proxy"—a folklore genre that my Muslim friends called "miraculous stories of the Qur'an." They comprise a variety of narratives in which the actual Qur'anic book often plays a role. Here is one of them, reported to me on different occasions and in slightly different versions:

> There was once a man in the house. It was in the Upper Egypt. He went to sleep and there was a surge in electricity that caused a spark [in some versions he forgot to blow out his candle] and his house caught on fire. Everything got burnt. His house and all that was inside. But when people were digging in the debris, they found a *mushaf*. Its covers were singed, but the pages inside were intact. It was a real miracle!

Curious about the accuracy of this story, I asked some of the Azhari sheikhs about their interpretations. Some dismissed it as an example of people's ignorance, others simply looked up to the sky, conveying with this gesture the idea that they were not sure what to think about it, but "Allah knows best." Yet like the old *hadith* narrated in *The Excellences of the Qur'an* and its renditions in other sources, these vernacular "miraculous stories of the Qur'an"—although incidental from the jurisprudential point of view—are not completely inconsequential. Apart from highlighting in a common imagery the power of the Qur'an as a divine message, they persist in making the distinction between the immaterial word of the Qur'an and its physical mediator less certain. In contemporary times and on a popular level, they reanimate the precarious question of where the immateriality of the Qur'anic message ends and where the materiality of a human-made *mushaf* begins, testifying to the fact that on the level of practice, and for a number of reasons, it is much harder to make this distinction stable.

In this vernacular genre of "miraculous stories of the Qur'an," apart from the narratives about the *mushaf* that withstood destruction by fire, there is also another strand that includes examples of situations in which the materiality of the Qur'anic book is evoked. These are typically stories about a pious person who was saved from danger by the tangible book itself. I have heard the following narrative told in reference to different military conflicts in which Egyptian soldiers have taken part in the past:

> There was a man who went to war. He was very pious and read his Qur'an a lot. One day he was in a battle and he got hit with a bullet. People thought he was dead, but he survived because the bullet got stuck in the mushaf he carried in the pocket on his chest.

This may be a "translation" of popular stories among Evangelical Christians in America related to a physical copy of the Bible, but the origins of this story, whether local or foreign, should not distract us from what it does in the Egyptian context.[9] As in the narratives about the *mushaf* that withstood burning, it reflects the difficulty of reconciling the tradition in which materiality of the Qur'anic book is taken seriously—like the examples recorded in *fada'il al-Qur'an*[10] that encouraged the practitioners to embellish the Qur'anic text, look at it during the recitation, or not to take it into the land of the infidels (a hard task in the age of globalization)—with the more contemporary interpretations and *fatwas* that treat the material instantiations of the Qur'an as having less theological weight. Against the opinion of sheikhs who prefer to dampen attentions to the material body of the text, this story features a man who is saved not because he recited the Qur'an from memory, but because he had the physical and tangible book with him. At the same time, the narrative cautiously leaves a margin for an alternative interpretation that does allow one to bypass the *mushaf* by assigning the agency directly to God—it was Allah who saved the pious soldier by letting the bullet hit the book, which happened to be the Qur'anic book.

However, such stories, whether accepted or ignored by religious scholars, do not have any political significance and do not stir up any serious discussions in the public realm. They are recounted via the internet or at informal gatherings and circulate as "maybe true" urban legends. Their power lies not in their credibility as much as in the discursive space they create for negotiation of different understandings about how important the material body of the message is and about the various degrees and conditions under which this tangible object participates in the blessings bestowed by the Qur'an itself. The presence of such stories in urban folklore does not call for any authoritative responses or pronouncements. On the contrary, because of the flexibility of their interpretations they can still be incorporated into sermons or speeches and used at occasions that are meant to remind people, in simple words, about the power of the Qur'an. These are ordinary stories told in ordinary circumstances, when the precise meanings and singular interpretations are not essential.

In contrast to such "free-floating" narratives, the events surrounding pastor Terry Jones's "Burn the Qur'an Day" required Muslim leaders to make a much more serious commentary on the physical presence of the book. It was the material body of a concrete object that allowed the message to be assaulted and, therefore, any reference to the Qur'an necessarily involved the *mushaf* as well. It was in this moment of crisis in which the entanglements of the message and its mediator became more pronounced, revealing some interesting tensions and making the old theological debates about the materiality of the Qur'an once again relevant. In terms of their content, the reactions of Muslims in Egypt to the abuse of the book ranged from those who felt that the destruction of the *mushaf* was for all intents and purposes equivalent to the destruction of the Qur'an itself, to those who adhered to the traditions found in *hadiths* and other narratives that treated the *mushaf* as nothing more than merely an index of the Qur'an, to those who, for a number of reasons, tried to downplay the materiality of the book by "dematerializing" it.

"Dematerializing" the Book

I spent a lot of time perusing the main Egyptian newspapers (*al-Ahram, Ruz al-Yussif, al-Yum 7, al-Fajr,* and *al-Masri al-Yum*) and news websites around the dates of the burning incidents. I expected them, as had happened before, to be much more exact in quoting any official statements made by VIPs than their American counterparts. Many of the articles focused on the responses of the American government and other important world leaders to those events and often used this subject to ponder more broadly current "American-Middle Eastern" relations. Those articles were always rich, sometimes disturbing, and often indicative of the depths of misunderstanding, ignorance, and resentment on both sides. Because of the breadth of their content, I mainly concentrated on the responses directly addressing the *mushaf* and on the official statements issued by the Azhari leaders, as they should, at least in theory, set the theological tone for the rest of Muslims in Egypt.

Incidentally, when Terry Jones burnt *mushafs* in 2010 and again a year later, he did not know that he was putting leaders of al-Azhar in a very precarious position. His iconoclastic acts demanded a Muslim answer that was as theological as it was political in its nature, and the answer certainly had to be diplomatic in style. Of course, as representatives of an important and influential Muslim institution, the heads of al-Azhar could not ignore the situation altogether, but they had to be very careful about how they framed their responses. The circumstances were tense and fraught with pitfalls. The burning incidents took place during a time of increased tensions in the country between the Coptic Christians and Muslims, including violence and bombings. The power of Muslim Brotherhood was on the rise, challenging al-Azhar's authority. In the midst of all of this theological and civil unrest, and with Mubarak's regime falling apart around them, the leaders of al-Azhar were expected to condemn the acts of burning Qur'anic books. Everybody knew that these would become political statements as well. After all, they had the potential to worsen Christian-Muslim relations within Egypt and beyond, as well as to jeopardize the Egyptian-American economic arrangements.

However, by censuring these acts the *'ulama'* did something else as well. Not only did they once again acknowledge the central status of the Qur'an in Islam, but they also implicitly admitted that the material instantiations of the message matters, somehow. Again, I want to emphasize that the political scope of the *'ulama*'s responses was wide and complex, and I do not wish to minimize it. But those responses also raised a question important for this project, which is: how is one to reject an unacceptable action without paying too much heed to the direct object of this action? This is not a trivial inquiry. For one thing, excessive attention to the act of abusing Qur'anic books could have had a further ripple effect in the form of continued violence, and the leaders of al-Azhar did not want that to happen. Secondly, speaking too much about the material object of the offensive act would not have been theologically correct either.

As reported by newspapers and news agencies, the response of the then-*Mufti* of al-Azhar, 'Ali Goma'a, was exemplary of the judicious approach taken by the officials of the institution and was as diplomatic as could be expected from a person in his position. He denounced the incineration of the Qur'anic text as a form of racism (without specifying, however, in what respect) and called for Muslims to stand together against depictions of Islam as a religion of violence and terrorism, showing the world the truth of Islam and the wisdom of upholding Muslim rights. He also denounced any form of violence and called for avoidance of extremism, as it was not a part of Islam that assumed a posture of tolerance and moderation. He emphasized that resisting injustice should be done by legitimate means and that living in the contemporary world required sharing, participating, and contributing to its civilization by ordinary people and their leaders as well. The *Mufti* also encouraged the engagement of Islam with science in order to benefit from technological achievements of our age. It is the role of '*ulama*' to instruct future generations in the ways of moderate Islam, he pointed out, and concluded that harmony in Islam depended on consensus between scholars and citizens alike. The Qur'anic book itself had very little presence in 'Ali Goma'a's speech, and the whole incident was eclipsed in his statement by a more general concern about the situation and role of the Muslim *umma* (community) within the contemporary world.

Grand Sheikh al-Tayyeb echoed some of these sentiments as well, repeating that the calls to burn the Qur'anic books were a form of racism and that they would have disastrous consequences for the relationships between people and for the preservation of peace, as they would inevitably anger the Muslim community. But he also footnoted his statement by saying that the Qur'an had been memorized by Muslims through centuries, and it would continue to be memorized until the end of time, as it had been promised in the Qur'an itself. By adding this point, Sheikh al-Tayyeb clearly shifted the emphasis away from the actual book to the immateriality of the eternal message and the obligation of committing it to memory.

Two years later, however, his speech had a different tone. In his response against the burning of *mushafs* in Bagram, Afghanistan, he said that a mistreatment of Qur'anic books is a "red line" for any Muslim who will defend al-Qur'an al-Karim with his blood and life. Al-Tayyeb stated that scholars at al-Azhar were extremely annoyed with such barbaric behavior. He followed this with a demand that American aggressors stop the assaults on Muslim people that had been taking place under the guise of a "war on terror." In al-Tayyeb's opinion, the only way to abate violence in Afghanistan was for Americans to leave the country, as the French had eventually done in the nineteenth century after their occupation of Egypt. He warned that promises of leaving the country should be followed by actions, because people nowadays have changed and would not be deceived by words only. He also connected this incident of book abuse with another one that took place two hundred years ago. He said, "The military had committed this crime before, when the horses of French occupiers entered [al-Azhar] and abused the Qur'anic copies there, and [the soldiers] were not satisfied with ripping them apart, but also insulted them in a barbaric way." He ended by calling, "Enough, aggressors! Let the people determine their own destinies and choose their own path! Do not add Bagram to the record of Guantanamo [another instance of the books' abuse], the record of shameful actions that history will not forgive."[11]

Al-Tayyeb's speech focused on the political situation in Afghanistan, but significantly, it also involved the material body of the Qur'anic book in a much more direct way than previously. First of all, the Grand Sheikh referred to "mistreatments of the Qur'an," which was done through the abuse of the book. He warned his American audience that Muslims were ready to give up their lives in defense of the Qur'an, which again referred to the physical mistreatment of the *mushaf*. He also recalled another historical episode in which Qur'anic codices were abused. As a result (and unlike his previous statement two years earlier), the clear distinction between the immaterial revelation of the Qur'an and its material mediator was harder to make, with the *mushaf* noticeably standing in for the Qur'an. Truth be told, the Grand Sheikh's second response to Western abuse of the *mushaf* was more in line with popular sentiments expressed by ordinary Egyptian Muslims, but at the same time, it was somewhat less typical of the overall tone expressed by Egyptian religious leaders on that matter.

Because of the theological implications, the Egyptian *'ulama'* discourage paying too much attention to the *mushaf* as an object, because in their opinion, it diverts practitioners' attention away from the message and gives an impression that Muslims are mistaken about the real source of the *mushaf*'s power, which is Allah. So in order to avoid this potential confusion, some *'ulama'* have taken part in a strategy that might be described as an effort to "dematerialize" the book. They have done this by more openly disengaging the content of the book from its material form—focusing on the message and downplaying the book. This was the main point of a presentation given by the former deputy of al-Azhar, Sheikh Mahmud 'Ashur, at a conference that examined the problem of responses to religiously meaningful objects. At a symposium organized in response to "Burn the Qur'an Day" in America by the Islamic Sufi Forum entitled "Islamic Symbols: Between Sanctification and Profanation," Sheikh 'Ashur expressed an opinion, which Egyptian newspapers called a "surprise of a high caliber," that the burning of the Qur'anic copies was not a "disaster" (*musiba*) after all. He said:

> We as Muslims burn the Qur'an when its pages wear out. [This is, indeed, an acceptable practice to dispose of old *mushafs*.] We also burn *mushafs* that are distorted. This is not a call to burn, but the problem of the poor condition of Muslims and their alienation from the content of the Qur'an.[12]

From Sheikh 'Ashur's point of view, the issue of "burning the Qur'an" had distracted Muslims away from a more significant problem, which was the lack of "activation of the Qur'anic message" in people's lives. In this opinion, the Qur'an should be applied to one's moral behavior rather than displayed as an object in one's living room to gain blessings, or kept for adornment, or used in other superficially religious ways. This is contrary to the wisdom sent in the Qur'an, 'Ashur declared.

During the same conference, another participant, 'Imar 'Ali Hasan, gave a similar presentation. He emphasized the less-accepted (but more "logocentric") part of the *sunna*, which claimed that there were no written copies of the Qur'anic text during the time of the Prophet. In spite of this state of affairs, the scholar reminded his audience, the message of the Qur'an had nonetheless endured. Not surprisingly, both of these viewpoints met with mostly critical responses from readers of the internet news websites that had reported on conference and its content. The critics saw 'Ashur's and Hasan's words as attacks "on the book of Allah." The much less immanent concept of the Qur'an offered by these two scholars clearly did not fit within the idioms of semiotic ideology operating among the majority of Egyptian practitioners.

The efforts to dematerialize the book—or, at a minimum, to make it more transparent—have taken place not only among some of the religious leaders in Egypt but also among those graduates of al-Azhar who have been drawn to a more puritan strand of Islam percolating into the country from the Gulf, Saudi Arabia in particular. The graduates who embrace the Salafi vision of Islam (which rejects a large portion of what they perceive a "folk" Islamic tradition) feel very uncomfortable with any discussion of the Qur'an in relation to its material medium. This is because an emphasis on the forms of material mediation of the Qur'anic text sounds too much like idolatry and, by extension, one more example of the "western assault on Islam," as one particularly conservative Salafi sheikh implied in a rather tense conversation with me. According to his interpretation of Islam, the suggestion that Muslims pay close attention to the material Qur'an is a false accusation that should not be tolerated. More than anyone else today, many Salafis are emphatic that the *mushaf* acquires its importance solely from the fact that it indexes the Qur'anic message, but in and of itself this index is insignificant.

Paper Burns... Again

Yet efforts of Egyptian religious leaders to sort out the proper degrees of intimacy with the *mushaf*, including steps toward a disengagement of the message from its material instantiation in order to prevent any associations with idolatry or magic, are diffused and incapacitated by rules built upon the Muslim tradition that call for a particular treatment of Qur'anic books. A semiotic ideology that accommodates the idea of a tangible book participating in the power of the message has to operate within a broader field of religious practices that sustain and perpetuate it. These practices are especially effective if they engage the book's material form in a variety of ways, further stabilizing a particular set of convictions about the importance of the Qur'an's material instantiations. Earlier, I mentioned a bundling effect that allows books to be handy and to burn easily at the same time. This propensity of paper to burn—fortuitous for those who want to burn the Qur'anic book as a form of protest—has an additional effect on religious practice in Egypt. It allows Muslims to easily dispose of old Qur'anic copies in a legally accepted way. My own encounters with this particular etiquette were frequent and took many forms. Among the many examples in my field notes, this was my favorite episode, as it also highlighted the contingent nature of ethnographic fieldwork.

I was walking to pick up our kids from school. On the edge of the street curb, in a pile of rubbish, I noticed a burnt piece of paper with a characteristic *tashkil* and numbers of *ayas* still visible on the unscorched fragments. I leaned to pick it up. It was one of those little booklets (*juz'*) with the Qur'anic text. Evidently, someone tried to burn it and didn't make sure that it was fully gone. There was a young Egyptian couple walking right behind me. When the man saw me picking up the paper, he glanced at my hand and, passing by, asked,

"What is it?"

"An *aya* from the Qur'an," I replied, thinking about putting the paper in my bag. He said,

"Give it to me."

I handed over the tiny scratch of paper.

"Do you have a lighter?" He asked, touching his pockets, visibly looking for one.

"No," I said. "I don't smoke."

"Ok, I will keep it then. Thank you," he added, putting the piece in his jacket. They speeded up, getting ahead of me.

This was not the only occurrence in which the importance of the proper disposal of the Qur'anic text came up. The first time it happened, I was printing out pages of an article that included quotes from the Qur'an in Arabic. A man waiting in line to print remarked, "If you have any pages that you don't need, I'll take them. They need to be burnt." I heard this kind of statement many times during my years in Egypt, as it is one of the legally acceptable ways of disposing of a *mushaf* that is not usable anymore. (The other ways include burial in a ritually clean place or donation to a mosque.) This etiquette is formed in the basic religious education taught to Egyptian children and publicly confirmed, in one example, on the al-Azhar's *fatwa* website. There one may find the opinion issued by *Mufti* 'Ali Goma'a:

> A *mushaf* that is good for reading should not be burnt because of its inviolability [*hurma*]. But if it becomes unsuitable for reading it may be burnt, as [this opinion] is maintained by a majority of scholars.[13]

The *fatwas* related to the official disposal of Qur'anic copies by burning—and there are many of them on various religious educational websites, articulating more or less the same opinion—are based on a careful analysis of *hadiths* available on this subject in the writings of classical scholars representing different schools of religious law. One of the narratives most often quoted in these situations is a well-known and widely accepted *hadith* referenced by al-Bukhari that recalls the story of the first official codification of the Qur'anic manuscript in the times of caliph 'Uthman Ibn 'Affan. That codification provided an important precedent for later legal rulings on the matter of proper disposal, as 'Uthman Ibn 'Affan ordered the Qur'anic copies that were unfitting in the eyes of the editorial committee to be burned:

> Hudhaifa Ibn al-Yaman came to 'Uthman at the time when the people of Sham and the people of Iraq were waging war to conquer Armenia and Azerbaijan. Hudhaifa was afraid of their [the people of Sham and Iraq] differences in the recitation of the Qur'an, so he said to 'Uthman, "O chief of the Believers! Save this nation before they differ about the Book [Qur'an] as Jews and the Christians did before." So 'Uthman sent a message to Hafsa saying, "Send us the manuscripts of the Qur'an so that we may compile the Qur'anic materials in perfect copies and return the manuscripts to you." Hafsa sent it to 'Uthman. 'Uthman then ordered Zayd Ibn Thabit, 'Abdullah Ibn al-Zubayr, Sa'id Ibn al-As, and 'Abd al-Rahman Ibn Harith Ibn Hisham to rewrite the manuscripts in perfect copies. 'Uthman said to the three Qurayshi men, "In case you disagree with Zayd Ibn Thabit on any point in the Qur'an, then write it in the dialect of Quraysh, as the Qur'an was revealed in their tongue." They did so, and when they had written many copies, 'Uthman returned the original manuscripts to Hafsa. 'Uthman sent to every Muslim province one copy of what they had copied, and ordered that all the other Qur'anic materials, whether written in fragmentary manuscripts or whole copies, be burnt.[14]

This *hadith* is considered to be an essential part of Muslim religious history as well as a legal precedent to induce a more general rule of conduct when one wants to dispose of objects containing the Qur'anic text. Unsurprisingly, then, it was evoked by one of the Egyptian weekly magazines, *al-Fajr*, at the time of "Burn the Qur'an Day" controversy. It accompanied an editorial on the matter of this incident in Florida, as an ancillary clarification and a suitable reminder of the ethical difference between the two types of Qur'an burning.[15]

I could see the legal principle of burning the unwanted copies of the Qur'anic text applied not only to the book or its pages, but also in less ubiquitous circumstances, like this peculiar evangelism project of hanging certain *ayas* from the Qur'an printed in English, Arabic, and French from the branches of an old willow tree on Road 9—a street in the Ma'adi suburb of Cairo, well known for its international restaurants and upscale shops. The printed sheet read in pidgin English at the bottom: "If you want to destroy this paper, please by burning because it may include words about Allah (His Highness) or Prophet Muhammad. And to leave it better... Thank You for your understanding." The author of this project indicated that the need to burn the paper came from the fact that it contained "words about Allah or Prophet Muhammad," not necessarily because these were direct citations of the Qur'anic *ayas*. However, this might have been a matter of poor translation into English rather than a different understanding of the nature of these quotes and their relationship to paper.

"Rematerializing" the Book

The protocol of burning unusable copies of the Qur'anic text belongs to a wider set of rules known as *adab al-Qur'an*—the etiquette of the Qur'an—which includes a large number of guidelines on how to properly handle the book. I will speak of *adab al-mushaf*, the rules of conduct that pertain to touching, storing, or using Qur'anic books, in the next chapter. But for now, let's specifically consider the acts of burning *mushafs* in regard to the meaning they acquire within a semiotic ideology in which the material body of the message can at times become contentious, thus further undermining efforts to easily disengage the text from its material form.

The rule of respectfully discarding Qur'anic copies by burning them performs a number of tasks. First, it obviously refuses to accept the modern distinction between the text and the book so easily taken for granted in Euro-American culture. Second, it allows us to better understand why practices that engage the book's materiality performed by non-Muslims are scrutinized and taken very seriously by Muslim communities at large. Third, they complicate the efforts toward the dematerialization of the book, such as the statements made by al-Azhar officials mentioned earlier in this chapter, or the opinions expressed at times by the Salafi-oriented practitioners who call for a "return to the tradition of the righteous forebears," thus calling into question many practices accepted and carried out by the majority of Egyptian Muslims.

Let's begin with the first task. Burning *mushafs* as a form of disposal is not simply a symbolic gesture or a matter of choice; it is a religious obligation. Muslim practitioners in Egypt go to great lengths to make sure that this is, in fact, done to any paper carrying the Qur'anic message. Moreover, this is also a practice where the materiality of the book intersects with politics on a governmental level. The religiously sanctioned disposal of *mushafs* also includes any kind of misprinted Qur'anic material created as a by-product of regular book printing activities. Any printing press found guilty of not taking proper care of such remains can be fined, although they can also be fined for burning trash within the city limits. This means that the best way to discard such books or pages is by burning them in the desert, which is a rather cumbersome activity, as one of the press workers I talked to admitted with a sigh. Whether disposed of by individuals or companies, these copies of the Qur'anic text participate directly in the transactions that undoubtedly strengthen the relationship between the text and the book that mediates it.

Thus, the well-documented classical tradition of discarding the *mushaf* in particular ways is maintained by contemporary practices of its disposal, indexing the divine status of the book's content and leaving a space for different understandings of *whether, when,* and *how* indexing becomes something closer to a matter of oneness. Varying semiotic ideologies operating in Muslim communities produce discrete responses. The dogma that the Qur'anic revelation is the verbatim words of Allah instantiated on paper means that it can be debated how exactly that instantiation is taking place. But, as long as it is done, any other forms of physical activity involving the *mushaf* will have to be investigated as well, including the intention with which this activity has been done. In other words, on an ethical level the burning of *mushafs* performed by Pastor Terry Jones in Florida was not the same as the burning of *mushafs* performed by Muslims in Egypt. In the first case the intention was to destroy the material books so that they are obliterated. In the other, the destruction of old *mushafs* was done with anticipation of new ones to come.

However, the fact that the physical body of the Qur'anic message has to be disposed of in a particular way—an ordinance among other book-centered rules of the etiquette—inevitably collapses the power of the message and its material body into one. As a countermeasure against this problem, Muslim scholars have to periodically admonish practitioners about the proper ways of using the *mushaf* in other circumstances, lest the people be confused about what constitutes the right forms of engagement with the book's material form. So keeping a *mushaf* in the car for protection is not a proper activity, but keeping it in the car as a reminder of God's providence is fine. Sleeping with it under one's pillow to deter headaches is not a proper thing to do, but keeping it by one's bedside to pray when the headache comes is correct. Giving a pendant in a shape of a *mushaf* as a gift is discouraged, but giving a *mushaf* as a gift is encouraged. This list could go on and on and illustrates the predicament of negotiating the forms of Qur'anic mediation on a daily basis and the constant diligence of religious authorities to monitor these activities in addition to the usual task of interpreting the Qur'anic content.

Given the number of Qur'anic books sold in Egypt every year and the established presence of multiple *mushafs* in most Egyptian households, it is inevitable that this negotiation will constantly take place with varying results and sometimes completely new effects. An expensive *mushaf*, even if used for reading, may be displayed at home in a prominent place. The same owner may decide to use a cheaper copy in the car for reading as well as protection. Another spare copy brought from the *hajj* might be placed in his shop window to extend the book's *baraka* (blessings) in other locals as well. This flexibility in tapping into the apotropaic power of the book would not be as easily possible two hundred years ago. Where *mushafs* abound—handled in officially prescribed ways, of course—the allure to perceive the Qur'anic book as more than just a "reminder" of the Qur'anic message is tenacious. Whether the blessings are immanent in the book, or just from what the book indexes, or both, on the level of practice these theological distinctions do not matter as long as they are effective. From this point of view and in the eyes of many Egyptian practitioners, the scholarly reminders to discern the exact source of power appear to be beside the point. The material Qur'anic text is important, somehow.

Prophet's Medicine

"The repudiation of the material is always a selective process," says Matthew Engelke in his ethnography of religious transactions that aim at making some material objects less substantial. "What sustains projects of immateriality in religious practice is always the definition of what counts as materially dangerous."[16] That said, I would argue that in the case of the Qur'an and its instantiations, instead of defining "what counts as dangerous," it is more precise to speak of what is defined as forbidden or acceptable within the bounds of the discursive tradition with which the practitioners can engage. The difficulty to repudiate or to negotiate materiality in the context of *sunna* that are based on the codification of an enormous body of authoritative actions is best exemplified by the discussions surrounding two very popular customs of making *hagabs* (amulets) for protection and writing Qur'anic *ayas* with honey, saffron, and water to obtain healing. These customs are not only popular in Egypt, and both of these practices have advocates as well as opponents. The arguments for which they are rejected or accepted nicely illustrate the mechanisms by which the traditional knowledge of *sunna* is applied. This is because Islamic tradition in its richness provides evidence for both the renunciation of objects and substances as well as their acknowledgment and value. In the context of the use of Qur'anic *ayas* for healing purposes, the selective process of accepting or repudiating the material is tied, then, to a number of factors, including the kinds of substances with which the *ayas* are written as well as the prerogative of the narratives that support these transactions.

Interestingly, the use of honey, saffron, and water in religious healing practices conveniently dovetails with contemporary discourse about natural health and natural healing methods that is rapidly spreading in Egypt. Arabic literature on that subject is available in many bookstores and small book and magazine stands scattered throughout the streets of Cairo. Over the past decade or so, shops that sell organic and natural products have appeared in more affluent areas in the city as well as the stands, booths, and makeshift businesses catering to poorer consumers. Among the increasingly popular Egyptian self-help books and brochures on how to improve one's health, there are many that discuss the advantages of consuming honey as a form of natural, organic, scientifically confirmed remedy. They range from books written by professional doctors to publications prepared by herbalists and amateur writers, in which the authors promote the use of honey as a cough suppressant, as a treatment for "corrupted phlegm in the stomach and to soften the general constitution of the body," as a way to increase appetite, and, when drunk regularly with water, as a safeguard against infections. Some of these books advertise honey as a detoxicant for drug users, as an antitoxin to treat the accidental eating of poisonous plants, and as an effective medicine for cuts, burns, hangovers, sore throat, and sleeplessness. It can also be used as a natural skin moisturiser.[17] One pamphlet in particular recommended drinking it with hot water as a remedy for dog bites and rabies. All in all, the range of ailments claimed to be cured by honey is indeed very wide.

What singles honey out in the lists of natural remedies is that it has a religious genealogy as well. The publications on the benefits of bee products are often accompanied by reports that indicate the Prophet's love for honey, recorded in major collections of *sunna*. And not only did he take pleasure in consuming it, but he also recommended it for medical purposes, as noted in the major collections of *hadiths Sahih al-Bukhari, Sahih Muslim*, and *Jami' al-Tarmidhi*:

> A man came to the Prophet (peace be upon him) and said, "My brother is suffering from loose bowels." He said: "Let him drink honey." So he drank it. Then, the man came and said: "O Messenger of Allah (peace be upon him)! He has drunk honey, but it has only made him worse." So the Messenger of Allah (peace be upon him) said: "Let him drink honey." So the brother drank it. Then the man came and said: "O Messenger of Allah (peace be upon him)! I gave him some more to drink, but it has only made him worse." The Messenger of Allah (peace be upon him) said: "Allah has told the truth, and your brother's stomach has lied. Give him honey to drink." So the man gave him more honey to drink and the brother was cured.[18]

This report is supported in many medical contexts by two less authoritative *hadiths* recorded by Ibn Majah, who described the Prophet as saying, "You should take the two that bring healing: honey and the Qur'an,"[19] and "Whoever eats honey three mornings each month, will not suffer any serious calamity."[20] Such collectively supported narratives about the consumption of honey not only for pleasure but also for therapeutic purposes have reverberated with the reports of modern pharmacological research about its health benefits, thus persuasively synchronizing the authority of a religious tradition with the authority of modern medical science. Self-help publications effectively combine the *sunna* narratives, like the one about the Prophet curing a man suffering from diarrhea, more general quotes from the Qur'an that mention honey, and ethnomedical and allopathic research in order to promote the taking care of one's health as a holistic endeavor in which religious wisdom is merged with and additionally supported by scientific knowledge. Books about *al-tibb al-nabawi*, the Prophet's medicine, have their niche in terms of their audience and places of dissemination, including the vicinity of al-Azhar Mosque where, among many other spices and natural remedies, jars of honey and books on how to apply it can be purchased at the same time.

Like honey, the use of saffron as a food spice, medicinal herb, and dye has a long history in the Middle East, and contemporary pharmaceutical studies have confirmed its therapeutic properties as well. Its beautiful and vibrant orange-yellow hue is very unique and impossible to obtain through other natural pigments. Also, like honey, saffron appears in various collections of *hadiths*, although mainly in the narratives prohibiting its use as a dye, as it is, according to the Qur'an, characteristic of the garb worn by Christians. However, there are a few sources that mention it in a medicinal context. It is recalled as an ingredient used in a recipe, supposedly dictated by the Prophet himself, that recommends writing specific verses of the Qur'an in saffron on the surface of a bowl, then dissolving the writing in water, preferably from the Zamzam spring in Mecca, and drinking it for healing purposes.[21] In spite of the rather weak provenience of this *hadith*, the practice of writing Qur'anic *ayas* in saffron is popular in Egypt and even more common in Gulf countries, and the instructions on how to write a *ruqya* (incantation) with saffron can be easily found on YouTube, if one wants to know how to do it.

These three substances—honey, powdered saffron diluted in water, and water by itself—have been commonly used in healing transactions that, in spite of exposing the Qur'anic *ayas* to digestible matters, cannot be easily repudiated. Their occurrence in the *hadiths* above and others in which the Prophet's companions are reported to have used honey, saffron, or water in similar ways creates a precedence and makes both the transaction and the substance permissible. An additional layer of endorsement is cumulatively provided by further instructions in using honey, saffron, and water for writing of the Qur'anic *ayas*, communicated by the scholars of the formative era. For instance, Imam Ibn al-Qayyim's (d. 751/1350) *Provision of the Hereafter*[22] in which he ponders the action of drinking water in which the Qur'anic *ayas* had been dissolved, and finds this transaction permissible, is now cited along other *hadiths* as a proof of the lawfulness of this practice. Given this precedence, many Egyptian *fatwa* websites include a verdict allowing this particular transaction, indicating that the question of ingesting Qur'anic *ayas* is still relevant, quite popular, and permissible.

However, even those who support the conviction that honey, saffron, and water in conjunction with Qur'anic verses can produce healing results admit—perhaps recognizing the slippery slope of mingling the message with the matter—that it is better to pray over the honey, saffron, or water and, then to drink it, instead of using these materials for writing. "Can you tell me how to make a *ruqya* (prayer or intention written down on a piece of paper) with honey?" I inquired of the owner of a bee products booth across the street from the al-Azhar Mosque. "Why do you want to make a *ruqya*?" he replied. Scooping his hands as if he were going to inhale an invisible substance, he said, "Just pray over it, make an intention, and eat it."

Hagabs

While *ruqyas* made out of honey or saffron are permissible among all Muslim legal schools (though perhaps not encouraged), writing Qur'anic verses on paper and wearing them in the form of an amulet (*hagab* or *tamima*) is more disputable. The *hadiths* and other sources that report this transaction are rather contradictory, and so it is possible to argue both for or against the practice. In their rejection of or contingent acceptance of it, contemporary sources of legal opinions "digested" for popular use in the mass media and on websites reflect the complicated landscape of religious politics and alliances. *Hagabs* and *tamimas*—like the prayer beads described by Younes Saramifar[23]—belong to a group of objects that draw a line between those who support the more selective and definite visions of Islam promoted by sheikhs from Saudi Arabia and those who adhere to the more "object-friendly" interpretations of Islamic tradition.

Undeniably, the growing presence of religious television channels available from the Saudi Kingdom and Saudi financial support for building religious schools and clinics in Egypt have been gradually changing local understandings of what correct Muslim practice should be in Egypt. Al-Azhar itself, perhaps looking for allies against the authoritarian tendencies of the Egyptian military government, has opened itself over the past few years to Saudi influences (and lucre), creating an increasingly contested space where the question of correct practice regarding Qur'anic amulets is more likely to be officially debated in the future. But today there is still a clear distinction between the Azhari and Saudi takes on this tradition. Overall, the official *fatwas* and personal commentaries posted in Egyptian media are much more sympathetic to the practice of procuring talismans when compared to those posted on the Saudi websites. The Egyptian sites support the legality of this transaction by highlighting the traditional narratives that affirm this practice directly or at least imply its permissibility, although they also make it clear that it is only the Qur'anic amulets that are acceptable.

Like incantations that visualize the Qur'anic *ayas* for the purpose of ingestion to improve health, amulets containing written Qur'anic verses are expected to work in a similar manner—to protect from harm and to bestow blessings and health on their users. A number of my friends wear such *hagabs* containing verses that are regarded to be particularly potent, including the famous *ayat al-Kursi*:

> Allah—there is no deity except Him, the Ever-Living, the Sustainer of [all] existence. Neither drowsiness overtakes Him nor sleep. To Him belongs whatever is in the heavens and whatever is on the earth. Who is it that can intercede with Him except by His permission? He knows what is [presently] before them and what will be after them, and they encompass not a thing of His knowledge except for what He wills. His Throne [Kursi] extends over the heavens and the earth, and their preservation tires Him not. And He is the Most High, the Most Great (Q. 2:255).[24]

Users of *hagabs* often wear them in little leather pouches and are very particular about when and where they are worn, making sure that they take them off when entering the bathroom, for example.

The following *fatwa*[25] answering a question whether it is permitted to wear *hagabs* was posted on the Dar al-Ifta' website (the branch of al-Azhar responsible for issuing *fatwas*) in 2014. It was not signed by any *mufti* in particular, but it is rather long and elaborate, citing a number of sources that permit the wearing of talismans on certain conditions:

The term "amulet" (tamima) has two meanings: one—the beads attached by the Arabs to their children for protection against the evil eye, [a practice that] has been abolished by Islam;[26] two—a piece of paper on which a verse from the Qur'an has been written and attached like a necklace for blessings.[27] It is part of Muslim doctrine that what has been created cannot affect other creations out of its own will [as opposed to God's permission]. So whoever believes in the possibility of such effects coming not from Allah, he engages himself in polytheism [shirk]. The Sheikh of Islam, Ibn Hajar al-Haytami [d. 973 AH/1566 CE], said, "This is ignorance and error, and one of the greatest sins. And even if it is not shirk, it leads to it, as it is only Allah the Highest that gives benefits and withholds, prevents and defends."[28]

However, if one does not believe that amulets affect out of their own will, then there are two cases: either they are made of the Qur'an or not from the Qur'an. If the ones not from the Qur'an are made from prayers, and litanies, and good words, this is permissible. But if they are the opposite—in the language of talismans and unrecognizable Arabic or in another language—then this is not permissible.

The amulets from the Qur'an, and what falls under this category of prayers, litanies, and good words, according to the assembly of scholars of *fikh* (Maliki, Hanafi, Shafi'i, and according to a narration about Imam Ahmad [Ibn Hanbal]) are permissible. They inferred it from the words of Allah the Highest: "And We send down of the Qur'an that which is healing and mercy for the believers, but it does not increase the wrongdoers except in loss" (Q. 17:82).

The Imam al-Qurtubi [d. 671 AH/1273 CE] in his book Tafsir al-Qurtubi[29] said that the scholars differed about what it means that the Qur'an is a healing [shifa']: one—that it is a healing for the hearts as it removes ignorance and doubt, and opens the heart to understanding of wonders and things that lead to Allah the Highest; two—a healing from actual sickness by incantations and prayer of protection, and so forth.

So the written protective amulets, as mentioned, are not prohibited. So, for a Muslim to wear it with an intention of obtaining blessings is fine, as according to words of the Highest "And this [Qur'an] is a Book We have revealed [which is] blessed, so follow it and fear Allah that you may receive mercy" (Q. 6:155).

[…] So whoever wears the Qur'an should be guided by Allah and not by anything else. Because it is Allah who should be desired in the healing by the Qur'an.[30]

In addition to these examples, there are nine other instances cited in this *fatwa* that indicate the permissibility of making amulets containing written verses of the Qur'an *in certain circumstances*. Birgit Meyer says that in order to understand "what things do" we need to generate "detailed insights into the different modes through which relations between people and things are shaped and transmitted in particular settings."[31] In the Muslim context, these *fatwas* act as one of the mechanisms through which the proper relationships between objects and things are established. They make it clear which forms of engagement with the material instantiations of the Qur'anic text, and on what conditions, are endorsed. Only the endorsed amulets can do "the job" properly. Others encroach into the murky territory of magic and idolatry. It is important to notice that the permissibility of making amulets with the Qur'anic text hinges upon the practitioner's correct understanding of the basic Islamic principle of *tawhid*—the absolute oneness of Allah. As the author of the *fatwa* explains, objects cannot be expected to act of their own accord; they can only be animated through the creative power of God. Moreover, what is ingested disappears immediately while the amulets (at least the unlawful ones in the eyes of religious authorities) attempt to usurp the power of the message through the text that is not read or recited.

Yet the idea that the power of the message can be somehow contained and manipulated to one's advantage is very appealing. Therefore, every now and then the Egyptian newspapers report stories of people who have been arrested on the premise of using the Qur'anic text in practices that were meant to sow harm and discord in the community. Similarly, reports of the Qur'anic books being found in "suspicious circumstances"—being bundled up and covered in strange substances or left in forbidden spaces—are not that rare. These incidents are usually ascribed to a local *sahir* (a magician or person that has dealings with *jinns* or demons) or a person who attempts to tap into the undisputed power of the Qur'an by employing its mediator (*mushaf*) for gains that breach the ethical rules of the community and promote antisocial values, such as jealousy or revenge. A *sahir* usually acts on behalf of a client who desires to secretively benefit through means that are considered wrong or at least disputable by the majority of the client's neighbors. Yet one thing that differentiates a contemporary *sahir* from his antecedents is that now he has easy access to the object of his manipulations—cheap editions of the Qur'anic books that can be inexpensively bought at any mosque, bookstand, bookstore, and peddler in the city.

The *sunna* and the *fatwas* based on them that are meant to regulate the relationship between the immaterial Qur'an and its material mediators produce, then, a double effect. On the one hand, they instruct the practitioners about the proper understandings and uses of the Qur'anic books vis-à-vis the message they mediate. On the other, they open the door to potential abuses of the *mushaf* that are enabled by the very materiality of the book—the fact that it is made out of paper, written, printed, or perforated; and that it is small, portable, flammable, and often inexpensively made. These particular material features of the Qur'anic books have been at the forefront of my story so far. However, my examination of the *mushaf* as an object would be deficient if I did not address in my last chapter another turning point in the ways in which the Qur'anic message is materially mediated. Let's now talk about the *mushaf* of bytes.

9

Body, Gender, and How to Enact "Electronic Qur'ans"

The basic premise of this chapter is simple: in practice, things are "enacted" and their meaning is created.[1] As I emphasized earlier, the acknowledgment that the Qur'an is the words of Allah does not only happen through speech. Muslims not only say that the Qur'an is unique, they also enact it through what they do with the *mushaf* as an object, through the acts of recitation, exegesis, display, burning, calligraphy, making amulets, and so on. The reality of something utterly other is brought into being through what is done with something very familiar, common, and tangible—a book. However, when the technology that mediates that text changes, the practices that enact it inevitably change as well to accommodate this new and unprecedented materiality of the text. The question is: how? And what happens, theologically, as a result of it?

This is what I want to explore in this chapter: the enactments that specifically engage a new materiality of the Qur'an—digital technology. I want to see what things emerge as a result of this evolution, especially since digitization of the Qur'anic text is a relatively new phenomenon. The attempts to reproduce the Qur'anic text in a digital format have been taking place for about three decades. But only within the last twenty years or so have software and apps companies started selling electronic editions of the Qur'an in Arabic. This incorporation of the digital as a form of Qur'anic mediation is not neutral, though. On a certain level, a digital *mushaf* changes the ways in which people perceive the text and redefine the practices that surround it. A book made of paper is not the same as the Qur'anic text on the screen of a phone. A text visible on the page is not accessed in the same way as a digitized version under a plastic cover. By surveying instances in which the Qur'an is enacted through the daily routines of worship and piety known as "the etiquette of the *mushaf*," and by inquiring into what happens when the *mushaf*—the book itself—is gone, I want to once again examine the complexity of the relationship between the text and the object that mediates it.

Etiquette of the *Mushaf*

Let's begin with the forms of rapport long established between practitioners and their printed Qur'anic copies known as *adab al-mushaf*. Outlining this rapport first, especially the issue of who and on what conditions can handle the Qur'anic copies, will allow me to better highlight recent transformations that have taken place as a result of the incorporation of the Qur'anic text through a medium that contains memory chips and internet access instead of pages and binding. So let's focus first on the etiquette of the Qur'anic book.

A quick search online for the word "Qur'an" shows that in popular English, the Qur'an is often referred to as the Muslim "holy book" or the "Holy Qur'an." Yet strictly speaking—as we already know—the Qur'an is not a book. Nor it is "holy" in the common understanding of this word. Neither the book nor the message is "holy" in the way Christians refer to the Bible. In the Arabic language, the word *muqaddas* (holy) and its derivatives do not index the Qur'an or its tangible body. Perhaps this is because *al-kitab al-muqaddas*—the "holy book"—is the phrase already reserved by Arabic-speaking Christians to describe their own scripture, the Bible. My friends in Egypt never spoke of the Qur'an or a *mushaf*'s holiness but instead would emphasize the notion of "deference" (*ihtiram*), which should be directed toward the book that contains the text of the Qur'an. The word *ihtiram* etymologically comes from the root *harima* "to be prohibited, to be forbidden, to exclude, or withhold," which in some of its derivative verbal forms has the connotation of describing something set aside or inviolable. But rather than relying solely on the semantic field of this word, I suggest we turn to the actual practices of *ihtiram* performed by Qur'anic users, people who read and handle Qur'anic copies in the course of their daily activities. Let's think of them as meaning-making enactments of the Qur'an expressed through the etiquette of the *mushaf* or *adab al-mushaf*.

What practitioners know about *adab al-mushaf* comes from lessons at the mosque, education at home, mass media programming, and self-study. This knowledge pertains to multiple situations in the course of daily activities, not only strictly pietic ones. Over time, I trained myself to pay attention to the small gestures of *ihtiram* that surrounded the *mushaf* in private and public spaces. I learned to notice that a *mushaf* was not left open turned upside down, was not covered with other books and objects, and was not left on the floor or on a table with food. I watched these acts of deferment implemented every day through gestures of *ihtiram*. I saw my friends and strangers uncover a *mushaf* that was accidentally buried under other things, pick it up, move it, put it away; I learned where and when it could be left undisturbed, at least as much as life in crowded and polluted spaces allowed. In the discussions about the Qur'an, I was given many examples of what not to do with the *mushaf*: I was warned not to wet my finger with my saliva when turning the pages; not to read it in bed; not to sit on, sleep with, or lean upon a *mushaf*; not to throw it; not to put anything between its pages except empty sheets of paper; and not to scribble notes in it. Producing commentaries on the Qur'an, I was reminded, has always been considered a very profound religious activity and cannot be compared with the marginal notations of a personal and private character added by a layman for later study or edification. Although it may be interpreted in several ways, the essential principle—as one of the sheikhs put it—is not to "mix into the Qur'an what is not of it." (In the past, different styles of script were occasionally used to differentiate the Qur'an from "what is not of it," such as writing the Qur'an in proper *naskh* but writing the inter-linear translations in Persian in *ta'liq* script.) In other words, it is preferable not to blend the text of the Qur'an with non-religious texts or random objects. For the same reason, citations from the Qur'an in religious writings are usually fully vocalized and separated from the rest of the text by brackets or other forms of font enhancement. Sometimes ordinary acts of respect would take me by surprise or frustrate me. I remember the moment of awkwardness when my friend Rahab's mother conspicuously removed a pair of golden earrings I accidentally put on her *mushaf*. I also remember incidents in one of the university libraries where I worked, where an anonymous patron would persistently and daily remove a *mushaf* from the lower shelf (where its call number would require it to be) to the top shelf, out of cataloging order. How are all these different transactions conceptualized? They are situated in a broader set of religious tenets that take us back to the early theological questions of the relationship between the Qur'an and the *mushaf* and speak more directly to the rules of purity and prohibition articulated in Islam in relation to the human body and space.

Qur'anic copies available on the Egyptian book market, whether small and plain or large and decorated, have a similarly titled cover that simply says "al-Qur'an al-Karim." Usually, nothing else appears there except this austere-looking but meaningful phrase. A few specialized *mushafs*—such as the *Mushaf of Fourteen Schools of Reading* by Sheikh al-Ma'asarawi I mentioned earlier—may include additional subtitles that indicate some academic content, but ubiquitous copies are simply titled "al-Qur'an al-Karim (The Noble Qur'an)." Yet occasionally, a slightly different wording can be spotted on the covers: "*The Glorious Qur'an. None Touch It Except the Purified.*"[2] This extra line in the title is actually a part of *sura* fifty-six, verse seventy-nine in the Qur'an, which says: "Indeed, it is a noble Qur'an (77) In a Book well-protected (78) None touch it except the purified (79)."[3] Apart from the Qur'anic text, the same pronouncement appears in another source, a famous *hadith* attributed to 'Amr Ibn Hazm according to whom the Prophet Muhammad said: "No one touches the Qur'an except the pure."[4] How does this phrase pertain to *adab al-mushaf* and why might it appear on the book's cover?

The Qur'anic text occasionally, and rather enigmatically, refers to the existence of a book called *Umm al-Kitab*, the "Mother of the Book" (for example, *Surat al-Ra'd* 13:39, *Surat al-Zukhruf* 43:4). Preserved on a tablet in heaven and adorned with precious stones, this primordial text is the wellspring for the Torah, the Gospels, and the Qur'an. The different terms used to refer to this book are somewhat equivocal. Sometimes it is simply called "the Book," sometimes "the Preserved Tablet," and sometimes "the Mother of the Book." Verse seventy-eight above speaks of a "Book well-protected" and it is commonly understood that "the Book" in this case refers to the heavenly "Mother of the Book," not the Qur'an. It is not clear, however, whether the pronoun "it" that appears in the next verse (79) points to the Qur'an or to the Book well protected from which the Qur'an descended. The Qur'anic text mentions that "the Mother of the Book" is protected in heaven by angels who are perfectly pure creatures.

Thus the passage quoted on the cover of the *mushaf* may be read in two ways. Strictly speaking, it may mean that only the angels can touch the heavenly book from which the Qur'an originated. Some scholars propose such an interpretation, pointing to the story of an exchange of letters that took place between the Prophet Muhammad and the ruler of a certain non-Muslim tribe. These scholars argue that if verse seventy-nine referred to the Qur'an, then, being familiar with this prohibition, the Prophet would not have sent letters containing passages from the Qur'an to infidels who were not in a state of *tahara* or ritual cleanliness.⁵ More broadly, then, the most popular interpretations maintain that verse seventy-nine speaks of the Qur'an and therefore of the earthly *mushaf* because, as some scholars have pointed out, no human can touch the abstract message. Although Muslim scholars have not unanimously accepted the *hadith* of Ibn Hazm as fully trustworthy, most *'ulama'* have traditionally supported it as being reliable enough and that there is no indication in his *hadith* that the phrase "none touch it except the purified" refers to anything else but the material and tangible books that contain the Qur'anic text.⁶

These arguments seemingly take us away from the transition of the Qur'anic text into a digital format. Yet they are important to the contemporary debates that surround the electronic versions of the Qur'an, especially those generated by women. So before I come back to the Qur'an in bytes, I need to speak more of the concept of purity in regard to *mushaf*.

"None Touch It Except the Purified"

The *hadith* of Ibn Hazm has become one of the key narratives cited in the debates of a very practical nature: is it permissible to touch a *mushaf* without making ablutions? As with the interpretations of verse seventy-nine, no unanimity prevails among Muslim scholars on this matter, but most accept Ibn Hazm's words to mean that an impure person is prohibited from touching the book. Yet depending on the school of law and debates that prevail within each of them, scholars disagree about what degree of impurity precisely prevents one from touching a *mushaf*.⁷ But according to widespread opinion, two basic rules apply: non-Muslims are not in the state of *tahara* and therefore should not touch a *mushaf*, and Muslims should be in the state of *tahara* when handling the book. A Muslim practitioner puts herself in a state of major impurity (*al-hadath al-akbar*) through sexual activities, menstruation, giving birth, and physical contact with a corpse, or a minor state of impurity (*al-hadath al-asghar*) through, for instance, using the bathroom, falling asleep, or vomiting. In order to remove a major state of impurity one has to perform *ghusl* (full ablution), washing the entire body. A minor impurity calls for *wudu'* (partial ablution), in which only certain body parts need to be cleansed. Ablutions must be performed before prayers and before reading the Qur'anic text.

Many classical scholars recognized the difficulty of following the rules of purity in all circumstances and at all times. A well-known example cites the case of pupils in the Qur'anic schools who, if the rules were upheld, would have to perform ablutions after every urination or defecation, which would disrupt the class and take too much time away from instruction. Therefore different provisions and exceptions, such as holding or touching the book with other objects or between the outer parts of one's palms, have been made to reconcile the rules of purity with daily exigencies. These provisions and exceptions have become incorporated into daily routines and are even more necessary as transmigratory life in Cairo makes following the rules more cumbersome. For instance, the long hours of commuting to work could be spent reading the Qur'an, but making the required *wudu'* beforehand is not always possible (although it must be said that squeezing private reading of the Qur'an between other tasks, such as commuting to work, may be a particularly modern and postmodern practice). It is, therefore, left to the conscience of individual practitioners how to reconcile *adab al-mushaf* with the contingencies of rapidly changing and accelerated urban lifestyles.

From many examples that illustrate the practicalities of dealing with a *mushaf* while fulfilling the rules of *tahara*, I will discuss the ones that accentuate a changing environment in which the etiquette of the *mushaf* must be applied, requiring contemporary practitioners to make decisions, including uneasy decisions that may indicate whether their allegiances lie with people or things. I know that I was at times the cause of such dilemmas. When I traveled with Rahab, a spunky girl in her twenties, to her family's cabin on the shores of Marsa Matruh, I was merely an exchange student, not aware of the rules that guided the handling of a *mushaf*. At the end of the day, I sat on a comfortable bed and stretched lazily, not being able to decide if I was too tired to read anything. Out of the corner of my eye I saw a book on the bedside table and picked it up. It was a *mushaf*. I flipped through the pages absentmindedly. Rahab walked into the room and saw the book in my hands.

"Do you mind putting it away?" she said somewhat sheepishly, "you are... you know... you're not clean."

"I just washed my hands," I replied, not sure what she meant.

"That's not it." She was clearly uneasy. "You are... you are not a Muslim, so... you shouldn't touch it."

Rahab did not want me to hold the *mushaf*. Perhaps because we were such good friends she felt able to bluntly ask me to put it away, although it was not a comfortable request to make. In my interactions with other people, I occasionally saw a fleeting hesitation and an almost instinctive jerk of the hand in a protective gesture when I reached for a *mushaf*. Once or twice it was silently removed from my hands with a quick but telling motion. But Rahab was one of few who candidly referred to my impurity.

"A *mushaf* shouldn't be sold to any non-Muslim," said Hisham, another close friend and a bookseller. "It's a book just for Muslims. It can't be touched by any person who is not Muslim and he is not washed, pure." Hisham's familiarity with a large number of reports (*hadith*) related to the rules of purity was actually rather unusual. But his mother was a French convert to Islam and I knew that discussions about what constitutes proper Muslim practice were far more common in his household than in many other homes to which I was invited over the years. "For instance," he explained in the eager tone of a person who wanted to make sure that I quite understood the importance of his example,

> 'Umar al-Khattab, when he was not yet Muslim, entered the house and found his sister, who was Muslim, holding some scripts in her hands and reading the Qur'an. He wanted to see them, but she asked him to wash first and then allowed him to read it. But one can't sell a *mushaf* to anybody who won't use it properly, who won't put it in a proper place, and it's my responsibility as a seller because I give it to him.

Fortunately, Hisham did not object to studying the Qur'an with me and allowed me to hold the book under his watchful eye.

Marcel, an American living temporarily in Cairo, described a scene that neatly illustrated the conflict of choosing between the book and the friend even more vividly. Late one morning Marcel's friend 'Abd Allah knocked at his door. In a pile of things he brought was a gift, a *mushaf* that contained both the Arabic text and its English translation. 'Abd Allah was in a hurry so he handed the *mushaf* to Marcel, quickly turning around on his way out. But halfway through the turn he was suddenly arrested by a thought. "You have taken a shower since you had sex last time, haven't you?" he said, looking in a meaningful way at Marcel's girlfriend coming into the room. Marcel was not Muslim (although his friend perhaps had hopes for his conversion, judging by the gift he elected to bring). So in the hierarchy of states that cause impurity, 'Abd Allah chose to focus *not* on the fact that Marcel was a *kafir*, a person inherently incapable of fulfilling Muslim requirements of purity, but instead addressed the kind of impurity that his friend could actually remove by taking a quick shower. Such situations, however, additionally complicate the logic of *tahara* in a modern, international, and multicultural city like Cairo, where constant adherence to purity is already hard to exercise.

Gendering Blood

Because semen and blood are impure substances in Islamic tradition, they should not come in contact with the *mushaf*. As a non-Muslim, I was not in a state of purity (*tahara*), but neither was Rahab when she asked me to put down the *mushaf* that evening in Marsa Matruh. She immediately picked up two other books from the coffee table and, using them as tongs, carried the *mushaf* out of the room. "I'm having my period," she said in a matter-of-fact voice, responding to the surprised look I threw at her behavior. By not touching the Qur'anic text while menstruating, Rahab followed the rules of handling the *mushaf* habituated by many generations of Muslim women. These rules today, apart from constituting a habitus of a good *Muslima*, are publicly articulated in a variety of venues, including the al-Azhar *fatwa* website. Under the keywords: "menstruating women" and "reading the Qur'an" there is the following clarification:

> Question: What is the ruling on menstruating woman entering the women's prayer room in a mosque to participate in studying and memorizing the Qur'anic verses, memorizing the Qur'an [in general], and touching the Qur'an during this period?
>
> Answer by Prof. Dr. 'Ali Goma'a [who served as Grand *Mufti* of Egypt between 2003–2013]: It is not permissible for a menstruating woman to enter the mosque for any purpose other than passing, because the Prophet (peace and blessings of Allah be upon him) said: "I do not permit a menstruating or impure person to enter the mosque," narrated by Abu Dawood. It is not permissible for a menstruating woman to touch the mushaf or to read the Qur'an. However, the Maliki [school of law] permits the woman to read a little of the Qur'an without touching the mushaf, so that she does not forget it.[8]

This is a well-known guideline; nonetheless, not all women simply take for granted this particular bodily comportment with the Qur'anic book, as prescribed by the predominant legal schools (*madhabs*) in Egypt. Women's religious education in Egypt has significantly expanded over the last couple of decades, familiarizing them with many classical writings and interpretations. The growing piety movement has produced female practitioners who want to learn more about their religion.[9] By rejecting modern and secular values promoted by the Egyptian government, and trying to oppose various social pressures, they turn to religion for empowerment. These women choose to submit to Islamic principles with diligence and conscious decision-making, including judgments about what to do and what to avoid in their time of menstruation.

Apart from indicating various levels of religious reflexivity, the attitudes of my female friends and acquaintances to the issue of touching a *mushaf* during periodic bleeding bespeak of growing diversification in the attitudes toward one's own body. Some women, like Rahab, consider menstruation as a state of major impurity and simply accept the ruling that in that state they cannot physically read the Qur'an. Others are unsure about how to think of their own menstruating bodies, perceiving the prohibition not so much a matter of ritual uncleanliness, but rather as a sort of tradition that should, nevertheless, be upheld. And some women, conveying that a prohibition of touching the book makes them feel somehow "dirty," question the rationale behind this practice and find creative ways around the rules that would separate them from the actual text. Some distinguish touching the text itself from touching the blank corners of a page. And a few, like Dalia (the same one who reported a "wrong" *mushaf* to the university guards), consider menstruation a biological function that should not prohibit a pious woman like herself from cultivating—as she described it—a personal relationship with Allah, including holding the words of the message mediated in a tangible way by a *mushaf* without any restrictions. A girl who was not afraid of forcefully expressing her opinion using salty language, Dalia once told me:

> I read the Qur'an. I touch the *mushaf*, not the Qur'an. I do everything. The only things I don't do when I'm in menstruation are: I don't pray the formal prayer—because the formal prayer requires ablutions—and I don't fast. Otherwise I...again...there are different sheikhs who are giving their opinions or *fatwas* about this. And 99% of the sheikhs that have given *fatwas* about this are men. They don't menstruate, so they don't know what the hell they are talking about! The point is that a believing person, a practicing person would not want to cut the relationship with God because she is menstruating. You can be in menstruation a quarter of your life. There is no *hadith*, no single verse that says "do not deal with the Qur'an when you are in menstruation." So I don't give a damn about these *fatwas*.
>
> Mind you, I don't make my own *fatwas*...One of the great scholars, which is Ibn Hazm, gave a *fatwa* that there is no problem concerning this. The only verse related to this is the "*junub*." It is different than menstruation. "*Junub*" is...a man and a woman have an intimate relationship. A Muslim, a man or a woman, after they finish their intercourse they have to shower. To refresh the body and to clean the private parts from the liquids. But if you did not take a shower you are "*junub*."

In this case you should not enter a mosque or deal physically with the Qur'an. Why in this case is there a rule? If you are in *"junub,"* it takes five minutes to take a shower. But when you are in menstruation you can be in menstruation for a week. You see the difference?

The history of Islamic *fikh* is just like the history of the world, it's very—what do you call it—patriarchal? "Dhukuri," masculine... Men have control of the words and you will find it, for instance, among the priests. You know more about the priesthood—even the pope of the Vatican is a man. The same here, the Sheikh of al-Azhar is a man. You will find throughout history that most of the people who wrote *fikh* were men, so you need to read the Qur'an or read the *hadith* of the Prophet for yourself.

The knowledge gained from studying works by classical scholars allows women like Dalia to speak about these texts in ways relevant to their own needs and interests. In most cases, their readings of scriptural tradition result in emphasizing and de-emphasizing parts of the tradition to accommodate their uniquely feminine points of view. Dalia supported her decision to read the *mushaf* during menstruation by emphasizing the absence of more precise regulations concerning that matter in the Qur'an itself, affirming the less common exegesis of the verse "none touch it except the purified" and questioning the opinions of influential scholars, such as Imam al-Nawawi (d. 676 AH/ 1277 CE), who strictly forbid touching the *mushaf* during menstruation.

Imam al-Nawawi, a well-known scholar of jurisprudence, wrote in his widely popular *Guide to the Etiquette of Dealing with the Qur'an*: "He who exposes the *mushaf* to impurities becomes an infidel."[10] By impurity, Imam al-Nawawi meant not only the ritual uncleanliness caused by menstruation, sex, or a number of other activities, but also the qualities of particular places. For instance, he—as well as many other scholars of *fikh*—considered bathrooms spaces of particular concern, where a *mushaf* should not be brought nor the Qur'an recited. One day, when I went to service my cell phone at a neighborhood store, I saw someone putting al-Nawawi's ruling into practice. A customer in the waiting room had a pocket-sized *mushaf* in a black briefcase on his lap (some practitioners think that a bag with a *mushaf* inside should not rest on the floor, either). After a while, he decided to use the bathroom. He opened the bag and handed his *mushaf* to a customer sitting next to him. When he returned, he took the *mushaf* from the hands of the helpful stranger and put it back in his briefcase. The owner of the *mushaf* could not know whether the stranger had performed *wudu'* but religious legal provisions stipulate that it is permissible to hand a *mushaf* to a person without a *wudu'* rather than to let it be exposed to impurities in a public bathroom.

One last piece of ethnographic material I have chosen includes both a practical display of *ihtiram* and an illustration of the dynamic existing between printed and written Arabic letters, two techniques of inscription that are much more entwined than their equivalents in the places where Latin script is used. My friend 'Ali was already waiting at the metro station when I arrived, and we headed for Cafe Beano's, our usual meeting place. Most of the customers were congregating around the tables outside, enjoying an occasional cooling breeze, rare in the summer. 'Ali and I sat inside with our books and laptops spread out on a table. The waiter brought us chai latte and a small espresso. With a big smile, 'Ali pulled out of his bag a *mushaf* and handed it to me saying, "It's like the one we used yesterday. You can have it."

I took and opened it. It had the familiar, beautiful font of *Mushaf* al-Shimarli. "Did I tell you that Sa'ad likes this *mushaf* because of its calligraphy?" I asked.

"What do you mean?"

"I mean that it was handwritten first and then kind of 'scanned.'"

"I didn't know that. How do you know that it was handwritten?"

"It has the calligrapher's name on the first page," I replied, "and also some of the letters have shapes you would not be able to reproduce with computer software. Now that you know it's special, do you want it back?" I joked.

"No, it's yours," he said and with a swift move kissed it and raised it to his forehead touching it slightly. Then he handed it over to me.

Once again, I want to emphasize that my attention to the corporeal presence of the book articulated so far through this ethnographic monograph should by no means suggest that the Islamic legal pronouncements standing behind the rules of *adab al-mushaf* assign any priority to the book over the Qur'anic message. Yet the same pronouncements about the etiquette of the Qur'anic book attest to the fact that it is very hard to demarcate a clear boundary between the intangible, eternal words of Allah and their material mediators in the form of perishable ink, paint, paper, and script. On a practical level, this fluid relationship between the message and its mediator becomes most obvious when the medium that conveys the message is drastically changed. The introduction of digital technologies in the dissemination of the Qur'an provides us with the opportunity to ask: how does a profound transformation in medium circumscribe the message? How does one enact a "digital Qur'an" according to the rules of *adab al-mushaf* and what are the results of this enactment? How does one reconcile purity, menstruation, and electronics?

Digitizing the Qur'an

Although it is extremely useful for the dissemination of texts, ironically it is the digital technology itself that has for so long been the obstacle to creating the virtual Qur'an. In spite of growing interest in the digitization of the Qur'anic text, the spread of new technologies and skills, and the creation of digitally encoded Arabic fonts in the Muslim world, efforts to render the Qur'an in a digital format have spawned numerous conundrums for programmers and religious authorities. Although practitioners with access to computers and other electronic devices saw the benefits of using a digitized Qur'anic text, it was the programmers' inability to properly reproduce it in an electronic format that impaired its initial spread. Even though electronic programs that allowed typing in Arabic have been used for over thirty years, the complexity of the Qur'anic script and grammar prevented programmers from creating software that would allow them to render the text in a way that followed the calligraphic conventions of handwritten and printed copies using the 'Uthmanic orthographic rules. In other words, initially the Qur'an was only available in the form of *a digitized picture* but it was not available as an *independent, copyable,* and *searchable text* that might be practically used in various computer applications for study and edification. The essential question was: how is one to properly encode the Qur'an in a computer as text? This problem was multifaceted.

First, discussion over the simplification of Qur'anic spelling that could have alleviated some of the challenges facing computer engineers working on the Qur'anic text eventually came to a dead end.

Adherence to particular calligraphic styles in printing did not help matters, either. As we've seen earlier, although there was no *sunna* (written tradition) that assigned particular styles of writing for the Qur'anic text, officials at the *Mushaf* Committee have chosen not to allow any innovations in that regard, perhaps out of conviction that new font designs responded to different communicative needs of the public that were not relevant to the dissemination of the Qur'anic text. The calligraphic styles used over the centuries for writing *mushafs* and imitated through lithographic and offset printing (which themselves have facilitated continuation of many calligraphic traditions in mechanically reproduced texts of the Qur'an) have produced their own regimes of authority and authentication that would be hard to recreate through a font style that did not participate in the tradition of Qur'anic calligraphy. "The paths traced by calligraphic scripts, movable type, and digital fonts carve different spaces of meaning," notes J. R. Osborn.[11] This is particularly true when we consider how the introduction of typographic print in Egypt disrupted the semantic system of distinct calligraphic styles and their fields of signification by visually unifying texts belonging to different spheres of religious, political, and economic practice. With the introduction of printing, a variety of calligraphic styles that communicated different contents of the text were replaced by one uniform printing font that lost its capacity to convey meaning through format. However, as we saw in the story of *Mushaf* Fu'ad, the state of disruption in the case of the Qur'an was not permanent. The Qur'anic typeface eventually (re)created its own distinctive visual format that in many ways was much more grounded in the preprint scripts than in then-contemporary secular printing, full of innovative "non-Qur'anic" designs.

Third, although letters of the Arabic alphabet were first encoded alongside ASCII (the American Standard Code for Information Interchange) and later included in ISO (International Standards Organization) encoding standards were significantly simplified and the codification did not include any of the additional layers of the Arabic script and excluded a number of diacritics.[12] A number of bigger corporations (like IBM, for instance) addressed this inadequacy by creating separate encoding systems that represented non-Latin scripts in a more correct way, but the texts written in those coding systems were not transferable from one digital environment to another without causing distortion of the text. These distortions included placement of diacritic marks over incorrect letters, which changed the meaning of the words. This was, of course, especially problematic for transferring the Qur'anic text.

By the end of the twentieth century, the Unicode system emerged as an answer to the problem. Its major advantage was that it helped to include many more variations of Arabic letters and a much larger number of diacritics.[13] However, as a seminal tool of the digital revolution, the Unicode system used worldwide for encoding texts in different writing systems was nonetheless grounded in a typographic, Latin-script-based tradition of assigning a particular code to a particular letter in a sequential order.¹⁴ One of the developers of Arabic digital fonts, the Dutch linguist and designer Thomas Milo, aptly summed up the challenge faced by graphic designers who wanted to create an Arabic script in a digital format: "Writing Arabic involves more than just lining up letters. The connected letters assimilate with each other. They are highly adaptable, which makes it impractical to describe each variant individually. In Arabic script the graphic unit of writing is the letter compound: a string of connected letters."¹⁵ Unfortunately, the programs initially developed for writing in Arabic, which Milo described as the "visual equivalent of Beethoven's *Für Elise* played by cell-phone," reproduced the structure of Latin script, treating letters as isolated graphemes, which resulted in a visually simplified form of type that did not include *tashkil* or any other signs uniquely characteristic of the Qur'anic text, setting aside aesthetic concerns entirely. However, Milo treats the Qur'an as a test case because it is unlike any other text and, therefore, uniquely difficult to reproduce electronically. His argument is that if you can represent the Qur'anic text accurately then you can represent any other Arabic accurately. This position, however, is contested by some designers and coders.¹⁶

Nevertheless, in the early electronic texts in Arabic the elements of the text that could be reproduced were too easily shifted around when transferred to different file formats or search engines. For instance, one of the most common problems was the unstable position of *fatha* ó, *kesra* ọ, *damma* ó, *sukkun* ó, *tanwin damma* ó, *tanwin fatha* ó, *shadda* ó, and *tanwin kesra* ọ, which are placed on a secondary baseline in relation to the main line of graphemes. These little *tashkil* signs were (and still are in many programs, including the one I am using to type this book) notoriously hard to place over the correct letters. So the Qur'anic text written in such software was not only lacking many specifically Qur'anic signs, it was also easily distorted and altered because each letter was treated by the software as an individual sign, uncorrelated with the rest of the diacritics and letters around it. Although finally good enough to represent contemporary Arabic script, Unicode still did not support all the variants and diacritics needed to create the Qur'anic text.

By that point, changes in religious visual culture had already taken place. In particular, they were prompted by Qur'anic printed editions popular in Egypt, such as the *Mushaf* Fu'ad or the *Mushaf* al-Shimarly, and in general by the modern aesthetics of secular texts to which readers were already becoming accustomed. The reading habits of Muslim practitioners had changed. People wanted to read the text of the Qur'an that was "legible" and "print-like," and they wanted it to be user-friendly like other easily accessible and usable non-religious electronic texts. Therefore, the push to digitize the Qur'an in Egypt did not come at first from institutions, such as al-Azhar, but through the grassroots initiatives of individual practitioners who were concerned about both orthography and usability of the text. The early attempts to create searchable digitized texts of the Qur'an were undertaken not by calligraphers, artists, or publishers, but by computer engineers and programmers,¹⁷ which, in return, prompted religious authorities to step in.

The response of Azhari scholars toward this new digital medium was cautiously supportive. What the *'ulama'* wanted to consider this time was not whether the new technology was suitable for the dissemination of the Qur'anic text, but rather how to reconcile the benefits of digitization with preservation of the graphic format of the message already adopted for print. Members of the *Mushaf* Committee did not endorse software editions that did not graphically replicate the authorized printed texts in a satisfactory way. They could not recommend such a simplified, prone-to-error, and "uncontrollable" Qur'anic text as a primary source for reading or memorizing the Qur'an. But the *'ulama'* had no objections to digitized Qur'anic texts that were scanned from handwritten or printed *mushafs*. Such a solution, although less than ideal for computer specialists, was initially very satisfactory for the members of the *Mushaf* Committee. Accidental glitches or alterations of the content of the message were not possible when the text was fixed in a format that could not be edited. However, what protected the text from distortion at the same time made it difficult to quote or reproduce fragments of the Qur'an, which Muslim practitioners wanted to do.

Authenticity and Authority Again

The popularity of Muslim religious websites has exploded over the past decade. In the unstable political environment of recent years, many young Egyptians have been feeling more inclined to express their religious views on discussion boards and blogs devoted to Islamic doctrine and practice than in public. A formal display of arguments required quotes from the Qur'an but this was problematic on the internet because copying and pasting the Qur'anic words did not necessarily preserve the text's correct format. Even text that was fairly stable in one digital environment might be completely jumbled up and full of illegible signs when transferred to another program, computer, or electronic device. Technically, it was not difficult to copy and paste the Qur'anic text, but the results were often disastrous. From this perspective, the ease of transferring text from one format to another, or from one electronic device to another, was ironically one of the biggest stumbling blocks to disseminating the digitized Qur'an. For religiously motivated programmers, the challenge was to create a program in which the Qur'anic text would be stable, editable, and transferable, but not easily manipulated.[18]

The online digitized Qur'anic text presented one more problem for scholars. Given the complexity of the process of authentication for printed *mushafs*, how could the issue of correctness be addressed in the internet, where the circulation of an unlicensed text is easy? Moreover, how could the institutionalized forms of text control—like the procedures of authentication described earlier—be replicated on the digital level? The channels of bureaucratic control over the publishing houses have long been established, but similar systems of authentication were not yet available for copies circulating on the internet. Within this milieu, the most pressing questions that emerged were those of how to create a new form of "*isnad*" for the electronic copies of the Qur'an, how to protect the integrity of the text in the process of transfer from one environment to another, and how to evaluate the existing copies for their correctness.

Badr 'Orabi, one of the language consultants for Egyptian software companies, explained the dilemma in this way:

> The easiness of writing and modifying the electronic text, and the easiness of its editing—whether for review and licensing purposes or not—means that

any institution or individual who wants to change the electronic Qur'anic text (deliberately or by accident) can do it without difficulty. In this case the only way to ameliorate the consequences is to review the original text again and to obtain a new license. And sometimes—I do not say always—the authorities giving a permit overlook the additional review after the initial acceptance of the text arrangement has been given because an extra revision requires time, money, and effort which they do not need to spend.[19]

In 'Orabi's opinion, the lack of standardized control over electronic texts of the Qur'an and the problem of lumping them together with reviews of the text on paper were to be blamed for the chaos existing among the digital copies of the Qur'an. By that he meant that there had been an influx of Qur'anic software from abroad that users could easily download, but al-Azhar could not check for correctness. 'Orabi suggested that a solution to this problem might be achieved if the multiple and diverse efforts of small companies producing electronic Qur'anic texts were unified into one large company that would deal with the specificities of the Qur'anic text in an electronic format. But this solution was not welcomed by those for whom the production and dissemination of digitized Qur'ans was not only a pious activity but also a source of income. Besides, theoretically the only institution authorized to carry out such an enormous undertaking was al-Azhar. But al-Azhar's ability to invest money in large religious projects has been long undermined by the removal of profit-making *awqaf* (donated lands and properties) from their supervision. The financial independence of al-Azhar ended at the beginning of the nineteenth century when Muhammad 'Ali took control over the *waqf* revenues to pay for his extensive program of national modernization. Succeeding rulers of Egypt were not inclined to let go of such a lucrative source of income; neither was the new, republican government, which confirmed the governmental control over the finances of al-Azhar by placing *awqaf* under the administration of the Ministry of Religious Endowments in 1961.

Unsurprisingly, then, one of the first officially endorsed programs that would allow the searching, copying, and pasting the Qur'anic text without distortion of the position of the letters, or changing them into numeric signs and symbols, was created at the King Fahd Qur'an Complex in Saudi Arabia.[20] A few years ago, its team of engineers released to the public domain a font application that is also compatible with Unicode. The Qur'anic application is available for free on the Complex's website and has been developed specifically for the text of the Qur'an according to *al-rasm al-'Uthmani* following the reading of Hafs. The shape of the letters are, as in the printed *mushaf* al-Madina, designed by the calligrapher 'Uthman Taha, but in its style and composition the script is far from artistic. It is based on the one-letter code system and therefore does not imitate features of Arabic handwriting beyond its loose adherence to *naskh*, despite being designed by a calligrapher. Its primary function is to reproduce, without distortion and in different digital environments, all of the graphemes present in the Qur'anic text.

Also, Thomas Milo and his company DecoType[21] have been successful in developing new ways of encoding Arabic script that allow the preparation of a fully marked

Qur'anic text while strictly following the rules of Arabic calligraphy. A few years ago, he and a group of engineers from his DecoType company were able to develop a plug-in called "Tasmeem" that operates inside WinSoft's Middle Eastern version of Adobe InDesign.[22] Instead of treating Arabic glyphs as separate units, this program—unlike most products available on the digital market—offers a unique method of seeing the text in a multi-linear dimension where parts of letters and *tashkil* form combinations of graphemes in relative positions to each other. The basic unit in Tasmeem is not a letter but a carefully analyzed calligraphic pen stroke translated into a digital code. In other words, instead of redesigning the Arabic letters to make them compliant with the typographic bias of most text editing programs, Milo and his team reworked the technology to fit the demands of traditional Arabic calligraphy. As a result, his team produced a text that very closely imitates the dynamic legato features of Arabic handwriting, while remaining searchable and compatible with the international Unicode system.

It is telling that for the first two font types reproduced using Tasmeem, Milo chose the calligraphic style *naskh* and the print typeface of the *Mushaf* Fu'ad (which he called the *Emiri* font),[23] allowing computer users to type both kinds of text: secular and religious. Presenting the debut of Tasmeem on his website, Milo wrote that it was finally possible to create a Unicode-based, searchable Qur'anic text with the familiar appearance of today's printed editions, which was typographically stable and orthographically flawless, regardless of the operating system or the type of web device.[24] Yet some contemporary Arab font designers have criticized DecoType's philosophy of modifying technology in order to embrace the principles of calligraphy—so useful in printing the Qur'anic text. They would have preferred that he explore new directions in font rendering rather than emphasizing proper Qur'anic representation. Nevertheless, DecoType's invention has been used to create a new national symbol—the first digital Omani *mushaf*, called the *Mushaf* Muscat that has also been approved by al-Azhar.[25]

However, institutionally sponsored electronic versions of the Qur'an still compete with those produced by for-profit companies like DecoType that are attuned to the digital market and offer a broader range of design, functionality, and features. These private companies are also able to upgrade their applications faster. Therefore, the discussions about how to secure the Qur'anic text in the digital environment have continued and are not likely to disappear any time soon.

"Electronic Qur'ans"

Electronic devices that mediate the digital Qur'an assume many forms and types: from small, portable, and multifunctional cell phones and tablets, uni-purpose Walkman-like mini-players, or pen-like reading devices designed specifically to teach non-Arabic-speaking Muslims how to recite, to laptops and stationary computers with touch screens and CD and DVD players that can display the Qur'an interactively. Each of these electronic devices mediates the Qur'anic text in particular ways and elicits different forms of engagement with the message.

The Korean- and Chinese-made devices advertised and available on the Egyptian market, such as the "PenMan Holy Qur'an" or the "Iqra'a Digital Qur'an," are perhaps the most versatile in terms of their content, portability, and application. Because of their convenient size and multifunctionality, they can be read and listened to in various locations and circumstances. Depending on the model, they feature exegetic explanations, tools for memorization (such as the automatic repetition of marked passages or different speeds of recitation), dictionaries, translations into other languages, guidelines facilitating proper recitation, and various search options. For instance, the Penman Digital Qur'an contains the Qur'anic text in Arabic, six different voice recordings by famous reciters, translations of the Qur'an in eight languages, commentaries, books of *hadith*, a device showing the Qibla direction for prayer, prayer times for each day of the year, the ninety-nine names of Allah, a guide to *Hajj* and *'Umra* (two types of pilgrimage), and a brief story of the Qur'anic revelation. Additionally, this "digital Qur'an" has a "stylish slim design, built-in stereo speaker, earphone jack, and a rechargeable battery." It costs about a hundred US dollars and resembles a handheld Nintendo game console. The most sophisticated models come with extra memory, allowing users to store pictures, create recordings, and convert files. They are advertised as "the best gift for a Muslim learner who wants to study the Qur'an." These devices are often brought to Egypt from the Gulf, having been exported from China and Korea, and al-Azhar can exert only limited control over their circulation and use. Only in particularly egregious cases is the *Mushaf* Committee able to intervene. And it did when a Chinese company put forward a plan to produce a device that featured a recitation of the Qur'an subtitled by text transliterated into the Latin script, which of course was not acceptable to the *'ulama'* on the committee.[26]

Most specialized software available for computers and laptops is designed for textual study and requires above-average knowledge of the Qur'anic text, its grammar, orthography, and schools of recitations. Reading the Qur'an in such specialized software presupposes an academic engagement with the text that entails pausing, rereading, and analyzing the content, and an emphasis on "immersion" in the text through sound is not a priority. It is used by scholars at al-Azhar and students of the Qur'anic sciences.

Since phone applications are by far the most accessible, these constitute the most popular form of the digitized Qur'an in Egypt. They are available for free or for a moderate fee from various websites and Islamic organizations, but they offer a less diversified range of functions. However, because the number of smartphones in Egypt has been steadily rising, reaching at this point about 27 million users,[27] mobiles have become the most popular platform for the display of the Qur'anic text. These statistics may not be the most reliable, but even if taken with a grain of salt, they give us a picture of a society where a smartphone is an increasingly common object to use. In 2012, 92,000,000 cellular phones were reported to be in use in Egypt,[28] while the population of the country was about 82,000,000. Most phones now come with a screen that allows the display of pictures and text. The number of phone applications available on the market with the text of the Qur'an, its recitation, commentaries, and other options is also growing very fast. Such apps are easily available and also inexpensive, quickly multiplying the number of users of the "electronic Qur'an."

Unlike the specialized Qur'anic computer software, the applications used on tablets and mobile phones are more likely to be used for reading that does not necessarily include pausing to analyze or study the content. This affectual reading—reading that is likely to elicit an emotional response from the reader and is often connected with the movement of the reader's lips and silent or half-silent recitation—allows the reader to access the text visually and aurally in a more senses-engaging way. Some phone applications include the option of listening to one's favorite *qari*, a Qur'anic reciter, and following the highlighted verses at the same time. These types of phone software are popular with younger Muslims who read the Qur'anic text "on the go" in buses, in the metro, and during breaks between other activities.

New Questions, New Solutions

A Muslim practitioner once told me that a computer is an ideal medium for the Qur'an because it makes the Qur'anic text immaterial. The assumption is that a digitized text, unlike a *mushaf*, has no physical body. This is a very common assumption. That said, the use of various electronic devices to mediate the Qur'an nonetheless engenders questions that directly engage the material bodies of these new mediators. The most common concerns are those that require the practitioners to revisit the rules of Qur'anic etiquette and adapt them to the new technology. These include inquiries such as whether it is permissible to have a Qur'anic application on the phone, whether it is permissible to delete such an application, and most commonly, whether one has to perform ablutions before listening to or reading from a digital device containing the digital Qur'anic text, whether one is allowed to use such an electronic device while menstruating, and whether one is allowed to bring a phone with the Qur'anic application into the bathroom.

The scholarly answers given to these concerns hinge on the question of whether an electronic device constitutes a *mushaf*. After a period of initial hesitation, the conclusion that a phone should not be treated like a *mushaf* began to prevail, and I've seen that position reflected over the past few years in casual conversations and on Egyptian and Saudi internet *fatwa* websites. Fewer and fewer scholars insisted that the rules of *adab* should apply in the same way to both objects, the book and the phone alike; most have followed the argumentation implied by an anonymous anecdotic "*fatwa*" circulating on the internet:

> A man asked a sheikh whether it was permitted to bring a mobile phone with the Qur'anic verses to the bathroom. The sheikh answered, "It is permissible because the verses are in the memory of the phone."
> The man asked again, "But sheikh, we are talking about the Qur'anic verses and the most beautiful names of Allah, and you are saying that it is permitted to take them to the bathroom?" The sheikh replied,
> "Have you memorized any verses from the Qur'an?"
> "Yes," said the man.
> "Well then," retorted the sheikh, "when you go to the bathroom, leave your head by the door and then step in."[29]

However, a *fatwa* on the subject of "electronic Qur'ans" featured on the al-Azhar website is more ambiguous and indicates that any difference between the *mushaf* and an electronic device is still somewhat debatable.[30] Al-Azhar's *fatwa* reminds practitioners that every letter read from the Qur'an brings the reader ten blessings. This applies to the letters read on the electronic screens as well, even if the reader has not performed the ablution (*wudu'*)—with a few exceptions, including menstruation. But, says the same *fatwa*, reading from a paper copy of the *mushaf* is better than reading from an electronic device, and touching the Qur'anic text on an electronic screen is not the same as touching the paper *mushaf* because the text on a screen appears there as on a surface of water or a mirror. The purity required for touching the paper *mushaf* is not obligatory in this case because touching the screen is like touching the Qur'an's shadow. In conclusion, the *fatwa* states that reading from the paper *mushaf* engages the touch and the eye more than reading from the phone.

To further clarify the questions of difference between a *mushaf* and an electronically mediated Qur'an, al-Azhar issued a statement that expressed its support for a *fatwa* given by a Saudi preacher, Muhammad Ibn Saleh, who ruled that it is necessary to be in a state of ablution while touching a phone or any other electronic device that contains the Qur'an *only* when the verses appear on the screen. "In the case when the Qur'an shows up on the screen of the phone the same rules that guide handling of a regular paper *mushaf* apply, as it came in the precious *aya* 'No one touches it except the pure.'"[31] The Head of the Association of Scholars and Preachers at al-Azhar, Sheikh Ahmad Qandil Turkiyya, confirmed this decision, saying: "A person without ablutions is not prohibited from handling a device and using it because it is not a written *mushaf* and he does not touch the verses with his hands, merely the device. However, if a Qur'anic verse appears on the screen this instance requires prohibition of touching, as indicated by the *aya*."[32]

Many conversations surrounding electronic devices implicitly or explicitly compare the memory of electronic devices carrying the Qur'anic text with human memory. Sometime later I heard a version of the anecdotic *fatwa* reproduced above, told in a more straightforward manner: "A man asked a sheikh whether it was permitted to bring a mobile phone with the Qur'anic verses to the bathroom. The sheikh answered, 'It is permissible because the verses are in the memory of the phone.'" In such a case the rules that guide *ihtiram* toward the object did not apply unless the Qur'anic text is manifest on the surface of the screen. So it seems that the physical presence of the text on the screen of the phone has become the key element that sheikhs take into consideration when addressing the etiquette of electronic devices.[33] An Azhari graduate gave me a related example, this time addressing computers: "If the Qur'an is visible on the computer screen you can't sit in front of it with your feet on the table directed towards the screen but if the text is not there you may do it if you want to." So unlike a closed book, a turned-off electronic device or application dematerialize the message.

An anthropological approach before the material turn would be to treat all of these entanglements of deference and purity as reflections of the extraordinary nature of the Qur'anic message. But I cannot simply overlook the material mediation of the *mushaf* in the fabric of religious practice, affect, and knowledge because not all rules of *tahara* (purity) that apply to the act of reading from the book apply to recitation. In other words, the limitations on interaction with the object are stricter than limitations on the circumstances in which the text may be recited. In 2004, the previous Grand *Mufti* of al-Azhar, 'Ali Goma'a, declared in his *fatwa* number 485 that "it is not forbidden to recite the Qur'an without ablution with the exception of touching it according to the words of the Highest: *Only the pure can touch it*."[34] Similarly, a *fatwa* issued on the popular internet site "Islamweb" states:

> God willing, there is nothing wrong with touching a cassette tape or an electronic *mushaf* [on which the sound is recorded] by a person who did not perform ablutions because the conditions that forbid [touching a *mushaf*] regard only to a written one, in an Arabic calligraphy. [A recording device] preserves the voice of a specialized reciter who preserved the words of the Qur'an in his heart.[35]

The *fatwas* Azhari scholars issue are authoritative but this does not mean that they constitute a law. Disagreements are possible and practitioners may question the grounds on which a pronouncement was established. The novelty of the "electronic Qur'an" issue creates a fertile environment for the exchange of opinions between scholars and public alike. The readers' comments that appeared below the article summarizing the Azhari standpoint reflect a continued lack of consensus about how to approach the Qur'anic text mediated by a mobile phone in spite of the official *fatwas* issued in Egypt and Saudi Arabia. "Sheikh al-Munjid, may Allah protect him, has reviewed the issue together with the Sheikh 'Abd al-Rahman al-Barak, may Allah protect him," wrote a reader from Jordan,

> deciding on the permissibility of reading the Qur'an from the electronic *mushaf* without *tahara*. They also permitted touching the screen on the grounds that the screen constitutes a barrier. It is true [that] what came in the *fatwa* news from al-Azhar is a hasty [move] on their part because [other] sheikhs pronounced it permissible. I think that an [increased] rigorism in that matter is not good. There is also a previous *fatwa* by Sheikh 'Othaymin, may Allah preserve him, that gives permission, too.[36]

Another reader questioned altogether the interpretation of the *aya* "no one touches it except the pure" as the basis for the ruling, pointing out that grammatically this verse does not represent an imperative form but merely a statement that needs to be considered in the context of the surrounding sentences. Since the statement came as a part of a rebuttal against those who claimed the Qur'an to be a *jinn*'s doing, it is only natural to understand it to mean that the pure who have access to it are angels. Moreover, if non-Muslims were not allowed to touch the *mushaf*, the second caliph 'Amr Ibn Khattabb would have never converted, as he expressed his desire to embrace Islam only after having read—and touched—the Qur'anic text preserved by his sister. Most readers who responded with comments to the article about the Azhari *fatwa* thought that the requirement of ablutions when the Qur'an appears on the screen was not well justified and therefore unnecessary, although this *fatwa* does make the use of the Qur'anic text preserved in a mobile phone easier in comparison to a book—unlike a *mushaf*, a phone can be brought to the bathroom. A Palestinian woman emphasized this point in her comment:

> I think it should be stressed that having the Qur'an on my phone helps me to read while traveling without having to carry a *mushaf* with me. If I put it [a *mushaf*] in my purse it would prevent me from going to the bathroom. And if I put it in a pocket it may fall out on the floor. So I prefer the phone. I like to listen to it when I'm traveling or having my period. So the Qur'an on the phone, whether the sound or text, is the best.[37]

The opinion that a phone is not a *mushaf* allows woman in particular to negotiate their access to the Qur'anic text during menstruation. In other words, for women the advent of the Qur'anic phone and tablet applications has opened up an entirely new way to access the Qur'an without transgressing the rules of *adab al-mushaf*. The following vignette, like the post of the Palestinian reader under the al-Azhar's *fatwa*, reflects the way in which digital technology can be appropriated by Muslim women to serve their particular religious needs.

All seats in the women's carriage were already taken when I got on the metro at Tahrir Square in Cairo. I was steered to the corner by the current of flowing bodies, where a young woman was sitting with an open mobile phone in her hand. The bright screen displayed lines of *ayat*—the Qur'anic verses. Every now and then, she slid her finger over the glass, "turning the pages over." Not so many years ago the same young woman would have been holding a small paper copy of the Qur'an. Now, to see her gazing at the lit phone screen was nothing out of the ordinary.

"I know it's a strange question," I addressed her, "but why do you like reading the Qur'an on your mobile?"

She looked up at me with a slight surprise.

"Oh, it's just a matter of convenience," she replied, "and I can read it without ablutions even when I have my period." Then, she promptly returned to looking silently at the screen.

Since mobile phones and tablets on which the Qur'an is recorded do not come under the same rules as the *mushaf*, this also means that other rules of purity do not apply in the same way, either. As we have seen, the rationale behind both is that the letters of the Qur'an in these devices are "different" than the letters in the non-electronic *mushaf*, whether handwritten or printed. Thus, menstruating women follow the opinions expressed by the sheikhs of al-Azhar that an electronic device constitutes a carrier *and* a barrier for the text. The plastic case or glass screen is a safe barrier, as it cannot be traversed: one cannot directly touch the digital letters, as they appear and disappear from display, not being "fixed" on the page. For that reason, menstruation has no effect on the practical use of the Quranic text in a digital device because, from a legal point of view, digital letters are less material than those in print.

This opinion has been disseminated not only by preachers in the mosques and *fatwa* websites, but also by women's electronic periodicals and news web portals, such as the popular *Masrawy* website that in 2016 published a *fatwa* by the Grand Sheikh Dr. Ahmad al-Tayyeb:

Question: Is it permissible for a menstruating woman to read the Qur'an from any source other than the *mushaf*?

Dr. Ahmad al-Tayyeb, Sheikh of Al-Azhar, replies: Imam Malik allowed the reading of the Qur'an without touching the mushaf during the menstrual cycle, so that the inability to read does not lead to forgetting the Qur'an. Based on this, it is permissible for a menstruating woman to read the Qur'an from any source other than the *mushaf* in order to be rewarded [with blessings], even if it is daily. It is known what the answer is to the question, if the case is as stated. And God Almighty knows best.[38]

I suggested at the beginning of this chapter that practices of *ihtiram* (deference) directed toward the book, including the practices of ritual and physical cleanliness, enact the Qur'an. I also described the ways in which the Qur'an is enacted through the practices of handling a physical book and changes to the etiquette directed toward the object that emerge when the Qur'anic text becomes mediated through digital devices, rather than a book. I think it is important, then, to ask what happens to the Qur'an when its enactments suddenly become quite different from the ones carried out by previous generations of practitioners. Annemarie Mol, an anthropologist of practice, suggests that when we foreground the practices surrounding things we are able to track how those things come into being. If the practices differ, new things appear and the realities are multiplied. Instead of a passive thing in the middle seen from multiple perspectives, we are faced with new things constantly coming into being. Yet the multiple objects do not fall apart, but as she puts it, they "tend to hang together somehow."[39] For Muslim practitioners, the Quran in a phone that can be touched without ablutions is not suddenly different from the Quran in a *mushaf* that cannot. This change slowly happens because new practices that have the ability to create new realities are always entangled with older practices that stabilize things, give them a kind of inertia, and make them "hang together." The practices that enact the Qur'an can turn it into something else just as much as they have the power to sustain it. Even as the Qur'an is changing into digital form, the meaning and material uses of earlier manuscript and printed forms are also changing (handwritten *mushaf* becoming *makhtut*). Both the future-oriented digital practices and history-oriented *makhtut* practices are turning the material Qur'an "into something else." But the accelerating use of technology in accessing the Qur'anic message prompts an important question: how much longer will the *adab al-mushaf* be relevant to the Qur'an, and when or if it ceases to be germane to Muslim practice, what will this change do to the way the Qur'an itself is understood and interpreted?

Conclusion

In a classic article, "The True Meaning of Scripture," Wilfred Cantwell Smith noted that "We cannot understand the Qur'an, and its role in human history, without an adequate understanding of scripture as a major matter in human affairs, individual and social; and we cannot in turn develop a serious concept of scripture, obviously, unless it be one that comprehends, *inter alia*, the Qur'an."[1] Cantwell Smith was not a book historian. He was a religious studies scholar who thought like an anthropologist—he insisted that in order to understand the Qur'an as scripture, we also need to understand when and how it intersects with the lives of individual human beings (and groups of human beings) who read, interpret, and follow it in historically and socially distinct circumstances. Cantwell Smith called this web of intersections "human affairs." He was right in his suggestion not to study the Qur'anic message separately from the ideas and desires of those who live by it.

But human affairs are not just the affairs of humans. Human affairs also include things with which humans entangle themselves in the process of living out their scripture. As Severin Fowles concludes, "By attending to things in themselves, we stand in a much better position to understand people in themselves, due to the inescapable conclusion that people and things are mutually constitutive."[2] This has been the focus of my story—the multitude of entanglements between the users, makers, and custodians of Qur'anic books and other people and things, a historically particular constellation of objects and bodies, habits and interests, technology and culture. I tracked its various actors: fonts, scholars, mobile phones, publishers, orthography, tradition, readers, and of course, the *mushaf* itself, mapping out circuits of their agency and work. None of these actors had total control over the events I described, and each of them contributed in a unique way to this narrative, at the center of which there is the Qur'anic book.

I began with a description of the concerns that surrounded the decision to render the Qur'anic text in print. From today's perspective, printing may have seemed to be an inevitable next step in the history of Qur'anic communication, but at that point in time it was neither obvious, nor that necessary, especially regarding dissemination of the Qur'an. The objections mounted against this project were related to two important issues: the methods of authorization and the technological shortcomings in the representation of the text. By that point, inscription of the Qur'an was firmly grounded in the calligraphic tradition and orthographic canon that were not easily transferable onto this new medium. And for a few decades, the problems of printing the Qur'an in a typographic format were greater than its benefits. However, an alignment of calligraphy and lithographic printing allowed Muslims to largely alleviate the deficiencies of fast multiplication. Most of the Qur'anic texts produced in Egypt in the nineteenth century—with the exception of *mushafs* from Bulaq—were produced as lithographies. At the same time, the growing number of printed Qur'anic copies relegated the handwritten *mushafs* to the role of manuscripts—books made by hand as opposed to books made by a machine. This distinction put Qur'anic manuscripts in the category of books whose material characteristics prevail over the content. Before printing, manuscripts were something else, but certainly not museum objects.

By the beginning of the twentieth century, printed copies of the Qur'an were becoming more common but were often of poor quality, so this problem needed to be addressed in a more regulatory manner. In Egypt it was done in two ways: first, by publishing an edition prepared by a committee of scholars from al-Azhar with an extensive commentary on the rules followed and corrections proposed in this edition. Thus for the next fifty years or so, *Mushaf* Fu'ad gained its authority not only through the power of the committee that prepared it, but also through its own ubiquity. Second, the quality of Egyptian *mushafs* was regulated by creating an institutional board of reviewers responsible for the content and craftsmanship of printed Qur'anic books, which, by that time, were being published in the thousands. However, control over the quality of these *mushafs* was directly related to the interests and benefits of the publishers who printed the Qur'anic text for profit. The increasingly poor quality of the books and complaints by their users put pressure on religious authorities to tighten their control over publication by turning to the Egyptian parliament to reinforce state laws regarding Qur'anic printing, which obviously complicates the sacred/secular divide that is often assumed in contemporary American politics. The pressure to control the quality of *mushafs* in Egypt also came from the outside as a by-product of the undertaking to create error-free and defectless copies of the Qur'an at the King Fahd Complex in Saudi Arabia. The influx of their *Mushaf* al-Madina into Egypt problematized Qur'anic production for Egyptian publishers such as al-Shimarly, who championed their own editions of the Qur'an, reprinted *Mushaf* al-Amiri, or copied other, less common, old editions.

The description of the circumstances in which *Mushaf* al-Madina has become prevalent in the Middle East also addressed the remaking of the soundscape culture in the region by promoting a particular tradition of Qur'anic reading and allowed me to point out that writing and printing should not be seen as sequential, but as complementary. Uthman Taha based his *handwritten mushaf* on the calligraphy of a *printed* Qur'anic edition. His *calligraphed* edition was catered for an audience whose visual reading habits were trained by *typographic fonts*. A similar interdependent relationship can be observed between some of the "electronic Qur'ans" and their calligraphically designed content. The more the materiality of the message is removed and made non-essential, the more it returns and resurfaces in unexpected and new ways.

The digitization of the Qur'an also created room for the rethinking of some of the practices that until recently had focused on fairly inexpensive, paper copies of the Qur'anic text. The etiquette of the *mushaf* had to be realigned with the new materiality of the Qur'anic mediator. The enactments of the Qur'an became enriched by a new host of practices introduced by *fatwas* that worked as a mechanism of realignment between old practices and new technology. Unlike books, digital devices allowed Muslim women to access the Qur'anic text in ways they had not been able to before. Similarly, printing in Braille allowed vision-impaired Muslims to access the Qur'an in a new, more tangible, manner. Like digitalization, Braille technology required a different set of alignments, as it did not permit publishers to copy the Qur'anic blueprint, the consonant base with its diacritics. The materiality of *mushaf* printed in Braille needed to be taken into consideration when deciding whether such a book can indeed be called a *mushaf*. Theology and technology intersected again over the perforated dots.

Why *Mushaf*?

In writing this account of Qur'anic books in Egypt, I have had three goals in mind. First and most broadly, I wanted to draw attention to the way in which objects and technology make us do things, to write a "thick description" of this process (in the senses proposed by Alder and Latour[3]), and to respond to the question of how Islam becomes present in the public through material, tangible forms.[4] If publishers have difficulties printing the Qur'an because new technologies cannot accommodate the traditional spelling, we can't *only* blame the situation on designers and engineers. If the same words written on a page and displayed on the screen of a mobile phone do not evoke the same responses, we have to admit that this difference is not *just* a matter of changing sensibilities. Digitized Qur'anic texts provisionally contained in electronic devices mediate the Qur'anic message in different ways than books. They evoke different expectations and cause different reactions; they appeal to different demographic groups and occupy different social spaces, ultimately instigating the production of new knowledge. As Webb Keane points out, our reactions to objects do not depend entirely on our dispositions, knowledge, emotions, and so on. We enter into relationships with objects and our actions are often modified, limited, encouraged, or thwarted by their material qualities.[5] Therefore, objects do not only stand for something else—an idea, a belief, or a desire—they also provoke action. The Egyptian *Mushaf* Committee came into being precisely because there was a need to make sure that a mechanically reproduced *mushaf* does not contain orthographic mistakes. Egyptian parliament members spent many hours of their working time meeting with publishers and al-Azhar officials, discussing the circumstances of the production of *mushaf*s. Electronic *mushaf*s have brought changes in the understanding and application of traditional etiquette toward the "digital Qur'ans." These events, of course, may be explained in terms of human action shaped by cognitive processes and performed upon material objects. But seeing them as a result of interactions between things and people opens up a new arena for understanding the politics of objects and highlights still barely explored forms of human/non-human becoming. Yet my story of the physical and tangible object—its script, paper, and forms of making and using— should not be read as some version of material determinism. I do not suggest that the material characteristics of the *mushaf* are the exclusive cause of the described events. Rather, my emphasis on the ways in which technology intermingles with religious practice is meant to make the picture of "human affairs" more complete by connecting people's concerns, reactions, and doings to the material world that surrounds and bears upon their actions.

My narrative's second goal, which was also general, was to contribute to a corpus of anthropological literature on religion that treats religious practice as meaning-making that is entangled with materiality by necessity. This choice has been dictated by the fact that, as Webb Keane again reminds us, "religions may not always demand beliefs, but they will always involve material forms. It is in that materiality that they are part of experience and provoke responses, that they have public lives and enter into ongoing chains of causes and consequences."[6] By attending to materiality and to practices involving things, we can trace the processes through which meaning is constructed, including the domains of power (a path marked out by Talal Asad in *Geneologies of Religion*).[7]

Finally, I wanted to explore an unoccupied niche in the anthropology of Islam that had been created by a historically conditioned lack of interest in the practices surrounding material copies of the Qur'anic text. Unlike other scriptures like the Torah, the Bible, and Buddhist or Hindu texts whose material forms and effects have recently received some attention (especially by James Watts,[8] Dorina Miller Parmenter,[9] Brent Plate,[10] and other scholars associated with the Iconic Books project at Syracuse University[11]), the *mushaf*, not only in the history of its production but also in its use, has been overlooked. My ethnographic story fills this vacuum by bringing to scholars' attention the multitude of religious, political, and economic spheres within which *mushafs* operate in Egypt. We should again remember that these spheres were never purely religious, economic, or political. The difficulty to compartmentalize the reality of which I was writing was one of its main characteristics. Cautioned by Latour to avoid explaining what I encountered by the presence of enigmatic social forces, I stuck to the tangible book, its circulation and use, and the debates generated by its physical form. These realms might have otherwise been left unnoticed had I not chosen this peculiar method of materializing them through the materiality of the *mushaf* itself.

Notes

Preface

1 Peter Stallybrass, "Material Culture: Introduction," *Shakespeare Studies* 28 (2000): 124.
2 Annemarie Mol, *The Body Multiple: Ontology in Medical Practice* (Durham: Duke University Press, 2002), 31–3.
3 Talal Asad, "The Idea of an Anthropology of Islam." *Occasional Papers Series* (Washington, DC: Center for Contemporary Arab Studies, Georgetown University, 1986): 14.

Introduction

1 أبو الفداء إسماعيل بن عمر بن كثير، تفسير القرآن العظيم، مجلد ٧ (بيروت :داركر،١٩٦٦): ٤٨.
2 In his study of Qur'anic recitation, Patrick Eisenlohr calls this phenomenon *transduction*. He means that both the transformation of energy from one material modality into another as well as all bodily sensations and attendant psychic phenomena produced in the act of sonic immersion. In the words of his interlocutors, it is "the sensation of being profoundly seized and moved by the voice" that happens to those who recite or listen to Qur'anic chanting. Patrick Eisenlohr, *Sounding Islam. Voice, Media, and Sonic Atmospheres in an Indian Ocean World* (Oakland: University of California Press, 2018), 9.
3 I do not use this plural form throughout the book, though. In order to make the text more accessible, I use an Anglicized plural form *mushafs*.
4 Walter Benjamin, "Unpacking My Library," in *Illuminations* (New York: Schocken Books, 1969, [1931]), 59–67.
5 Donald F. McKenzie, *Making Meaning: "Printers of the Mind" and Other Essays* (Amherst: University of Massachusetts Press, 2002), 200.
6 Roger Chartier, *The Order of Books: Readers, Authors, and Libraries in Europe between the Fourteenth and Eighteenth Centuries* (Stanford, CA: Stanford University Press, 1994), 3.
7 Ibid.
8 Patrick Hanan, Judith T. Zeitlin, and Lydia He Liu, *Writing and Materiality in China: Essays in Honor of Patrick Hanan* (Cambridge, MA: Asia Center for the Harvard-Yenching Institute, 2003).
9 J. R. Osborn, *Letters of Light: Arabic Script in Calligraphy, Print, and Digital Design* (Cambridge, MA: Harvard University Press, 2017).
10 Bjornar Olsen, "Material Culture after Text: Re-membering Things," *Norwegian Archaeological Review* 36, no. 2 (2003): 100.
11 Ken Alder, "Introduction: Focus: Thick Things," *ISIS* 98 (2007): 80.

12. Bruno Latour, *Reassembling the Social: An Introduction to Actor-network-theory* (Oxford: Oxford University Press, 2005), 72.
13. Olsen, "Material Culture after Text," 97.
14. Latour, *Reassembling the Social*, 53.
15. Jeremy Stolow, *Orthodox by Design: Judaism, Print Politics, and the Artscroll Revolution* (Berkeley: University of California Press, 2010), 124; in another article, Stolow says, "This metanarrative [about the disembedding of religion by media] is structured around the assumption that the mere expansion of modern communication technologies is somehow commensurate with a dissolution of religious authority and a fragmentation of its markers of affiliation and identity." "Religion and/as Media," *Theory, Culture, and Society* 22, no. 4 (2005): 122.
16. Roland Barthes, "Jeunes Chercheurs" quoted in James Clifford, "Introduction: Partial Truths," in *Writing Culture: The Poetics and Politics of Ethnography*, ed. James Clifford and George Marcus (Berkeley: University of California Press, 1986), 1.
17. Latour, *Reassembling the Social*, 39.
18. Marshall McLuhan, *Understanding Media: The Extensions of Man* (New York: The New American Library, 1964), 23.
19. W. J. T. Mitchell, "There Are No Visual Media," *Journal of Visual Culture* 4, no. 2 (2005): 262.
20. Latour, *Reassembling the Social*, 64.
21. The first date follows the Muslim calendar; the second date follows the Gregorian calendar.
22. Travis Zadeh, "Touching and Ingesting: Early Debates over the Material Qur'an," *Journal of the American Oriental Society* 129, no. 3 (2009): 444.
23. Travis Zadeh, "'Fire Cannot Harm It': Mediation, Temptation and the Charismatic Power of the Qur'an," *Journal of Qur'anic Studies* 10, no. 2 (2008): 50–72.
24. Ibid.
25. Zadeh, "Touching and Ingesting."
26. Al-Juwayni, Imam al-Haramayn. *A Guide to Conclusive Proofs for the Principles of Belief* (كتاب الإرشاد إلى قواطع الأدلة في أصول الاعتقاد), trans. Paul E. Walker (UK: Garnet Publishing, 2000), 72–3.
27. Hala Auji, *Printing Arab Modernity: Book Culture and the American Press in Nineteenth-century Beirut* (Leiden: Brill, 2016), 12.
28. Since I wrote these words, apart from Travis Zadeh, a few other scholars have begun mentioning the *mushaf* as an object of pietic practice in their work on the Qur'an. For instance, see Ingrid Mattson, *The Story of the Qur'an: Its History and Place in Muslim Life* (Malden, MA: Blackwell Publishing, 2008).
29. Daniel A. Madigan, *The Qur'an's Self Image: Writing and Authority in Islam's Scripture* (Princeton, NJ: Princeton University Press, 2001): 3. Angelika Neuwirth also emphasizes the oral nature of the Qur'an. For instance, Angelika Neuwirth, "Two Faces of the Qur'ān: Qur'ān and Muṣḥaf," *Oral Tradition* 25, no. 1 (2010): 141–56.
30. The official website of the King Fahd Glorious Qur'an Printing Complex http://qurancomplex.gov.sa/

Chapter 1

1. One of the exceptions is Nile Green's article, "Journeymen, Middlemen: Travel, Transculture, and Technology in the Origins of Muslim Printing," in which he

discusses how "movement and interaction of a definable circle of men and their machines" contributed to different trajectories of print development in Iran, India, and Egypt. *International Journal of Middle East Studies* 41 (2009): 203–24.

2   Kathryn Schwartz, "Meaningful Mediums: A Material and Intellectual History of Manuscript and Print Production in the Nineteenth-century Ottoman Cairo" (PhD dissertation, Harvard University, 2015), 7.

3   Auji, *Printing Arab Modernity*, 7.

4   The idea that printing in the Middle East was "lagging" behind its European counterpart is expressed in academic texts on this subject even in more recent works. For instance, Yasemin Gencer, "Ibrahim Müteferrika and the Age of the Printed Manuscript," in *The Islamic Manuscript Tradition: Ten Centuries of Book Arts in Indiana University Collections*, ed. Christiane Gruber (Bloomington: Indiana University Press, 2010), 155.

5   Osborn, *Letters of Light*, 103.

6   See, for instance, Michael W. Albin, "Early Arabic Printing: A Catalogue of Attitudes," *Manuscripts of the Middle East* 5 (1990–1991): 114–22.

7   Zadeh, "Touching and Ingesting," 444.

8   Michel-Rolph Trouillot, *Silencing the Past: Power and the Production of History* (Boston, MA: Beacon Press, 1995), 29.

9   Ibid., 25.

10 For a similar point of view see Richard N. Verdery, "The Publications of the Bulaq Press under Muhammad 'Ali of Egypt," *Journal of the American Oriental Society* 91 (1971): 129–32.

11 خليل صابات، تاريخ الطباعة في الشرق العربي. (القاهرة: دار المعارف بمصر، الطبعة الثانية، ١٩٦٦ [الطبعة الاولى ١٩٥٧]):١٤٦.
    See also Geoffrey Roper, "The History of the Book in the Muslim World," in *The Book: A Global History*, ed. Michael F. Suarez and H. R. Woudhuysen (Oxford: Oxford University Press, 2013), 544.

12 اسماعيل سراج الدين و خالد عزب، وعاء المعرفة: من الحجر إلى النشر الفوري (الاسكندرية: مكتبة الاسكندرية، ٢٠٠٧): ٨٣. كذلك: سراج الدين، اسماعيل. مطبعة بولاق. الاسكندرية: مكتبة الاسكندرية، ٢٠٠٥. محمود محمد الطناحي، "أوائل المطبوعات العربية في مصر. في: ندوة تاريخ الطباعة العربية حتى انتهاء القرن التاسع عشر (القاهرة: منشورات المجمع الثقافي، ١٩٩٦). ابراهيم عبده، تاريخ الطباعة والصحافة في مصر خلال الحملة الفرنسية ١٧٩٨–١٨٠١ (القاهرة: مكتبة الأداب، ١٩٤٩).

13 خليل صابات، محمود محمد الطناحي، "أوائل المطبوعات العربية في مصر". في: ندوة تاريخ الطباعة العربية حتى انتهاء القرن التاسع عشر (القاهرة: منشورات المجمع الثقافي، ١٩٩٦): ٣٥٩.

14 A *multazim* or contractor system by which the Egyptian government allowed its subjects to commission privately financed printings from its presses. See Schwartz, "Meaningful Mediums," 14.

15 Angela Nuovo, "A Lost Arabic Koran Rediscovered," *The Library* 12, no. 4 (1990): 273–92.

16 Brett Wilson, *Translating the Qur'an in an Age of Nationalism: Print Culture and Modern Islam in Turkey* (Oxford: Oxford University Press, 2014), 34.

17 Sheila Blair, *Islamic Calligraphy* (Cairo: The American University in Cairo Press, 2006), 29.

18 This characteristic, apart from being articulated in the Arabic sources on calligraphy, was already noticed by a German traveler to the Middle East in the eighteenth century. See Carsten Niebuhr, *Travels through Arabia and Other Countries in the East* (Reisebeschreibung nach Arabien und andern umliegenden Ländern), trans. Robert Heron (Edinburgh, 1792), 2, 261.

19 I thank J. R. Osborn for letting me use this idea, which he demonstrated in his book *Letters of Light*, 95.
20 Muhsin Mahdi, "From the Manuscript Age to the Age of Printed Books" in *The Book in the Islamic World: The Written Word and Communication in the Middle East*, ed. George N. Atiyeh (Albany: State University of New York Press, 1995), 1.
21 Osborn, *Letters of Light*, 97.
22 Michael W. Albin, "Printing of the Qur'an," in *Encyclopedia of the Qur'an*, ed. Jane Dammen McAuliffe (Leiden: Brill, 2001), 265.
23 Roper, "The History of the Book in the Muslim World," 547.
24 خليل صابات، ٢٩-٣٠.
25 محمود أغا ناظر القلمخانة قدم عرضًا لمجلس الجهادية مضمونه أنه سئل عن كمية ما يلزم لتلاميذ القلم المذكور من أجزاء القرآن الكريم ومن سائر اللوازم، فأجاب بأنه يلزم لهم أربع ختمات وستون لوحًا. فقال أهل المجلس: ينبغي أن يحرر من طرف علم من طرف حضرة بك أفندي ناظر الجهادية إلى عمر أفندي ناظر المهمات بأن يصرف الأشياء المذكورة للتلاميذ حيث كانت لازمة لهم. الوقائع المصرية، العدد رقم ٣٣٨ الصادر في ٤ شعبان ١٢٤٧هـ/٨ يناير ١٨٣٢م.
26 أبو الفتوح رضوان، تاريخ مطبعة بولاق ولمحة في تاريخ الطباعة في بلدان الشرق الأوسط (القاهرة: المطبعة الاميرية القاهرة، ١٩٥٣، ١٩٤٢): ٢٧٨.
27 See, for instance, a popular historiography website http://www.toraseyat.com, an article entitled:
رحلة طبع "المصاحف المصرية" من الانتشار حتى الاندثار
28 For instance: Amit Bein, *Ottoman Ulema, Turkish Republic: Agents of Change and Guardians of Tradition* (Stanford: Stanford University Press, 2011); Thomas F. Carter, "Islam as a Barrier to Printing," *The Moslem World* 33, no. 3 (1943): 213–16.
29 أبو الفتوح رضوان، ١٩.
30 George N. Atiyeh, "The Book in the Modern Arab World: The Cases of Lebanon and Egypt," in *The Book in the Islamic World: The Written Word and Communication in the Middle East*, ed. George N. Atiyeh (Albany: State University of New York Press, 1995), 285.
31 Wilson, *Translating the Qur'an in an Age of Nationalism*, 56–64.
32 Ibid., 67. Interestingly, however—says J. R. Osborn—Cevdet never asked for nor received a *fatwa* authorizing him to print a *mushaf*. *Letters of Light*, 160.
33 Nedret Kuran-Borçoğlu, "Osman Zeki Bey and His Printing Office the *Matbaa-i Osmaniye*," in *History of Printing and Publishing in the Languages and Countries of the Middle East*, ed. P. Sadgrove (Oxford: Oxford University Press, 2004), 36–7.
34 Wilson, *Translating the Qur'an in an Age of Nationalism*, 72.
35 يوسف إليان سركيس، معجم المطبوعات العربية والمعرّبة. الجزء الثاني. مكتبة الثقافة الدينية (١٩٢٨-١٩٣٠): ١٤٩٩-١٥٠٠.
36 Alder, "Introduction," 82.
37 For the rules of writing the Qur'anic text, see, for instance, Jan Just Witkam, "Twenty-nine Rules for Qur'an Copying: A Set of Rules for the Layout of a Nineteenth-century Ottoman Qur'an Manuscript," *Journal of Turkish Studies* 26, no. 1 (2002): 339–48.
38 انه بمناسبة طبع المصحف الشريف يلزم استقدام ناظر المطبعة وسؤاله عما إذا كانت أجزاء المطبعة مصنوعة من جلد الكلب أم لا وترسل الإفادةعن ذلك الى حبيب افندي في آخر ذي القعدة سنة ١٢٤٨ (٣٠ ابريل سنة ١٨٣٣) دفاتر المعية بتركي، دفتر رقم ٥٠، وثيقة رقم ٥٣٧، ص ٩٤، محفوظات عابدين. واستشهد في أبو الفتوح رضوان، ٢٧٩.
39 For a more detailed discussion of the issue of impurity and Qur'anic printing, see Mohammed Ghaly, "The Interplay of Technology and Sacredness in Islam: Discussions of Muslim Scholars on Printing the Qur'an," *Studies in Ethics, Law, and Technology* 3, no. 2 (2009): 1–24.

40 وقد بلغ من العناية بطبع القرآن أن خصص جزء من مطبعة بولاق لطبعة خاصة عرف باسم "مطبعة المصحف الشريف" وكان لها رئيس مستقل في أبو الفتوح رضوان، ٢٨٢.

41 الإفتاء المصري: من الصحابي عقبة بن عامر إلى الدكتور علي جمعة. عماد أحمد هلال. الجزء الثالث (مطبعة دار الكتب والوثائق، القاهرة ٢٠١٥): ١٣٦٤-١٣٩٠.

42 Andrew Archibald Paton, *A History of the Egyptian Revolution, from the Period of the Mamelukes to the Death of Mohammed Ali; from Arab and European Memoirs, Oral Tradition, and Local Research* (London: Trübner & Co., 1870), 245.

43 إن المصاحف المطبوعة منع بيعها وشرائها لكثرة غلطتها ولحانتها وتحريف كتابتها في جملة مواضع فيصير اعدامها بالوجه المستحسن شرعا. وأما ما يجري في حق من يضبطه معه مصاحف مثل ذلك فما أن ما وجد معه من ذلك جرى مجازاته فهكذا إذا وجد أحدا معهم مصاحف مثل ذلك يجري مجازاتهم بحسب ما يتضح. أفادة نمرة ٣٤٧ من المعية الكتخداوية لمحافظة الإسكندرية في ١١ شعبان سنة ١٢٧٠ (٨ مايو سنة ١٨٥٤) وجه ١٣١ دفتر مجموع أمور إدارة وإجراءات مجلس الأحكام ص ٢٦٤ محفوظات عابدين. استشهد به في أبو الفتوح رضوان، ٢٨.

44 ديوان الداخلية

45 أبو الفتوح رضوان، ٢٨١.

46 فهرست الكتب العربية المحفوظة بالكتبخانة الخديوية، جزء ١ (القاهرة ١٨٨٧)، ٢.

47 سركيس، ١٥. – ١٤٩٩

48 Maṭbaʿat Ḥasan Aḥmad al-Ṭūkhī 1882 (complete *mushaf* and 30 parts), 1883, 1884, 1886; Maṭbaʿat Muhammad Abū Zayd 1882, 1883, 1884, 1891; Maṭbaʿat Sayed ʿAli 1884, 1885; Maṭbaʿat al-Sheikh Sharaf 1890, 1891; Maṭbaʿat al-Sayed Ḥasan al-Sharīf 1888; an edition by al-Sheikh Muhammad Raḍwān [al-Makhallalātī] 1891; a Moroccan edition 1894, 1900; Maṭbaʿat' Abd al-Khālaq Ḥaqqī 1893, 1896, 1897, 1899, 1900, 1901, 1902, 1903, 1904. These dates are approximate, as they were recorded according to the *hijri* calendar.

49 عايدة نصير، حركة نشر الكتب في مصر في القرن التاسع عشر (القاهرة: الهيئة المصرية العامة للكتاب، ١٩٩٤)، ٤٤٥.

50 Albin, "Printing of the Qur'an," 266.

51 Ian Proudfoot, "Lithography at the Crossroads of the East," *Journal of the Printing Historical Society* 27 (1998): 127.

52 Ian Proudfoot, "Mass Producing Houri's Moles, or Aesthetics and Choice of Technology in Early Muslim Book Printing," in *Islam: Essays on Scripture, Thought, and Society*, eds. P. G. Riddell and T. Street (Leiden: Brill, 1997), 164. See also Moinuddin Aqeel, "Commencement of Printing in the Muslim World: A View of Impact on Ulama at Early Phase of Islamic Moderate Trends," *Kyoto Bulletin of Islamic Area Studies* 2, no. 2 (2009): 18.

53 Francis Robinson, "Technology and Religious Change: Islam and the Impact of Print," *Modern Asian Studies* 27, no. 1, Special Issue: How Social, Political and Cultural Information Is Collected, Defined, Used and Analyzed (Cambridge: Cambridge University Press, 1993), 233.

54 Wilson, personal communication.

55 Robinson, "Technology and Religious Change," 234.

56 Wilson, *Translating the Qur'an in an Age of Nationalism*, 40.

57 أبو الفتوح رضوان، ٩٠.

58 Ibid., 81–89.

59 Walter Henry Medhurst, *The Missionary Herald* 25 (1829): 192-3, quoted in Proudfoot, "Lithography at the Crossroads of the East," 121.

60 Proudfoot, "Lithography at the Crossroads of the East," 127.

61 H. von Dewall (1857) "[Berigten:] Eene Inlandsche Drukkerij te Palembang‹." *Tijdschrift voor de Indische Taal- Land- en Volkenkunde uitgegeven door het Bataviaasch Genootschap van Kunsten en Wetenschappen*, deel 6/n.s. deel 3

62 Proudfoot, "Lithography at the Crossroads of the East," 127.
63 H. Von Dewall (1857): 196–7 in Jeroen Peeters, "Palembang Revisited: Further Notes on the Printing Establishment of Kemas Haji Muhammad Azhari, 1848," *International Institute for Asian Studies Yearbook* (1995): 182.
64 Roper, "The History of the Book in the Muslim World," 547.
65 الافتاء المصري.
66 For example, *mushaf* from al-ʿĀmira al-Sharfiyya (item 340); *mushaf* from Maḥbūb Hindāwī wa Sharīka (item 464), Library of Mashyekhat al-Azhar.
67 Private conversation with Kathryn Schwartz.
68 But, possibly, penned by a calligrapher ʿAbd al-Khālaq Ḥaqqī, not al-Makhallalāti himself.
69 سركيس، ١٤٩٩-١٥٠٠.
70 For instance, the 1886 edition printed by Muhammad Abū Zayd that is not mentioned in Sarkīs' list, Library of Mashyekhat al-Azhar (item 692).
71 In private collection.
72 Ibid.
73 Item 323, Library of Mashyekhat al-Azhar.
74 Roper, "The History of the Book in the Muslim World," 544.
75 Item 756, Library of Mashyekhat al-Azhar.

Chapter 2

1 Kathryn Piquette and Ruth Whitehouse, "Introduction: Developing an Approach to Writing as Material Practice," in *Writing as Material Practice: Substance, Surface and Medium*, eds. Kathryn Piquette and Ruth Whitehouse (London: Ubiquity Press, 2013), 1–13.
2 Marcel Mauss, *The Gift: The Form and Reason for Exchange in Archaic Societies*, trans. W. D. Halls (New York: W. W. Norton, 1990 [1923]).
3 It is a common form to address men in Egypt.
4 الهيئة المصرية العامة للكتب
5 Al-Sayed al-Qaftanji (السيد القفطانجي) (paper presented at the Conference of Calligraphers at Bibliotheca Alexandrina in Alexandria, 2014).
6 Sarah Eissa, "Killing Calligraphy," *Al-Ahram Weekly Online* (December 16–22, 2010) http://weekly.ahram.org.eg/2010/1027/fe2.htm (accessed March 1, 2013).
7 The conquest of Central Asia opened the Muslim World to contact with China. Methods of papermaking were transferred through lands today known as Uzbekistan. The new technology was perfected and subsequently spread to Iraq, Syria, Egypt, North Africa, Sicily, and Spain. Jonathan Bloom, *Paper before Print: The History and Impact of Paper in the Islamic World* (New Haven: Yale University Press, 2001), 8–9.
8 Eric Gill, *An Essay on Typography* (London: J. M. Dent & Sons Ltd., 1941), 33.
9 Tim Ingold, "Materials against Materiality," *Archaeological Dialogues* 14, no. 1 (2007): 16.
10 Eissa, "Killing Calligraphy."

11 Saif-Ur-Rahman Dar, *The Roots of Muslim Calligraphy in Arabia, Iran, and Pakistan* (Pakistan: University of Peshawar, 1981), 7.
12 The Arabic Qur'anic Corpus http://corpus.quran.com/translation.jsp?chapter=24&verse=35.
13 Such individualized products of personal piety can be viewed in the collection of manuscripts stored at Sayeda Zaynab Mosque in Cairo.
14 The history of calligraphy in the Middle East occasionally includes names of women from notable families who became famous for their artistic skills in copying Qur'anic text.
15 For most calligraphers, making a living by copying Qur'anic text required speed, without the luxury of time for a slow, spiritual contemplation of each stroke of the pen. Calligraphy was also an important skill in the business of making jewelry and other ornamental objects.
16 فيه جو في كل الخط
17 A visual representation of the sound. This remains an issue for digital applications discussed later in the book.
18 Elementary textbooks are vocalized to help children to learn to read. Some religious classics (for instance the *hadith*) can also be vocalized to avoid misreading.
19 Al-Qaftanji.
20 مجلة حروف عربية
21 وزارة الثقافة والشباب وتنمية
22 الرسم العثماني
23 لجنة المصحف تحت مجمع البحوث الإسلامية
24 Kenneth M. George, "Ethics, Iconoclasm, and Qur'anic Art in Indonesia," *Cultural Anthropology* 24 (2009): 589–621.
25 Blair, *Islamic Calligraphy*, xxvi.

Chapter 3

1 See, for example, Fawzi M. Tadrus, *Printing in the Arab World with the Emphasis on the Būlāq Press in Egypt* (Qatar: University of Qatar Press, 1982), 71.
2 On commodification of early Qur'anic books see Delia Cortese, "The Commodification of the Muṣḥaf in the Early Centuries of Islam," in *Writing and Writing: From Another World and Another Era*, eds. Robert M. Kerr and Thomas Milo (Cambridge: Archetype, 2010), 41–66. For a modern example of commodification of the Qur'anic text and the dilemmas produced by it, see Gregory Starrett, "The Political Economy of Religious Commodities in Cairo," *American Anthropologist* 97, no. 1 (1995): 51–68.
3 السعيد داود ، النشر العائلي في مصر: دراسة تأصيلية (دار التيسير: القاهرة، ٢٠٠٨)، ٩٤.
4 Ibid., 96.
5 نصير، ٤٣٥.
6 Four editions mentioned by Sarkīs and two confirmed by the copies kept at Mashyekhat al-Azhar: al-Makhallalāti 1886 and Siluman 1907 (published in 15- and 30-part editions). Muhammad Abu Zayd also printed another edition prepared by Sheikh Muhammad Sulīmān al-Safaṭī.
7 On the technical aspects of setting a typographic text in Arabic, see Titus Nemeth, *Arabic Type-making in the Machine Age: The Influence of Technology on the Form of Arabic Type, 1908–1993* (Leiden: Brill, 2017).

Notes

8. Item number 198, Library of Mashyekhat al-Azhar.
9. "إرشاد القراء والكاتبين إلى معرفة رسم الكتاب المبين"
10. "الوقف والابتدا"
11. شيخ معهد القراءات بالأزهر الشريف
12. عبد الفتاح القاضي، تاريخ المصحف الشريف (مكتبة القاهرة: القاهرة، ٢٠١٠)، ٥١.
13. Various editions of this *mushaf* show that al-Makhallalāti did not make these changes all at once, but they were gradually added or removed from subsequent versions.
14. Although other lithographic editions were also popular, such as the ones by 'Abd al-Khāliq Ḥaqqī or Hasan Ahmad Ṭūkhī.
15. وكان هذا المصحف هو المتداول بين أهل العلم والقراء.. المعول عليه عندهم المقدم دون سائر المصاحف لما اشتمل عليه من المزايا السابقة، بيد أنه لم يبرز في صورة حسنة تروق الناظر، تنشط القارئ، لرداءة ورقه، وسوء طبعه، إذ أنه طبع في مطبعة حجرية. عبد الفتاح القاضي، ٥٢.
16. السعيد داود، ١٤٥.
17. One of Qadroghli's *mushafs*, initially printed by Subīḥ, was later reprinted in 1981 by a publishing house called al-Anwar al-Muhammadiyya.
18. For instance, an edition published in 1951/52 under the approval of al-Azhar I saw in a private collection.
19. السعيد داود، ١٥٠.
20. نظارة المعارف العمومية
21. Purportedly, the *mushaf* produced by Osman Zeki Bey, reproduced according to the seventeenth-century calligrapher Ḥāfiẓ 'Uthman, did not strictly adhere to the 'Uthmanic *rasm*.
22. شيخ المقارئ المصرية محمد علي خلف الحسيني
23. عبد الفتاح القاضي، ٥٣.
24. Personal conversation with a worker from al-Amiriyya.
25. This name is sometimes confused with the handmade *mushaf* penned especially for the king and also known among calligraphers as *mushaf* Fu'ad.
26. "It was done in an elegant print compared to other contemporary *masahif* and was received with great acceptance by the broader Muslim community"—this is how *mushaf* Fu'ad is described today by an Egyptian seller in an online antiquities store called *The Souq*, where this first edition was available for purchase for a significant amount of money.
27. عبد الفتاح القاضي، ٥٦.
28. Walter Benjamin, "The Work of Art in the Age of Its Technological Reproducibility," in *Selected Writings Volume 3, 1935–1938*, trans. Edmund Jephcott, Howard Eiland, and Michael W. Jennings (Cambridge: The Belknap Press of Harvard University Press, 2002), 104.
29. Brinkley Messick, *The Calligraphic State: Textual Domination and History in a Muslim Society* (Berkeley: University of California Press, 1993), 127.
30. The first one took place in the second Islamic century when the differences between the 'Uthmanic and other, non-'Uthmanic *rasms* (such as *rasm* of Ibn Mas'ud) were still reviewed by Muslim scholars but in the third Islamic century *'ulama'* began to limit possible variants to those attributed to 'Uthman only.
31. مذكرة بشأن تيسير القراءة العربية الصحيحة بحروف الطباعة الحالية وضبطها بحركات الشكل المعروفة اللازمة للنطق الصحيح مرفوعة إلى حضرة صاحب المعالي رئيس مجمع الملك فؤاد الأول للغة العربية من محمد نديم، مدير المطبعة بدار الكتب المصرية، ١٩٤٨.

    A handwritten copy of this document is available at the National Library Dar al-Kutub in Cairo
32. مجمع الملك فهد لطباعة المصحف الشريف

33 "فلم وثائقي عن مجمع الملك فهد لطباعة المصحف الشريف،" http://www.youtube.com/watch?v=VY4Eg8_smEs (accessed April 7, 2011). See also "The *Muṣḥaf* al-Madīna and the King Fahd Holy Qur'an Printing Complex," *Journal of Qur'anic Studies* 1, no. 1 (1999): 155–8.

34 وزارة الأوقاف السورية

35 أحمد غاوي، "عثمان طه: كتبت أربع نسخ للمصحف فنشر منها الملك فهد عشرات الملايين في العالم،" الرياض، ٢٣ نوفمبر ٢٠٠٦. http://www.alriyadh.com:8080/203788

36 مدرسة الخطوط الملكية

37 السعيد داود، ٩٧.

38 السعيد داود, ٩٨

39 احمد صبري زايد. تاريخ الخط العربي وأعلام الخطاطين. (القاهرة: دار الفضيلة، nd)، ٢٩٩.

40 The earlier problems with typeset printing were later solved in many publishing houses by mechanical phototypesetting that did not require setting the letters by hand, speeding up the process, and improving the accuracy and correctness of the text.

41 A statement placed on the official website of King Fahd Complex says: "Copyright: Based on the approval of His Excellency the Minister of Islamic Affairs, Endowments, Da'wah and Guidance, General Supervisor of the King Fahd Qur'an Printing Complex. The Qur'an Printing Complex is honored to present to the Muslim public a complete free digital copy of *Mushaf* al-Madīnah published by the Complex, in the following formats: Adobe Illustrator files, PDF files, High quality images, True Type Font. *Mushaf* al-Madīnah in these previous formats can be used for free in all personal, commercial & individual businesses, in works of governmental departments & agencies, in the publications of both private and national institutions, also suitable for Qur'an printing, digital publishing, & for media use, can be used also in websites, software, and other similar intermediates. We ask Allah that He renders this blessed project beneficial to all Muslims." http://dm.Qurāncomplex.gov.sa/copyright-2/.

42 محمد علي عنز. "توحيد جهة الطباعة ضرورة لسلامة المصحف من الأخطاء،" الأهرام (٥ نوفمبر ٢٠١٠): ١١.

43 "حكم أخذ مصحف من مسجد ووضعه في مسجد آخر،" رقم الفتوى: 100457. مركز الفتوى islamweb.net، ١٠ أكتوبر ٢٠٠٧ http://fatwa.islamweb.net/fatwa/index.php?page=showfatwa&Option=FatwaId&Id=100457.

Chapter 4

1 Birgit Meyer, "There Is a Spirit in That Image: Mass-produced Jesus Pictures and Protestant-Pentecostal Animation in Ghana," *Comparative Studies in Society and History* 52, no. 1 (2010): 100. See also Birgit Meyer and Annelies Moors, *Religion, Media, and the Public Sphere* (Bloomington: Indiana University Press, 2006).

2 رجاء النمر، "الانتخابات وطباعة المصحف الشريف،" الاخبار (٢٨ مايو ٢٠١٢): ٢٠.

3 أخطاء أو تحريف

4 غرفة صناعات الطباعة والتغليف

5 Ken Alder, "Making Things the Same: Representations, Tolerance, and the End of the Ancient Regime in France," *Social Studies of Science* 28, no. 4 (August 1998): 503.

6 It's important to remember that manuscript copies also had errors, but they were individual errors and easy to correct on the margins of the text.

7 وزارة العدل

8 سلوى عثمان، "الطباعة تفتح النار على شيخ الأزهر وتجريمه أخطاء المصحف،" البلد (٢٢ مايو ٢٠١٢).
http://www.el-balad.com/170170/altbaah-tfth-alnar-aly-s.aspx#sthash.NJ5TJMwl.dpuf

سليم علي، "صناعة الطباعة تشكل لجنة لزيارة الطيب لبحث قرار تجريم أخطاء طباعة المصحف،" اليوم السابع، ٢٦ مايو ٢٠١٢.
http://www1.youm7.com/News.asp?NewsID=688624&SecID=24&IssueID=0#.U-Jza0hPZ8s

وائل المزيكي، "غرفة الطباعة تناقش مقترح قانون لتجريم أخطاء طباعة المصحف،" اخبار اليوم، ٢١ مايو ٢٠١٢.
http://www.akhbarelyom.com/news/newdetails/34924/1/0.html#.UnvtCCSE4zm

9 رئيس لجنة الشؤون الدينية بمجلس الشعب

10 "فى حالة تطبيق القانون فان جميع مطابع المصحف فى مصر ستكون مهددة بالتوقف وبذلك سنفتح الباب لدول أخرى لطباعة المصحف مثل الصين ودول شرق آسيا وهو ما يهدد بضياع هيبة الأزهر الشريف." سلوى عثمان، "الطباعة تفتح النار على شيخ الأزهر وتجريمه أخطاء المصحف،"

11 لجنة الثقافة والإعلام

12 "لسنا أقل من المملكة العربية السعودية التي يتم طباعة المصحف فيها، وفقا لمواصفات ومعايير مع تطبيق العقوبات على المخالفين." اتحاد الناشرين ينتقد فرض الأزهر لرسوم جديدة على طباعة المصحف،" (٢٩ مايو ٢٠١٢).
http://news.egypt.com/arabic/permalink/2248214.html

13 مجمع البحوث الإسلامية

14 عائشة زيدان، "صناعة الطباعة تناقش أخطاء طباعة المصحف،" مصرس (١٣ يونيو ٢٠٢١).
http://www.masress.com/elwady/17849

محمد فتحي، "الناشرون ينتقدون الأزهر لفرضه رسوما جديدة على طباعة المصحف،" الأهرام الرقمي (٣٠ مايو ٢٠٢١).
http://digital.ahram.org.eg/Policy.aspx?Serial=916281

سليم علي، " تأجيل اجتماع أصحاب مطابع "المصحف" مع "الأزهر" للأحد المقبل،" اليوم السابع (٧ يونيو ٢٠١٢).
http://www1.youm7.com/News.asp?NewsID=698595&SecID=24

15 الأخطاء المهنية ناتجة من إهمال

16 عائشة زيدان، "صناعة الطباعة تناقش أخطاء طباعة المصحف."

17 محمد ربيع غزالة، "شيخ الأزهر: تذليل كل الصعوبات من أجل طباعة المصحف الشريف،" الأهرام المسائي.
http://massai.ahram.org.eg/Inner.aspx?ContentID=57045
فوقية ياسين، "الطيب: تذليل كافة الصعوبات من أجل طباعة المصحف الشريف،" البلد (٠١ يونيو ٢٠١٢).
http://www.el-balad.com/187177/altybsnzll-kafh-alsaobat.aspx

18 "البرلمان المصري يدعم عقوبة الخطأ في طباعة المصحف،" عرب نت ٥ (٣ يناير ٢٠١١).
http://www.arabnet5.com/news.asp?c=2&id=76430#.T8ahEL-Qx-I

19 يوسف محمد،"مكتبة بالحسين تعرض مصاحف بها أخطاء مطبعية،" مصرس (١٩ أغسطس ٢٠٠٨).
http://www.masress.com/youm7/36659

20 He became the President of Parliamentary Council for Religious Affairs two years later. He had also worked at the Islamic Research Academy at al-Azhar supervising, among others, the Department of mushaf. In 2005 he was briefly arrested for participation in demonstrations against American "insults against the Noble *Mushaf*."

21 ياسر حمود "يكشف أخطاء في طباعة المصحف الشريف،" نافذة مصر (٣ مايو ٢٠١٠).
http://www.egyptwindow.net/news_Details.aspx?News_ID=8056

22 لجنة المصحف الشريف

23 "اشتريت المصحف بعد أن انبهرت بتجليده وطباعته، لكن بعد القراءة لاحظت تغييراً فى معانى آيات السور وتشابهها فى معظم الآيات، ولولا حفظى للقرآن ما كنت اكتشفت تلك الأخطاء. [...] فور اكتشافى الأخطاء ذهبت

بالمصحف إلى دار النشر التى طبعته فقال لى أصحابها: "المصحف اللى مش عاجبك ده وزعنا منه 10 آلاف نسخة، منها 3 آلاف نسخة للمساجد ولم يشك أحد منه'، فذهبت به إلى مشيخة الأزهر بالدراسة ولم يهتم بى أحد." http://www.almasryalyoum.com/node/1167671

24 Bruno Latour, "*From Realpolitik to Dingpolitik—An Introduction to Making Things Public.*" http://www.bruno-latour.fr/node/208.
25 وزارة الأوقاف
26 "القانون رقم 102 لسنة 1985 بشأن تنظيم طبع المصحف الشريف والأحاديث النبوية." http://www.ug-law.com/downloads/law102-85.pdf
27 لجنة مراجعة المصحف الشريف
28 "المعصراوي: أخطاء المصاحف سببها دور النشر،" مصرس (5 أبريل 2009). http://www.masress.com/moheet/100000
29 In comparison, early printed Bibles were full of typographical errors, such as the famous "Wicked Bible" published in England in 1631 that says, "Thou shalt commit adultery." Statements such as al-Hakim's show that Islamic scholars were well aware of the tricks of printing (as well as its potential benefits).
30 محمد علي عنز، 11.
31 هبة خالد، "المعصراوي: نشر الآيات القرآنية على الإنترنت أمر بالغ الخطورة ... وفرصة لتحريفه،" الرأي (20 يناير 2011). http://www.alraimedia.com/alrai/Article.aspx?id=251094&date=20012011
32 IPR Strategic Business Information Database, accessed May 12, 2003.

Chapter 5

1 Dick Houtman and Birgit Meyer, *Things: Religion and the Question of Materiality* (New York: Fordham University Press, 2012), 7. See also Birgit Meyer, "Materializing Religion," *Material Religion* 4, no. 2 (2008): 227 and "Medium," *Material Religion* 7, no. 1 (2011): 58–64.
2 Historians have also given credit to other scholars for these improvements, such as Nasr Ibn ʿAsim (d. 89 AH/707 CE) and Yahya Ibn Yaʿmur (d. 129 AH/746 CE).
3 Abdel Haleem, "Qurʾanic Orthography: The Written Representation of the Recited Text of the Qurʾan," *Islamic Quarterly* 38, no. 3 (1994): 172.
4 جلال الدين السيوطي، الإتقان في علوم القرآن (المملكة العربية السعودية: مركز الدراسات القرآني،nd)، 2199.
5 كتاب المقنع في معرفة مرسوم مصاحف أهل الأمصار
6 التنزيل
7 عقيلة أتراب القصائد في أسنى المقاصد
8 عنوان الدليل في مرسوم خط التنزيل
9 الإتقان في علوم القرآن
10 Haleem, 173–9.
11 الليل الليل
12 قالوا
13 يسأل- يسل
14 زكوة زكاة
15 يومهم – يوم هم؛ فيما – في ما
16 Houtman and Meyer, 2.
17 شيخ عموم المقارئ المصرية
18 مدير إدارة شؤون المصاحف بالمسجد الحرام

19 مليون مصحف بالمسجد الحرام، دي ون جي
   http://www.d1g.com/forum/show/4855761
20 مصحف المساحة والأميرية: تعريف بهذا المصحف و اصطلاحات الضبط (القاهرة: المساحة والأميرية)، ١٣٤٢.
21 شعبان محمد اسماعيل. رسم المصحف وضبطه: بين التوقيف والاصطلاحات الحديثة (القاهرة: دار السلامة، ١٩٩٩)، ٨٢-٨١.
22 مجمع اللغة العربية بالقاهرة
23 Erik Jan Zürcher, *Turkey: A Modern History* (London: I.B. Tauris, 2004), 188.
24 Youssef Mahmoud, "On the Reform of the Arabic Writing System," *Journal of Reading* 23, no. 8 (1980): 728.
25 عبد الحي الفرماوي، كتابة القرآن الكريم بالرسم الإملائي أو الحروف اللاتينية: اقتراحان مرفوضان. (القاهرة: دار التوزيع والنشر الإسلامية، ١٩٩١)، ٣٣.
26 Ibid., 54.
27 Yannis Haralambous describes three of the projects submitted to the competition in his article "Simplification of the Arabic Script: Three Different Approaches and Their Implementations," in *Electronic Publishing, Artistic Imaging, and Digital Typography: Proceedings of the 7th International Conference on Electronic Publishing*, eds. Roger D. Hersch, Jacques André, and Heather Brown (Berlin: Springer, 1998), 138-56.
28 عبد الحي الفرماوي، ١٦.
29 For more information on the script reform, see Osborn, *Letters of Light*, Chapter 5.
30 شعبان محمد اسماعيل، ٦٣.
31 شعبان محمد اسماعيل، ٦٣.
32 عبد العزيز سعيد الصويعي. الحروف العربي تحفة التاريخ وعقدة التقنية. (الدار الجماهيرية للنشر والتوزيع والإعلان، ليبيا) ١٩٨٩، ٨١-٨٢.
33 كلية أصول الدين
34 شعبان محمد اسماعيل، ٨١-٨٢.
35 مجلات الأزهر
36 هيئة كبار العلماء بالمملكة العربية السعودية
37 اللجنة الدائمة للبحوث العلمية والإفتاء
38 شعبان محمد اسماعيل، ٨٣-٨٦.

Chapter 6

1 See Charles Hirschkind, *The Ethical Soundscape: Cassette Sermons and Islamic Counterpublics* (New York: Columbia University Press, 2006).
2 For instance الصلواة
3 أثر
4 It is part of Thomas Milo's argument that *nuqta* and diacritics should be digitally coded as separate forms.
5 مطابع خادم الحرمين الشريفين
6 See also Abdel Haleem, "The Blind and the Qur'an/المصحف بخط برايل," *Journal of Qur'anic Studies* 3, no. 2 (2001): 123-5.
7 السعودية: طباعة مصاحف جديدة خاصة بالمكفوفين!
   http://www.farfesh.com/Display.asp?catID=179&mainCatID=147&sID=84244
8 J. R. Osborn says, "Some of the most successful typographic systems for Arabic script reform, such as the CSV Codar system also adopted this strategy, in which *tashkil* were interspersed between consonants." Personal communication, 2019.

9 محمد مرسي، "الأزهر يدشن مشروع تسجيل القرآن الكريم بلغة الإشارة وطريقة برايل،" أوركيدزا (٢٩ مايو ٢٠١٢).
http://orkidza.com/Middle-East/Egypt/2012/5/28/114
For more information on the topic of unification of the Arabic sign language, see Kinda Al-Fityani's dissertation: "Deaf people, modernity, and a contentious effort to unify Arab sign languages." https://oatd.org/oatd/record?record=california%5C%3Aqt23n5f0h5

10 نحو مصحف برايل مصري بدون

11 استجابة لتطلّع الملايين من المكفوفين لاقتناء كتاب الله الكريم مطابع خادم الحرمين تنتهي من طباعة المصحف بطريقة "برايل." "إذ إن هناك ملايين من المكفوفين يتطلعون إلى اقتناء كتاب الله الكريم بطريقة برايل، وخاصة أئمة المساجد والخطباء والمدرسين وطلبة العلم، وستستمر في أداء مسؤولياتها بطباعة القرآن الكريم بطريقة برايل." "استجابة لتطلّع الملايين من المكفوفين لاقتناء كتاب الله الكريم: مطابع خادم الحرمين تنتهي من طباعة المصحف بطريقة برايل،" المواطن (٢ يوليو ٢٠١٣).
http://www.almowaten.net/?p=36472

12 ""إبصار" تواجه عبء تأمين "مصاحف برايل" لمستفيديها من المكفوفين." الإقتصادية، ١٢ يوليو ٢٠١٢.
http://www.aleqt.com/2012/07/12/article_673805.html

13 فوانيس رمضان، "المصحف الشريف بطريقة "برايل"... وقصة مطبعة مصرية جميع عمالها من معدومي البصر،" الرأي (٢١ سبتمبر ٢٠٠٨).
http://www.alraimedia.com/Articles.aspx?id=69090

14 "يشير مدير المطبعة... إلى أن مراحل طباعة المصحف الشريف بطريقة برايل تبدأ بترجمة كتابة القرآن الكريم إلى الكتابة البارزة على لوح صفيح، وذلك بتلاوة القرآن الكريم على أحد المكفوفين المتخصصين في الكتابة بطريقة برايل الذي يحول ما يسمعه إلى حروف مكتوبة بالخط البارز." فوانيس رمضان، "المصحف الشريف بطريقة "برايل"... وقصة مطبعة مصرية جميع عمالها من معدومي البصر."

15 The Qur'anic text translated into another language is also considered to be only a translation or a commentary to the Qur'an in Arabic. It is not the Qur'anic message itself. See, for example, Carl Ernst, *How to Read the Qur'an: A New Guide, With Select Translations* (Chapel Hill: University of North Carolina Press, 2011), 71–2.

16 هو مصحف نفسه.

17 قسم الفقه والدراسات العليا بكلية الشريعة بجامعة الإمام محمد بن سعود الإسلامية بالرياض.

18 ظهر لنا مما سبق أن الرأي الراجح هو وجوب التزام الرسم العثماني في كتابة المصحف, وأما كتابة الآيات في غير المصحف للمتعلمين من الصبيان وكذا في الصحف والمجلات فيجوز كتابتها بغير الرسم العثماني, وما سبق خاص في الكتابة المرئية. وأما نظام برايل أو يسمى بالخط البارز فهل ينطبق عليه نفس الحكم، أو هو رموز محددة لا علاقة لها بصورة الرسم العثماني أو الإملائي دعت إليها ضرورة معينة. وأن ما يقال عن استبدال الرسم العثماني بالرسم الإملائي لا ينطبق على استبدال الرسم العثماني بنظام برايل ؟ عبد الله الخميس، "كتابة القرآن الكريم بنظام برايل للمكفوفين،" almoslim.net، (٤ نوفمبر ٢٠٠٦).
http://www.almoslim.net/node/83459

19 Interestingly, Ibrahim Müteferrika made a very similar claim with regard to print in his list of ten reasons for Ottoman printing. J. R. Osborn, personal communication, 2019.

20 عبد الله بن منيع

21 وذكر الشيخ عبد الله بن منيع عضو هيئة كبار العلماء "لقد عرض علينا موضوع كتابة المصحف بطريقة "برايل"، غير أننا توقفنا عن إصدار أي قرار حوله"، ولفت إلى أن أعضاء مجلس هيئة كبار العلماء، اختلفوا حول إعطاء مصحف برايل أحكام المصحف القرآني، مؤكدا على رفض مجلس الهيئة اعتباره مصحفا. "السعودية: الانتهاء من طباعة مصحف برايل وسط تحفظ كبار العلماء،" العربية (٢٨ ديسمبر ٢٠٠٧).
http://www.alarabiya.net/articles/2007/12/28/43470.html

22 محمد الحسين سلامة، "حكم الالتزام بالرسم العثماني ومدى جواز الكتابة الإملائية في كتابة آيات القرآن الكريم،" نور الشرق (٥ يوليو ٢٠١١).
http://mahamadelhosseny.blogspot.com/2011/07/blog-post_8415.html

Chapter 7

1. Messick, *The Calligraphic State*, 117.
2. On the list of 'Uthmanic *mushafs*, there is a copy the Russians had taken from Samarkand in the mid-nineteenth century and kept for some time in the Imperial Library in St. Petersburg. This *mushaf* attracted the attention of Orientalists and Muslims alike and has significantly contributed to ongoing disputes about the origins of the Qur'anic text. In 1905, a facsimile edition of this manuscript was printed, distributed as a gift to foreign diplomats and sold to bibliophiles. After the October Revolution, Lenin donated the manuscript to Muslims in the city of Ufa but in 1924 it was moved again, this time to Tashkent where it has remained ever since. Numerous scholars have run a range of radiocarbon tests on the Samarkand manuscript with different results. In 1997 the Muslim Board of Uzbekistan nominated it to the UNESCO "Memory of the World" register, an international initiative to protect valuable examples of the world's documentary heritage. Apart from the *mushaf* kept in Tashkent, there are a number of codices that bear names of the caliphs 'Uthman and 'Ali but most manuscript specialists describe them as forgeries. See the citation on the "Memory of the World" UNESCO website: http://www.unesco.org/new/en/communication-and-information/flagship-project-activities/memory-of-the-world/homepage/
3. Behnam Sadeghi and Mohsen Goudarzi, "Ṣanʿāʾ1 and the Origins of the Qur'an," *Der Islam* 87, no. 1–2 (2012): 1–51.
4. Tradigital http://www.tradigital.de/products.htm
5. Here an analogy can be made to book collectors in the West who display leather-bound copies, first-edition reproductions, or facsimiles of famous works of literature by the Easton Press, the Franklin Library, or the First Edition Library in their homes.
6. Yasin Hamid Safadi and Martin Lings, eds., *The Qur'an: Catalogue of an Exhibition of Qur'an Manuscripts at the British Library, 3 April–15 August 1976* (London: British Library, 1976).
7. D. S. Rice, *The Unique Ibn al-Bawwab Manuscript in the Chester Beatty Library* (Dublin: Emery Walker, Ltd., 1955), 79–80.
8. Nevine El-Aref, "Egypt Requests French Auction House Stop Sale of Qur'an Manuscript," *ahramonline* (June 2, 2013). http://english.ahram.org.eg/NewsContent/9/43/72963/Heritage/Islamic/Egypt-requests-French-auction-house-stop-sale-of-Q.aspx
9. "Qur'an Auction Halted after Egyptian Protests," *Daily News Egypt* (June 6, 2013). http://www.dailynewsegypt.com/2013/06/06/Quran-auction-halted-after-egyptian-protests/
10. "Azhar Aims to Recover Qur'an Manuscript," *Egypt Independent* (June 6, 2013). http://www.egyptindependent.com/news/azhar-aims-recover-Quran-manuscript
11. I have heard rumors that this *mushaf* has been returned to Egypt.
12. Nina Burleigh, *Mirage: Napoleon's Scientists and the Unveiling of Egypt* (New York: HarperCollins Publishers, 2007): 86–7.
13. This ad is no longer available online but the pages were advertised under the eBay item number 19df0f8298.

Notes

Chapter 8

1. David Morgan (ed.), *Religion and Material Culture: The Matter of Belief* (London: Routledge, 2010), 2.
2. Webb Keane, "On Semiotic Ideology," *Signs and Society* 6, no. 1 (2018): 64–87.
3. Webb Keane, "On the Materiality of Religion," *Material Culture* 4, no. 2 (2008): 230–1.
4. فضائل القرآن
5. الإتقان في علوم القرآن
6. كتاب تأويل مختلف الحديث
7. Zadeh "Fire Cannot Harm It," 54.
8. Ibid.
9. My husband heard a Coptic version of this story when he was teaching at the American University in Cairo. During a battle in the 1973 Arab-Israeli War, an Egyptian Coptic soldier was shot in the chest but was saved because the Bible he was carrying in the pocket of his army jacket stopped the bullet. When the Coptic soldier later examined his Bible, he was astounded to see that the Israeli bullet had pierced the Bible's pages, only to stop at Isaiah 19:21–22 (ESV): "And the lord will make himself known to the Egyptians, and the Egyptians will know the lord in that day and worship with sacrifice and offering, and they will make vows to the lord and perform them. And the lord will strike Egypt, striking and healing, and they will return to the lord, and he will listen to their pleas for mercy and heal them."
10. Asma Afsaruddin, "The Excellences of the Qur'an: Textual Sacrality and the Organization of Early Islamic Society," *Journal of the American Oriental Society* 122, no. 1 (2002): 1–24.
11. "الطيب" لأمريكا: حرق المصحف خط أحمر وعليكم بالرحيل بمن أفغانستان." http://www.elshaab.org/thread.php?ID=17159
12. "مفاجأة من العيار الثقيل.. وكيل الأزهر السابق: حرق القرآن «ليس مصيبة الأنباء»."(٢٠ سبتمبر ٢٠١٠). https://www.masress.com/moheet/16570
13. حرق أوراق المصحف القديمة http://www.dar-alifta.org/AR/ViewFatwa.aspx?ID=11151 16/06/2005
14. *Sahih al-Bukhari*. https://sunnah.com/bukhari/66/9
15. أحمد عبد المقصود، "لماذا حرق عثمان المصحف؟" الفجر (٢٠ سبتمبر ٢٠١٠).
16. Matthew Engelke, "Dangerous Things. One African Genealogy," in *Things. Religion and the Question of Materiality*, eds. Houtman Dick and Birgit Mayer (New York: Fordham University Press, 2012), 40.
17. محمد صديق خليفة، علاج نفسك بالأعشاب والأغذية القرآنية (دار قطوف للنشر والتوزيع القاهرة)، ٢٠١٠.
18. https://sunnah.com/urn/673850
19. https://sunnah.com/urn/1274970
20. https://sunnah.com/ibnmajah/31
21. Zadeh, "Touching and Ingesting," 464.
22. زاد المعاد
23. Younes Saramifar, "Objects, Object-ness, and Shadows of Meanings: Carving Prayer Beads and Exploring Their Materiality alongside a Khaksari Sufi Murshid," *Contemporary Islam* 12, no. 1 (2018): 39–55.
24. The Arabic Qur'anic Corpus. http://corpus.quran.com/translation.jsp?chapter=2&verse=255

196　Notes

25　The official website of Dar al-Iftā' al-Maṣrī http://www.dar-alifta.org/ar/ViewResearch.aspx?sec=fatwa&ID=110
26　النهاية في غريب الحديث والأثر (1/197، ط. المكتبة العلمية).
27　حاشية الجمل على شرح المنهج (1/76، ط. دار الفكر).
28　الزواجر عن اقتراف الكبائر (1/274، ط. دار الفكر).
29　الجامع لأحكام القرآن (10/316، ط. دار الكتب المصرية).
30　الجامع لأحكام القرآن، للقرطبي (10/320).
31　Meyer, "There Is a Spirit in This Image," 299.

Chapter 9

1　Annemarie Mol, *The Body Multiple: Ontology in Medical Practice* (Durham: Duke University Press 2002), 31–3.
2　لا يَمَسُّهُ إلا الْمُطَهَّرُونَ
3　The Arabic Qur'anic Corpus. http://corpus.quran.com/translation.jsp?chapter=56&verse=79
4　https://sunnah.com/malik/15
5　ناصر بن أحمد بن النجار الدمياطي. حكم مس المصحف بغير وضوء (القاهرة: مكتبة أولاد الشيخ للتراث، ٢٠٠٥): ٢٢.
6　Ibid., 17–29.
7　Ibid., 27.
8　http://www.dar-alifta.org/AR/ViewFatwa.aspx?sec=fatwa&ID=11392. See also http://www.dar-alifta.org/AR/ViewFatwa.aspx?sec=fatwa&ID=12343.
9　Saba Mahmood. *Politics of Piety: The Islamic Revival and the Feminist Subject* (Princeton, NJ: Princeton University Press, 2012).
10　"ولو ألقاه (المصحف) مسلم في القاذورات، صار الملقي كافرا." الإمام أبو زكريا يحيى بن شرف النووي. التبيان في آداب حملة القرآن (القاهرة: دار السلام، ٢٠٠٢)، ٣٠٩.
11　J. R. Osborn, "Narratives of Arabic Script: Calligraphic Design and Modern Spaces," *Design and Culture* 1, no. 2 (2009): 300.
12　Osborn, personal communication, 2019.
13　Osborn, *Letters of Light*, 170.
14　Difficulties of transferring the Arabic graphemes into a software based on the typographic model are well exemplified in Yannis Haralambous, "Typesetting the Holy Qur'an with TEX." https://www.academia.edu
15　Thomas Milo, "Authentic Arabic: A Case Study. Technical and Aesthetic Challenges" (paper presented at the 20th International Unicode Conference, Washington, DC, January 2002): 3. See also Thomas Milo, "Arabic Script and Typography: A Brief Historical Overview," in *Language, Culture, Type: International Type Design in the Age of Unicode*, ed. John D. Berry (New York: ATypI, 2002), 112–27. There are many designers and coders, however, who disagree with Milo, and the arguments about how to best represent the Arabic script in an electronic format continue.
16　For more information about the debates surrounding the electronic design of the Arabic script, see Osborn, *Letters of Light*, Chapter Six.
17　Jon W. Anderson maintains that it is incorrect to perceive the use of digital technology in the Middle East only in terms of its consumption, pointing to the new areas of production and design that actively change the social engagement with technology in that part of the world. "Producers and Middle East Internet

18. See, for instance, Mohsen A. Rashwan et al., "Data Preparation and Handling for Written Quran Script Verification." Conference Paper (October 2016). https://www.researchgate.net/
19. بدر محمود ابراهيم عُربي، " كتابة المصاحف الالكترونية: مشاكل والحلول. مجلة البحوث و الدراسات القرآنية.": ١٨٦.
    http://jqrs.qurancomplex.gov.sa/
20. "مجموعة الخطوط الحاسوبية"
    http://fonts.qurancomplex.gov.sa
21. https://www.decotype.com/
22. "Tasmeem Manual," Deco Type, 2006. http://www.decotype.com/pdfs/Tasmeem_Manual.pdf
23. At this point, there are a number of designers who have created digital versions of Arabic typeface based on the font used by al-Amiriyya. For instance, الخط الأميري https://www.amirifont.org/
24. Ibid.
25. مصحف مسقط
    https://www.mushafmuscat.com/
26. "الأزهر يؤيد فتوى سعودية أوجبت الطهارة قبل لمس «قرآن الجوال».. ويمنع تداول المصحف الصيني،" الشرق الأوسط (١١ اكتوبر ٢٠١١).
    http://www.aawsat.com/details.asp?section=17&article=644426&issueno=12005#.U1_I3MeaF8s
27. https://www.statista.com/statistics/467747/forecast-of-smartphone-users-in-egypt/
28. ICT Indicators in Brief Arab Republic of Egypt Ministry of Communications and Information Technology. http://www.mcit.gov.eg/Upcont/Documents/Publications_1992012000_Eng%20Flyer-August2012-last.pdf
29. سبلة عمان، ٢ يناير ٢٠٠٩.
    http://www.s-oman.net/avb/showthread.php?t=367870
30. http://www.dar-alifta.org/AR/ViewFatwa.aspx?sec=fatwa&ID=13248
31. "اتفق الأزهر مع فتوى الداعية السعودي محمد بن صالح المنجد بوجوب الطهارة قبل لمس قرآن الهاتف الجوال أو الأجهزة الإلكترونية المشغلة للقرآن الكريم، مؤكدا في مجمل رده أنه في حالة ظهور القرآن على شاشة الهاتف الجوال ستنطبق عليه نفس أحكام المصحف العادي الورقي، وفقا لما جاء في الآية الكريمة «لا يمسه إلا المطهرون»." الأزهر يؤيد فتوى سعودية أوجبت الطهارة قبل لمس «قرآن الجوال».. ويمنع تداول المصحف الصيني،" الشرق الأوسط ١١ اكتوبر ٢٠١١.
    http://www.aawsat.com/details.asp?section=17&article=644426&issueno=12005#.U1_I3MeaF8s
32. "لا مانع من حمل الجهاز لغير الطاهر واستخدامه لأنه ليس المصحف المكتوب، فهو لا يلامس الآية بيده فهو مجرد جهاز، أما إذا ظهرت الآية القرآنية على الشاشة فإنها في هذه الحالة تأخذ حرمة المس الذي أشارت إليه الآية الكريمة." الأزهر يؤيد فتوى سعودية أوجبت الطهارة قبل لمس «قرآن الجوال».. ويمنع تداول المصحف الصيني،"
33. مثلا، المشيقح، خالد بن علي. "دخول الحمام بأجهزة تحتوى على القرآن الكريم." طريق الإسلام ١٦ يناير ٢٠١٢. http://ar.islamway.net/fatwa/36228
    الرفاعي، خالد عبد المنعم. "دخول الخلاء بالجوال." طريق الإسلام ٥ سبتمبر ٢٠١٢.
    http://ar.islamway.net/fatwa/39023
34. "لا مانع شرعًا من قراءة القران بغير وضوء ومع عدم مس المصحف عملا بقوله تعالى: (لَا يَمَسُّهُ إِلَّا الْمُطَهَّرُنَ)." "قراءة القرآن بدون وضوء،" رقم الفتوى: ٢٢٦، دار الإفتاء المصرية (١٣ مايو ٢٠٠٩).
    http://www.dar-alifta.org/ViewFatwa.aspx?LangID=1&ID=266

35 "فإن مس المحدث للمصحف الإلكتروني أو المسجل على أشرطة الكاسيت لا حرج فيه إن شاء الله تعالى، لأن شروط منع مس المصحف للمحدث أن يكون مكتوباً، وأن يكون بالخط العربي، أما المصحف المسجل فإنه ليس بمكتوب؛ وإنما ثبت فيه صدى صوت القارئ بطريقة يعرفها أهل الاختصاص، فصار أشبه بالقرآن المحفوظ في الصدر، فيجوز لصاحبه الدخول به في الحمام، ويجوز لمسه من المحدث والجنب والحائض. والله أعلم." "حكم لمس المصحف الإلكتروني بدون وضوء،" رقم الفتوى: ٣٢٤١٠، مركز الفتوى Islamweb.net (٢٤مايو٢٠٠٣). http://fatwa.islamweb.net/fatwa/index.php?page=showfatwa&Option=FatwaId&Id=32410

36 "الشيخ المنجد حفظه الله كان يراجع الأمر مع العلامة الشيخ عبد الرحمن البراك حفظه الله وفي الأخير تقرر منهم جواز قراءة القرآن من المصحف الألكتروني بدون طهارة وجواز مس الشاشة على اعتبار أن الشاشة هي حائل.. وإن كان صحيحا ما جاء في الخبر من الفتوى من الأزهر فهذا تسرع منهم لأن المشايخ أفتوا بالجواز وأعتقد أن التشدد في هذا الأمر غير جيد كما أن هناك فتوى سابقة من الشيخ العثيمين رحمه الله بالجواز أيضا.." "الأزهر يؤيد فتوى سعودية أوجبت الطهارة قبل لمس «قرآن الجوال».. ويمنع تداول المصحف الصيني."

37 "اعتقد هنا انه فيه شئ من التشديد لاني انا موجود في جوالي القران الكريم وهذا يساعدني على قرائته اثناء السفر دون اللجوء إلى حمل مصحف معي لاني اذا وضعته في شنطة اليد سوف اضطر لدخول الحمام واذا وضعته في شنطة الملابس سوف تلقى في الأرض فيجوال شي بنسبة لي وانا احتاج ايضا لسماعة اثناء السفر أو الحيض في القران المسموع أو المكتوب على الجوال افضل شئ." " الأزهر يؤيد فتوى سعودية أوجبت الطهارة قبل لمس «قرآن الجوال».. ويمنع تداول المصحف الصيني."

38 هل يصح للحائض أن تقرأ القرآن من أي مصدر غير المصحف؟ السبت 16 يناير 2016. http://www.masrawy.com

39 Mol, *The Body Multiple*, 9.

Conclusion

1 Wilfred Cantwell Smith, "The True Meaning of Scripture: An Empirical Historian's Nonreductionist Interpretation of the Qur'an," *International Journal of Middle East Studies* 11, no. 4 (1980): 490.

2 Severin Fowles, "People without Things," in *An Anthropology of Absence: Materializations of Transcendence and Loss*, ed. Mikkel Bille, Frida Hastrup, and Tim Flohr Sorensen (New York: Springer, 2010), 23–41.

3 Bruno Latour, "Can We Get Our Materialism Back, Please?" *Isis* 98 (2007): 138–42. Alder, *Introduction*.

4 See, for instance, Annelies Moors, "Popularizing Islam: Muslims and Materiality—Introduction," and other articles in the issue of *Material Religion: The Journal of Objects, Art and Belief* 8, no. 3 (2012): 272–9.

5 Keane, "On the Materiality of Religion," 230–1.

6 Keane Webb, "The Evidence of the Senses and the Materiality of Religion," *Journal of the Royal Anthropological Institute* 14, no. 1 (2008): 124.

7 Talal Asad, *Genealogies of Religion: Discipline and Reasons of Power in Christianity and Islam* (Baltimore: The Johns Hopkins University Press, 1993)..

8 James Watts, *Iconic Books and Texts* (Sheffield: Equinox, 2013). See also his *How and Why Books Matter: Essays on the Social Function of Iconic Texts* (Sheffield: Equinox, 2019).

9 Dorina Miller Parmenter, "Material Scripture," in *The Oxford Encyclopedia of the Bible and the Arts*, ed. Timothy Beal (New York: Oxford University Press, 2015), 24–35.

10 S. Brent Plate, ed., *Key Terms in Material Religion* (London: Bloomsbury Academic, 2015).

11 http://jameswwatts.net/iconicbooks/.

References

Print Publications in English

Afsaruddin, Asma. "The Excellences of the Qur'an: Textual Sacrality and the Organization of Early Islamic Society." *Journal of the American Oriental Society* 122, no. 1 (2002): 1–24.

Albin, Michael W. "Early Arabic Printing: A Catalogue of Attitudes." *Manuscripts of the Middle East* 5 (1990–1991): 114–22.

Albin, Michael W. "Printing of the Qur'an." In *Encyclopedia of the Qur'an*, edited by Jane Dammen McAuliffe p. 265–276 Leiden: Brill, 2001.

Alder, Ken. "Making Things the Same: Representations, Tolerance, and the End of the *Ancient Regime* in France." *Social Studies of Science* 28, no. 4 (1998): 499–545.

Alder, Ken. "Introduction: Focus: Thick Things." *ISIS* 98 (2007): 80–3.

Al-Qaftanji, al-Sayed (السيد القفطانجي). Paper presented at the Conference of Calligraphers at Bibliotheca Alexandrina in Alexandria, 2014.

Anderson, Jon W. "Producers and Middle East Internet Technology: Getting beyond 'Impacts.'" *Middle East Journal* 54, no. 3 (2000): 419–31.

Aqeel, Moinuddin. "Commencement of Printing in the Muslim World: A View of Impact on Ulama at Early Phase of Islamic Moderate Trends." *Kyoto Bulletin of Islamic Area Studies* 2, no. 2 (March 2009): 10–21.

Asad, Talal. "The Idea of an Anthropology of Islam." In *Occasional Papers Series*, 1–24. Washington, DC: Center for Contemporary Arab Studies Georgetown University, 1986.

Asad, Talal. *Genealogies of Religion: Discipline and Reasons of Power in Christianity and Islam*. Baltimore: The Johns Hopkins University Press, 1993.

Atiyeh, George N., ed. *The Book in the Modern Arab World: The Cases of Lebanon and Egypt*, 233–53. Albany: State University of New York Press, 1995.

Auji, Hala. *Printing Arab Modernity: Book Culture and The American Press in Nineteenth-century Beirut*. Leiden: Brill, 2016.

Bein, Amit. *Ottoman Ulema, Turkish Republic: Agents of Change and Guardians of Tradition*. Stanford: Stanford University Press, 2011.

Benjamin, Walter. "Unpacking My Library." In *Illuminations*. New York: Schocken Books, 1969 [1931].

Benjamin, Walter. "The Work of Art in the Age of Its Technological Reproducibility." In *Selected Writings Volume 3, 1935–1938*, translated by Edmund Jephcott, Howard Eiland, and Michael W. Jennings, 101–33. Cambridge: The Belknap Press of Harvard University Press, 2002.

Blair, Sheila S. *Islamic Calligraphy*. Cairo: The American University in Cairo Press, 2006.

Bloom, Jonathan. *Paper before Print: The History and Impact of Paper in the Islamic World*. New Haven: Yale University Press, 2001.

Burleigh, Nina. *Mirage: Napoleon's Scientists and the Unveiling of Egypt*. New York: HarperCollins Publishers, 2007.

Cantwell Smith, Wilfred. "The True Meaning of Scripture: An Empirical Historian's Nonreductionist Interpretation of the Qur'an." *International Journal of Middle East Studies* 11, no. 4 (1980): 487–505.

Carter, Thomas F. "Islam as a Barrier to Printing." *The Moslem World* 33 (1943): 213–16.

Chartier, Roger. *The Order of Books: Readers, Authors, and Libraries in Europe between the Fourteenth and Eighteenth Centuries.* Stanford, CA: Stanford University Press, 1994.

Clifford, James. "Introduction: Partial Truths." In *Writing Culture: The Poetics and Politics of Ethnography*, edited by James Clifford and George Marcus, 1–26. Berkeley: University of California Press, 1986.

Cortese, Delia. "The Commodification of the *Muṣḥaf* in the Early Centuries of Islam." In *Writing and Writing: From Another World and Another Era*, edited by Robert M. Kerr and Thomas Milo, 41–66. Cambridge: Archetype, 2010.

Dar, Saif-Ur-Rahman. *The Roots of Muslim Calligraphy in Arabia, Iran, and Pakistan.* Pakistan: University of Peshawar, 1981.

Eisenlohr, Patrick. *Sounding Islam. Voice, Media, and Sonic Atmospheres in an Indian Ocean World.* Oakland: University of California Press, 2018.

Engelke, Matthew. "Dangerous Things. One African Genealogy." In *Things: Religion and the Question of Materiality*, edited by Houtman Dick and Birgit Mayer, 40–61. New York: Fordham University Press, 2012.

Ernst, Carl. *How to Read the Qur'an: A New Guide, with Select Translations.* Chapel Hill: University of North Carolina Press, 2011.

Al-Fityani, Kinda. "Deaf People, Modernity, and a Contentious Effort to Unify Arab Sign Languages." PhD dissertation, University of California, San Diego, 2010.

Fowles, Severin. "People without Things." In *An Anthropology of Absence: Materializations of Transcendence and Loss*, edited by Mikkel Bille, Frida Hastrup, and Tim Flohr Sorensen, 23–41. New York: Springer, 2010.

Gencer, Yasemin. "Ibrahim Müteferrika and the Age of the Printed Manuscript." In *The Islamic Manuscript Tradition: Ten Centuries of Book Arts in Indiana University Collections*, edited by Christiane Gruber, 155–93. Bloomington: Indiana University Press, 2010.

George, Kenneth M. "Ethics, Iconoclasm, and Qur'anic Art in Indonesia." *Cultural Anthropology* 24 (2009): 589–621.

Ghaly, Mohammed. "The Interplay of Technology and Sacredness in Islam: Discussions of Muslim Scholars on Printing the Qur'an." *Studies in Ethics, Law, and Technology* 3, no. 2 (2009): 1–24.

Gill, Eric. *An Essay on Typography.* London: J. M. Dent & Sons 1941.

Green, Nile. "Journeymen, Middlemen: Travel, Transculture, and Technology in the Origins of Muslim Printing." *International Journal of Middle East Studies* 41 (2009): 203–24.

Haleem, Abdel. "Qur'anic Orthography: The Written Representation of the Recited Text of the Qur'an." *Islamic Quarterly* 38, no. 3 (1994): 171–92.

Haleem, Abdel. "The Blind and the Qur'an/المصحف بخط برايل," *Journal of Qur'anic Studies* 3, no. 2 (2001): 123–5.

Hanan, Patrick, Judith T. Zeitlin, and Lydia He Liu, eds. *Writing and Materiality in China: Essays in Honor of Patrick Hanan.* Cambridge, MA: Asia Center for the Harvard-Yenching Institute, 2003.

Haralambous, Yannis. "Simplification of the Arabic Script: Three Different Approaches and Their Implementations." In *Electronic Publishing, Artistic Imaging, and Digital*

Typography: Proceedings of the 7th International Conference on Electronic Publishing, edited by Roger D. Hersch, Jacques André, and Heather Brown, 138–56. Berlin: Springer, 1998.

Hirschkind, Charles. *The Ethical Soundscape: Cassette Sermons and Islamic Counterpublics*. New York: Columbia University Press, 2006.

Houtman, Dick and Birgit Mayer, eds. *Things: Religion and the Question of Materiality*. New York: Fordham University Press, 2012.

Ingold, Tim. "Materials against Materiality." *Archaeological Dialogues* 14, no. 1 (2007): 1–16.

Al-Juwaynī, Imām al-Ḥaramayn. *A Guide to Conclusive Proofs for the Principles of Belief* (كتاب الإرشاد إلى قواطع الأدلة في أصول الاعتقاد). Translated by Paul E. Walker. Reading, UK: Garnet Publishing, 2000.

Keane, Webb. "The Evidence of the Senses and the Materiality of Religion." *Journal of the Royal Anthropological Institute* 14, no. 1 (2008): 110–27.

Keane, Webb. "On the Materiality of Religion." *Material Culture* 4, no. 2 (2008): 230–1.

Keane, Webb. "On Semiotic Ideology." *Signs and Society* 6, no. 1 (2018): 64–87.

Kuran-Borçoğlu, Nedret. "Osman Zeki Bey and His Printing Office the *Matbaa-i Osmaniye*." In *History of Printing and Publishing in the Languages and Countries of the Middle East*, edited by P. Sadgrove, 35–57. Oxford: Oxford University Press, 2004.

Latour, Bruno. "From Realpolitik to Dingpolitik—An Introduction to Making Things Public," 2005. http://www.bruno-latour.fr/node/208.

Latour, Bruno. *Reassembling the Social: An Introduction to Actor-network-theory*. Oxford: Oxford University Press, 2005.

Latour, Bruno. "Can We Get Our Materialism Back, Please?" *Isis* 98 (2007): 138–42.

Madigan, Daniel A. *The Qur'an's Self Image: Writing and Authority in Islam's Scripture*. Princeton, NJ: Princeton University Press, 2001.

Mahdi, Muhsin. "From the Manuscript Age to the Age of Printed Books." In *The Book in the Islamic World: The Written Word and Communication in the Middle East*, edited by George N. Atiyeh, 1–15. Albany: State University of New York Press, 1995.

Mahmood, Saba. *Politics of Piety: The Islamic Revival and the Feminist Subject*. Princeton, NJ: Princeton University Press, 2012.

Mahmoud, Youssef. "On the Reform of the Arabic Writing System." *Journal of Reading* 23, no. 8 (1980): 727–9.

Mattson, Ingrid. *The Story of the Qur'an: Its History and Place in Muslim Life*. Malden, MA: Blackwell Publishing, 2008.

Mauss, Marcel. *The Gift: The Form and Reason for Exchange in Archaic Societies*. New York: W. W. Norton, 1990 [1923].

McKenzie, Donald F. *Making Meaning: "Printers of the Mind" and Other Essays*. Amherst: University of Massachusetts Press, 2002.

McLuhan, Marshall. *Understanding Media: The Extensions of Man*. New York: The New American Library, 1964.

Medhurst, Walter Henry. *The Missionary Herald* 25 (1829): 192–3.

Messick, Brinkley. *The Calligraphic State. Textual Domination and History in a Muslim Society*. Berkeley: University of California Press, 1993.

Meyer, Birgit. "Materializing Religion." *Material Religion* 4, no. 2 (2008): 227.

Meyer, Birgit. "There Is a Spirit in That Image: Mass-produced Jesus Pictures and Protestant-Pentecostal Animation in Ghana." *Comparative Studies in Society and History* 52, no.1 (2010): 100–30.

Meyer, Birgit. "Medium." *Material Religion* 7, no. 1 (2011): 58–64.
Meyer, Birgit and Annelies Moors, eds. *Religion, Media, and the Public Sphere*. Bloomington: Indiana University Press, 2006.
Miller Parmenter, Dorina. "Material Scripture." In *The Oxford Encyclopedia of the Bible and the Arts*, edited by Timothy Beal, 24–35. New York: Oxford University Press, 2015.
Milo, Thomas. "Arabic Script and Typography: A Brief Historical Overview." In *Language, Culture, Type: International Type Design in the Age of Unicode*, edited by John D. Berry, 112–27. New York: ATypI, 2002.
Milo, Thomas. "Authentic Arabic: A Case Study. Technical and Aesthetic Challenges." Paper presented at the 20th International Unicode Conference, Washington, DC, January 2002.
Mitchell, W. J. T. "There Are No Visual Media." *Journal of Visual Culture* 4, no. 2 (2005): 257–66.
Mol, Annemarie. *The Body Multiple: Ontology in Medical Practice*. Durham: Duke University Press, 2002.
Moors, Annelies. "Popularizing Islam: Muslims and Materiality—Introduction." *Material Religion: The Journal of Objects, Art and Belief* 8, no. 3 (2012): 272–9.
Morgan, David, ed. *Religion and Material Culture: The Matter of Belief*. London: Routledge, 2010.
"The *Muṣḥaf* al-Madīna and the King Fahd Holy Qur'an Printing Complex." *Journal of Qur'anic Studies* 1, no. 1 (1999): 155–8.
Nemeth, Titus. *Arabic Type-making in the Machine Age: The Influence of Technology on the Form of Arabic Type, 1908–1993*. Leiden: Brill, 2017.
Neuwirth, Angelika. "Two Faces of the Qur'ān: Qur'ān and Muṣḥaf." *Oral Tradition* 25, no. 1 (2010): 141–56.
Niebuhr, Carsten. *Travels through Arabia and Other Countries in the East* (Reisebeschreibung nach Arabien und andern umliegenden Ländern). Translated by Robert Heron. Edinburgh, 1792.
Nuovo, Angela. "A Lost Arabic Koran Rediscovered." *The Library* 12, no. 4 (1990): 273–92.
Olsen, Bjornar. "Material Culture after Text: Re-membering Things." *Norwegian Archaeological Review* 36, no. 2 (2003): 87–104.
Osborn, J. R. "Narratives of Arabic Script: Calligraphic Design and Modern Spaces." *Design and Culture* 1, no. 2 (2009): 289–306.
Osborn, J. R. *Letters of Light: Arabic Script in Calligraphy, Print, and Digital Design*. Cambridge: Harvard University Press, 2017.
Paton, Andrew Archibald. *A History of the Egyptian Revolution, from the Period of the Mamelukes to the Death of Mohammed Ali; from Arab and European Memoirs, Oral Tradition, and Local Research*. London: Trübner & Co., 1870.
Peeters, Jeroen. "Palembang Revisited: Further Notes on the Printing Establishment of Kemas Haji Muhammad Azhari, 1848." *International Institute for Asian Studies Yearbook* (1995): 181–90.
Piquette, Kathryn and Ruth Whitehouse, eds. "Introduction: Developing an Approach to Writing as Material Practice." In *Writing as Material Practice: Substance, Surface and Medium*, edited by Kathryn Piquette and Ruth Whitehouse, 1–13. London: Ubiquity Press, 2013.
Plate, S. Brent, ed. *Key Terms in Material Religion*. London: Bloomsbury Academic, 2015.
Proudfoot, Ian. "Mass Producing Houri's Moles, or Aesthetics and Choice of Technology in Early Muslim Book Printing." In *Islam: Essays on Scripture, Thought, and Society*, edited by P. G. Riddell and T. Street, 161–84. Leiden: Brill, 1997.

Proudfoot, Ian. "Lithography at the Crossroads of the East." *Journal of the Printing Historical Society* 27 (1998): 113–31. Al-Qaftanji, al-Sayed (السيد القفطانجي). Paper presented at the Conference of Calligraphers at Bibliotheca Alexandrina in Alexandria, 2014.

Rice, D. S. *The Unique Ibn al-Bawwab Manuscript in the Chester Beatty Library*. Dublin: Emery Walker, Ltd., 1955.

Robinson, Francis. "Technology and Religious Change: Islam and the Impact of Print." *Modern Asian Studies* 27, no. 1, Special Issue: How Social, Political and Cultural Information Is Collected, Defined, Used and Analyzed, Cambridge University Press (February 1993): 229–51.

Roper, Geoffrey. "The History of the Book in the Muslim World." In *The Book: A Global History*, edited by Michael F. Suarez and H. R. Woudhuysen, 524–52. Oxford: Oxford University Press, 2013.

Sadeghi, Behnam and Mohsen Goudarzi. "Ṣanʿāʾ 1 and the Origins of the Qurʾān." *Der Islam* 87, no. 1–2 (2012): 1–129.

Safadi, Yasin Hamid and Martin Lings, eds. *The Quran: Catalogue of an Exhibition of Quran Manuscripts at the British Library, 3 April–15 August 1976*. London: British Library, 1976.

Saramifar, Younes. "Objects, Object-ness, and Shadows of Meanings: Carving Prayer Beads and Exploring Their Materiality alongside a Khaksari Sufi Murshid." *Contemporary Islam* 12, no. 1 (2018): 39–55.

Schwartz, Kathryn. "Meaningful Mediums: A Material and Intellectual History of Manuscript and Print Production in the Nineteenth-century Ottoman Cairo." PhD dissertation, Harvard University, 2015.

Stallybrass, Peter. "Material Culture: Introduction." *Shakespeare Studies* 28 (2000): 123–9.

Starrett, Gregory. "The Political Economy of Religious Commodities in Cairo." *American Anthropologist* 97, no. 1 (1995): 51–68.

Stolow, Jeremy. "Religion and/as Media." *Theory, Culture, and Society* 22, no. 4 (2005): 119–45.

Stolow, Jeremy. *Orthodox by Design: Judaism, Print Politics, and the Artscroll Revolution*. Berkeley: University of California Press, 2010.

Tadrus, Fawzi M. *Printing in the Arab World with the Emphasis on the Būlāq Press in Egypt*. Qatar: University of Qatar Press, 1982.

Trouillot, Michel-Rolph. *Silencing the Past: Power and the Production of History*. Boston, MA: Beacon Press, 1995.

Verdery, Richard N. "The Publications of the Bulaq Press under Muhammad ʿAli of Egypt." *Journal of the American Oriental Society* 91 (1971): 129–32.

Watts, James, ed. *Iconic Books and Texts*. Sheffield: Equinox, 2013.

Watts, James. *How and Why Books Matter: Essays on the Social Function of Iconic Texts*. Sheffield: Equinox, 2019.

Wilson, Brett. *Translating the Qurʾan in an Age of Nationalism: Print Culture and Modern Islam in Turkey*. Oxford: Oxford University Press, 2014.

Witkam, Jan Just. "Twenty-nine Rules for Qurʾan Copying: A Set of Rules for the Layout of a Nineteenth-century Ottoman Qurʾan Manuscript." *Journal of Turkish Studies* 26, no. 1 (2002): 339–48.

Zadeh, Travis. "'Fire Cannot Harm It': Mediation, Temptation and the Charismatic Power of the Qurʾan." *Journal of Qurʾanic Studies* 10, no. 2 (2008): 50–72.

Zadeh, Travis. "Touching and Ingesting: Early Debates over the Material Qurʾan." *Journal of the American Oriental Society* 129, no. 3 (2009): 443–66.

Zürcher, Erik Jan. *Turkey: A Modern History*. London: I.B.Tauris, 2004.

Online sources in English

"Auction Halted after Egyptian Protests." *Daily News Egypt* (June 6, 2013). http://www.dailynewsegypt.com/2013/06/06/quran-auction-halted-after-egyptian-protests/

"Azhar Aims to Recover Quran Manuscript." *Egypt Independent* (June 6, 2013). http://www.egyptindependent.com/news/azhar-aims-recover-quran-manuscript

Eissa, Sarah. "Killing Calligraphy." *Al-Ahram Weekly On-line* (December 16–22, 2010). http://weekly.ahram.org.eg/2010/1027/fe2.htm

el-Aref, Nevine. "Egypt Requests French Auction House Stop Sale of Quran Manuscript." *ahramonline* (June 2, 2013). http://english.ahram.org.eg/NewsContent/9/43/72963/Heritage/Islamic/Egypt-requests-French-auction-house-stop-sale-of-Q.aspx

Haralambous, Yannis. "Typesetting the Holy Qur'an with TEX." https://www.academia.edu

ICT Indicators in Brief Arab Republic of Egypt Ministry of Communications and Information Technology. http://www.mcit.gov.eg/Upcont/Documents/Publications_1992012000_Eng%20Flyer-August2012-last.pdf

IPR Strategic Business Information Database (accessed May 12, 2003).

King Fahd Complex Official Website. http://dm.qurancomplex.gov.sa/copyright-2/

"Memory of the World." UNESCO. http://www.unesco.org/new/en/communication-and-information/flagship-project-activities/memory-of-the-world/homepage/

"Number of smartphone users in Egypt from 2013 to 2019 (in millions)" Statista. https://www.statista.com/statistics/467747/forecast-of-smartphone-users-in-egypt/"Quran

The Qur'anic Arabic Corpus. http://corpus.quran.com/

Rashwan, Mohsen A. et al. "Data Preparation and Handling for Written Quran Script Verification." Conference Paper (October 2016). https://www.researchgate.net/

Sunnah. https://sunnah.com/

"Tasmeem Manual." Deco Type, 2006. http://www.decotype.com/pdfs/Tasmeem_Manual.pdf

Tradigital. http://www.tradigital.de/products.htm

Print Publications in Arabic

أبي داود (السجستاني)، أبو بكر بن. كتاب المصاحف، محرر محبّ الدين عبد السبحان واعظ. بيروت: دار البشائر الإسلامية، ٢٠٠٢.

الإفتاء المصري: من الصحابي عقبة بن عامر إلى الدكتور علي جمعة. عماد أحمد هلال. الجزء الثالث مطبعة دار الكتب والوثائق، القاهرة ٢٠١٥. ١٣٦٤-١٣٩٠.

اسماعيل، شعبان محمد. رسم المصحف وضبطه: بين التوقيف والاصطلاحات الحديثة. القاهرة: دار السلامة، ١٩٩٩.

بن كثير، أبو الفداء إسماعيل بن عمرر. تفسير القرآن العظيم، مجلد ٧. بيروت :دار الفكر،١٩٦٦.

خليفة، محمد صديق. علاج نفسك بالأعشاب والأغذية القرآنية. دار قطوف للنشر والتوزيع القاهرة، ٢٠١٠.

داود، السعيد. النشر العائلي في مصر: دراسة تأصيلية. دار التيسير: القاهرة، ٢٠٠٨.

الدمياطي، ناصر بن أحمد بن النجار. حكم مس المصحف بغير وضوء. القاهرة: مكتبة أولاد الشيخ للتراث، ٢٠٠٥.

رضوان، ابو الفتوح. تاريخ مطبعة بولاق ولمحة فى تاريخ الطباعة في بلدان الشرق الاوسط. القاهرة المطبعة الاميرية.بالقاهرة، ١٩٥٣ [١٩٤٣]

زاد، أحمد صبري. تاريخ الخط العربي وأعلام الخطاطين. القاهرة: دار الفضيلة، nd.

سراج الدين، اسماعيل. مطبعة بولاق. الاسكندرية: مكتبة الاسكندرية، ٢٠٠٥.

سراج الدين، اسماعيل، وخالد عزب. وعاء المعرفة: من الحجر إلى النشر الفوري. الاسكندرية: مكتبة الاسكندرية، ٢٠٠٧.
سركيس، يوسف إليان. معجم المطبوعات العربية والمعرّبة. الجزء الثاني. مكتبة ،الثقافة الدينية ١٩٢٨-١٩٣٠.
السيوطي، جلال الدين. الإتقان في علوم القرآن. المملكة العربية السعودية: مركز الدراسات القرآنية، nd.
صابات، خليل. تاريخ الطباعة في الشرق العربي. القاهرة: دار المعارف بمصر، الطبعة الثانية ١٩٦٦ [الطبعة الاولى١٩٥٧].
الصويعي، عبد العزيز سعيد. الحروف العربي تحفة التاريخ وعقدة التقنية. الدار الجماهيرية للنشر والتوزيع والإعلان، ليبيا،١٩٨٩.
عبد المقصود، أحمد. " لماذا حرق عثمان المصحف؟" الفجر (٢٠ سبتمبر ٢٠١٠).
عبده، ابراهيم. تاريخ الطباعة والصحافة في مصر خلال الحملة الفرنسية ١٧٩٨-١٨٠١. القاهرة: مكتبة الآداب، ١٩٤٩.
عنز، محمد علي. "توحيد جهة الطباعة ضرورة لسلامة المصحف من الأخطاء." الأهرام (٥ نوفمبر ٢٠١٠):١١.
الفرماوي، عبد الحى. كتابة القرآن الكريم بالرسم الإملائي أو الحروف اللاتينية (اقتراحان مرفوضان). القاهرة: دار التوزيع والنشر الإسلامية، ١٩٩١.
الفرماوي، عبد الحى. رسم المصحف: بين المؤيدين والمعارضين. القاهرة: مكتبة الأزهر، ١٩٧٨.
فهرست الكتب العربية المحفوظة بالكتبخانة الخديوية. القاهرة ١٨٨٧، جزء ١، ص. ٢.
القاضي، عبد الفتاح. تاريخ المصحف الشريف. القاهرة: مكتبة القاهرة، ٢٠١٠.
محمود محمد الطناحي، "أوائل المطبوعات العربية في مصر. في: ندوة تاريخ الطباعة العربية حتى انتهاء القرن التاسع عشر (القاهرة: منشورات المجمع الثقافي، ١٩٩٦): ٣٥٣-٤٣٨.
مصحف المساحة والأميرية: تعريف بهذا المصحف و اصطلاحات الضبط.القاهرة: المساحة والأميرية، ١٣٤٢.
نديم، محمد. مذكرة بشأن تيسير القراءة العربية الصحيحة بحروف الطباعة الحالية وضبطها بحركات الشكل المعروفة اللازمة للنطق الصحيح مرفوعة إلى حضرة صاحب المعالي رئيس مجمع الملك فؤاد الأول للغة العربية من محمد نديم، مدير المطبعة بدار الكتب المصرية، ١٩٤٨.
نصير، عايدة إبراهيم. الكتب العربية التي نشرت في مصر في القرن التاسع عشر.القاهرة: قسم النشر بالجامعة الأمريكية بالقاهرة، ١٩٩٠.
النمر، رجاء." الانتخابات وطباعة المصحف الشريف." الأخبار (٢٨ مايو ٢٠١٢): ٢٠.
النووي، الإمام أبي زكريا يحيى شرف. التبيان في آداب حملة القرآن. القاهرة: دار السلام، ٢٠٠٢.
الوقائع المصرية، العدد رقم 338 الصادر في 4 شعبان 1247 هـ/8 يناير 1832م.

Online Sources in Arabic

"«إبصار» تواجه عبء تأمين «مصاحف برايل» لمستفيديها من المكفوفين." الإقتصادية (١٢ يوليو ٢٠١٢).
http://www.aleqt.com/2012/07/12/article_673805.html
"اتحاد الناشرين ينتقد فرض الأزهر لرسوم جديدة على طباعة المصحف." (٢٩ مايو ٢٠١٢).
http://news.egypt.com/arabic/permalink/2248214.html
"استجابة لتطلّع الملايين من المكفوفين لاقتناء كتاب الله الكريم: مطابع خادم الحرمين تنتهي من طباعة المصحف بطريقة برايل." المواطن (٢ يوليو ٢٠١٣). http://www.almowaten.net/?p=36472
"الأزهر يؤيد فتوى سعودية أوجبت الطهارة قبل لمس «قرآن الجوال».. ويمنع تداول المصحف الصيني،" الشرق الأوسط (١١ اكتوبر ٢٠١١).
http://www.aawsat.com/details.asp?section=17&article=644426&issueno=12005#.
U1_I3MeaF8s

References

"البرلمان المصري يدعم عقوبة الخطأ في طباعة المصحف." عرب نت 5 (3 يناير 2011).
http://www.arabnet5.com/news.asp?c=2&id=76430#.T8ahEL-Qx-I

حرق أوراق المصحف القديمة
http://www.dar-alifta.org/AR/ViewFatwa.aspx?ID=11151 16/06/2005

"حكم أخذ مصحف من مسجد ووضعه في مسجد آخر." رقم الفتوى: 100457. مركز الفتوى islamweb.net، 10 أكتوبر 2007.
&http://fatwa.islamweb.net/fatwa/index.php?page=showfatwa&Option=FatwaId
Id=100457

"حكم لمس المصحف الإلكتروني بدون وضوء." رقم الفتوى: 32410، مركز الفتوى Islamweb.net 24 مايو 2003.
&http://fatwa.islamweb.net/fatwa/index.php?page=showfatwa&Option=FatwaId
Id=32410

خالد، هبة. "المعصراوي: نشر الآيات القرآنية على الإنترنت أمر بالغ الخطورة ... وفرصة لتحريفه،" الرأي (20 يناير 2011).
http://www.alraimedia.com/alrai/Article.aspx?id=251094&date=20012011

الخط الأميري https://www.amirifont.org/

الخميس، عبد الله. "كتابة القرآن الكريم بنظام برايل للمكفوفين." almoslim.net (4 نوفمبر 2006).
http://www.almoslim.net/node/83459

دار الإفتاء المصري http://www.dar-alifta.org/ar/ViewResearch.aspx?sec=fatwa&ID=110

رحلة طبع "المصاحف المصرية" من الانتشار حتى الاندثار http://www.toraseyat.com

الرفاعي، خالد عبد المنعم. "دخول الخلاء بالجوال." طريق الإسلام 5 سبتمبر 2012.
http://ar.islamway.net/fatwa/39023

رمضان، فوانيس. "المصحف الشريف بطريقة «برايل» ... وقصة مطبعة مصرية جميع عمالها من معدومي البصر." الرأي (21 سبتمبر 2008).
http://www.alraimedia.com/Articles.aspx?id=69090

زيدان، عائشة. "صناعة الطباعة تناقش أخطاء طباعة المصحف،" مصرس (13 يونيو 2012).
http://www.masress.com/elwady/17849

سبلة عمان، 2 يناير 2009 http://www.s-oman.net/avb/showthread.php?t=367870.

"السعودية: الانتهاء من طباعة مصحف برايل وسط تحفظ كبار العلماء." العربية (28 ديسمبر 2007).
http://www.alarabiya.net/articles/2007/12/28/43470.html

"السعودية: طباعة مصاحف جديدة خاصة بالمكفوفين!"
http://www.farfesh.com/Display.asp?catID=179&mainCatID=147&sID=84244

سلامة، محمد الحسين. "حكم الالتزام بالرسم العثماني ومدى جواز الكتابة الإملائية في كتابة آيات القرآن الكريم." نور الشرق (5 يوليو 2011).
http://mahamadelhosseny.blogspot.com/2011/07/blog-post_8415.html

"الطيب" لأمريكا: حرق المصحف خط أحمر وعليكم بالرحيل من أفغانستان"
http://www.elshaab.org/thread.php?ID=17159

عثمان، سلوى. "الطباعة تفتح النار على شيخ الأزهر وتجريمه أخطاء المصحف." البلد (22 مايو 2012).
http://www.el-balad.com/170170/altbaah-tfth-alnar-aly-s.aspx#sthash.NJ5TJMwl.dpuf

غربي، بدر محمود ابراهيم. "كتابة المصاحف الالكترونية: مشاكل والحلول. مجلة البحوث و الدراسات القرآنية." : 187. http://jqrs.qurancomplex.gov.sa/

علي، سليم. " تأجيل اجتماع أصحاب مطابع "المصحف" مع "الأزهر" للأحد المقبل." اليوم السابع (7 يونيو 2012).
http://www1.youm7.com/News.asp?NewsID=698595&SecID=24

References

علي، سليم. "صناعة الطباعة تشكل لجنة لزيارة الطيب لبحث قرار تجريم أخطاء طباعة المصحف. "اليوم السابع (٢٦ مايو ٢٠١٢).
http://www1.youm7.com/News.asp?NewsID=688624&SecID=24&IssueID=0

غاوي، أحمد. "عثمان طه: كتبت أربع نسخ للمصحف فنشر منها الملك فهد عشرات الملايين في العالم." الرياض، ٢٣ نوفمبر ٢٠٠٦. http://www.alriyadh.com:8080/203788

غزالة، محمد ربيع. "شيخ الأزهر: تذليل كل الصعوبات من أجل طباعة المصحف الشريف." الأهرام المسائي.
http://massai.ahram.org.eg/Inner.aspx?ContentID=57045

فتحي، محمد. "الناشرون ينتقدون الأزهر لفرضه رسوما جديدة على طباعة المصحف." الأهرام الرقمي (٣٠ مايو ٢٠١٢).
http://digital.ahram.org.eg/Policy.aspx?Serial=916281

"فلم وثائقي عن مجمع الملك فهد لطباعة المصحف الشريف." Accessed April 7, 2011
http://www.youtube.com/watch?v=VY4Eg8_smEs

"القانون رقم 102 لسنة 1985 بشأن تنظيم طبع المصحف الشريف والأحاديث النبوية."
http://www.ug-law.com/downloads/law102-85.pdf

"قراءة القرآن بدون وضوء." الرقم ٢٢٦، دار الإفتاء المصرية (١٣ مايو ٢٠٠٩).
http://www.dar-alifta.org/ViewFatwa.aspx?LangID=1&ID=266

"مجموعة الخطوط الحاسوبية."
http://fonts.qurancomplex.gov.sa/

محمد، يوسف. "مكتبة بالحسين تعرض مصاحف بها أخطاء مطبعية،" مصرس (١٩ أغسطس ٢٠٠٨).
http://www.masress.com/youm7/36659

مرسي، محمد. "الأزهر يدشن مشروع تسجيل القرآن الكريم بلغة الإشارة وطريقة برايل." أوركيدزا (٢٨ مايو ٢٠١٢).
http://orkidza.com/Middle-East/Egypt/2012/5/28/114

المزيكي، وائل. "غرفة الطباعة تناقش مقترح قانون لتجريم أخطاء طباعة المصحف." اخبار اليوم، ٢١ مايو ٢٠١٢.
http://www.akhbarelyom.com/news/newdetails/34924/1/0.html#.UnvtCCSE4zm

المشيقح، خالد بن علي. "دخول الحمام بأجهزة تحتوى على القرآن الكريم. " طريق الإسلام ١٦ يناير ٢٠١٢.
http://ar.islamway.net/fatwa/36228

"مصحف مسقط" https://www.mushafmuscat.com/

"المعصراوي: أخطاء المصاحف سببها دور النشر،" مصرس (٥ أبريل ٢٠٠٩).
http://www.masress.com/moheet/100000

"مفاجأة من العيار الثقيل.. وكيل الأزهر السابق: حرق القرآن ليس مصيبة الأنباء." (٢٠ سبتمبر ٢٠١٠).
https://www.masress.com/moheet/16570

"مليون مصحف بالمسجد الحرام،" دي ون جي
http://www.d1g.com/forum/show/4855761

"هل يصح للحائض أن تقرأ القرآن من أي مصدر غير المصحف؟ السبت (16 يناير 2016).
http://www.masrawy.com

ياسر حمود "يكشف أخطاء في طباعة المصحف الشريف،" نافذة مصر (٣ مايو ٢٠١٠).
http://www.egyptwindow.net/news_Details.aspx?News_ID=8056

ياسين، فوقية. "الطيب: تذليل كافة الصعوبات من أجل طباعة المصحف الشريف." البلد (١٠ يونيو ٢٠١٢).
http://www.el-balad.com/187177/altybsnzll-kafh-alsaobat.aspx

Index

'Abbas I 27, 58, 63
'Abd al-Qadir 'Abdallah, Muhammad 39, 44
'Abd al-Rahman, Abu 101
'Abd al-Rahman Effendi 26
'Abd al-Rahman family 58, 72–3
'Abd al-Rahman, Muhammad 72
'Abd al-Salam, 'Az al-Din Ibn 107
'Abduh, Khaled 84–6
'Ajaj, Husayn Amin 39
'alamat al-wuqf (signs of punctuation) 61, 100–1
'Ali, Muhammad 20–1, 23–4, 27, 31, 34, 38, 58, 65–6, 169
'amiyya (Egyptian dialect) 105
'aqida (creed) 10
'ilm al-naqt (science of diacritics) 97
'ilm al-rasm (science of the consonant baseline—*rasm*) 98
'Umar al-Khattab 161
'Uthman, Hafiz 25, 104

Abu 'Amr Ibn al-'Ala' 'an Hafs al-Duri 104
Abu 'Ubayd 141–2
Abu Dawood 162
Abu Razin 9
Abu Talib, 'Ali Ibn 101
Abu Zayd, Muhammad 28, 34, 59, 61
adab al-Qur'an/adab al-mushaf (etiquette of the Qur'an/ *mushaf*) 149, 157–9, 161–2, 165, 175–6
al-Ahram 18, 40, 42, 85, 91, 135, 143
al-Akhbar 82–3
al-Amiriyya 21, 59, 63–70, 105, 130
al-Azhar 18, 24, 53, 64, 68–9, 81, 88–9, 92–4, 98, 106, 109, 135, 144, 167–9
al-Baqi, 'Ali 'Abd 85–6
al-Baqillani, Abu Bakr 106
al-Basri, Hasan 9
al-Dani, Abu 'Amr 98
al-Diba'a, Muhammad 'Ali 68

al-Du'ali, Abu al-Aswad 96
al-Fajr 143
al-Haddad, Muhammad 'Ali Khalaf al-Hussayni 66–7
al-Halabi, Ahmad al-Babi 58
al-Haytami, Ibn Hajar 155
al-Jari, 'Abd al-Baqi 27
al-Juwayni, Imam al-Haramayn 10
al-Khamis, 'Abd Allah 122–3
al-Kutubkhana al-Khidiwiyya 28, 30
al-Ma'asarawi, Ahmad 90–2, 100, 159
al-Mahdi, al-'Abbasi 34
al-Marakashi (Ibn al-Bina'), Abu al-'Abbas 98
al-Masabki, Niqula 21
al-Masri al-Yum 87, 143
al-Mustaghfiri 9
al-Najar, Muhammad 'Ali 68
al-Najud, 'Asim Ibn Abi 101
al-Nawawi, Imam 9, 164
al-Qadi, 'Abd al-Fattah 61, 66, 68
al-Qaftanji, al-Sayed 39–41, 49
al-Qarmuti, Jabar 83
al-Qayyim, Imam Ibn 153
al-Qurtubi, Imam 155
al-rasm al-imla'i (the conventional orthography) 121–4
al-Sakhawi, al-Din 109
al-San'ani, 'Abd al-Razzaq 9
al-Shatibi Imam 98, 109
al-Shimarli, Ahmad 86
al-Sijistani, Abu Dawud 8
al-Solammi, Abu 'Abd al-Rahman 101
al-Suyuti 98, 141
al-Tamimi, Ahmad 27
al-Tayyeb, Ahmad 84–7, 92, 145, 175–6
al-tibb al-nabawi (medicine of the Prophet) 152
al-Tukhi, Hasan Ahmad 34
al-Wadi 85
al-Waqa'i' al-Masriyya 23

al-Yum 7, 85, 143
al-Zarkashi, Badr al-Din 98, 107
al-Zuhdi, 'Abdallah Bik 52
Alder, Ken 5, 26, 179
Arabic Language Academy in Cairo 105–6, 108
Asad, Talal 11, 180
ASCII (the American Standard Code for Information Interchange) 166
Atatürk, Kemal 105
Auji, Hala 11
Azhari, Muhammad 32–3, 58

Bab al-Khalq 127, 133–4
basmala (a common phrase *bismillahi ar-rahmani ar-rahim*—in the name of God, the Most Merciful and Compassionate) 42, 47–8, 50, 108
Basyuni, 'Abd al-Halim 68
Benjamin, Walter 3, 68
Bibliotheca Alexandrina 17, 21, 39
Blair, Sheila 54
books as objects 3, 127–8
Bulaq (Printing Press at Bulaq) 21, 23–4, 26, 28–9, 31–2, 34, 58, 64, 67, 69, 178

calligraphy 37, 43, 51, 54, 69, 166, 169
Cevdet, Ahmet 25
Chamber of Printing Industries 82, 84–6
Chartier, Roger 3
Clifford, James 7

dabt (diacritics) 61, 66, 94
Dar al-Mushaf 73–4
Dawud, al-Sa'id 72
de Paganini 21–2
DecoType 169–70
diacritics 6, 32, 35, 49–50, 53, 59–61, 65–66, 68, 95–8, 100–2, 109–11, 116–17, 119, 166–7, 179
diwani (a calligraphic style) 43, 45

Egyptian Supreme Council of Antiquities 134

fada'il al-Qur'an ("excellent qualities of the Qur'an") 9, 141–3
Fanton, Aristidis 24
farsi (calligraphic style) 32, 45

Faruq I 68
Fatah Allah, Hamza 70
fatwa 24, 30, 75, 102, 110, 121, 123, 143, 148, 153–6, 162–3, 172–3–175, 179
fikh (jurisprudence) 11, 155, 164
Fowles, Severin 177
fusha (literary Arabic) 105

Geertz, Clifford 5
George, Kenneth 53
ghusl (full ablution) 160
Gill, Eric 41
Goma'a, 'Ali 119, 144–5, 148, 162, 174,

Haddad, Muhammad Sa'ad Ibrahim 73
hadith (narratives about the deeds and saying of the Prophet Muhammad) 8, 11, 24, 26, 109, 131, 141–3, 148–9, 152–3, 159–61, 163–4, 171
Hafs 'an 'Asim 101–4
hagabs (amulets) 151, 154–5
Hamdullah, Sheikh 25
Hanan, Patrick 4
Haqqi, 'Abd al-Khalaq 28
harakat (marks for vowelization indicating declension) 32, 38, 48–9, 63, 96, 102
Houtman, Dick 95

i'arab (markings of declension) 96, 102, 117
i'jam (dots above and below the *rasm* that make distinction between the letters) 97, 102, 117
Ibn 'Abbas 10
Ibn 'Affan, 'Uthman 8, 18, 59, 61, 66–7, 69, 96, 110, 117, 129, 148
Ibn Abu Shayba, Abu Bakr 9
Ibn al-Bawwab 132
Ibn al-Nadim 69
Ibn Anas, Malik 9, 98, 109
Ibn Durays 9
Ibn Hanbal, Ahmad 141, 155
Ibn Hazm 160, 163,
Ibn Hubaysh, Zirr 101
Ibn Ka'ab, 'Ubayy 101
Ibn Khaldun 106
Ibn Khattabb, 174
Ibn Majah 152
Ibn Mas'ud, 'Abdallah 101
Ibn Muqla 132

Ibn Najah, Abu Dawud Suliman 98
Ibn Qutayba 141
Ibn Sallam, Abu 'Ubayd 9
Ibn Thabit, Zayd 18, 101, 148,
Ibrahim Basha, 58
Ibsar 120–1
Iconic Books 180
ihtiram (deference) 158, 164, 173, 176
ijaza (a license to teach Qur'anic recitation) 31
Ingold, Tim 41
Islamic Research Academy 85–89, 93, 104, 119
isnad (a chain of Qur'anic transmission) 31, 34, 57, 59, 69, 168

Ja'afar Bik, Muhammad 67, 70
Jami' al-Tarmidhi 152
Jones, Terry 1, 3, 139–41, 144, 150
juz' (section) 33–4, 59, 64, 147

kashida (a type of calligraphic ornamentation) 47
Kazan, Hilal 52
Keane, Webb 140, 179–80
Kemal, Namik 24
kerning 46
khata' (error) 84,
khatt (calligraphy) 38, 40, 65, 112, 122,
King Fahd Complex 71, 73, 76, 92–4, 101, 120–1, 169, 178
kiswat al-Ka'aba (a cover on Ka'aba) 52
kitab (book) 9, 158–9
kufi (a calligraphic style) 44, 48, 51, 72

Latour, Bruno 5–6, 8, 88, 179–80
Law Number 102 86, 88
Lisan al-'Arab 38
lithography 30, 34–5, 61

Madigan, Daniel 11
Majallat al-Azhar 109
Makhtuts (manuscripts) 127–37, 176
masahif (pl. of *mushaf*) 2, 8, 98, 109
mawlid (Prophet's birthday) 2
Mayer, Birgit 81, 95, 155
McKenzie, Donald F. 3
McLuhan, Marshall 7–8, 19
Medhurst, Walter Henry 32,

Mehmed, Şekerzade Effendi 25
Messick, Brinkley 68
Miller Parmenter, Dorina 180
Milo, Thomas 167, 169–70
Mitchell, W. J. T. 7
Mol, Annemarie 176
Morgan, David 139
Mu'tazilites 10
Mushaf al-Madina 57, 71–7, 89, 100, 103–4, 169, 178
Mushaf al-Makhallalaati 28, 34, 59, 61, 98
Mushaf al-Mu'allim 73
Mushaf al-Shimarli 71, 73–5, 77, 89, 93, 167
Mushaf Committee (Committee for the Review of the Noble *Mushaf*) 53, 68, 88–92, 100, 111, 119, 166, 168, 171, 179
Mushaf Fu'ad 57, 65–70, 101–2, 130, 166–7, 170, 178
Mushaf Hafiz 'Uthman 104
mushaf in Braille 113, 118–24, 179
mushaf in Malay 32, 58
Mushaf of Fourteen Schools of Reading 91, 159
Mustafa, Muhammad Effendi 58–9, 62, 72

Nadim, Muhammad 70
Nadim, Mustafa 70
Najib Basha, Ibrahim 70
naskh (calligraphic style) 32, 43, 45, 49, 52, 65, 70, 121, 158, 169–70
nasta'liq (a calligraphic style) 43
Nossir, Ayda 28

objects as actors 4, 88
objects as mediators 7
Olsen, Bjornar 5–6
orthography 67, 96, 99, 104, 111
Osborn, J. R. 4, 166
Osenat, Jean-Pierre 134–5
Ottoman *mushafs* 25

Palembang 32–3
Paton, Andrew Archibald 27
Piquette, Kathryn 37
Plate, Brent 180
Proudfoot, Ian 32–3

Qadroghli, Mustafa Nazif 63
Qalun 'an Nafi 104

qari' (reciter) 2, 101
qira'at (recitations/readings) 69, 102–4, 115, 119, 121

Radwan, Abu al-Futuh 24, 27
Ramadan (month of fasting) 2, 18, 33, 61
Rashad, Muhammad 85
rasm (consonant base of the Arabic language) 59, 61, 66, 94, 96–9, 102, 106–7, 109, 111–12, 114–24, 169
Robinson, Francis 30–1
Roper, Geoffrey 34
ruqa'a (a calligraphic style) 43, 45
ruqya (incantation) 153
Ruz al-Yussif 143

Sa'id Basha 27–8, 58
Sahih al-Bukhari 11, 21, 148, 152
Sahih Muslim 11, 152
Sami Basha, Amin 70
Sarkis, Yussif 25, 28, 34
Selim III 20
Sha'ib, 'Abd al-Rahman 39
Shalabi, 'Asim 85
Shilu Basha 70
Smith, Wilfred Cantwell 176–7
Subih (Printing Press) 34, 62
suhuf (bound pages) 2
sunna (Prophetic tradition) 11, 21, 88, 131, 146, 151–2, 156, 166
Syed, Soraya 52

ta'aliq 158
tafsir (exegesis) 68
Tafsir al-Baydawi 34

Tafsir al-Jalalayn 34
Taha, 'Uthman 71, 74–5, 169
tahara (purity) 9, 22, 26, 33, 160–2, 173–4
tajwid (type of recitation) 1, 100
talaqqi (method of Qur'anic transmission) 31
tartil (type of recitation) 2
tashkil 50, 61, 89, 102, 111, 116–17, 119, 167, 170
Tasmeem 170
tawhid (oneness of Allah) 10, 156
technique of the body 37, 40
thuluth (a calligraphic style) 43, 45, 48
Tradigital 130–1
Trouillot, Michel-Rolph 19–20
Turkiyya, Ahmad Qandil 173
typography (letterpress printing) 29, 35, 59, 65, 166, 178

Umm al-Kitab 159
UNESCO 135
Unicode 166, 170
Union of Book Distributors 84–6

Warsh 'an Nafi 104
Watts, James 180
Wilson, Brett 25, 30–1
wudu' (partial ablutions) 164, 173

Zadeh, Travis 8, 19
Zaghlul, Hussayn 65
Zaki Basha, Ahmad 70
Zarkashi, Muhammad ibn Bahadur 98
Zeki Bey, Osman 25, 104

www.ingramcontent.com/pod-product-compliance
Lightning Source LLC
Chambersburg PA
CBHW072233290426
44111CB00012B/2081